Industry of Identity Deficit

and

Cannibalization of Time Matrices

INDUSTRY OF IDENTITY DEFICIT

and

Cannibalization of Time Matrices

Betsy U. Chang

Printed in Victoria, Canada

National Library of Canada Cataloguing in Publication Data

Chang, Betsy U., 1954-
     Industry of identity deficit and cannibalization of time matrices
     Includes bibliographical references.
     ISBN 155212810-5
1. Group identity. 2. Globalization—Social aspects.
3. Multiculturalism. 4. Culture—Philosophy. I. Title.
II. Title: In defense of cultural identity.
HM1271.C48 2001   306'.01   C2001-900325-0

This book was published *on-demand* in cooperation with Trafford Publishing.
On-demand publishing is a unique process and service of making a book available for retail sale to the public taking advantage of on-demand manufacturing and Internet marketing. **On-demand publishing** includes promotions, retail sales, manufacturing, order fulfilment, accounting and collecting royalties on behalf of the author.

Suite 6E, 2333 Government St., Victoria, B.C. V8T 4P4, CANADA
Phone   250-383-6864   Toll-free   1-888-232-4444 (Canada &US)
Fax   250-383-6804   E-mail   sales@trafford.com
Web site www.trafford.com   TRAFFORD PUBLISHING IS A DIVISION OF TRAFFORD HOLDINGS LTD.
Trafford Catalog #01-0210   www.trafford.com/robots/01-0210.html
10   9   8   7   6   5   4

In memory of

Forrest E. Mars Sr., an American who exemplified filial piety
and
Hahn Changgi, a Korean who exemplified patriotism.

Contents

It is Not Growing Like a Tree
In bulk, doth make man better be;
Or standing long an oak, three hundred year,
To fall a log at last, dry, bald and sere:
 A lily of a day
 Is fairer far in May
Although it fall and die that night—
It was the plant and flower of Light.
In small proportions we just beauties see;
And in short measures life may perfect be.

—Ben Jonson (1573-1637) *

*From *Immortal Poems of the English Language*, An Anthology, Oscar Williams, ed., (Simon & Schuster, 1952) p. 79.

Acknowledgements

I am indebted to Prof. Isaiah Berlin (1909–1997), whose teachings provided much of the illumination in the writing of this book. He represents all that could be desired in a father figure, in the largesse of his mind and in his generous sharing of experiences and insights in the hope of a better future for mankind. His texts are like an arc bent towards the realistic, descriptive and sensible versus idealistic, predictive and statistical, so that one is pulled in, drawn out and let go, freer to explore the unknown. They are author-dependent, substance-driven, timeless, enriched, fortified, anchored and incorporable, rather than impersonal, neutral, neutered, volume-driven, trendy, formulaic, axiomatic or dogmatic with force-fitted, finite, predetermined and disposable answers that come with endings, guarantees, promises and much hype. As the elderly Chinese gentleman helping me find his books at a bookstore in Hong Kong wryly commented, "I like his work because Russians write with feeling." Prof. Berlin cannot be thanked without acknowledging the contribution of Prof. Henry Hardy, who made sure that the falling tree would be heard.

I am also very indebted to all of my teachers at King George V High School in Hong Kong, Central Piedmont Community College in Charlotte, North Carolina, University of North Carolina at Chapel Hill, and the School of Management at Northwestern University, Evanston, Illinois. In retrospect, I have found the pursuit of knowledge to be a perspicacious and sensitizing endeavour in perspectivism and pluralism.

The twenty years of working in various corporate environments in many countries provided a unique opportunity for understanding and studying human behaviour in many contexts. I would like to share my three rules in life, formulated during my time with Xerox:

1. Talk is cheap - when one's word no longer serves as one's bond.
2. There is no free lunch - where presumption of entitlements prevail.
3. Focus and make best effort - because it is too easy to lose sight of one's direction and sense of balance.

Working at Xerox was a most fortuitous and unique experience of a distinct corporate culture which served well as a standard in subsequent corporate milieux. I am grateful for the opportunity of learning APL (a programming language) with Xerox Learning Systems, which I had extensive experience in applying to multidimensional matrices made possible by the availability and access to well-maintained centralized databases. This work left a deep impression and resulted in other benefits, including the writing of this book. Only by being outside the 24/7 loop, in safe harbour, could this book have become, which was made possible by Laurent K.C. Lam.

Betsy U. Chang
Vancouver, June 2001

This book is a response to (1) the reports of the killing of James Byrd Jr., 49, a resident of Jasper, Texas, on Sunday morning, June 7, 1998 and (2) the coupling of identity deficit with the industries of identity, which will continue to compound social problems while disproportionately filling the coffers of commercial interests. While reading the interviews with the three young men who killed James Byrd Jr., it struck me that they all seemed to be afflicted with severe identity deficits and that a kind of 'industry' of hate is thriving by feeding and exploiting this unsatisfied need. What can explain the cruelty inflicted by these men in beating, shredding and decapitating someone who caused them no harm?

This is not solely an American issue, as I have seen variants of the phenomenon in many other countries in our age of technology and globalization. Nor is this an anti-American treatise, but far from it, as I have studied, worked and lived in the U.S. long enough to have experienced a full spectrum of the human spirit there. However, racism inflicts a much deeper wound in America than anywhere else, since it compounds and exacerbates the traditional divides of religion, class, age and gender as well as modern divides of numerous social, economic and political constructs or isms. Secondly, the U.S. carries the greatest consumption and wastage weight, so that its ways affect many others; and thirdly, its military and industrial combines set in motion multiplier effects in conflict escalation and de-escalation.

Within a couple of generations (marked by the UN Declaration of Human Rights and the Korean War), the U.S. has moved from internationalism, intellectualism and humanitarianism to entrenched unilateralism, provincialism and materialism accompanied by the information or mass media age but without a cultural ideology supported by an organic language of relationships, which enable crossing the species barrier to a human culture. With increasing U.S. mass media ownership convergence and global amplification, even ancient cultures teeter toward the inorganic bling-bling of capitalism and scientism versus awakening to the complex web of organic lifeforms. Language of relationships, rites and duty, which immunizes against individualism, buckles under the weight of commerce, litigation and inalienable rights, resulting in winner-take-all mindsets that proliferate as totalitarian, intransigent, impermeable and involute archetypes. Co-existence that rests upon the principle of compromise or giving way becomes unfashionable as might takes over as the prime mover and problem-solver, without courage, taste or style. All kinds of isms are embraced except that of 'organicism' as suppression of compassion induces inorganic illusions of infallibility and immortality and paves the way towards maximum wastage.

Americanism rotates within a heady and headstrong mixture of Greek individualism and humanities; Roman institutionalism and might-is-right; authoritarian and liberal orthodoxies of 18th-century Western European vintage; each bundled with its respective family of values, a supporting cast of power props, garbs and conscripts sporting schmaltzy shtik and spiel; all wrapped up in refined political and economic ideologies, terminologies and rights in a win/lose power grid that is unswayed by passions and resolves inspired by change of hearts or minds, since they are designed for rule by rulers, spun from another time, lineage and place or non-indigenously evolved or ersatz. This set-up enables lives to be endlessly and efficiently produced, processed and expended for concepts and dollars that conveniently crowd out or stand in for human family values, a social ideology or a recognition that every relationship entails some qualification, compromise and impediment of individual liberty, in consideration of and for personal identity.

In the absence of a cultural identity or language of relationships, personal identity is as ad hoc as political concepts of absolute individual rights. Such rights are then wedded to inorganic structures that impede and circumvent meaning derivations since these meanings can neutralize, over-ride or undercut being ruled by rulers and their rules, which in turn anoint authority and organizations designed to stymie change and to preserve the status quo. So the pursuit of liberty, equality, happiness and justice is not the hallmark of a cultural identity, but is designed for its vitiation, subordination, pre-emption, dissolution, expiation and denial, for the sake of political power aspirations, interests, concepts or illusions, whereby self-service revolves around denial of self or deindividualization that is as oxymoronic as running in place faster and harder as the clock runs out. In such a milieu, much ado is made of character, which is rendered as finite packaged goods, conjecture, caricature, anecdote, spectacle and witness, when it is something as elusive as stepping into another person's shoes to access and record private thoughts and feelings of the inner being in a particular time and setting. Seeing reality from another individual's perspective defies quick and definitive authentication so that what remains is an examination of the projected fragments of a life as an accumulation of words and deeds (quality and variety or calibre and repertoire of personas) shaped by an attitude that has learned both the art of compromise and mechanics of killing over a lifetime.

While size and extensions in singular dimensions, such as inch-wide and mile-deep or mile-wide and inch-thick exposure, give rise to a sense of stability, sprawl comes with a reduction in the sense of a centre, coordination and versatility in coping with change. Fixed, rigid, static, arrested or limited development takes its toll, especially at the fringes, so that harm, be it from absolute power, fanaticism, or stupidity arises from carelessness, heedlessness, callousness or incapacity and inadequacy of hearts that have not been anchored by or found an indivisible loyalty, integrity or union of a centred and stilled heart, aligned to a culture of life that rarely loses its way or is at a loss in knowing how to spend or value its time (the Chinese ideogram for loyalty appears on the cover in red). Sincerity comes in many guises as there are many who are sincere in their lies, and loyalty along with a plethora of other values pivot upon the purpose being served, so that the practise and outcome of these values are distinct from knowing what they are in the binary context of good and evil or right and wrong.

I would encourage the reader to take a critical stance to refute, support, modify and revise the point of view expressed in this book for the purpose of achieving greater understanding and clarity of consistencies and paradoxes of beliefs, practices and identity. It is my hope that knowledge, especially in regard to self-knowledge, will lead to greater possibilities for self-mending in that many of our wounds are largely self-inflicted. This uniquely human trait should be a sufficient and necessary cause for teaching, developing and nurturing mindfulness and self-mending throughout life, leading onto a path of serenity with an appreciation for the harvest of collaboration, especially in solitude over extended times.

This book represents the bundling of some of the strands of time that have passed through one mind so that it is likely to be even only in oddness and is a result of selective memory mining covering many times, countries, traditions, studies and peoples, focusing on the critical nature and nurture of identity. It represents one permutation or perception of reality shaped by the torque of a trinity of muse, angst and ethos over several decades. It is a product of much left unsaid and unaired due to either premature or inappropriate times, places and occasions, but nevertheless has been developing, forming and turning on its own accord. Like revenge being best dished out cold, this *bildungsroman* (striving for normalcy) has been tempered, calibrated and humoured enough to turn out one dish or outlook for minimum recoil and wastage. Its purpose is to mindshare in order to inform, irritate and imprint other trinities (whose angles may sum to less, equal, or greater than 180° as an on-going function of warps, bumps or irregularities in the individual's sense of the time/space continuum) in their iterative, incremental and integrating processes over space and time. Hopefully, the viewpoints expressed are more than singular and for sure, less than universal, in that dissents and consents are equally preferable to abstentions.

Its theme is anti-ism or multi-ism or against impediments to individual potentials and identity realizations, which are often shortchanged by set-in-stone, bottomless-trawling (indiscriminate catch-all) and humourless mindsets, paradigms and illusions, especially emanating from unilateralism, isolationism and absolutism in all their maniacal and fanatical manifestations, equally sporting spontaneity, originality and righteousness, all over the map. There are five gears at work in this book; *iota*, representing the minutiae, incrementality or individuality; *delta*, the factors of change; *sigma*, the summation of these elementary changes or the big picture; *quad*, catenating the quandary and the response that in turn fashions and furnishes the *quoins* (keystones) of the realm or the sense of reality, mediating the perceiver and the perceived. The big picture represents the story spinning and collating centre that cuts, copies, pastes and formats in order to fabricate and preserve self-serving illusions so long as the isthmus of compassion is denied, blocked, choked, excised or otherwise rendered impassable through shortfalls in purpose formulations, contextual libraries, acuity in reflections, imaginations or permeabilities. Thus each player is equipped with an escapement mechanism that varies in gear-ratios, sizes and shapes, which like a good watch best functions with regular attention or maintenance so as to prevent malfunctioning or gridlock, seizure and shutdown, especially from *folie de grandeur* (megalomania) or short-sightedness. The few and select individuals, beliefs and principles that we hold dear and sacred are not rendered so by incessant articulation of the depth and breadth of our feelings but only demonstrable in how they are reflected and incorporated in our day-in and day-out specific performances or culture.

What is held sacred unravels, comes undone or is torn asunder when we trade off any one of these against each other or at the expense of one or more as means to an oftentimes illusory or unbecoming end. Dawn is ushered in with the lifting of the "crocus veil" as Homer inimitably describes the stirrings of time, so long ago.

It is written in the author's unadulterated style or voice which may entail various levels and degrees of unraveling insofar as the markings of the convolutions have purposely been left in place. Where and when such unreadability, indigestibility and incorporability do occur, it is solely due to the shortcomings of a singularity's inner personal language. While the author appreciates the currency of style, she respectfully declines to assign a higher rank or weight to this very appealing user-friendly and eye-catching factor over materiality, texture and tone. In essence, the message should carry the day and the burden of satisfying truth or trust conditions of each individual reader, irrespective of the 'looks', nominal categories, principles and promises of the messenger, information bundle or time matrix.

It may also be an interesting counterpoint in the inside-out and outside-in continuum of the narrative traditions. There are as many types of readers as there are listeners. Quoting from *Coleridge: Darker Reflections*, by Richard Holmes (p. 123): "...an amusing definition of types of listeners: sponges, sand-glasses, strained bags, and lastly, the Great-Moguls Diamond Sieves who retain everything that is valuable and forget the rest."

Question: What difference can one life or singularity make?
Answer: Less than nothing to more than Time.

This book addresses two contiguous fronts: (a) the conflict over globalization which is often equated with Americanization (or capitalism) under the guise of non-contextual (American) principles of liberty, equality and justice as absolute values; and (b) the increasingly popular and expanding lexicon of multiculturalism. While there exists a mountain of literature spanning several millennia in both Western and Eastern traditions covering the development of ideas concerning liberty, equality and justice, there is a distinct lack of understanding and appreciation of what these principles mean in their many different contexts.

These are mostly practiced in the sole context of I, in which case these principles really serve no purpose. There is, at the same time, an abdication of personal responsibility while assigning blame to others. Scapegoating, denial or rationalization has evolved into an art form. Doesn't the education of the young reside with parents first and foremost? If one is just a slave to one's appetite, which is the case under the mantras *just be yourself, be natural, do as you please*, for example, where is liberty or free will since there appears to be no choice involved? Nihilism, a twisted sliver of Nietzsche's philosophy, is an extension of such a simplistic outlook, tinged with malevolence, operating in an either/or (binary) framework predicated upon a deterministic beginning and end but foiled by the only certainty that change and therefore compromise are constant. The seesaw of deconstruction and destruction versus the challenge of construction and creation is evident in the comparison of works representative of the periods before, during and after 1770-1830. The cusp of the 19th century is marked by industrialization, imperialism and nationalism culminating in civilization demarcated by the advent of spheres of military power, technological deployment and gun-boat diplomacy subjugating ever-greater masses of people and their lands. We live today with the values created, developed and transmitted from this period in Western Europe which have altered and reshaped cultures by ending extended family structures.

How democratic are international laws, economic interests, scientism, technocentrism and efficiency as defined and promulgated by one group designated as the horse (fixed variable) that draws the cart of all other goods, interests and human cultures (contingent and dependent variables)? Democracy is good for business and business excels at deluding the masses from seeing the sword of Damocles or the flip-side of economic growth, which is enslavement of life, and very few human cultures can be said to have weaved democracy and *laissez-faire* into their social ideologies. More importantly, what is the magic equation that defines equivalent, equal and identical and how does it get solved into 1 or 0 when incommensurable variables are set up against a uniform, indiscriminate and inhuman measure of dollars and cents, so that distinct cultures are processed into a goose-step march into the same hominizing and monetizing spirals. Are only the children in economically poor countries deliberately maimed, chained or sold into slavery, or is there as much or more efficient and abundant trading of human flesh in the rich and civilized monotheistic countries? Which monotheistic countries have a majority of their population emulating the lifestyle of their godheads, let alone their thoughts, languages and deeds in their daily lives as translations, translocations and time distort and dilute them? Can how and what they see themselves to be, be so dramatically different from how and what the others see as their representation if there is clarity, integrity or honesty within and without in the individual, group or national identity? Such disconnects seem to suggest that the processes and details of truth conditions or correspondence to objective, independent or third party facts vary widely individually, wherein truths or principles are interchangeable with assertions or propositions. Such individual responses demonstrate that certain and fixed lies are preferable to uncertain and shifting truths since there can be no responsibility when there is no thinking and choice in having deferred to authoritarianism of secular or non-secular laws or even of majority or personality, respectively dyed in absolute tautology. What x-entity says must be true because x said it.

There can be no dialogue since winning rather than reaching a common understanding is paramount. Social ideology of culture that governs attitude, conduct and words in context of relationships, especially within the family, becomes increasingly critical in languages that do not have these sensibilities embedded within them, so that the individual inclinations no longer take ultimate precedence or priority. Patriotism shrink-wrapped in flag-waving nationalism for asymmetric exploitation in profit maximization under the guise of absolute ownership by purchase, self-anointment and legal rights percolates without generational communion with the soil that courses through the veins from rootings and renewals that absorb the essence of earthly flavours. Reverence, gratitude and humility remain just remote concepts as relativism or the incessant need to compare, rank and categorize is the antithesis of compassion and Oneness that obliterates such unilateral imposition of boundaries. If there is no transition with varying degrees of incorporation and reflection to stimuli that can range from no response and ill response to reciprocal response for consideration, then compassion that requires no consideration in return is unlikely to root and remain moot.

Even as societies progress from hereditary rank and privilege to those of merit and achievement, hierarchy is still defined and operational. To be simple-minded in interpreting equality is to be frustrated and arrested in development, because equality is earned within specific social contexts: equality is not an absolute, stand-alone entitlement. While there is much talk of social justice and many believe themselves to be its advocates, to the extent that the effort is externally and financially oriented in the absence of commonly held values, it is misguided and misdirected. To approach social justice requires individual self-awareness from a specific cultural as well as universal perspective with their attendant priorities and precedents, along with the great discipline (caution and restraint) one needs to engage the external and other realities. The prerequisite for such engagement is the attainment of compassion with an equal measure or excess of humility, in absence of any expectation of reciprocity. Trying to act compassionately without an appreciation or incorporation of these two requirements is more likely to result in merely joining the ranks of Job's many mourners. (Too much humility is, of course, pride.) Since such a state or orientation of good faith appears largely absent and undeveloped from the most vociferous advocates of justice, it is not likely to prevail.

Progress towards justice can be made at an individual level by acknowledging much that one has in common and one's commonality with the rest of humanity. But to the extent that multiculturalism is embraced, it will appear to be even more elusive when what is right and the exertion of rights collide where group boundaries increasingly overlap. Multiculturalism is a form of oxymoronic pluralism in that what is unsettling, strange and unfamiliar is not given an equal opportunity to remain so, but is increasingly marginalized, exterminated or homogenized into blandness and tastelessness. The position of pro-life is increasingly uncoupled from the context of pluralism or co-existence. This, combined with the prevailing attitudes of winning at any cost and of my way or no way, coupled with social Darwinism and capitalism, make compromise a *non-sequitur*—the result of thwarted willfulness causing incalculable damage, manifesting both internally and externally since id solutions to id-originated problems only compound it.

When compromise takes on such negativity, not only peace and harmony but reconciliation and resolution of differences become a non-starter. Culture (a means to effect peaceful co-existence), which is the result of and provides remedy for differences among differents, recedes, and only might and money remain, so that human beings become less humane or genuine. Without cultural context, self-discipline or self-control over appetite gives way to its over-satiation. Commoditization of all aspects and stages of life subsume and subordinate all other non-economic parameters, too easily filling the void with the seduction and apostasy of traditional institutions and traditions. Perhaps in addition to the three supposed benefits of work (prevents boredom, avarice and poverty, none of which necessarily holds, but rather, justifies being tethered to the treadmill) *à la Voltaire*, it also imparts a sense of identity as materialism takes centre stage so that industry is identity as other derivatives of identity wither away. The importance of identity can perhaps be best appreciated in its absence, as when people cannot identify or identify with their work because of its intangible nature or because they have no control or input into it since their own creativity and uniqueness are deemed unnecessary. They are merely dispensable and interchangeable cogs in the wheel driven by paper shufflers and money movers.

Multiculturalism, like many utopian visions, serves to lock in the existing status quo, and only serves to create an illusion of harmony while diverting attention away from the disconnect between its appealing lexicon widely spewed into the public domain with the thoughts and deeds in the private one. In this state of denial, not only are symptoms difficult to detect, but possible solutions addressing causes of conflict are absent, since the problem has largely been defined out of existence. Thus, it is an expedient banner which seems to imply that articulation and reminders to not discriminate and to tolerate and celebrate differences, whereby all cultures are equal, will result in a just and harmonious society. Societies which tend to promote and espouse multiculturalism (versus humanism), implicitly or explicitly, tend not to have a robust cultural paradigm *in situ* that can claim a heritage over space, time and membership of significant substance, duration and size. Thus, multiculturalism results in an ad-hoc approach to any specific culture or cultural independence or inconsistency, all under the illusion of liberty, equality and justice, as money becomes the measure of all, and all become equally marginalized philistines.

When government is corrupt or when taxes and other levies are too high and innumerable, accompanied by a mountain of laws, there is an equal likelihood of a vast and parallel shadow or sub-terranean economy flourishing, equally staffed and managed by hooligans, bums and bullies (principals) and their supporting cast of collaborators, affiliates, menageries and coteries, including lawyers, accountants, enforcers, sycophants and submitters with values that mirror and justify their *raison d'être*—like any other societies. Thus subversiveness is chronic, grey, diffuse and elusive in its economic, political and social manifestations, with each subversive element serving as means and ends of diversity and singularity (black and opaque or white and transparent holes) which are consistently overlooked, low-balled, under-estimated and misunderstood. Not surprisingly, for the pro-human cultured minds that retrospect, reflect and re-iterate upon the organic principles of life, the nation-state, the military-industrial combines and the mass profit-raking entities of homogenizing fanaticism and propagandism in both the secular (scientism and capitalism) and non-secular (monotheism) spheres, represent the quintessential symbols of subversion and enslavement of life or the apotheosis of inhumane cultures. The monolithic and leviathan institutions by their prolific, protected, above suspicion, beyond reproach, multi-platform and shielded nature and design with rules of their own making, make for challenging despumation (skimming scum) indeed.

While much blame is cast on poverty as a major factor contributing to declining educational standards and increasing violence, perhaps this reflects on the pervasiveness of the need for money and material-based explanations and solutions. Studies of many countries where extremes of poverty have been the norm for most of the population through centuries do not indicate such causal linkage. When life becomes increasingly defined along a singular axis of money, it becomes the sole solution to its many ills and needs; this makes it seem feasible to produce a baby in one month by getting nine women pregnant. Throwing piles of money—while simple, visible and measurable—is not likely to dent a problem of non-materialistic causes and results, both of which are complex and immeasurable, residing in organic, cultural, intellectual and emotional domains.

Pluralism does not lend itself to absolute values and rights, so that rather than promulgating these as the be all and end all by various groups, a common shared process for problem-solving (along Hegel/Tao lines), to mitigate fear, friction and *frisson*, needs to be emphasized and incorporated into the education of the young. The philosophy of pluralism infers that not all needs, values or goals can be absolutely satisfied and that some harm, disappointment or dissatisfaction is inevitable, though perhaps mitigable. Critical thinking involves, at a minimum, considerations of materiality, perspective and context, coupled with need for compassion, tolerance and compromise, with consequences involving the individual, the family and others.

Thus, in a multicultural or pluralistic society, process tends to transcend espoused values so that its élite tend to be masters of its legal (dominant) language and process, with content and purpose being secondary and often obscure since the origin and nature of both are not based on multiculturalism or pluralism. One cannot navigate or negotiate without mastery of the *lingua franca* in a multicultural society. Even communications technology is predicated upon a standard or protocol of increasing complexity, breadth and depth of application, for transmission, reception and hand-off synchronicity with built-in but limited and defined range for tolerance and filtering out of noise prior to loss of signal integrity and content breakup.

Humans are designed with an impressively tolerant bandwidth, enabling survival in a multiplicity of conditions, achieving an independence or transcendence of merely the physical conditions in the compromise to live. Our physical endurance is separate and yet an extension of the intellectual, emotional and spiritual dimensions finding their match in the robustness and resilience of the life force or *chi* as it is called in Taoism. In the past, people endured much physical poverty and suffering from social oppression and material scarcity, against which endurance was the only recourse for survival. This was assuaged by living in a culture with various tonics for the soul, including food, drink, music, song, dance, crafts and story telling. Life was thus imparted and imbued with a sense of meaning and joy.

Endurance, like learning, is an internal process since our perceptions and sense of self are individually complex and unique permutations. Progress cannot happen if what is unfamiliar or difficult is automatically rejected as a result of totalitarianism, brain-washing or mass-conditioning. Unless we can endure ourselves as well as others, we can only resort to neutralizing each other and ourselves (new isms denouncing old isms), rather than overlapping and over-layering cumulative and collective experiences and knowledge through eternity. Discipline in any one dimension benefits cultivation of endurance in many others. Lack of discipline or endurance weakens the entire organic system, making it vulnerable and susceptible to breakdown whether due to internal or external causes. The heart may be a lonely hunter but it is not a loner, nor can it exist alone for long.

To live is to endure suffering through discipline which safeguards humanness and human dignity. To deny a child discipline is to deny it life. Suffering need not be induced because as life unfolds, so do the challenges and difficulties encountered, in turn shaping and forming endurance at all stages and directions. Endurance can blossom from nurturing of the heart with guidance for developing and strengthening the capacity for compromise and discipline. It is not achieved through operational conditioning, reward and punishment, or any transactional processes involving material and temporal barter. Irrespective of where an individual is born or resides, the sense of the centre and centredness is universal and equal in all beings. So too, the inner and outer forces exert equal influences. In Chinese writing, China is referred to as the Middle Kingdom, reflecting that there is existence and reality only in the middle way, and that to flourish is to compromise.

Tolerance is a test and demonstration of tensile strength and tensility, not a symptom of flaccid apathy, acquiescence or submission. Where intensity and duration of suffering and its corollary, endurance, prevail, culture will be found at its most definitive and deeply-etched manifestation where the force of life is pushed and pulled until it coalesces into a palpable heart, holding and anchoring the centre in all directions and dimensions through eternity. The ancient and Eastern practice of determining site location, form and name attests to a way of life that incorporates a desire for harmoniousness and serenity encapsulated in Confucian social harmony, Buddhist spiritual harmony and Taoist universal harmony. The seven notes within the conventions of five lines, five rests and three clefs musical grid contain an infinite repertoire for completeness in expression with tempo, temper and temperament notations; the seven colours combine for an infinite array of visually launched experiences within the narrow band of visible light to deliver similar kaleidoscopic effects; the seven strokes or mysteries of the Chinese ideogram representing eternity is just that; and Confucianism as well as many ancient oral traditions and languages position the named within a musical power grid to promote and produce social and cosmic harmony. Without defining relationships, words and rules for rapprochement and concordance, there is an absence of orientation, understanding and discipline; tensility stays fixed and unplayable as there is no reference to any chords and keys; and no meaning, joy and wonder are released and realizable.

The thought process for naming peoples, places and spaces, like the names themselves, has symbolic significance and meaning from a cultural perspective as well as incorporating the perceived attributes of the named. The modern and Western process is an antithesis of this way of life, with profit and efficiency maximization being the goal. The inversion of values is epitomized in the monumentalization and mythification of political and billionaire figures and entities, reflected in the nomination process for all kinds and types of public structure and space. Such transactional commemorative transformations of the organic and material into inorganic and artificial (and vice versa) are perfectly captured in the proliferation of images for bills, coins, stamps and other collectibles. This is an example of how a cultural backdrop, or its absence, provides moral and ethical contexts in natural, universal and eternal perspectives.

The importance of time and timing is literally lost on those who spend it, often mindlessly, versus those who measure and monitor its usage minutely by parsing seconds in order to generate user session statistics for billing as well as for marketing purposes to further increase usage—to bill and grow being the twin *sine qua non* of commercial fitness and finesse. The numerous pricing plans with 'unlimited time offer' results in mindless disposal of what is invaluable, irreplaceable and limited. This unlimited time offer converges with the increasing usage of terms like *killing time* and *getting wasted*, along with the proliferation of their many associated activities. There is a schism between the jingle of unlimited time, have it all, do it all, and be all, versus an individual's sense of never having enough time or running out of time. For all the sophisticated, user-friendly technology that is available, one that really is helpful, is the kitchen timer.

Mindfulness is a chronological event, and when the value and essence of time are lost, there is no continuum or memory, only mindless existence where life seems both too short and long, bypassing the sense of the moment. Anything for free has the greatest appeal for those without appreciable values, skills or talent coupled with lack of will or wherewithal and without the prospect of any. They tend to be unable to distinguish the merit of a honest day's labour, servitude or begging from unmerited pay-offs, shameful gain or theft. This propensity for free (loss leader) is reflected in the pursuit of the material when it is fully exploited by separating pain from gain. A red flag should pop up any time the term *free*, is encountered, especially by the young and the impressionable.

Captive audience and user base thus represent a predatory amassing of time which, with varying subtlety and seductiveness, establishes a faith-like belief in the users (prey) that the benefits invariably exceed the price paid and the opportunity cost. Such transactions involve exchanging the real and material for the unreal and immaterial through artifice (illusion) and the artificial (money). The number of zeros following various measures of market size serves as a useful inverse indicator of the mindfulness of its product and service consumption, which in turn produces trend growth or the cream of all revenue.

No one else could capture, control and define time with the thoroughness, disingenuousness and ingenuity of sweeping commerce and its superlative *time is money* maxim as well as the many variations and inversions (unlimited time offers) upon this theme. There can no longer be any pride in work or workmanship if there is no honour or dignity in how one spends time when *it's only money* and valued monetarily. Time, space and being are demarcations and manifestations of creation, just as non-time, -space and -being are of non-creation. This alchemic and anemic conversion of time voids it of sacredness, flattens its pulse, and denies its incommutable nature and independence from will. Similarly, the 24-hour day and various instruments used to measure time do not bear any significant relation to the eternal cosmic flow of time on the side of creation we know something about. The only point about time is not to waste whatever allotment has been made available.

The burden and challenge for parents as well as public, social and educational entities—to develop critical thinking skills and common protocols—arguably are far greater in a multicultural setting than in a monocultural one, albeit that both face the certainty of constant change and the impact of globalization. Any concept of family values that is not mirrored in the language and lacks a code of conduct defining hierarchy along with attendant duties (obligations and responsibilities) is meaningless or futile. The primary challenge for parenthood in this context would appear to be one of modeling duty-in-action, signaling and symbolizing through songs and stories, and guiding through postures and mannerisms, day-in and day-out. A formidable feat for anyone in all times! While respect and love from children are not necessarily earned, lack of nurturing can result in their irretrievable loss since children tend to see the world in terms of black and white, taking appearances at face value since the veil of illusion or familiarity does not mask but represents reality.

Since we can only learn what we do not already know, the tautology of 'I can only know what I know to be true' pre-empts and precludes any learning. Rather than deepening, expanding and illuminating the mind over time, its state of ignorance, infallibility and shallowness are pre-served and guarded. Such compulsive behavior pivots and thrives upon prejudice or pre-judgement so that rather than commune in the moment with the text at hand, it is bypassed, rejected or libelled out-of-hand. This cultivated habit defines the self outside the nexus of cause and effect as well as disconnecting thought, word and deed, resulting in non-integrity. Self-knowledge that can lead towards coherence and balance remains undeveloped, unmanifested and unexamined so that even self-interest is not served but quite the reverse. In a world of all or nothing, non-sever-ability is presupposed and unforgiving so that any disagreement with some parts of the work results in rejection of the lot. Since many great works (and people) have idiosyncrasies, paradoxes or internal inconsis-tencies (syncretism), other worlds do not come into view, so that there is no convergence of perceptions from various vantages to release truths. What is seen or shown is irrelevant versus the particulars of vantage. The fixed and paramount perch of the self excludes the minimum conditions for processing any other perspectives. When there are only assertions of the self accompanied by the maximum suppression and denial of others, truths and lies become interchangeable as the mind flees or flips as it goes increasingly off course, snipped of moral agency and principle. Assertions are passed off as truths without meeting any condition of truth. The sole remaining inescapable reality is the march and mark of time from which the self finds escape, relief and consolation in windowless and dark rooms tethered to consuming mass products and services that efficiently evis-cerate individuality. Artificial memories that are as un-unique as they are shallow, are continuously looped, repackaged and stroked by systems whose batteries are always fully charged by an inexhaustible supply of consumers staying in their comfort-zones, clinging onto the innocence and illusions of youth and the familiar, long gone by. The illusion of democracy is relentlessly maintained while its inefficiencies and imprac-ticalities are flattered and flattened by the synergy of two organized to the max binary systems whose totalitarian objectives of absolute might and right meld seamlessly. Thus capitalism and monotheism reach their pin-nacle, waving a brand of power patriotism divorced from any particulars of the land or life.

Democracy with its rule of majority comes no closer to truths since every possible vote is neither cast nor counted equally and much that transpires does so behind closed doors. Regardless of how finely capped, robed or rigged, the majority decision is only memorable for its outcome with the reasoning being as contorted and couched as it is unrecallable and unscintillating in the dustheap of the past. The antithesis of right is not neccesarily wrong but meaninglessness, as apathy is to love or compassion, not hate. The principles of family and social relationships exert a force over an infinite range, being independent of individual weight and measure. The relative strength or weakness of such a force pivots upon and radiates from an understanding of inter-relationships and affinities that gives way to Oneness. Democracy has proven itself to be good for business as it cherry-picks family relationships and replaces them with brand loyalty and 'us versus them' mentality, which define identity through hate and intolerance. How free, able and willing are children to explore beyond the boundaries and attachments of the familiar to the many and the unknown? Probably in equal measure to the others in their vicinity and increasingly as fabricated by television and other mass-marketed propogandas, products and services.

The debate over abortion focuses on the unborn and unknowable rather than moral principles governing all existing lives. Such moral principles, when deeply felt and observed by the group, seem to be necessary but insufficient to stem the tide of greed and its twin, avarice. Rather than defanging the process of divorce and other social disputes of any economic incentives and disincentives, the volume and nature of litigation seem to revolve around money. The rituals of divorce and marriage should mirror each other, and be marked by the solemn and public exchange of the vows or repudiation of unity, witnessed by family, friends and elders. There are no guarantees of perpetual lifestyle and livelihood, only the bond of relationships in life or in marriage, and when the shame, dishonour and loss are equally felt by both partners, other paths beyond that of 'my way or no way' can be explored.

The assigning and changing of names and titles, given ritually at birth, marriage and even posthumously in many cultures, have meaning in relative position and identity significance for the named in his/her relationships to others as in the saying *nomina sunt omina*, meaning 'names are portents'. The prevalence of the 'my way or no way' impasse, as if each party were an omnipotent deity, is interesting when even God as described by the prophets allows for free will, folly and mistakes, encouraging the practice of atonement and forgiveness while condemning forgetfulness. Duty and its stygian bond may be oppressive and feel like hell but its denial and discard do not give rise to a free pass from such a destination, self-inflicted or otherwise. The Socratic teaching 'to know thyself' and Buddhist 'there is no self' (*anatman*) can perhaps be reconciled by the Confucian to Kantian concept of duty that transcends and yet forms the self in being of service to others. The teachings of Confucius (*K'ung Fu-tzu*) address the structure, function and dynamic of identity matrices for the purpose of organic unity within a culture which evolves through time. The Hindu concept of *dharma* that unites principle, passion and purpose of life rests upon self-knowledge as sufficient and necessary pre-requisites, not self-love and self-esteem.

The extensive terminologies to indicate humaness and its flip-side suggest that many cultures consider becoming human to be a get-wise and with-it process. Such terminologies are not classifications of good and evil, but denote esteemable traits of nobility and wisdom versus baseness and ignorance in the context of a specific cultural sensibility. Other lifeforms are not disparaged but equally imbued and associated with these traits of character and behaviour. To be recognised as a human being is not a given, but is coupled with satisfying cultural standards and rites associated with status in various membership, capping and coming-of-age ceremonies. These rites confirm and bestow identity, status and privilege, as well as the reverse, because maintaining social positions depend upon household dynamics, balance, discipline, sophistication and cohesiveness as individuals of different hue, taste, wattage and charge move up/down and in/out, leaving their tinge through time. All great and sacred literature and testaments of the human experience attest to the fact that to live is to suffer and that compassion is the path towards co-existence and harmony.

While personal identity may not be the subject of great scrutiny for an individual, his or her self-perception plays a crucial role in its unfolding. People are no longer strictly defined by ethnicity and geography due to technological and economic trends which have resulted in increasing homogeneity in the sense that much becomes externally familiar and knowable. This is accompanied by a decreasing sense of identity and belonging, which could be called genuine cultural intelligence.

The need to belong has not dissipated, but has only become more particular and peculiar as evidenced by the proliferation of innumerable groups defined along an exclusionary single axis, qualifying membership by ethnic, religious, political, sexual, age or gender attributes (distinguishable in that they require no effort or signify no merit or status of any kind, which perhaps is their sole attraction) in an effort to compensate for and/or deny the fact that one is a part of a single human population with much more in common than one would like to admit. As globalization picks up momentum and mass, the industry of identity thrives on amplifying the Freudian notion of 'the narcissism of minor differences.' The revenue potential and windfall of filling the identity void that industry itself creates and defines, aided and abetted by corporate consolidation and technological empowerment, is self-perpetuating with winning formulae such as: consume and stay young, indulge the appetite and hang on to youth, and out with the old and in with the new. Under this banner, society's elders, with their sense of history and perspective[1] which humanizes and impregnates life with a sense of identity, cannot come into existence, thereby ensuring that the identity industry is safe and secure.

The entire nature of perceptual inputs and interfaces of identity formation is becoming increasingly inorganic and untethered from the family as well as the collective and cumulative memory of the community. The resulting output reflects rootlessness with a preference for asynchronous time/space experiences or illusions. There is no test for identity or self-knowledge or self-actualization, but the quest seems to require transcending the self or going beyond the I into the Universal Self. Numerous secular and non-secular texts describe this quest,

---

1. The German poet Goethe once said, "he who cannot draw on three thousand years is living hand to mouth." Jostein Gaarder, *Sophie's World* (Berkley Publishing Group, 1996), pp. 164, 300.

such as the Hindu Upanishads which refers to the Self as the Greater Atman or one's true nature. Art in this context would seem to be a sensory medium that attempts to impart a glimpse of enlightenment and thereby provide comfort and solace beyond the loneliness of the lone I.

The entertainment media has only one purpose: to increase access and usage fees by hooking an ever increasing number of users while increasing user session. While millennia of civilization indicates an effort to integrate the self into humanity, modern technologies, with their pull-down menus (captive and limited options) and individualization (bounded imagination), disintegrates the self into anonymity—albeit under the guise of originality plastered with the word 'creative'. There is much frenzy in short-selling, short-circuiting and short-changing off-the-shelf identities, accelerating the formation and deformation cycles, so that a balanced perspective over time is undestined and unformed. There is no incremental rapport or digestion of repertoire, only displacement and passive throughfare of images. The Coleridgean 'willing suspension of disbelief' becomes a *nonsequitor* in a top-down mechanically projected reality versus the bottom-up organically reflected realities as industry of individual effort gives way to industry of identity.

The industry of identity feeds upon and is, in turn, fed by the escalating politics of identity or nano-issues or 1/6 of a nano-issue, each entity taking on similar stripes and practices, eroding the purpose of government and civic roles and functions which require inclusive outlooks of greater depth and field of perception beyond the highly refined ability to self-obsess. Thus the same reasons for separation of church and state apply to commerce and state, perhaps even more so and with greater urgency in the age of globalization and the mass media. Many of these self-imposed, self-defined or inherent categorizations are characterized and pushed to extremes by radical individualism or 'I-centricism', which is referred to as 'a culture of one' in this book.

While this may be an oxymoron, it becomes all too real in the pursuit of absolute self-autonomy, and manifestations of this seem to be gaining favour with individuals who perceive themselves to be under threat of losing their distinct place, however tenuous or unmerited their status may be. Radical individualism is not only confined to acts of violence, sensationalized with wall-to-wall media coverage, but fosters the creation of a large pool of loners of all ages, across economic and ethnic parameters, increasingly accommodated by the prevailing economic paradigm of global capitalism and technological developments, enabling isolationistic lives and lifestyles.

Behind the preeminence of consumerism is a vast information-sifting mechanism which, on the macro level, entices consumer groups by efficient and expedient segmentation and, on a micro level, tracks, stalks and hawks transactional and personal data of individuals. Technological developments enable the keepers of marketing information to slice and dice their data-bases with ever greater finesse. The proliferation of delivery mechanisms (transportation systems, mega-malls, 500+ television channels, the Internet, efficient communications technology, electronic funds transfer), all characterized by speed and ease of use, not only encourages and facilitates what is purchased, but sets the pace since consumers are hooked and per-suaded to keep up, in lock-step, to the call of the Pied Piper. The metronome of consumption imperceptibly picks up pace and volume: mindlessness, complaisance and acquiescence are often the result. Is this desirable? Those who most loudly and eloquently extol the simplicity and simple-mindedness of the peasants are interestingly never of that group themselves. Perhaps ignorance is bliss, but from whose point of view? What human endeavours illustrate this enlightened state of mind for the masses?

Totalitarianism comes in many guises and shapes; perhaps none is as enticingly packaged and marketed as consumerism. *Mea culpa* now means its exact opposite: *it is not my fault because I couldn't help it* and *I am just a victim of my personality or forces beyond my control*. Small wonder, then, that games of chance, gambling and lotteries proliferate when cultural context is absent from choice, whether rational, irrational or radical. If a lifetime of net wages totals $1.5 million, to sustain $720 billion wagered annually in the U.S. (where 11 million people are addicted to gambling) or $2 billion per day, requires an amassment and disposal of over 1,300 wage-lives per day. This is only a fraction of one side of the time and energy convergence and consump-tion equation that also includes all of the activities for nurturing, sustaining and perpetuating the revenue circulatory systems for 'wagers', all quantified, processed and normalized as dollars. The revenue potential and profitability of this industry is perhaps only exceeded by the legal and illegal trade in drugs and other weapons or means (guns and isms) of mass destruction and enslavement. Thus the feeding trough runneth over to satisfy the rapacious and ravenous appetite of the time cannibals and their cannibalization systems.

Information technology not only makes available a vast quantity of data in all forms, but in the process of gathering, packaging and ranking data, allows for instant comparisons, with a resulting proliferation of lists of all kinds (e.g., corporate rankings, individual wealth, philanthropy, educational institutions, bestsellers in various categories, countries and populations). There does not appear to be much that can escape this process of commoditization, including charity. How much does charity remain an affair of the heart and not just another media spectacle, notable only for its celebrity and charity-ball A-lists? Given the value of the free global media exposure, puffing up of status, pumping up of the ego and commemoration by posterity, charitable donations appear to be a break-even exercise with the added benefit of their dollar-for-dollar matched tax reduction on the bottom line.

In the U.S. where equality is much touted as a right and a virtue, a clearer distinction and demarcation of inequality looms large, resulting in a greater sense of prevalent and prevailing social injustice. Even in countries where equality and individualism have been de-emphasized or made non-existent in the cultural text, the Americanization of the popular media propels these to take on the status of absolute rights, circumventing or even obliterating many traditional values. The United States has the most ethnically diverse population base in the world, epitomizes capitalism and individualism, provides the necessary platforms for democracy, and elicits the strongest reaction and recognition—yet it lacks a genuine cultural paradigm. No other country has citizens who identify themselves with hyphenated identities so frequently: African-American, Irish-, Italian-, Chinese-, Jewish-, Hispanic-, Indian-, etc.

But what is '-American'? These categorizations of various nationalities and ethnicities with '-American' suggest that this term does not lend itself to association or identification with these attributes of identity, but rather that which is of greater inclusiveness capturing all that precedes it, i.e. transcends or is somehow incompatible with nationality and ethnicity or that which is empty of identity content on its own. Some example of this is the identity imbued in a reversal of these terms as in French-Jew, Hungarian-Gypsy, Japanese-Korean. Culture, which is intricately coupled with ethnic groups within geographic boundaries, predates and is distinct from ethnocentrism or nationalism; Americanism is not and cannot be rooted in nationalism. And yet the nature of identity, although not fixed, is neither frangible nor fungible. While cultural identity and intelligence may not be missed, they still play an essential role, even in absence, which cannot be circumvented or displaced in a piecemeal fashion with other identities.

The U.S. offers a refuge for those who cannot belong where membership is predicated upon nationality or ethnicity, and where social ascendancy is curtailed by static traditions. Claiming to be an '-American' implies a subscription to a cultural paradigm not grounded upon precepts common to all other cultures, but which necessarily still needs to serve similar functions. Unlike '-Jew', '-American', is an inorganic political construction as rich in meaning as political science and political art. If the American culture is essentially a culture of laws (as it likes to remind other nations that it considers lawless or backwards) which presupposes prudence and therefore rationalism, then there is a greater burden for the society to ensure preservation and promulgation of these values since rationalism is not necessarily a natural state or inherent characteristic from birth. What passes as, or constitutes, reason can be as individualistic, subjective or relative as there are people, with innumerable mutual exclusivities. If culture imparts a sense of belonging, with commonly held beliefs and values, individualism and self-autonomy are its antithesis; and yet in practice these seem to epitomize Americanism that celebrates individuality above family and private property above community. The incomprehensible rage associated with killings of the last few years as reported by the popular press seem to reflect a huge disconnect between numerous and complex individual needs, especially of the young. These crimes cover a full spectrum of Americana from rural outbacks to city streets, inside homes, schools, police stations, corporate offices and foreign postings, involving all ages across the income, educational, ethnic and lifestyles spectrum. These are swept aside when a society values and seeks instant gratification, entertainment, celebrity and the new which are better served by forgetting rather than understanding, resolving and forgiving.

Non-American cultures are characterized by apparent homogeneity of the population and the seemingly endless means devised and employed to differentiate, ranging from extreme and elaborate external displays (e.g., body mutilations, accessories and dress) to subtle distinctions (e.g., mannerisms, rituals, forms of speech and address) made along the axes of duty and honour of defined relationships or status. America is characterized by the non-homogeneity of its population and an aversion to class stratification, but the need to differentiate still prevails predominantly on the 'look' and economic axes. In indigenous cultures, the look or a bundled first impression is a given, encapsulating components of identity and status very quickly, comprehensively and non-verbally, as a result of 24/7 (around-the-clock, seven-days-a-week) cultural assimilation and millennia of cultural evolution. Many indigenous spoken languages are also embedded with identity as a function of relationships. But in the U.S. the look is anything but given, and the need to move beyond this immediate and superficial categorization is greater, because it cannot serve as a primary determinant of identity in a country of such diversity. While looks cannot convey as much and as saliently as in some traditional cultures, the media continue to place the greatest weight on this one factor, so that in practice the one factor that should recede becomes the primary focal point, determining the terms and conditions of engagement in many situations (social, economic, political), often with lifelong consequences.

More importantly, what constitutes the collective and cumulative memory of Americans, so essential to the formation and evolution of a cultural paradigm? The practice of associating with a broad category of skin colour is a uniquely American phenomenon. How does a colour designation signify or imbue one with the attributes and constituents of an identity, let alone a cultural paradigm? White-American can be an amalgamation of many ethnic backgrounds, not necessarily all of European ancestry and, like white light, the result of many colours. Colour is, after all, only an illusion of the mind which interprets the play of light wave lengths or particles through the red, green and blue filters: it serves a purpose of expression or nominalism but does not contain any element of virtue or value. Catch-all stereotyping by referral to continents such as Asia, Africa or Europe is absurd when one considers the cultural divide that distinguishes each country within these regions, as well as the internecine strife within each country. Each country maintains and subscribes to its distinct cultural paradigm. A European heritage can be intellectual but not cultural because too many values collide, as evidenced by the history of European countries, as is the case with all other continents.

Americanism and racial purity or racial categorization is a contradiction in terms. As can be seen in many countries claiming some degree of racial purity, a cultural paradigm does not revolve around such concepts as what one's race is or how many races comprise one's lineage. What cultural paradigm one subscribes to is distinct and separate from race. While America can be said to consist of a racially diverse population of many individuals with mixed nationalities, this does not translate into a workable amalgamation or synthesis or syncretism of numerous cultural paradigms, let alone understanding or tolerance of all of these distinct cultures. Not only is the concept of pure-breed or half-breed absurd at a physical level, but increasingly at an intellectual level, as global communications disperse many ideas and points of view. The American experience can be viewed as a template for global direction towards a single population, requiring greater tolerance of differences and greater understanding of commonalities. Being of German, French, Spanish, English, Chinese, African descent does not result in a knowledge or familiarity with all these cultures and their values, let alone tolerance for them: racial diversity does not equal cultural diversity because the former is an individual physical expression and experience of the one (static and singular), whereas the latter is an interactive and evolving collective intellectual, emotional and perhaps spiritual development of the one and the many. This requires learning of some kind (dynamic and numerous), just as responsibility (parental) does not give rise to aptitude, knowledge to wisdom, or lifestyle to (virtuous) life.

According to Voltaire, 'If God did not exist, it would be necessary to invent him', since the meaning of life, i.e., why am I here?, cannot by definition come from man himself due to its circular nature, no matter how clever its circularity or metaphysics/metamatters. The devotion and insistence for an external, all-powerful, singular homocentric God is much more pervasive in Western traditions compared to examples of Ancient or Eastern beliefs and traditions of Egyptian, Persian, Greek, Indian, Chinese, Nordic, Celtic or Teutonic origin with their numerous non-homocentric images or purely symbolic representations. Whether or not there is an answer to life's meaning, the matter cannot be bypassed or unengaged, so that pursuit of self-knowledge is a timeless affair and matter of the heart above and beyond merely limiting downside risks or ensuring reciprocity, involving experiences and perceptions transcending time and space. Yet, how is disengagement from time and space possible? The teachings of thinkers, sages and saints would indicate that it cannot be achieved without great effort towards stillness through meditation or prayer, becoming a strand of time in the eye of space, ultimately approaching and recognizing commonness (universality) and nothingness (infinity).

Because most countries enjoy (or are burdened with) millennia of cultural heritage, those who seek other paths, voluntarily or involuntarily, need a place of refuge. The U.S. is the primary provider of relief for the many who are not so specifically aligned or inclined. Many of those who live in the U.S. do so because they do not or cannot belong anywhere else. In a way, it is a country created for this purpose. But it is not a free pass to unequivocal individualism with entitlements of absolute liberty, equality and happiness or justice. Being an American entails a greater awareness and tolerance of others than in all other countries, not the reverse. Therefore citizenship unpredicated upon nationality requires a greater degree of mandatory education regarding its values and obligations beyond paying taxes and not running afoul of the law (for example, compulsory community or national service).

The lack of a specific cultural paradigm in the U.S. is exacerbated by the fact that the term 'culture' is used in a wide variety of contexts, most notably to denote popular entertainment or consumer products and services, created and reinforced by the pervasive and all-encompassing mass media, securing and establishing their foothold and footprint on all sensory platforms. Culture is symbolized and epitomized by visual spectacles and is divorced from its moeurs (manners, customs, behaviours). The very term 'cultural icons' would be puzzling to people of traditional cultures because it is a contradiction in terms: culture lives in the hearts and minds of its belongers, not in image-worship and image-creation which are manifestations and extensions of inflated human personalities and forms masquarading as Truth. While the original intent may have been to use icons to draw and retain religious believers, the mass media machinery has usurped the original intent while taking iconography and iconism to new heights and twists. The terms 'cultural icons' and 'iconoclastic' are ironically used interchangeably by advertisers for symbols of consumerism or industry, while the term 'cultural gap' is used to cover and obscure the credibility and knowledge gap by anyone who cannot or does not want to acknowledge or understand a different perspective.

The heart of most traditional cultural paradigms is the family unit, which is based upon consanguinity or its defined equivalents through marriages and adoptions. Kinship, therefore, forms the core of the values hierarchy, not rationalism, nationalism or patriotism, nor how well-educated or strong one is. Consanguinity can be oppressive and inescapable, but, like life itself, it poses challenges and obstacles. Enculturation—the acquisition of cultural intelligence—sets up a way of coping with factors beyond one's control without causing harm or disharmony to the one and the many. In the U.S. the family structure is increasingly disassociated from consanguinity, which is increasingly viewed as being incompatible with the pursuit of individual liberty and equality as well as material prosperity. Instead, families are mostly viewed as marketing and political concepts with cultural contexts only relevant in these applications. Family members are no longer individuals but, rather, consumers or voters to be categorized, sorted, counted, summarized, weighed and valued by income (spending and donation track-record and potential), ethnicity, gender and age. However, unless the family is understood, appreciated and valued for itself, and unless its functions and perpetuation are ensured, the importance and relevance of the family will also diminish for even marketing and political purposes.

But the trade-off does not diminish or abrogate the functions that consanguinity provides; the cultural void continues to grow, seductively and amply fed by consumerism and drowned out by a lot of noise, so that its wane and absence go unnoticed. Because culture is no longer an all-pervasive reality and the traditional transmission mechanisms and content are largely AWOL, many aspects of society need to be drawn into the enculturation exercise, especially in the K-12 schooling years which still remain largely compulsory, in order to fill the gap and the void. Countering the obsolescence of the traditional family structure and social hierarchy that are non-monetarily defined and non-barterized (i.e., not a derivative of a market economy where *quid pro quo* reigns, and the trade relationship is defined as fair market exchange of values, where everything and anything can be bought and sold), requires shifting the primary emphasis from the traditional 3 R's to those of relationships in the various stages of life.

There is instead an exponential growth industry of merchandising spirituality along with virtual, pseudo and temporary families, or affiliations staffed by counselors peddling advice and remedies to emulate the traditional transmitters of cultural values. Cultural values used to be transmitted and driven home by and through all formal and informal structures and functions throughout society. Beginning with the parents, extended family, educational systems and secular entities, these structures and functions encompassed just about every point of contact or interaction with the outside world. Non-secular entities, particularly Christianity, with its systematic ploy of cornering the authority market and paternalistic language, undermines family values and usurps or displaces the diversity of memories since faith based on supposition of free will is not conducive to being passed on without ever greater exertion of authority and imposition of its singular point of view which conveniently includes satisfaction, consolation and even reward for ceaseless punishment and suffering of the other or non-believers.[2] The mass media and distribution enable the mass production and marketing of indul-

---

2. "In order that the happiness of the saints may be more delightful to them and that they may render more copious thanks to God, first they are allowed to see perfectly the suffering of the damned...the Divine justice and their own deliverance will be the direct cause of

continued

gences which further amplify demand. Therefore as sacred texts become merely another off-the-shelf product with a price tag, their lustre becomes increasingly dull as the secular and non-secular converge and engage in the same practices in the same marketplace for same subscriber from Wall to Main Streets.

The modern want-to-be equivalents or 'enterprising charlatans unlimited' proliferate as self-help and how-to programmes and publications, therapy groups of all kinds, temporary shelters, foster care, daycares, nursing homes, prisons and Web sites, often characterized by less than a one-dimensional category and assuaged by anonymity. None of these offers an authentic path to the expression of cultural identity because the concept of *inter loco parentis* from its social context is missing, being entirely materially focused and due to the lack of integration and coherence among all the transmission vehicles and the transmitters.

The North American cultural identity is uniquely unfettered by ethnocentrism and nationalism by definition if not by heritage and practice, with the corollary of a greater burden on and of credibility, even perhaps authenticity. This latter aspect is the challenge of individualism, in that the right to life, liberty and pursuit of happiness rests upon an appreciation that the same rights shall be exercised by all others—equally, unobstructed and unimpeded. There is no one source of text, but only a profound search and need for commonality of purpose and value or common ground to extend the boundaries of inclusion towards universality while distinguishing the private and public spheres. This is the bedrock of individual humanity beckoning for a fillip beyond the 'I', so essential and necessary for understanding and approximating justice and order. In this context, a particular cultural paradigm can be viewed as an aid or enabling interface template for individuals to traverse and travail outside the self which is deemed to be not necessarily

joy of the blessed, while the pain of the damned will cause it indirectly...the blessed in glory will have no pity for the damned." St. Thomas Aquinas, *Summa Theologica* (III Supp.[xciv] pp. 1-3) as quoted in "C.S.Lewis, God and the Problems of Evil," Prof. Anthony Flew, *Philosophy Now*, April/May 2000, p. 29.

Author's Note: The fervour of evangelism in converting infidels to a particular monotheism in order to increase its subscriber base and decrease diversity finds its equal match in the degree of intolerance, disdain and hatred spawned and spewed. It seems an apt expression of an attenuated and much qualified love that exemplifies the antithesis of compassion.

intuitive or reflexive but necessary to be initialized and disseminated explicitly for each new generation. Since encounters of the new, unfamiliar and different are situational and infinite, the enabling interface template cannot be rigid or fixed, but must be capable of continuous development and improvisation based upon an underlying theme.

Multiculturalism, while an appealing concept, is anti-American in that it creates distinct, separate and unique group identities which side-step, distract and detract from syndesis.[3] This results in disunity and disharmony: minorities are equally marginalized and superficialized. Only vested interests are well-served and serviced where cultural context is both absent and unnecessary for its focus and purpose. The resulting jargon spewing out will be 'compassionate capitalism' and its variants. Humanism and identities based on non-ethnic and non-look aspects offer a road map consistent with being an American.

Making an effort to associate and acknowledge an individual first by name would be a start, rather than linking to religion, ethnicity, gender, age or other convenient and dehumanizing one- dimensional labels. An example of this is the phrase 'six million Jews' which immediately sets up a 'not us' disassociation, bereaving its lesson-value in both individual and universal contexts. The 'us versus them' is only a man-made construct or divide as are various other exercises in nomination, quantification and illustration which serve to elaborate differences for affect and effect to counter the ubiquitous us.

While the outside-in consequences of all the fine categorizations may hinge upon superficial perceptions, inside-out or culturally-driven paradigms have tended to immunize and transcend such superficiality and superciliousness until the advent of packaged image proliferation. The attitudes, values and beliefs are no longer driven by ethnicity linked with specific cultures but by

---

3. Author's Note: Syndesis: the state of being bound, linked, or connected together. Studying different ideas, languages, cultures and traditions can be a process of syndesis rather than discrete, unconnected and unrelated data arrays. This is similar to catenation of (computer) workspace which results in geometric modular expansion in both data carrying and programme application capacity. Syndesis thus is an expansion of mind space leading to exponential performance improvement and enhancement much as the value of a diamond steeply curves upwards with increases in size, brilliance and clarity. Colour is only valued for its absence which results in its maximum prismatic radiance.

artificial and totalitarian constructs, especially along political and economic dimensions entwined with quasi-religious overtones. Segmentation spawns by destroying and emulating the inside-out foundation of identity upon which it feeds by inserting and recycling its own nominations, images and definitions which are naturally, economically and efficiently self-serving. Thus the multiplier effect of choice-making (internally and externally) masks the homogeneity of the selection process as well as the choice itself, as the industry of hate thrives, unchecked. Competition which necessitates incessant comparisons annihilates any sense of standards by reducing everything into relativity, quantity and irreverence.

No culture is exempt from these nauseating and macerating scum and slime. It is not uncommon to observe that the negative sentiments held against various categories of others have been instilled, shaped and formed by mass media stereotypes or propaganda rather than based upon historical or experiential contexts, regardless of ethic origin. Such seeding of stereotypical images once *in situ* are rarely dislodged or balanced but more likely to become increasingly reinforced and fortified.

Rather than advocating a singular belief in one system, a study and understanding of no less than three are encouraged by the age of 18 or 21 as a rite of passage into majority status. This approach will increase the probability of mindfulness formation, development and maintenance, the *sine qua non* to sound choice-making at all times, in all places and in all occasion. Polymathical educational philosophy tends to encourage exploration beyond the three standard deviations into the realm of the infinite along both wings or tails of the bell-curve.

As Prof. Isaiah Berlin wrote, "the only freedom to which knowledge contributes is freedom from illusion."[4] It seems that only our firmly clenched attachment to illusions exceeds our grasping material possessiveness. This uniquely human trait and tendency for self-inflicted wounds should be a necessary and sufficient cause for teaching and cultivating mindfulness or self-knowledge for self-binding and healing throughout life, leading to serenity based upon confidence in and integrity of self-identity coupled with a sense of belonging.

---

4. Isaiah Berlin, *The Proper Study of Mankind: An Anthology of Essays* [1949-90] (Pimlico Edition, 1998), p.107.

For most people there is an implicit cultural identity which is an integral part of ethnicity and imparts a sense of personal identity. However, a disconnect between ethnicity and cultural identity has been created by the advent of global commerce, based on capitalism, which not only facilitates the flow of financial assets but also of people; by the pervasiveness of the mass media, with more of the same content in greater variety of format and controlled by the narrow interest of capitalism; and by information technology, increasingly driven and defined by capitalism in pursuit of greater profits.

The result is to forfeit or counterfeit personal identity, resulting in rootlessness and alienation. Personal identity becomes ad-hoc as does much else when novelty and disposability are valued, and integrity is rendered superfluous. Under the aegis of a laissez-faire market economy, amply complemented by the mass media, it is not surprising that hawkers of identity proliferate and thrive, peddling a comprehensive range of off-the-shelf identity products and services offering a full line from financial and physical to emotional and spiritual: economic identity and all its accouterment being the *sine qua non* in this edifying milieu. This is compounded by the re-constitutionalization, both in membership and frequency, of the family and the relative ease of relocation across continents, whether in pursuit of academic qualifications, economic opportunities (foreign and out-of-state students and employees being largely a phenomenon of American academic institutions and corporations), political freedom, or other personal goals. While external features retain similarities and expectations remain, the process of enculturation is fragmented and increasingly non-family defined or driven, as changes in its structure and stability have a dramatic and inevitable effect on its function and functionality.

An impression of multiculturalism, internationalism and cosmopolitanism is created, which externally reveals itself through familiarity with many aspects other cultures, as can be sensorily (or superficially) perceived (e.g., language, dress, cuisine, music, dance) as well as through sharing a similar ideological outlook in varying degrees of Westernization or Americanization. This is most pronounced in the younger segment of society, nurtured and brought up on a steady daily diet of television and various entertainment media, in the absence of parents or extended families. Even the education curriculum is tending towards homogenization based on achieving economic goals, and has become a supplicant to industry as a provider of trained labour based on identification of their future requirements; money has become the sole definer of status and power. To the extent that enculturation is an informal practice and its transmission curtailed or supplanted, what is readily absorbed and therefore familiar will take on the mantle of a cultural identity. A cultural identity, shaped and formed by this gleaning process, is likely to be extremely individualistic, with pride disproportionately related to its shallowness and demand for immediate satisfaction of wants unmatched by its ability as to means. An amplifying loop is set up, with frustration leading to unrestrained anger and hatred, resulting in reckless behaviour and feeding into feelings of alienation and, ultimately, loneliness.

In Chapters 4 and 5 an exploration of these concepts and their application are articulated and illuminated through reference to the Korean culture. The Korean culture is included as an example, not as an exemplar, of traditional or ancient cultures. The normative practice is described, and while it varies from household to household[5] therein, the underlying cultural theme of family and social bonds and values is ever present, being embedded in the language, with no shortage of terms denoting relationships which guide attendant demeanour and appropriate form and content of address, governing engagement and disengagement of the other. The intention is to show how a value system determines and affects one's relationships and forms a foundation for a code of conduct, with a sense of honour and dignity of the one and the many, rather than 'family values' as just a vague and vacuous concept or an expedient political sound bite. Truth, justice, charity, love, compassion, etc., without social context, are not operationally functional and remain just abstracts when disconnected and disassociated from day-to-day existence and experience. No culture is deemed to be superior; each culture has its own internally accessible and coherent set of values, and enculturation initializes a process of shaping a value hierarchy which evolves as the individual and society incorporate new knowledge and experience.

Values, whatever they are articulated to be, are only realizable in attitude and behaviour activated through relationship with the other, which is unlikely to be tension-free but rather contingent upon it. In this context, values are not ends but dynamic processing systems and linking interfaces

---

5. "All happy families are like one another; each unhappy family is unhappy in its own way." Leo Tolstoy, *Anna Karenina* [1877] (Signet Classics, 1961), p.17.

for tempering relationships with both the seen and unseen to mitigate temperamental inclination. In the trinity of the father, son and the holy spirit, it is the spirit that relates and imparts definition to the other. It is imageless and yet defines the fluid and infinite points of contact and degrees of separateness. The quality and quantity of inter-beingness and relatedness shape and form the manifestation of the potentiality for goodness and badness, transforming us gradually.

Regardless of what awaits at the end of this transformation process of endurance, alluvion and acclimation, we are better prepared for the inevitable encounter with the unknown, independent of our attribute and possession. The sages and elders, both secular and non-secular, attempt to temper our foolhardy and headlong rush or natural inclination toward the temporal and material by illuminating the sacredness of relationships. Since this sacredness is essentially ineffable, but penetrable with effort for those who attempt the journey towards completeness by infusing their lives with the non-temporal and non-material, their teachings are not for nought. The pursuit of whole-heartedness, in lieu of half-hearted existence, through the cultivation of a spiritual life is prone to be tenuous and elusive for those who cannot dignify and honour the relationships with their fore-mothers and -fathers, as well as teachers, let alone with others. Thus, in the quest for completeness and wholeness of the heart, to be human is neither natural nor unnatural, but attitudinal and relational.

Whether one believes in rationalism and self-determination, which imply a burden or freedom of choice, or in their opposites (emotionalism and fatalism), one's cultural identity plays a crucial role in life's journey. A cultural identity or a lack thereof can either facilitate and enhance or impede and reduce availability and perception of choice in how one deals with ambiguous situations. By providing a framework of materiality, context and perspective, a cultural paradigm provides varying degrees of comfort levels and safety zones to avoid or mitigate feelings of helplessness and hopelessness. The sea of life is as unpredictable and uncertain as any ocean journey, and just as experienced pilot needs to cope with both the known and the unknown, one must be as well-prepared as possible to minimize the probability of capsizing and avoid catastrophe.

What is relevant is not whether one believes that people are mostly irrational or subscribes to a chaos theory or chaotic outlook of some kind, but what value system is operational, manifesting itself in all aspects and varieties of encounters: should one's attitude and behaviours simply be irrational and chaotic because one perceives the world as such? Is this any kind of justification or explanation for unconstrained individuality? This is the distinction between delusion, illusion, detachment and denial, versus reality, illumination, engagement and acceptance, hinged on a personal sense of a specific cultural paradigm, transmitted by the family or by other means, such as formal education.

Studies of successful corporations reveal distinct corporate cultures. These did not just materialize randomly one day. As with corporate identity, individual cultural identity is an invaluable brand which one acquires over time through consistent exposure and effort. Like any viable marketing brand, it cannot be just a smorgasbord of random inputs. Commercial brands are invaluable assets of corporations, as are corporate identities. Enormous resources in talent, time and money are invested in their systematic development, innovation, enhancement, adaptation, projection, communication and protection. Many countries have Ministries or Departments of Culture to serve similar functions, although perhaps with fewer resources and flair or fervour than their corporate counterparts. One of the key factors for success in the corporate environment is an understanding of the corporate culture and its rules; employment is based on the understanding that these will be followed, beyond the policies and procedures manuals, which few but the internal auditors read or know about.

Likewise, cultural intelligence increases the odds of flourishing in the social community. While an individual cannot define or create a cultural identity, one can choose to emphasize or de-emphasize certain attributes to transcend stereotypes in order to gain entry to the other cultures in personal and professional endeavours. There can be a disconnect between ethnicity and cultural identity (permanent relocation), but not a disassociation or lack of one that is consistent and coherent within the operative cultural paradigm of residence or simply a self-constructed culture of one.

A cultural paradigm is like a well-designed computer programme which includes monitoring sub-routines to red-flag errors in processor output by setting defined parameters, along with default settings and override functions. For the most part, defaults and overrides are exceptions and when they are no longer so, the sub-routines need to be revised. Rules are no longer rules if all that transpires are exceptions. An individual's cultural paradigm also includes defaults and overrides as adjuncts to choice-making; these are also continuously updated and revised at both macro- and micro-levels, but not neglected, displaced or discarded in a random manner by random inputs.[6]

Irrespective of whether one acknowledges one's brand identity or not, its effects are inescapable; to deny or ignore its existence is likely to result in not only an internal schism or frustration and alienation, but carry a real penalty in all facets of life, including family, socioeconomic, political, and personal dimensions. In North America, a common and frequent response to the question, "Are you a Jew?"(or Chinese, Korean, Italian, Greek, Iranian etc), is, "No, I am a non-practicing or secular Jew" (or American or Canadian). Does this mean that they are practicing being a WASP, becoming something other than what they are, equating their professional affiliation, economic standing or political party membership with identity, or simply becoming more straight-jacketed and less human? This is the reverse of people who go around claiming to be Christians (or some other religion with their numerous sects vying for the top truth position) and yet practise so little or none of what this religion teaches or adhere to any of its imperatives. Since organic and

6. Author's Note: The premise that cultural identity is not a function of ethnicity is borne out by the effects of conditioning by asymmetric programming through the mass media and long term immersion in asymmetric social environments. The fear and intolerance of Blacks, Jews, Arabs, Indians, and Asians based on stereotypes and labels by each other and by peoples who have neither had any encounters with these others nor had historically antagonistic relationships cannot simply be justified as sentiments associated with the unknown. Another aspect of this is also evident in the similarities of the nature of these negative sentiments as well as the subject of such sentiments. In 'naturalized' Americans of various ethnic or cultural origins, the values and views held in common are quite homogeneous beyond just common language and duration of residence. The degree and depth of conversion into the culture of asymmetricism, anti-intellectualism and infantilism pivoting upon fear, hatred and intolerance, even of their own, by so many supposedly different categories of people only support their common needs to belong and to believe, preferably with quick and easy means and ends. Such attitudes are reinforced by the absence of studies in world history or a superficial skimming of it through rosy filters of nationalism and ethnocentrism spun by educational institutions, mass media, industries, parents and peers. These singular and single points of view tend to promulgate, proselytize and justify the use of force and might as acceptable means of conflict resolution since they tend to provide mass appeal and benefits for self-serving interests to ancillary benefit of providing grist for 'news' to special events and spectacles in continuous global 24/7 loops.

indigenous character traits that impart class, status and taste (flanges for social traction on the rails of time) in locales permeating with the toil and toll of predecessors are increasingly absent or displaced (literally and symbolically), the need for differentiation takes on the form of what are increasingly in-your-face outings and flauntings.

Not all Koreans (or peoples of other enduring cultures) can be said to be aware of their ancestral seat or adhere to the cultural ways which include ancestor reverence, filial piety, self-cultivation, capping ceremonies, and a working fluency in their mother-tongue, but this does not then make them into something other than Koreans, non-practicing Koreans, and surely not WASPs, even with multiple credentials or rounds of plastic surgery to look and sound WASPish. A particular trait that many who forge their identity share, other than being incoherent and without a sense of bottom, is an absence of poetry, non-resonance or tone-deafness. One is not commanded to honour and defend one's mother because she may be weak or strong, stupid or smart, rich or poor, good or bad, or some other categories or conclusions based on our own preferences, analysis (breaking down) and judgement, but solely because of who she is—someone whose heartbeat, voice and movement are indelibly imprinted into our own being or identity. A minimal proficiency in denial and splitting hairs, and not much else, oftentimes leads to displacing millennia of becoming for the momentary expediency, illusions and vanity of resetting the clock to zero or repeatedly wiping the slate clean for some kitschy self-concocted identity derived from mass pulldown menus, and settling for mediocrity, vulgarity, or the most common demoninator and the newest thing. Does the ability to commit identity *seppukku* or resort to *kamikaze* actions exempt anyone from categorization, fear, hate, disdain, or reproach by insiders and outsiders alike, or is this just opening more fronts for affronts leading to obduracy and all-out defence of self-created notions in the belief that anything self-originated must be fool-proof? This can result in dysfunctionality, non-relevance, marginalization, obsolescence and even incarceration and termination.

E pluribus unum: out of many, one. Can one culture—the language, values, arts, customs, food, dress, music, mannerisms, special days of observances—be selected above all others? Can it be an amalgamation of so many different cultures which, upon closer examination, reveals incompatibility at so many levels? Just as religious affiliations are mutually exclusive, so are cultural identities; two religious beliefs cannot reside in one body.

What ethnic threads are woven into the fabric of American culture? English, Irish, Scottish, French, German, Spanish, Italian, Russian and involuntary Africans in the past, and Mexican, Chinese, Japanese, Korean, Vietnamese, Iranian, Armenian, Lebanese, etc., more recently. What philosophical ideas permeate the American text? A meshing of the secular and sentimental values of 18th-century vintage: rationalism (age of enlightenment), nostalgia for the Republic, equality, liberty, empiricism, romanticism. If all this weren't schizophrenic enough, overlaid is the Christian religion and, topping it all off , the capitalist structure and its *coup de grâce*, the entertainment mega-empire, spawned to lull the fragmented (schizoid) mass into the chase of the material rather than materiality.

The Americanized Christian religion resembles a truncated pseudo-Christianity where rituals are divorced from faith due to the inconsistency in acknowledging the Divine power and existence of God when the goals are temporal and political. Christianity is reactive movement away from Judaism and towards a cult of the lowest common denominator as the entry bar is lowered or concocted anew to cater to narrowing categories of exclusivity and fashion. The term 'Judaeo-Christian heritage' is itself quite schizophrenic in the historical context of relentless persecution and slaughter. The means for achieving the goals of evangelism to maximize subscriber base are powered by cult of personalities who establish kleptocracies of their very own, propagating and promulgating by renting or owning media space. This results in the crowding out of charity (a Christian virtue) by political donations as political domination entwines with religious fervour, so that instead of helping the poor, weak and hungry, the rich, strong and overfed prevail.

This is the trend with all religions in their confrontation with modernity: fundamentalism no longer represents extremes of piety and virtue but extreme political ideologies, skirting and embracing fanaticism which breeds martyrs in service of political and temporal rather than virtuous and spiritual ends.

If the concept of heaven and hell convinced the masses to veer towards the good and virtuous, the removal of Divine judgement in practice seems to have laid to waste even the concept of the good and virtuous. What has taken thousands of years and countless lives to construct in order to understand the good and virtuous has been decimated in a matter of decades, demonstrating the power of modern efficiency and money. These new currencies of power are controlled and exercised by the few over the disillusioned and delusional masses. Philosophy which relies on calm, composed and collected thought through study also dies where frenetic activity around the making and spending of money prevails, and when the mere perception of being busy merges with status.

The conformity of consumerism unites people but is also their undoing, because the mantra of *I consume, therefore I am*, impedes or circumvents the pursuit of a higher awareness or different state of consciousness to maximize compassion in order to enable crossing the language and species barrier into the pool of moral life. One thinks *one culture is just as good as another* or *American is superior* without ever defining the culture to which one refers or even its profound meaning, with all the innumerable and interminable manifestations of culture.

The U.S. has never been a melting pot in that there is no oneness to assimilate into. It is a collection of tribes that have enough in common and common interest to mesh together an economic political structure. The tribes in the early days at least shared Eurocentrism with common looks and philosophical outlooks. However, they were not very successful colonizers in so far as preserving their way of life in perpetuity. They faced the dilemma of not having a cultural identity, unlike the very successful imperial colonialists who transplanted their lifestyle and culture in its entirety, strictly preserving all of its features even more vigorously than the folks at home, doing their best to demonstrate its superiority and dumping or unloading it onto the indigenous people while maintaining strict segregation and hegemony on political power.

Since the first Americans fought and won the war over the imperial powers, they would have needed to forge a new, distinct and unique cultural identity. As long as there was some consensus on what the American culture was, with its Eurocentric leanings, a delusion could be maintained and judgements as to what was acceptable, tasteful or *de rigueur* could continue to be made and observed. But once the forces of capitalism took over and the U.S. became a magnet for the worldwide pool of labour, this delusion was replaced by a culture of the individual and the material.

This can be seen if one compares the American perception of and reaction to taxation with countries of similar economic development, such as the United Kingdom, France and Germany, as well as countries whose per capita income lags far behind, such as China and India. While there is a universal dislike and dodging of paying taxes, in the U.S. one notices that there is resentment and anger at foregoing a part of one's labour in the interest of others who are seen to have no relevance to oneself. In contrast, the other countries reveal an acquiescence and acceptance of one's responsibility to others and contributions to society as a whole. This seems to be a result of trade-offs made by respective societies: *the broad social stability of the group versus unbridled upward or unsecured downward mobility of the individual.*

The Constitution and rule of law would appear to have been adequate in an earlier time when memory and practice of one's cultural life (ethical frame-work) was still internally accessible. But relying so heavily (or solely) on the rule of law rather than, or in lieu of, cultural imperatives has its drawbacks, as evidenced by what happens when the influence of the cultural imperatives dissipates and disappears over many generations, removed from the centre both figuratively and literally, and lacquered over with the influx of so many other influences. A Caucasian-American can be mistaken for one of many European nationalities usually without eliciting a negative response, but being mistaken for an American seems to be especially unflattering to a European or Canadian.

What makes the U.S. unique among all other countries is that it has traded off and paid for economic power and status, fueled and propelled by immigration, by giving up what made an individual a belonger, i.e., the inalienable and incommensurate right to a cultural identity. Appropriate homage to Christianity is still paid on Sundays by some who still believe that they can be both a good Christian in faith and a capitalist in practice. So the irony is in the increased or all-pervasive obsession with the self, when that self is the vestigial remains of a cultural identity, or an artificial construct of one, or a schizophrenic amalgamation that does not exist meaningfully and holis-tically, so that its disappearance or destruction would matter. This has resulted in a continuous tug-of-war over matters like abortion, right to die, death penalty and gun control, in a milieu where life seems to have lost meaning and value,[7] not to overlook the incredible supply side, with 214,000 births per day worldwide.[8]

The American culture could be a unifying human culture girded by universal human values, demanding much individual effort to sustain the complex workings of a democratic system in its political, economic and social dimensions and aspirations which necessarily involve trade-offs and compromises. Its text is not chiseled onto a blank slate but floats upon a stream of human experience and humanistic principles. A rigid, narrow and fundamentalist reading and application of its text is to dishonour and distort its authors and their legacies which tend to be inclusive and dynamic. An exclusive and static approach is therefore self-defeating, being inconsistent and at odds with the purpose of the text which is neither the beginning nor the end, but a framework for an attitude of mindfulness.

What is the point of teaching that guns are lethal weapons without first teaching the value of human (and other) life and why it is wrong to kill? The ironic twist is that those who so fervently advocate the abolition of abortion seem to be equally fervent in their support of the death penalty and gun ownership. This is cultural schizophrenia spilling onto the political realm, with wholesale assault on, and abandonment of, the common sense and cause.

Instead of spending so much effort on whether to bring forth life or facilitate its termination, why not focus on what being human means in terms of its values and how to care for and nurture human life? The challenge is for scholars to reach a consensus and produce a completely secular set of texts for use from kindergarten through grade 12. Something so fundamental as the

7. Mohammed is often quoted as saying that the "greatest catastrophes are many children and meagre sustenance." D.S. Roberts, *Islam: A Concise Introduction* (Harper & Row, 1981), p. 121.

8. "78 million people are being added to the planet every year—95% in developing countries." *Planned Parenthood International News*, vol. 1 (September 1999).

Author's Note: One's birthday celebration is a humbling experience in the context of sharing this one special and personal day with over 200,000 people, multiplied by one's age, most of whom do not celebrate it, or even know of it, let alone with joy and happiness. The U.S. with almost 300 million people may be the third largest population but with a consumption and disposal multiplier of 30-50, it represents a resource depletion weighted population base of 9-15 billion people.

human need to belong via a cultural identity cannot be neglected or allowed to occur in some random fashion. Of equal importance is how to take care of and nurture human life, since parenthood does not equal ability to parent; 'biology is destiny' cannot carry with it such an ominous undertone and unmitigable destiny. Parenting in all cultures is a learned skill for both genders; there is nothing innate about its requirements.

Cultural values and child-rearing practices, whatever they turn out to be, are not being propagated and disseminated in a coherent and consistent manner from generation to generation. The causes are many, including the need for both parents to work, separation of extended families, lack of family ties, language and lifestyle barriers between generations, and lives that are saturated and consumed in artificiality. However, the individual's ability to navigate through life with adequate choice-making and life-nurturing skills cannot be left entirely to fate. A starting point could be the creation of a Book of Humanization (Human Ethics) that would evolve through the Talmudic or Buddhist tradition of rigorous, disciplined and qualified discourse. The Department of Education should be complemented by a Division of Humanity with responsibility for ensuring proper teaching material and teaching methods of humanizing values, human conduct and parenting skills.

How meaningful or useful is it to study anthropology, history, sociology, psychology and economics without a cultural and a human context, and an appreciation of what it means to be a human being today? Such contexts will dislodge these studies from being just concepts, far removed from one's reality, to ideas that have relevance in both meaning and application to one's daily life. What meaning do Eurocentric history lessons have for all the non-Caucasian students? What feelings are inspired by viewing pictures of the founding fathers in the rotunda of the Capital Building and other national monuments for those citizens not of European descent pre-WW II vintage? These disconnects increase as political monumentalism overtakes the com-memoration of great teachers and leaders of timeless and universal significance and appeal.

What would make American culture unique would be what it cannot con-sist of: specific ethnicity, son of the native soil, religion. The notion of a son of the native soil holds profound implications for the indigenous in the con-text of reverential attitudes and rituals associated with the land, for example, by many Native Tribes, as well as with many immigrants' continuous ties with their homeland, even if their place of birth is different. If these are not allowed, what is left is a common denominator of what it is to be a human being and what it takes to nurture one. Therefore, the American culture would be unique in formalizing what the beliefs, values, and practices of being human are, and what is needed for its physical and intellectual nourishment. Since the U.S. has been the champion of universal human rights and the main source of funds for the UN (which is located on U.S. soil, in its most vibrant and diverse city), it would be an extension and formalization of what it has initiated, preached and practiced, consistent with its *raison d'être* from its founding. Woodrow Wilson's concept of the League of Nations, proposed unsuccessfully after WWI but later forming the backdrop for the creation of the UN in 1945, and the Universal Declaration of Human Rights in 1948, championed by Eleanor Roosevelt, started a secular ecumenical movement bearing a distinctive made-in-America stamp.

Capitalism cannot serve as a cultural blueprint, not only because it is an economic theory, but because it carries its own seed of destruction; after all, what is the hope and dream of a capitalist but to dominate and control the market by doing away with competition and creating a monopoly, which means that a capitalistic culture will breed tyrants. Are the concentration of wealth, its synonymity with status and existence side by side with poverty and homelessness what Adam Smith, the Scottish moral philosopher and founder of modern political economy, had in mind when he prophesied that the U.S. would be one of the foremost nations of the world? If efficient use of resources results in profit maximization, isn't there a supposition that frugality and thrift be practiced, instead of lands and oceans filled with pollutants, waste and garbage?

In an economy where the stock market reigns supreme, PR (public relations/media spin), EPS (earnings per share) and P/E (price/earnings ratio) take precedence over ROI (return on investment) or ROA (return on assets) and cash flow. What does the denominator of ROA consist of? How are damages to human life and the environment,[9] depletion of non-renewable resources and costs to the community accounted for, beyond the nominal

---

9. "In the symbolic killing of the albatross, he found what might be called a 'green parable', the idea of man's destructive effect on the natural world, so that human moral blindness inadvertently introduces evil into the benign systems of nature, releasing uncontrollable forces that take terrible revenge." Richard Holmes, *Coleridge: Early Visions* (Penguin Books, 1989), p.173.

penalties, fees and termination pay? Are these non-assets tending towards zero, resulting in an infinite rate of return? Or is it in concept and actuality that these assets are of infinite value (invaluable) so that the rate of return tends to zero?

The Constitution, a product of 18th-century sensibility of equality and liberty, not only has these two values, which collide and conflict in practice, but has an insurmountable deficiency, in that it excluded three very visible and vital segments of its population: African slaves, the indigenous people, and the female gender. Another obstacle is its non-secular nature, which causes internal conflicts among believers and non-believers, with so many different interpretations as well as the discord with current and future pop- ulation profiles, which will only be more diverse and divergent regarding which god(s) are worshipped; it also presupposes prudence of man, on the basis of which it is formulated.

Finally, rationalism could be considered since the rule of law also pre- supposes a prudent man. But this assumes that someone is inclined to listen and at the same time enjoys adequate reasoning and reasonable faculties. Anyone who has encountered violence or fanaticism can explain just how useful an appeal to reason can be. How many different species know when to play dead, and by this act, are they making a compassionate appeal? Perhaps playing dead is more viable than appeal to reason.

The citizenry of the U.S. has never been indigenous or homogeneous (critical components of viable culture) and is today a teeming cross-sampling of humanity. It would seem that very few people immigrate to the U.S. for cultural reasons: most leave their homeland precisely because of rigid and static cultural paradigms preempted by the power structure to create social, economic, psychological and political barriers against access, entry and ascent by those outside the realm of privilege. The allure of a new beginning through emigration did not siphon off the prevailing élites of respective countries, where class and status were not purchasable commodities defined by the whims of the marketplace without any regard for traditions. The drive for social ascension and status were not left behind nor diminished but, rather, the reverse, with the fervour and conviction of the converted through reclassification of status as defined by capitalism and its ultimate symbol— money—flaunted by conspicuous consumption and ostentatiousness.

But still, there need to be some ties that can somehow bind the disparate mass, some cohesive and compelling supracultural, supranational and suprareligious force. The U.S. cannot have a Department or Ministry of

Culture or Religion as do many other countries, but it uniquely qualifies and has a profound need for a Department of Humanity to promote universal human values of Compassion, Tolerance and Compromise, and the nurturing needs of human life—critical life skills and values.

Those who would object can consider, as an alternative, a country with *Star Wars*, *Star Trek* and video-game-inspired virtual reality subcultures. It is happening. How many kids and young adults are using "may the force be with you" or the vulcan hand signal as a greeting? It's too tragic to be ridiculous that a movie can become the subtext for life and can even be considered as some kind of cultural or self identity. Even with all the theory, practice and relentless indoctrination of religious beliefs, individuality still transcends all, and sins and sinners abound and thrive. Of those who want unique and distinct status accorded their culture, ask what standard text they are using, how many hours are devoted each week to cultural lessons (including how to care for the young); as with all other external lessons, what happens at an individual home is the prerogative of the home dwellers. There is more than enough opportunity in and protection of the sanctity of the home and family that specific language, cultural, lifestyle or religious lessons and practices can still be retained and transmitted. The trade-offs to be made by the educational system are similar to those of the political system in that it must necessarily serve the needs of the many.

To career in a sea of opinions, muddle through or just wing it while depending on the vestigial remains of a European heritage whose expiration date has long past, is to not address the need for a cultural identity and thereby promulgate the culture of one, by default or design. The population is too diverse, with incommensurable cultures, languages and religions; and a laissez-faire policy will mean that the mass entertainment media will take over the hearts and minds of the people, without a system of checks and balances for conflict prevention as well as resolution. This will happen much sooner than later, with the acceleration of technological developments and services combined with affordability that is allowing and enabling ever-greater media accessibility and penetration.

Those remaining relatively unsusceptible or immune to the pull of the media and pseudo identity will be the separate and distinct ethnic and religious fundamentalist groups whose strong ideologies will be retained and differences amplified. Censorship and legislation will not stop this process, just as the war on drugs has not solved the drug problem. Perhaps one common language and one consistent, formal humanizing education will help in promoting what it is to be human and what human values and needs are, in the context of a civic milieu.

Instead of engaging in endless debates, there is much to gain and nothing to lose (or too much to lose) in implementing a systematic and structured educational curriculum that teaches humanism and parenting skills. The quest for identity is a re-iterative journey between 'I am me' in a singly initialized, differentiating individual context representing a unique permutation at any given moment in time and 'I am you'[10] in an integrating universal one, being the source and realm of innumerable possibilities for all times.

As language becomes increasingly an inorganic broadcast experience via radio, television and the Internet, its original purpose for engagement, recognition, communion and interchange with the other is lost. Families and schools are no longer custodians of the young and impressionable but captive revenue streams as technologies and commercial interests become transmitters, pacifiers and satisfiers of ends and means, replacing elders, teachers and teachings. Economic, political and religious interests tend to be antagonistic to family values, structures and traditions as they are formidably resistant to the mindlessness of an easy sale. Family values (duty, discipline, diligence, discretion, devotion) which affirm and define relationships cannot flourish without family structures that occasion and opportune realization of virtue, so that values that tend to prevail are those of non- or anti-family: winning at all and any cost whereby life is a contest of countable and displayable scores.

This venal, anti-family attitude is propagandized with great flourish and relish through consumer-friendly, Panglossian, mass-media programming which creates an illusion that there is no missing link or disorientation. Technologies enable and match the speedy and tidy repackaging, refurbishing and recycling with consumption and disposal, of the old as novel and radical,

---

10. "It was Hillel who responded to the scoffing request of a heathen to teach him the whole Torah while the heathen was standing on one foot: 'What is hateful to you, do not do to your neighbour: that is the whole of Torah; the rest is commentary'." Norman F. Cantor, *The Sacred Chain: A History of the Jews* (Harper Collins, 1994), p.35.

Author's Note: This book would be fine without its repeated and ironic references to superior genes and genetic stock of the Jews. (A version of this is to be found in Romans 13:19: "The commandments...are summed up in this one rule: Love your neighbour as yourself..." as well as in teachings of Confucius, Kant and other secular and non-secular texts.)

in the search and capture of new and impressionable minds to feed the revenue systems. Thus, what distinguishes sex and violence in the primacy of mindlessness as the masses are conditioned into the infallible unilateralism of I-centrism is the severance from, and non-recognition of, the other, resembling a sterile chicken minus a head or heart.

The Korean culture is not just an ancient one, with more than five millennia of history, but a robust one. It has retained its manners, customs and behaviours despite its internal tribalism and numerous external pressures, including invasions and influences from China. It has survived Japan's relentless attempts at eradication through systematic planned displacement, distortion and dislocation of its people, language, ethics and history, over several generations of inhumane colonial occupation which ended on August 15, 1945. The instigation and duration of such inhumanity was accommodated and enabled by the complicity, interests and practices of the Western powers in the last few centuries. Historical texts tend to be more noteworthy for what is left out or excised from collective memory than what is recorded for posterity, especially in regard to askance looks, silent nods and innuendos. The National Foundation Day is commemorated on October 3, tracing Korean heritage back to 2333 BCE and its founder, Tan-gun, marking millennia of history and the deep physical and emotional bond with the land drenched with the blood, sweat and tears of countless generations struggling for survival and independence. What internal logic has enabled this culture to withstand and weather so much turbulence, much as the Jewish and Celtic cultures have?

The Korean culture is based on three pillars of philosophical teachings, all emanating from the 6th century BC: Taoism (*Lao-tzu*), with its emphasis on man's position in nature and his acceptance of his place with grace and humility (the quality of acquiescence and reverence to nature); Buddhism (*Siddhartha*), with its emphasis on compassion for all sentient beings and the recognition that all suffer and are capable of suffering;[11] and Confucianism,

---

11. Author's Note: For humans, compared to other sentient beings, the idea 'to live is to suffer' has distinct significance in that human suffering can lead to enlightenment (understanding and compassion) or embitterment (delusion and *schadenfreude* or the seductive power of hate). Coleridge wrote:

> Remorse is as the heart in which it grows:
> If that be gentle, it drops balmy dews
> Of true repentance; but if proud and gloomy,
> It is a poison-tree, that pierced to the inmost
> Weeps only tears of poison!

–Coleridge: Darker Reflections, o.p.cit., p. 326.

with its emphasis on a code of conduct befitting and becoming of man, to promote social harmony and propriety. In summary, Buddhism represents the right path and mindful attitude; Confucianism, right conduct and ethical attitude; Taoism, right harmony and universal/eternal attitude and perspective. A culture and language that has an affinity for and incorporates these philosophic approaches is likely to be fused with moral context from which no belonger is exempt. While there may be latitudes, any serious breach is likely to result in grievous ignominy. It is a culture which seeks to guide the human spirit and aspirations, not confine and contain it with dogmatism and absolutism.

These give the culture its structural soundness and underpin all that flows from it. These outlooks were likely adopted and adapted because they were consistent with the cultural practices and shamanistic (spiritual) beliefs already in place. The specific forms of address, which define all of one's relationships, probably existed before the teachings of Confucius were officially codified. The prevailing agrarian society and shamanism probably connected readily with Taoism; Buddhism probably rooted deeply with a population that was no stranger to extremes of poverty and suffering. The *sine qua non* of humanness is represented in two Korean words of equal reverence, referenced almost daily: (1) *eu li*—the principles of righteousness, a moral sense, justice, morality; loyalty, integrity, obligation, faithfulness; a sworn relation and (2) *in jong*—human desire (passions), human nature; humaneness, sympathy, humanity. The moral context is embedded within the common spoken language. Higher priority and emphasis are placed upon a personal code of conduct and relative status in the context of cultural values than on equality and liberty of the individual. The public good, and the attendant social unity, peace and order, take precedence over individual rights and their exertion.

Many of the negative or destabilizing elements of human nature are identified and proscribed, as are the positive aspects prescribed and encouraged. There are some distinct values not subject to trade-offs even at the expense of self-preservation, transcending the well-being of one for that of the many. These are at the heart of all ancient cultural paradigms and considered inviolable or sacred by the belongers.

What characterizes the code of conduct model is its pro-social stance and the absence of legal enforcement mechanisms. It places the individual in a social context, demands consideration of others and an appreciation of cultural imperatives, such as respect for the elder and filial piety. The end is social harmony, but the means are not so much rigid as suggestive of human dignity. Although the economic, judicial, political and religious dimensions are not as exhaustively addressed, these cultural imperatives affect and transcend all of these, as well as other human endeavours in varying degrees.

The expressions in art (including literature, music and staged format) vary in degrees of cultural intelligence or proficiency required for understanding and appreciating the entertainment value, from simple and basic to extremely complex and symbolic. These are often adaptable for audiences of different ages, through myths, folklore, folk songs and folk festivals, reflecting the pervasiveness of the enculturation process. The Korean language has a surprising number of distinct dialects given the land mass and population size, but an abundance of the same terms whereby information sought and given involves an array of impressions converging a full range of sensations, feelings and sentiments, vividly portrayed and conveyed. It is an ideophonic language, especially in the use and sound of the circular and oscillating symbol 'o'. There are many references to human nature in context of honour, dignity and integrity, but also those pertaining to the organic world and the natural universe. It is more concerned with essence than with form.

A manifestation of respect for elders and filial piety is what is described as ancestor worship. In practice, it prescribes remembrance and paying of respect by the oldest son to his father (resembling the Kaddish) in accordance with the patriarchal social order of the past: it is formalized respect and recognition of precedence. This annual or biannual observance reaffirms one's position, ties and obligations to the family and serves as an occasion for renewing and strengthening family ties with the formal gathering of the clan. It is an affirmation of a belief in souls of the departed being ever present in the lives of the descendants and the undeniable atavism (evocation of ancestral person in the look and feel of a descendent) observed and experienced in real life. Age is also an occasion for family celebration and veneration with the 61st birthday signifying a milestone in the completion of a cycle and the beginning of another phase in life, as are each of the decades thereafter. One is considered a year old at birth and reckoning of one's age is not only driven by the individuality of a birthday but additionally tied to a larger context of the flow of time which affects all equally on New Year's Day.

The written Korean language is structurally coherent in its simplicity and internal logic. Although it is an invention of the mid-15th century (1443), it shows an intuitive understanding of multidimensional matrix algorithms with a clear focus on one objective: to have a purely phonetic content, since the spoken language comprehensively incorporated and expressed cultural values and practices. It would be revealing to study the precedents that went into a 15th-century King's motivation to create a truly user-friendly written language, which is not only a radical act beyond compare in terms of liberating the individual mind but also represents the pinnacle of democratic principles. It is not good news for man but good written language for man. King Sejong, the 4th and considered the greatest ruler of the Yi Dynasty, is honoured with commemoration of Han'gul (Korean written language) Day on October 9, at his tomb site. This sweeping democratic gesture is ironic in an ancient society steeped in scholarly stoicism, rituals, traditions, hierarchy and social rules governing all aspects of daily life and yet with no shortage of fierce independence and equally ferocious suppression in its history and people. The scholars of classic Chinese calligraphy and literature are revered and essential, but the activities and ripples of knowledge integration are infinitely expanded and participatory with an indigenous and mother-tongue complementary written language.

The most striking difference between Korean and English (as well as other written languages) is the all-pervasive, always capitalized, subjective 'I' and the universal, non-specific 'you' in the latter, compared with the infrequent, but contextual and implied 'I' and the specific, positional 'you' in the former. This difference is above and beyond differences in syntax; it reflects a fundamentally different way of thinking about 'I' and 'you'—in isolation or in social context and interaction. Whom one is addressing always dictates choice of words and appropriate forms of address. The language integrates and supports the cultural norm of respect for the elders, and affirms and validates social relationships. It is the difference between talking to or at someone in a unilateral or transactional manner versus relational communion charged with sensibility and sentiment within the language.

The strength and durability of the Korean culture is such that it can and does transcend the corrosive nature of capitalism. What other culture has this power against greed and corruption? All cultures have this counter-force because all appreciate the distinction between right and might (including tyranny of the majority and the mob, since what is popular is not necessarily right), imparting a sense of being and doing good, versus prevailing at all costs and being right. Greed and corruption exist in Korean society as in all other societies, but these may not be viewed in the same way by the belongers or insiders; there are checks and balances which are only operative on them, above and beyond the forces of law.

Greed and corruption are ever-present traits of human nature[12] (not to be confused with features of a culture or its values). They are exacerbated and accentuated by materialism and capitalism. Even criminals have a set of cultural values; culturally prescribed penalties are meted out, which can be even more severe and long-lasting upon generations than the prescriptions of the legal system. Commercial and criminal codifications are relatively recent and imported concepts, whereas the strict civil code of conduct has been both explicit and implicit within the cultural paradigm for over a millennium. In this context, corruption and greed for wealth and power, via the modus operandi of capitalism, can be viewed mostly as a means to achieve status or to fulfill a social need for acceptance and recognition, since status is no longer fixed by heritage, qualification or virtue.

Confucianism largely circumvents the need for massive legal codification in the belief that the personal code of ethics (which it prescribes in extensive detail as it pertains to daily life, according to defined social positions) will be sufficient for maintaining social harmony. This, of course, does not imply that greed and corruption are expunged from human nature; social justice is important but it is not the stated goal of Confucianism, where social harmony (peace and order) take precedence. There is no satisfactory resolution between justice and peace, but merely an effort to ameliorate and dissipate the percolating frustration and discontent of the individual and prevent it from turning into anger and hostility by emphasizing social propriety, as reflected in and by one's personal sense of dignity and honour, as well as through defined and established relationships. Interpretation and application of justice and reason can be as numerous and varied as individuals.

---

12. "The difference between a kleptocrat and a wise statesman, between a robber baron and a public benefactor, is merely one of degree...Kleptocracies with little public support run the risk of being overthrown, either by downtrodden commoners or by upstart would-be replacement kleptocrats seeking public support by promising a higher ratio of services rendered to fruits stolen." Jared Diamond, *Guns, Germs, and Steel* (W.W. Norton, 1999), p. 296.

Satisfying an individual's or a group's need for justice involves trade-offs based on some shared hierarchy of values. The means for achieving justice and harmony are many and run the gamut between right and might, there being no one definitive resolution between these goals. Cultural values and prescriptions are guideposts and rubrics (established customs and rules), offering a way to safeguard the one and the many. Social or individual sense and need for justice has been at the core of all conflicts. History is littered with destruction of indescribable scale—indiscriminate slaughter and misery inflicted upon the innumerable, while the instigators remain largely unscathed escaping retribution which would deliver the satisfaction of justice and closure. The need for justice under Confucianism, rather than being denied, is offered various means towards prevention and reconciliation, not absolute resolution, through the emphasis and precedence of social harmony and propriety.

Korean Cultural Identity in the Context of Modernity

Is life fair? It doesn't appear so, given the frequency one hears the utterance, *That's not fair!* Is there justice? There seems to be a growing awareness of the chasm between legal justice and moral justice, along with social and economic divides. But as the mass media amplifies these innumerable injustices, the problem is further exacerbated by relegating the meting out of justice to the public domain. Justice and fairness in this sphere is but a reflection of the much deeper private domain: virtues of compassion, patience and sympathy resonate firstly and mostly in the heart and mind of an individual. Just as delayed gratification is no longer operational, the idea of justice delayed or denied is itself seen as unjust. This need for instant justice or gratification of want combined with an absence of common sense or standards, along with absence of choice (self-responsibility and accountability), juxtaposed with inadequate decision analysis skills, overburden and overwhelm the legal systems.

Injustice, the corollary of evil and bad faith, is a part of life and living. One strives to act in accordance with a personal code of conduct based upon and shaped by one's cultural paradigm so as to minimize inflicting harm to others. A sense of balance is sought, while not expecting total and final resolution or vindication, i.e., absolute justice. What is relevant is not that there is a day of final reckoning in an existential or divine context, but only that one is initiated in and develops, over a lifetime, a multidimensional sense of what is just, guided by a moral compass: a pang or pain of conscience. A heart of stone is usually found residing with a rock-like brain just as thin-skinned is found with the thick-headed.

In modern times, political and social trade-offs may have been made for economic growth to benefit the many, but the cultural values of respect for knowledge and age, along with filial piety, remain intact. At first glance, some aspects of Korean culture may appear to be draconian. In some rare instances in life, one may be called upon to make a choice between incommensurable goals and values, the ultimate choice involving life and death. In the past, when resources were scarce (extreme poverty was the rule, not the exception, for most of the population, for most of Korean history) and one was faced with the impossible dilemma of making a choice involving sacrifice or betrayal, one had to make an unspeakable decision or risk losing all.

If one had only so much food and no prospect of any more, who should be fed first in the family? If a child had to be sold, conscripted or abandoned, which one should it be? If one could afford to send only one child for further education, which child should benefit? If one had limited land or wealth, who should inherit? Who could think dispassionately about such choices or live peacefully with the burden of such choice-making? When conflict among incommensurable values arose, the cultural paradigm facilitated a path forward without reconciling or resolving the conflict. While the choice may have been acceptable, it was not necessarily rational, irrational or radical but, rather, conservative or consistent with traditions. The burden and difficulty of choice were undiminished; moral agency was not sidestepped. A choice-making template was operational, with or without the explicit awareness by the choice-maker whereby precedents of predecessors predisposed choice. At the centre of a cultured identity is duty and loyalty to one's namesake that endures and evolves day by day over countless thousands of years.

Poverty is the daily reality for many in Korea and billions of people world-wide. It has been and will remain pan-endemic irrespective of political, social, economic or religious ideology, deception or illusion. Democracy is no panacea when so many opt out of the system, when each vote that is cast and manages to pass the counting hurdle is then discounted for population density or some other backdoor skewing schemes hidden from view. How representative of reality are labels for a gamut of organizations, movements and countries with words such as united, international, national, democratic, republic, fidelity, prudential, liberty, charity, sacred, holy, etc., on structure, constituent, purpose and principle? The schism between labels and reality is representative of the natural contiguity of imperialism and bullyism characterized by parasitic ingratitude, chronic insatiability and forgetfulness, ironically exacerbated and empowered by the age of information and technology. Terminologies parading as virtues and progress, like some *deus ex machina*, proliferate to serve and enforce the agenda of the few genuinely inhumane who view other lives merely as means to be harnessed with a morality that is tops-down driven and force fitted to be hardly ever questioned and unquestionably hard on the many. Who would really want to see a worldwide democratic system whereby each vote carried equal weight? Democracy will continue to benefit those who control the resources and means of production—the poor tend to have many more impediments to their vote, are easier to spook, dupe, con, neutralize, distract, harass and mobilize for interests not of their making nor benefit. The way the game is increasingly set up favours those with money and property who work, shape, set and bend the rules of political and legal systems to their will, so that poverty which has always been a difficult barrier to overcome becomes and impassable and insurmountable roadblock.

The cultural imperatives, by emphasizing the least harm to the many, provided a guideline for defining the priority of one's family relationships and offered some measure of relief and comfort from this burden. The choice-maker, most frequently the head of the household, was responsible for the well-being of all the members and bore total responsibility for the outcomes of choice-making. However, the choice itself was not based on some subjective or arbitrary standard. Priorities do not mean exclusion or exclusiveness, because kinship or family ties are an inclusive, lifetime commitment that one is born into, a bond that remains beyond death.

But such a detailed prescription for daily life has not resulted in a population characterized by sheep-like behaviour or docility. If anything, it is just the reverse. There is a greater intensity of emotions in expressing both joy and sorrow, a deeply etched *élan vital* (Henri Bergson, 1859-1941) that is much more palpable than in the West where there is supposedly much greater freedom of expression. This facilitates the full realization of the individual's potential (albeit by means which do not cause social disharmony) more than in a laissez-faire culture where *might* overshadows *right*. The scholar and the teacher are respected, almost revered, rather than economic or political power. This, in turn, ensures that the culture is not only preserved, but evolves in a consistent (not radical) way, unfettered by commerce and consumerism.

The Korean cultural identity is a demanding one. It appears to have been designed to challenge the individual. To be virtuous, not just engaged in prevailing in one's rightness, is perhaps what explains the ability of the intellect to discern multidimensionality in its encounters with the new, different, unknown and unknowable. There is no assumption made regarding whether a man is inherently bad or good: merely that being good and human require a lot of effort in a social context where disagreements or conflicts are inevitable. There is no suppression or denial of the individual: just the opposite, in a most profound way. What is also implicit in the blueprint of codifying one's behaviour and relationship to others seems to be the recognition of the corrosive effect of social isolation. (The danger of isolation is born out in comparing children who have been abused to those who have been isolated and neglected. Often the damage may be equivalent.)

Western philosophical thinking, from which springs the democratic form of government, is optimistic about the nature of man in that human beings are believed to be inherently good or at least perfectible. Democracy presupposes and demands a high degree of cooperative attitude and behaviour because liberty and equality require tolerance, compromise and recognition of the plurality of man and society. Democracy as a political construct, without a cultural blueprint to support and sustain these attitudes, will become a series of stalemates at best, or might-over-right at worst, independent of the economic model adopted but exacerbated in an extreme degree by capitalism.

Liberty without self-discipline, and equality without understanding and recognition of the pluralistic nature of man, are without merit in that liberty and equality, unconstrained by cultural imperatives, are ultimately neither serving the well-being of the individual nor society. This is evident in the single-mindedness of political entities driven by single issues, taking extreme positions that cannot even acknowledge the existence, let alone the validity, of positions which differ from their own. Freedom of speech and the press translate into *anything that sells* and *anything goes*. Commercialization of life is boundless because there are no longer any cultural stigmas. There is no strong centre, no capstan around which opposing points of view whirl but are commonly bound. There are only separate camps, and as positions become more singular, ever fewer are the opportunities for overlap.

Cultural identity is not a buffet where one picks and chooses just as one pleases; its parts work together and support each other. It is infrangible. It is a full course from which one partakes in varying portions, and to the extent that one foregoes complete dishes such as language or kinship ties, there are real consequences. To be culturally intelligent is to be aware of the consequences that ultimately determine or undermine morality and integrity in the specific cultural context; this is what makes it incommensurable with a self-construct which lacks and is characterized by absence of integrative coherence.

One must always bear in mind that a culture does not just arbitrarily happen one day. Centuries of observations, experience and knowledge are cumulatively integrated by the best scholars dedicated to the study of human nature, society and the environment. It's not mathematics or physics, but it is still no less a non-arbitrary or subjective discipline. A culture's purpose is not to be predictive, but, rather, preventive of inner and outer turmoil and disharmony. Cultures evolve (mostly at the centre, at their own pace and rhythm) as their belongers do, reflecting and incorporating the times as well as integrating new and qualified knowledge. While a plethora of platitudes may be tolerated with respect to those who insist on holding onto some romantic notion of themselves and their 'culture of one', who exert themselves simply because it is possible, without thinking of any kind (*I am capable of speech, so I will blurt out whatever I want*), the sacredness of cultural goals and principles still remains undisturbed.

Traditional cultures, far removed from the centre by generations, time and distance, may appear to be rigid in preserving the old ways, but the only difference is in the degree and means of observance of the same goals, principles, values and customs as in the place of origin. No amount of individual willpower or intellect can deny it or dent it or replace its one vital factor— humility. It is this lack of humility in all that has gone on before the one, which is at the root of all unspeakable brutality (viz. *I have the solution and I'm omnipotent*). Humility never stopped anyone from achieving his or her full potential as a human being; the greater the achievement and the greater the humility implied by the achiever, the more enhanced and revered are both the doer and the result.

Globalization and corporate consolidations accelerate ubiquity of technology and homogenization of cultures via Americanization and consumerism, under the aegis of all rights and entitlements, all the time.

Consumerism feeds upon mindlessness and the resulting easy sales. The growth in this segment of the population is evidenced not only by robust revenue streams but, more strikingly, on the increasing need for law enforcement and protection, sex, drugs, alcohol, tobacco, gun education and health services, along with entitlements and rights to all manner of nano-issues. While people continue to produce children, the absolute size and the percentage share of the parental responsibility or time-and-money pie steadily shrinks without focused attention on countering the mantras of *doing my own thing, I am for me and mine,* and *my way, at all and any cost.*

These developments point to a greater need to develop a body of study which will help to preserve and integrate incremental changes in the cultural paradigm. Then at least there is a central source of reference and guidance for the many, as the vessel for safekeeping these in perpetuity—the extended family—ceases to exist. As extended families living together or in close proximity decrease, consanguinity or kinship as definers and influencers of relationships and behaviour, diminish. Thus, teaching the responsibilities of parenthood and the skills required for rearing the young, as well as the transmission of cultural values and imperatives, need to be formalized into the entire educational system. That sex, drug and gun education programmes have been deemed necessary while the aforementioned subjects have not, mirrors the prevailing social mind-set or mindlessness.

Purpose in Family Structure and Function

On the surface, the structure of Korean society seems patriarchal. But this belies the complex matrix of relationships and principles that most Koreans are encultured in to navigate through life and society, covering:

1. Patrilineal and matrilineal relatives, older and younger siblings spouse and in-laws, mentors and classmates.

2. Various social arrays that intersect with the above as in relatives in step-functions both vertically and horizontally, as well as friends, associates and acquaintances of such (e.g., a matrix generated from one person's in-laws of spouse, sibling and children).

3. Civic, official and professional relationships.

4. Principles that run through the matrix of relationships, such as filial piety, reverence for ancestors, deference to teachers and elders, along with many other sentiments of an ancient culture, a few of which are listed in Appendices 4 and 5. Below the careful integration of Taoism, Buddhism and Confucianism, these old sentiments continue to flow.[13]

As children learn their mother tongue, they quickly learn unique and general nominations for a range of extended relatives and non-intimates. They are not taught self-love and self-esteem, but the value of relationships and how to honour them through the patterns of language and mannerism, especially in regard to those that are not optional but lifelong. Times, feelings and common sense will change and people will come and go, grow old, change and die, but the truth and sentiment of the relationships will always be a constant. Life seems to revolve around knowing one's relative position or possessing the means for quick and accurate assessment within a complex web, so that no offense is given or taken. In a society that values propriety for purpose of

13. Author's Note: Before Taoism, Buddhism and Confucianism, the primogenitor had a word to represent the idea of the Reverential Oneness of all life—*Hananim*—symbolizing the many in the one and the one in the many; one cannot see oneself except as a reflection from the others, so that the greater the clarity and transparency one projects, the truer the image that can be consolidated and created over time and relationships. Through interdependance and inter-relationships, independance and strength are gathered exponentially, versus the clumsiness and non-sensibleness of individualism or unilateralism. Thus the two focal points focus light both internally and externally as in ellipses and hyperbolas, with unambiguous loyalty to one's namesake that requires no waivers, excuses or favours. A child or progeny is a unique fusion of two equal halves, creating a repository of innumerable past, present and future lives, just as all that is passed on in the learning process represents many lifetimes of trials, errors and discoveries. Parents who are compassionate towards each other are in essence unconditionally accepting the child in whom they are equally vested and represented. It is difficult for a child to accept who he or she is if the respective parents seem to reject rather than accept each other as individuals when individualism takes centre stage oblivious to the purpose of the union that transcends and subordinates self-serving orientation and inclination of childhood. How does a child learn to value himself or herself when he or she is conditioned to despise or unilaterally judge one or both parents as in the saying—as you judge, so shall you be judged. Rather than defining oneself to be good independently, it may be more mean-

maintaining peace and order in public so highly, social breach brings dishonour and shame to the family name. The journey of life never ends as long as relationships exist.

The social enculturation process is like building up a nest of personal Boolean statements and operators linking relationships in numerous dimensions which becomes second-nature through daily practice and exposure. It forms a safety net that positions and counts all, not a web of fear that terrorizes and isolates the individual. One is born into a web of relationships as a connected, not a free, agent. The activities of an individual are similar to that performed by all other connective and specialized tissues associated with a viable organism. Self-identity is a creation of unlimited free-forming plagiarism befitting of a life which is a unique copy resulting from the union of two such others in a milieu composed of its most affiliated, familiar and similar, but not all necessarily like-minded. The mind is free to create new illusions rather than keeping old ones in stasis, and to play with mind-games or thought experiments (*gedanken*) which help release and push the self outwards. A well-trained spy or an ultimate outsider, over time, becomes the ultimate insider, just as a chameleon at rest does not need to change colour for the time being. Thus we make ourselves while meeting our

ingful in the long-run, if one begins by defining the state of health of one's many unbreakable relationships of blood and duty over which one exercises no control or choice. Constraints of short-term mentality can only play out in the context of a lifetime and lives that are contingent upon it. One is undiminished by agreeing, complimenting or praising as well as expressing gratitude and humility to another, but quite the reverse. As compassion is increasingly qualified and conditional, it is deformed and crippled, with similar effects on the fruit and outcome of relationships so that going off course over time increases exponentially. Without orientation and a centrepoint, pearls do not form to catch and reflect the light from the glow of the stars so that dimness and dullness increase as luminescence and translucence decrease. The fruit remains unripe and green on the vine of life and with the passage of seasons simply drops off, hard and bitter, only to rot, never to flower and bear new life. The Buddhist mantra in Korean, *guanseumbosal*, shapes the attitude of the mind towards openness and permeability through repeated reminders to listen with tenderness and care to the cries and whispers of all that live and suffer—understanding Oneness becomes synonymous with compassion. The non-indigenous and imported beliefs and ideas were thus Koreanized and transformed as much as the Chinese ideograms were, without sacrificing their original intent for the purpose of local functionality and integration.

makers. The game *I spy with my little eye* does not cease with childhood, but continues as long as the eyes can see. By keeping a sense of family or household central to daily life, Koreans and other ancient peoples have remained democratic throughout their history because diversity has always ruled over blind conformity to dogma and uniformity. Idiosyncrasies and distinctive diversity are preserved and transmitted as long as the family or household is strong. When family and household structures fall away, everyone is more susceptible to becoming an assembly-line product of the mass media and public education systems.

Why has the separation of Church from State been a concern in many enduring cultures? Certainly not because of the harm they will cause each other. Such concentration of power will not merely oppress the individual, but unleash an exponentially multiplied force of intolerance and hatred, not just double the amount of pressure for conformity as demonstrated many times by dictators with a divine bent. Such a union of equals brews a maelstrom of infallible dogmas with immutable administrative structures with unlimited military and police forces as means for suppression and eradication of dissent. We have been there, seen it and done it already. Just as the external show of conformity masked the rich complexity and diversity of life at home as unique as a mother's home cooking, the external show of cultural diversity or multi-culturalism is merely a façade for the weakening flame of individuality as equal mediocrity and uniformity diminish the repertoire of scents and tastes.

Children are taught many things to live and make a living, but it is a sense of origin that imparts direction for alignment with their dharma. Following is an example to illustrate the multi-faceted concept of the Dharma. The *intention* of an ancient culture is to live with the land as one of many through the language of relationships based on *principles* of Origin and Organicity as entry into the Art and Way of Life. It is a knowing of enoughness, adequacy and satiation. Many people of different origins have come to the New World with the passed-down-through-the-generations intention to rape, plunder and spoil the land and the diversity within. One point of view is to extol the 'spirit of temporal' exploration (an oxymoron), but another more powerful view is to condemn those intent on exploitation, enslavement and extermination of those who are different and impede self-serving purposes at any cost. The newcomers have found a common interest and shared intent (lowest and base denominator) at the expense of awakening and unfolding of individuality (dharma and highest principle). Thus in a country or any country of mass and massive military industrial combines, many become their aspects or copies as commensurable cogs in the wheel, enslaved in cycles of production, consumption and disposal of the immaterial and inorganic, all the while convinced that they are the masters of the universe. The land is innocent enough, but not the ways of the non-indigenous, non-genuine and disingenuous who do not contain the vast memory of enoughness through the millennia of living from and in the One. Equal dullness and dearth in collective and individual expressions of paeans and dirges tend to characterize such creations of modernity, thus displaying the enduring integrity and sensibility of the insensitive bully that passes and poses as some kind of character to be prized.

These people who seem to have an insatiable appetite for carnage, slaughter and mayhem tend to be the most squeamish about what they will eat. Their fare tends to be as far removed from their propensity for predatory and cannibalistic gore as possible, settling on peanut butter and jelly sandwiches or other organic-origin-disassociated processed and packaged foods. Their ethnocentrically bent noses turn up and away from naturally preserved, flavoured, textured and coloured foods in favour of those which are chemically doused. (In contrast, the ubiquitous Korean *kim-chi* and many other condiments and dishes vary from household to household and from season to season.) Their food practices maximize wastage as a result of eating very selective parts and being very selective about what animals will be eaten. Unlike many other cultures, they have not developed a minimum wastage approach to preparing their foods so that they are unlikely to eat chitterlings, feet, hoofs, heads, fins, skin, blood, marrow or fat, preferring hydrogenated, ground-up, reformed, colour- and flavour-enhanced and highly processed products. The closest thing they have to ritualized and shared tables seems to be the headless, stuffed birds served up on special occasions. The paucity and blandness as well as lack of imagination and symbolism in foodstuffs seem to be equally matched by the indiscriminate approach to slaughter and wastage for the single-minded purpose of killing or destroying for its own sake. This then gives rise to an industry of denial, categorization and rationalization dragging in various terminologies of unintended consequences, collateral damages and us-versus-them to justify the dead and the dying. The evil within is rarely acknowledged, confronted, questioned and reconciled, so that it is doomed for endless replay in a loop. One wonders what refined foods the butchers and their many collaborators have consumed throughout history amidst the blood-baths wrought for the greater and absolute good.

The time spent in childhood is too precious to be spent in faceless, mindless, linear and inorganic interfacing predominated by right angles. This will not teach children how to live, but rather to surrender their time in voluntary disarmament to live and die for a non-dharma (inorganic principles) that cannot be their own. What loss is there in not ever having surfed on the Internet by the hunter/gatherer given our experiences so far in the compatibility between the inorganic and the organic? When it concerns the well-being of our children, it does not matter how degrees of harmfulness are rationalized and categorized by labels and fine print. The only thing that matters is that it is harmless. There can be no guarantee against downside risks proffered by industry, church, supreme courts or state, because their interests are not for a single child or individual but for their own veiled agenda for power. The only safeguard is in our individual judgement and choice.

This is a war that can only be won when we value our children's time more than our own and teach them their personal history so they know where they are from. Learning history when it is played out like a movie or a fairy-tale tends to be unrelated to the central question of 'who I am' and more often than not fails to connect. The timeless tradition of word-of-mouth or oral transmission of culture represents the fidelity of sounds generated from the insides of an organic being to another such being. There are not the intermediaries of paper or money. A baby is soothed and calmed by the mother's presence and the caress of her voice, not by the specificity of her actions and words. Whether shaped by antiquity or modernity, young or old, living in the new world or the old, many hearts ache in realizing the full value of what is lost to them, yearning and reminiscing to be home again, but accepting the currents of history that carry them away from the centre, but only for the time being.

Spending time interfacing with the mass media breaks down and disarms our resistance against uniformity. This is achieved by deceptions of empowerment conveyed through shared experiences. Such mass production of memories or market-share is the godhead of mass media that thrives by dissolving personalities or marketing depersonalized products as personal experiences. Can an individual relate to six billion, million or thousand people and learn the lessons of humanity from such a large spoke of outside-in relationship? Lessons in connectedness and humanity are better hatched in the nest of inside-out ties of every day familial relations radiating out from the central, indisputable and full-blooded bond with mothers who give life. How deep and broad can minds and lives be when shaped by nationally televised events and kept informed by the faceless and lifeless downloads from the mass media? The bird is crippled before it has had a chance for flight, safe in the company of like-strangers, forever remaining a stranger to its dharma to fly. A culture of family awakens the warrior spirit in the child to live to its potential by discovering his or her dharma, not merely to kill or be killed.

The family is the first and foremost transmitter of cultural identity. The most powerful teaching, especially of the young, is by example through adherence to a consistent code of conduct and values by all family members, especially by the mother or the primary care giver. Conformity within a family unit is necessarily strict because each member in this relatively small group carries more weight than does society at large, thus, the metacentre is that much more sensitive and susceptible. The meanings of consanguinity form the basic template and foundation for subsequent belonging to various groups in many contexts, ranging from play and study groups at school to alumni, corporate, military, political, economic, social, religious and community affiliations.

If life is viewed as a bundle of strands of time charged with *chi* or life force, with a specific point of origin, sequence and length, the longest and strongest strands are those that tie back to mother (literally, via the umbilical cord) to father, then to siblings, to extended family members, and on to the public spheres, with special ties to the teachers who instill relatively greater strands of time. The flow of time is irreversible and unidirectional, and thus the ties and bonds of family with attendant priority sequencing are considered inviolable, certain and sacred. In a patriarchal society, as filial piety for a female is just as operative as for a male, the success of motherhood depends on how well the wife switches loyalty and belonging from her clan or family to that of her husband. Divided loyalty negates the very concept of loyalty. The cultural imperatives make very clear the order of priority or sequencing for weighing and weighting; it does not depend on anyone's subjective judgement of merit or plurality of loyalties.

This is due to three factors: (1) the one without experience is not likely to appreciate its value beyond what he or she knows so far; (2) discipline and harmony cannot be maintained if everyone's merit is to be questioned, debated and justified (the younger are simply not equal to or qualified for the task of passing judgement on the elders); and (3) no one can truly know another, regardless of the effort made to do so.

A younger person assessing or judging an elder as to his or her worthiness for respect and deferential treatment has a greater likelihood of making an error; in doing so, he or she demonstrates either simple-mindedness or sheer willfulness in not being able to comprehend or accept why respect of the elder is a good insurance policy against committing a social breach, which only reflects sadly on the younger person making it. Therefore, regardless of the rightness of the younger's judgement, the very act of judging is considered a transgression of propriety by what could be considered, at best, an immature and uneducated person or, at worst, one who is uncultured and ill-bred.

Code of conduct does not imply whether man is inherently good or bad; it merely commits him to ends and values which promote social harmony. It is a knowledge of 'what to do', not knowledge of facts. When there is conflict, deference to the elder's position is prescribed both as a means to prevent prolongation or escalation of conflict (disharmony) and as a means of saving face for both parties, in that there is no winning or losing as such, but only the culturally acceptable way of resolution. More importantly, there is no abdication of responsibility because it involves an act of choice. One is not positioned to say, *It's not my fault. I couldn't help it. I didn't know.*

For these reasons, willfulness is the antithesis of Korean virtue, as it is the trait of an untrained, uncultured, or uncivilized mind. No other behaviour is condemned as much as willfulness. A person who only feels vindicated in getting his or her way is destructive to the survival and integrity of the cultural identity. A parent who consistently demonstrates willfulness and takes great pride in getting his or her way has undermined respect for the elder (wisdom), filial piety (duty), dignity and honour for one's position and the positions of others (harmony)—three pillars of Korean conduct. In so doing, the person has sown seeds not only of his/her unfitness and unsoundness, but those of the progeny. This is why willfulness is not tolerated (aside from the fact that while a willful child is merely unattractive, a willful adult is inexcusable).

Willfulness is not to be mistaken for tenacity in pursuit of a goal. But even tenacity must be exercised with the objective in clear view and the knowledge of when to stop, instead of becoming blindly fixated on a position or path of pursuit when the end will not be met or when cost exceeds benefit. With willfulness there is not even a pretense of any objective; behaviour is driven purely by *what I want* or *my way* as opposed to *what you want* or *your way*, without addressing the why's and the what for's.

Therefore the role of the husband in discharging his filial duties and transmitting his family's way of life and his cultural identity to the next generation, and in facilitating his wife's role in this, is as important as that of his wife's, as the mother of his children. In a traditional patriarchal society, the husband's family takes priority, but not absolutely, and regardless of material wealth or perceived social status, a wife is defined by her husband's position in the context of his family as well as its social status. The wife must be consistent in her behaviour and attitude towards her husband and his family. To act otherwise and to set about fulfilling her own agenda would not only be deceitful and dishonourable, it would be a betrayal of the trust conferred on her as a member of his family.

Because of this potential for inflicting so much harm on the family due to its multiplier effect and the relative weight of each member in a smaller group (not only on current but future generations), the introduction of a new family member brings about intense scrutiny by the elders whose permission is solicited for membership. This recognition results in a sequential series of complex and ritualistic exchanges which run a parallel and symmetrical course for both parties, the significance of extended families being equally applicable and enduring. Any undermining of the family construct creates a tear in the social fabric. To the extent that economic independence is allowed to translate into independence from cultural imperatives, society will become increasingly uncivil and uncivilized, with the ascendancy of the culture of one defined along a singular economic axis.

In this age of gender equality, it is an important function of parents and teachers to teach and set appropriate examples in observing the code of conduct. The cultural integrity of Korea in no way rests upon subordination or subjugation of the female; it rests upon the value it places on the care of the young and therefore on the care giver. If one studied (and appreciated in depth) the conception of gender in the philosophy behind the prescribed practices, one would not find so simplistic an answer as to superiority or inferiority of gender. Age, qualifications, achievements or social status carry greater weight and take precedence over gender. Gender is not the overarching category definer of status or role assignment.

If the role of women as mothers were respected and valued, instead of slighted and demeaned, society as a whole would benefit. The commercialization and exploitation of women has created a schizophrenic female construct in which one person works both outside and inside the home while maintaining the image of a sex object. This fragmentation obviously undermines gender equality. Coupled with the mass media promotion of 'tarting up' to increase the consumption of beauty and fashion products and services, it exemplifies extreme commoditization and exploitation. Both men and women are fully capable of being the primary care giver, but caring and rearing of even one child is a full-time job requiring 24/7 attention. Such care can only be provided by time-sharing within a tight group and is incompatible or incommensurable with earning a paycheque. The legal age cut-off of 18 or 21 may relieve parents from legal liabilities, but their moral responsibilities remain; it is a lifetime commitment. Due to evolutionary and traditional cultural factors, women tend to have more capacity for, or opportunities to, develop the empathy essential in caring for a baby; however, it is not an emotion which is absent or impossible to develop in men.

Achieving material wealth is not guaranteed and pursuing it does not guarantee its attainment with any sense of finality, regardless of ability, effort or dedication; also, it is not as time-critical or time-determinate as is nurturing and rearing of the young. Material wealth is not the primary determinant of how well a child can be brought up; the psychological moment will not remain or present itself in quite the same way ever again. Paraphrasing *Pascal's Wager*[14] in reverse and recategorized: the upside is uncertain, limited to material gain and one-dimensional to the one (adult), while the downside is certain, unlimited in potential loss and multidimensional for the one (child) and the many.

Countries that profess to value equality have in practice set poorer examples in how women have been treated than countries that supposedly confine and relegate their female members to a subordinate or lesser role. One should consider or evaluate these key factors: (1) how women in general and motherhood are valued; (2) how well the primary care giver's role is defined within the family structure; and (3) the degree to which all or most members of the society adhere to cultural prescriptions in their individual, familial and social contexts.

14. *Pascal's Wager* (1623-62): "If you believe in God, and he exists, you have all to gain. If you believe in God and he does not exist, you have nothing to lose." D.W. Hamlyn, *A History of Western Philosophy* (Penguin Books, 1987), p.145.

Author's Note: Many problems or propositions can be weighed in terms of 'all to gain, nothing to lose' or 'nothing to gain, all to lose' variations with reference to specific materiality, perspective and context, as a rule of thumb for initiating, continuing, modifying, and most importantly, stopping, with regard to thoughts, words or deeds, consistent with one's self image and cultural paradigm.

A culture whose secular code of ethics is centred on individual duty impressed with filial piety, integrity, honour and dignity does not allow religious or metaphysical doctrines to undermine or usurp its precepts, which take precedence and are deeply enmeshed within the social fabric and language. The family and social hierarchies are not subject to religious dogmas because they are kept in check from encroaching on or eroding these balances of authority and responsibility. Religions and their institutions disrupt and displace state, social and family structures and hierarchies, especially when combined with any one or more elements of economic, political or military capital. Such combinations can be catastrophic or lethal for the state and cause much unhappiness for the people because religion itself is totalitarian and vindictive in essence, no matter how ornate, elaborate and attractive its man-made constructs in design. Christianity may have been antagonistic to Jews because they are of an organic and distinct culture, not easily subjugated. The velvet gloves may be thin or thick, but they all eventually come off to reveal the rigid and absolute dictates at the core. Some religions are integrated with the cultural template of their subscribers in all aspects of their daily life, while some are total strangers, creating schisms, fractures and fragmentations in life. Many religious orders, in a cause and effect context, have spewed much toxic fear and hatred and efficiently served to alienate man from himself, veering away from humanity as expressed through brotherhood and unity, remaining the most potent and divisive force created by man. The notion that 'God is dead' (Nietzsche 1844-1900), the flip-side being that God is subjective and subjugable, or the omniscience of any one individual is a *non sequitur* in the Korean cultural context, not even registering on the Richter scale. Religion is only virtuous to the extent that universal humaneness remains uncompromised in principle and practice.

Culture fuses the self and non-self in the context of public morality and the perspective of the universal and eternal, demanding and requiring self-knowledge and self-realization, whereas religious dogmas bypass this source of difficulty, conflict and confrontation by providing a top-down absolute answer. There is in ancient cultures much reverence, love and respect for wisdom, knowledge and significant individuals, but a deliberate and cautious check against deification, monotheism and mindlessness. The specific bulwark is against mindlessness which represents the antithesis of will that is cultivated in awe of the universal force of life.

Although the Korean culture has retained its distinctness through a long history of living next door to an ancient and formidable imperial power as well as modern colonization, occupation and warfare, how well it survives the forces of globalization, Christianization and the mass media rests solely with its people and their reverence for heritage, language and identity. For a nation of such independent, contentious, emotional, and yet stoic and free-spirited people, their culture imposes a heavy burden and demands great effort. But in return, it gives them the benefit of a common centre and purpose. There is no shortage of ingenuity in the many attempts at escape, but as the simple lyrics of the folk song *Arirang* say—If you go over the hillock, discarding and deserting your heart, you will soon fall (and lose your bearings).

The Korean life is a creative balance between tension and release,[15] with the self most present in public or moral context and most absent at play. There is much self-control, self-discipline or tensility discernible in various contexts of family, social and public relationships where mindfulness is *sine qua non*, but at specific occasions for relaxation and entertainment, most Koreans seem capable of experiencing the innocence and joy of children at play or an uncanny ability to ease into non-pretentiousness, non-factitiousness and natural earthiness. Spontaneous singing appears to be a national pastime and conveys a poignancy, rhythm and beat which are felt through the senses, beyond the stethoscope's limit.

There is both the pull and push of conformity and non-conformity. The former insists upon moral cultivation and respect for the absolute ties and bonds of family as an integral part of the cultural grid. The latter portrays alternative paths of freedom unconstrained by consideration of rules, duties or obligations. With attainment of maturity comes the understanding that there

---

15. "Most of my readers will have observed a small water-insect on the surface of rivulets, which throws a cinque-spotted shadow fringed with prismatic colours on the sunny bottom of the brook; and will have noticed, how the little animal *wins* its way up against the stream, by alternate pulses of active and passive motion, now resisting the current, and now yielding to it in order to gather strength and a momentary *fulcrum* for a further propulsion. This is no unapt emblem of the mind's self-experience in the act of thinking." Coleridge, *Biographia Literaria*, pp. 124, 125, quoted in Richard Holmes, *Coleridge: Darker Reflections*, op. cit., p. 397.

Author's Note: Just as a child learns to play with a ball by learning to relax his grip and let go, so that it is released and passed, to and fro.

is no sense of self removed from its various public contexts and that dynamic compromises (not just equalization, neutralization, averaging out or a 50/50 split) between these forces of doing what is right in the cultural context and doing what I want in the willful context, ultimately forms and shapes individual character or self-identity. These developments give rise to an appreciation of the meaning of dignity and honour in the context that a person's word is his or her most precious asset, originating from within with fidelity.

Serenity[16] is attained when these two paths tend to converge more and diverge less, usually with the onset of mid-life when mortality begins to be felt and appreciated with balance tipping in favour of experience, willpower and knowledge over physical strength, willfulness and expediency. Moral and ethical teachings serve a dual purpose of transmitting what is right with a code of conduct, but also in encouraging the development of willpower tensibility or expanding and deepening the zones of tolerance, always in the context of the heart. This is the opposite from the suppression or denial of the self as it leads to the true liberation of the self which can transcend itself through willpower, no longer a slave to appetites or illusions.

To read into Korean history is to sense the interim reality and recycling of tensions borne between the polarities of human nature: nobility, willpower and spiritual regeneration versus venality, willfulness and material decay. The Korean metaphor—you have to see the sky to grasp the stars—seems adequate enough in conveying the sense that to read is to discover and discern meaning. History shows the subversion, perversion, corrosion, corruption, conscription, oppression, suppression of ideas and words through manipulation of language of the many by the few in moral ineptitude and decay—and, vice versa, in moral leadership and cultivation—representing the unending tug of war between mindlessness and mindfulness.

Many of the factionalisms, fanaticisms and purges that fill Korean life, both past and present, cast scholars and others who live their lives and risk their reputations for ideas (be they philosophic or cultural) in the context of their political and public struggles. Throughout these confrontations,

---

16. "It emphasized the dynamic, almost explosive, concept that Coleridge had of Beauty; or rather Beauty as an explosion of energy perfectly contained. Moreover he linked this dynamic aesthetic with the moral nature of mankind: happiness required that we had the individual sense of 'free will' and 'spontaneous action', balanced between and reconciled with 'regular forms' of duty and obligation." Richard Holmes, *Coleridge: Darker Reflections*, op. cit., p. 361.

however, the values and practices of filial piety which include ancestor worship and funeral rites, respect for elders, teacher/student and fraternal/classmate relationships have been equally observed. As within other orthodoxies, the dispute, discord and discourse continue to be a matter of degree of observance and priority in practice, sustaining tensions rather than snapping or flaccidfying or ossifying the idea itself.

Korean Family Values in the Context of Democracy

Democracy is more of a political utopian idea rather than reflective of philosophic thoughts and traditions or the practice of state-craft. It foments best as a means for plebeian appeal in the physical struggle to wrest political power from the old oppressors. When the new inevitably becomes the old, democracy is no longer represented as an end, but becomes so highly qualified by non-democratic restrictions and conditions that the result preserves authority and order over democratic means or principles. This is the transformation process as political manifestos meet the reality of governance and order. Constant chaos is not the desired end purpose or characteristic of most human endeavours, struggles and world view, regardless of the intent of the One. Like most utopian schemes, democracy also turns out to share many totalitarian traits with rigid definitions, positions and rules. While the brief life of a Democracy in Athens in 500 BCE is selectively interpreted by historians, even within a relatively small population base there still was no equality, since slaves presumably were not at liberty to vote.

Philosophic ideas from Plato's *Republic* to Hobbes' *Of Liberty and Necessity* to Nietzsche's works, seem to suggest propensity towards authoritarianism and order. This preference is also reflected in the practice of nation building and national or generic identity formation, where uniformity of written and spoken languages is found along with shared beliefs, rituals and hierarchical family structures. For example, in modernity, successful nation building and superimposition of generic identity was achieved by Bismark, the Iron Chancellor, who administered a large measure of 'medicine that is good for you' to the fragmented masses of 19th-century Germany. This may be one of the reasons why so many departed for the U.S.—better to pack up and start anew than conform—which sentiment captures Americanism.

Since immigrants from many other countries share a similar impetus for leaving their homelands, the absence of a generic identity has come to be associated with liberty, equality and justice. This lack of association results in rough and raw edges around the absolutely individualistic and immature approach to these concepts in America. As each generation starts anew without lineal awareness and heritage, so the strands of time are disconnected. What is agreed upon is to throw out the Old World views so that each individual is at liberty to live in a New World. The end result is a society of Sisyphus, and no wonder Nietzsche and his association with nihilism is endearing and enduring in the popular culture, while his vast flip-side is not even given lip-service. All that is achieved is the validation of the obvious—what is new today is old tomorrow—without appreciating that it is time that transforms, linearly, non-repetitiously, and independently of our circadian or diurnal notion of time, synchronicity or chronology.

The relevance of studying the history of Korea is in understanding how a small country generated enough negentropic forces for survival and evolution of a generic identity against relentless agents of chaos (like the encirclement by today's mass media) from China, Russia and Japan, throughout its existence. For this purpose, whether the generic identity is three- or five-thousand years old or more does not matter; only that it has survived intact for a very long time. How have filial piety, reverence for mentors and deference to elders, as well as so many other shared attitudes and world views served to retain its sphere of influence? Perhaps the key lies in a language that is so infused with a code of conduct and matrix of values that its ideologies remain elusive to incessant judgement, subjugation and subversion, and therefore are not subject to death by a thousand cuts but, rather, are confluent spheres that touch and move the heart. The language forms a decentralized and intangible web that is equally and readily dispersed throughout the social network. Scholarship was paramount; but without lineage, status and prestige or nobility of family background (especially of the mother), it was in practice, impotent. The *sajo*, or proof of descent from four ancestors and its variations, served as a passport to social life. The *hojok*, or household register, served as an indisputable proof of identity or origin. This register acknowledged and recorded ties to an ancestral name and seat along with the strictly-defined position of members within a household as submitted by its corporate head to the official registrar. The Korean words signify that one was elevated to or disowned by the *hojok*, rather than the transactional terms of entry and removal. While patrilineal descent made up the bulk of proof, the background of the mother was the acid test or the deal breaker in many of these schemes. Variations occurred only in theme and enforcement through the Dynasties, not in principle. Rights were strictly coupled with rites and *primus inter pares* or the sensibility of heredity strictly observed with its wish- or self-fulfillment ripple-effect. While conformity was encouraged, the emphasis on self-cultivation as a central ideology of the society, discouraged blind compliance.

Even during long periods of political fragmentation and extreme poverty, the generic identity remained whole. Each successive Dynasty from the Old Choson Period (2333 BCE) to Shilla, Koryo and the last of Choson, had its distinctive view and flavour, but each transition stage was evolutionary and not achieved or sustained by total and complete repudiation and expunging of the past. Character judgements over the proper alignment of the inside-out and outside-in pictures for assessment of integrity are elusive for measurement without relational contexts. The strong emphasis on family lineal trunk or longitudinal roots does not result in fool-proof discernment of nobility or fitness, but increases its odds by the risk posed for the continuity of the family and clan status and prestige well into the future. As within most hierarchical societies, the risk of downward mobility exceeded the possibility of upward mobility, and maintaining the status quo was not a given, even if birthright was. Great importance was placed upon keeping a family registry, as well as keeping current the public registry by incorporating and officially recognizing new members. The purpose of all this record-keeping was not quantitative, analytic, political or economic, but primarily for generic identity survival and evolution.

The mother is at the heart of Korea's language, patriarchal structures and exhaustive rules for being human. She is the organic vessel of culture and the guardian of virtue or whatever the people have held dear and sacred from the beginning of their group identity formation. The philosophies of Taoism, Buddhism and Confucianism have been critically applied in order to preserve this heart of the people. Thus, the most powerful force of nature—the maternal instinct—is safely protected and harnessed for the benefit of the many, not suppressed or obliterated. It would be hard to find another nation with scholars who have taken the education of the people as a cause for a longer period of time or more passionately. It would be equally hard to find a society where so much of family life and resources is devoted to the education (nurture) of the young and where the voice of the elder is not silent, nor silenced.

For all the cries of government of, by and for the people in modernity, very few states or countries have adopted a motto of *In People We Trust*, preferring instead, *In God We Trust*. For Koreans the motto and rallying cry of the heart through the millennia of unceasing turbulence has been: *In Our Mothers We Trust* or *By Our Family We Live*. As Korean history shows, generic identity-building takes time and requires passionate, sustained and profound leadership.[17] The turning point in the durability and resilience of such an identity pivots on the peerless, subtle and fine olfactory senses of the people who can sniff out what is true or false in infinite guises. This organic detection system operates in the context of a pro-life philosophy with great

---

17. Author's Note: The German experience resulting from religious reformation can serve to illuminate the crisis in identity and the response of the scholars to bind and mend the wounds. The religious discord from the Diet of Worms (1521) set off a chain reaction, resulting in brutal destruction that lasted over many generations, of which The Thirty Years' War (1618-1648) was but one of innumerable violent conflagrations. From the ashes budded the creative search for a more resilient, versatile and inviolable sense of the human identity.

As much as the German philosophers admired the qualities of the individual, their reading of Western history, tradition and society resulted in favouring authoritarianism over individualism in the political balance of power. Nietzsche's works seem to articulate his predecessors' understated conclusion that God is not enough in countering the forces of mob violence, mediocrity and modernity. *But, they do not stop here.* It is merely a departure point. They then go into elaborate lengths to show how an individual can be the author and authority of his or her own life. They did not see their fellow man or woman as a master or a slave, but simply as a human being, whom they wanted to help in liberating from the tyrannies that he or she brings upon himself or herself, at a minimum.

The only force remaining after the removal of God from the equation balancing good and evil, is the human being. Thus, from Schiller, the Schlegel brothers, Schelling and Schopenhauer to Hegel and Nietzsche are intense and passionate rallying cries and bold sketches of the power of the individual as the only resort and the final retort against mediocrity. They all seem to be drawing out the foundation of a generic human identity, not based on national, religious, ethnic or any other categorization, but one that can withstand the *sturm und drang* of life without losing sight of the true north of the Centre Point, to which there is no counterpoint.

The whiplash of turbulence was all around for permeable, delicate and sensitive or Noble Minds, who played their best hand to navigate, steer and chart a course for safe harbour for all those willing to embark on the journey of Life. Perhaps the Founding Fathers could have used more of a German influence than the British and French vogues of Locke, Rousseau, Voltaire and others in the bookends between the renaissance and enlightenment genres.

continued

consistency or accuracy when not stressed, reshaped and blinded by sloth, vanity and the diversionary ploys of vested interest groups. The sniff test can overcome many of the illusions created by the pet food industry as to the appealing smell, taste, texture and wholesomeness of their well-packaged by-products, which perhaps only the manufacturers can identify by name and source. Sloth, above all the other vices, ensures perpetual unknowingness or ignorance in a state of callous, obdurate and indurate infallibility, at the sacrifice of imagination and other experiences, which can broaden and deepen the library of contexts and sensitivities to the nuances of other lives.

Christianity, in common with other isms, encourages the acceptance of self-inflicted wounds which result from staying within the tight box of dogmas and rules. In contrast, enduring generic identity discourages self-inflicted wounds by continuously processing relationship experiences as they affect the well-being of the self as it transforms through time. What is the point of being enlightened if one continues to be miserable most of the time? The purpose of learning must be to increase happiness, not just to collect and correct as

Perhaps the leaning towards British and French traditions excluded Germany from the orbit of American sensibilities, given their historical contexts and turbulence on both sides of the pond. But the final structure and mechanics of the government that emerges seems to mirror the conclusion—In People We Do Not Trust or Only Through Authority Can We Govern—of the German and many other thinkers and traditions.

Democracy holds out an illusion of life without rules but ends up building an alter of laws with homage to the Supreme Court as the ultimate arbiter. From liberty, equality and happiness rises the culture of laws and lawyers in which there does not seem to be much sense of joy or justice. The English and French philosophic strains seem bright and full of light with an optimistic presentation, and tend to deal with people in abstract and conceptual terms, couched and justified by tautological or absolute values useful for political manifestos to generate mass appeal and mobilization. However, once the political power struggle is over, the result leads to the same square of external authority and arbitration over what is right or wrong as agitations continue to multiply. It holds out promises of light, hope and glory that mask a pinhole of darkness. The German strand engages the individual in concrete and subjective reality of the state of oppression and holds out the possibility of personal contentment through intense self-discipline and development, so that the individual can become the arbiter of what is right or wrong. It looks pessimistic but points to the light at the end of the tunnel. This is an aspect that shares much in common with the Confucian teaching of life-long self-cultivation.

many facts as possible in a lifetime or to kill time. Enculturation is a process that encourages disengagement from activities that makes one unhappy with a disposition for serving no other purpose than that of a constricted self-serving win/lose dichotomy.

It insists upon the self to not self-obsess, but to enter into the web of social relationships where it can come into being. Time is not wasted in silly debates over whether the chicken or the egg came first. Time is not wasted in debates which can only be endless and futile, whereby various nominations of truths, such as ultimate virtues, values and ends, are engaged in by anyone, at any time, equally. Time is not laid to waste by severing the links to the past, but is extended indefinitely into the future. What has worked for ages flows through, and what has not, is changed. Over time the proportion of what is preserved and passed on increases so that change becomes increasingly infinitesimal and imperceptible. Only permeability and transience or mutability remain constant.

The past provides the longitudinal context for the present latitudinal experiences so that individual existence and coping matter for the community as a whole in the flow of time. Time is too valuable to be dedicated to over-work for over-consumption, because time is not asymmetric or unequal in its effect. No one attains immortality by remaining a child, a student and a younger, but through becoming a parent, a mentor, an elder, and thereby transmitting knowledge gained and distilled through a lifetime, for the purpose of increasing favourable outcomes as future generations continue to remember, endure and overcome in successive iterations and permutations. For humankind, procreation is one of the many possible acts of creation as we collaborate in infinite permutations of relationships, to create in dimensions beyond the temporal.

To the extent that individuals believe themselves to be kings or victims or masters or slaves, authoritarianism (relative assignment of authority with consensus of the governed) at best or totalitarianism (absolute dogma-driven with blind consent) at worst represent the political landscape. To the extent that peace and order for the many is the minimum state of affairs to be secured and maintained by the government, individuals have signed-off on attenuation of individualism. Any attempt at structured government is a declaration of war against unlimited individualism which feeds the belief in absolute self-assertion in liberty, equality and justice for self-serving ends which must be won at any cost. It is a prescription for chaos, entropy and decay or anti-life when universal principles are usurped as absolute principles for political process or change by the few. The only people who advocate democracy as a *form* of government by defining democratic principles are those whose purpose is to displace those in current positions of power, not for maximum and equal distribution of political capital. Democracy is not principle or end, but a movement of change or process that has never been instituted as a government structure because it is anti-structure in essence. Honest thinkers have advocated democracy only in principle, not form, because slaves working and living in peace and order have tended to be more pro-life in the long-run than freemen plundering or being plundered in chaos and unlimited destruction. This preference is also borne out by observing the admiration shown by many outside the armed forces for military leaders who are products of rigid hierarchies or anti-democratic organizations and practices.

With the non-clarification of principle and process there seems to be many means, but a broad statement or sense of common purpose seems missing from the social landscape. Pro-life terminology, not philosophy, is being articulated and linked to religion (a marriage of dogmas) to obfuscate how it is being used as a means to achieve a political agenda of hatred and intolerance. Pro-life philosophy which is reflected in the writings (in secular context) of Noble Minds and incorporated in many ancient cultures seems to attest to the how's and the processes of preserving diversity and becoming genuine human beings, not defining when life begins or ends and what the meaning of life may be, which is endlessly covered by teleology, ontology, cosmology and theology. They are interested in sharing their knowledge of the many paths and approximations to the Way, not in dictating the One and Only or Absolute Way.

Culture is defined by the *Webster's New World Dictionary* as "the ideas, customs, skills, arts, etc. of a people or a group, that are transferred, communicated, or passed along, as in or to succeeding generations." Thus, culture is by nature highly dynamic and can take on many different meanings depending on the situation. In each of the following examples it is reflected and expressed differently:

1. in a land mostly populated by non-indigenous and non-homogeneous populations,

2. for those whose place of birth or citizenship is different from their place of origin,

3. when there is decreasing permanence and sense of place, with increased relocations, combined with homogeneity of view (media, consumer goods, dress, and cityscape),

4. where traditional cultures no longer have an extended family and close-knit community for cultural transmission,

5. where traditional cultures are assailed by consumerism and the mass media,

6. where the colonial mask of culture creates a schism in the indigenous culture,

7. when there is no common spoken language between the generations, and

8. when it is common that marriage and the adoption of children bridge ethnicities.

Therefore, culture can mean many different things to different people. What passes for culture for some could be owning expensive objects of art and appreciating and imbibing the finer things in life that are beyond the intellect and pocketbook of the masses. The reference is to something that suggests exclusiveness: the more exclusive, esoteric, eccentric or expensive, the more cultured, aesthetic or refined. In a society that only appreciates what can be shown and dollarized or shown off, combined with a virulent mass media dedicated to showcasing the showing off, each entity feeding on the other, there is a predictable outcome: a sense of unreachability and unattainability around culture for the majority. This is precisely the opposite of a culture's purpose, which is to impart a sense of belonging to the greater whole, to be all-pervasive and inclusive in the daily life of all belongers. Rather than democracy, the result is plutocracy, which ironically is circular, traditional and back-to-square-one. But it is a plutocracy *sans* the cultural heart and organic language which characterize ancient civilizations.

"To thine own self be true" could be interpreted as to be consistent with one's cultural paradigm, in that one's identity is defined by the culture into which one is born, the traditions and customs of one's family, and one's position within it and the society at large, which then determines one's personal sense of honour and dignity, with their attendant code of conduct. One tends to approximate the cultural paradigm with which one has the greatest familiarity and affinity, i.e., that which one was initiated into and therefore connected with, in belongingness. It does not mean do as you like or be whatever you like. Polonius does not say to his departing son Laertes, 'Remember you are number one' or 'Do us proud' or 'Winning is every-thing' or 'Say and do anything to win' or 'Win at all costs'. He is instead warning against self-deception and self-nullification, which can constitute the most formidable, insidious and insular barrier against self-knowledge as a prerequisite to discerning the various shades and shadings of truths and lies. Any progress towards the pursuit or recognition of Truth is curtailed through self-censorship and unilateralism. This, combined with mass-delusion where-by all are equally labeled as special, gifted and talented without any content, context or progress, fosters anti-intellectualism for the masses. When knowl-edge is thus rendered null and void in the absence of teachings regarding precedents—relativism and asymmetricism prevail.

The world of art (including architecture) and all its manifestations are but the visible tip of a much greater mass below the surface; just as all the dimen-sions of an iceberg cannot be appreciated by what is visible above the ocean surface, so too it is with culture. The concept can be appreciated by under-standing the *corpus delicti* aspect of law: the foundation and substantiation of how's and why's, since justice mirrors the crime in being circumstantial and occasional. The source of its power is not consciously thought about, even by individuals belonging to very rigid cultures, because culture by nature and design becomes part of one's essence or intuitive sense. It cannot serve its function if the why's, how's, and what's of its directions are questioned and debated incessantly. The learning is deeply internalized throughout early childhood by lessons and schooling. A child who cannot move beyond why 2 + 2 = 4 or why an object is red (as a result of a disability or because the child is far too clever to accept an artificial construct or an absence of definitive proof of perception or simply untaught) cannot move on, and as a consequence of being stuck at this level, cannot see the necessity of proceeding and is unable to proceed. This is the domain of epistemology, but one does not need to understand the theory of knowledge to know, just as one does not need to understand physiology to feel pain. The effect of a cultural imprint is similar in that it provides a foundation for all learned behaviour and beliefs which are built upon it, but dissimilar in that lacking or not accepting this early on in life could endanger it.

Culture imprints a picture of the inner person, a vision of 'who I am', and gives it order and structure through a value system and attendant code of conduct which are consistent with the goal of survival, because in a human society the ones who survive or flourish are not necessarily the physically strongest. To survive means to fit in to (and be fitting of) the existing society and to understand how to harmonize with it: propriety, propriety, propriety. This external propriety is mirrored back to oneself in terms of personal honour and dignity: what it means to be a human being with an understanding of human values and human conduct. This symmetry gives robustness and coherence to the cultural paradigm and at the same time, poses the greatest cultural challenge to the individual: to balance and navigate between these two spheres of inner and outer harmony. Personal integrity is a measure of how consistently one lives and conducts oneself in a manner that is consistent with this inner picture, resulting from the interactions between these two spheres.

Not many people can succinctly or clearly answer the question—What do you want?—but whether one is engaged in pursuing what one wants or is drifting aimlessly, the code of conduct still applies. This is the primary function and importance of culture: to ensure social harmony while allowing for pluralities within an individual as well as pluralities of individuals. A culture is neither good nor bad, superior nor inferior. It works for the benefit of all belongers and is able to accommodate and tolerate misfits by its sheer mass (population) as long as the balance is maintained by most; there is a limit to how far the metacentre can shift without falling below the centre of gravity and sinking. A life, whether well-lived or not, whether spent in service to others or not, should at least, at a minimum, not have caused any harm.

The cultural imprint is similar to that of the Processor Command Language (PCL). It is an inner supralanguage of a higher order rank that is global and universal; it both precurses and supersedes any subsequent outer language or experience. It is superior in its ability to override impulsive thoughts and actions, spoken or otherwise, and provides a platform for all other sub-routines and their interaction. This is the inner voice of the culture and perhaps, its magic. It is a moral compass aligned with the cultural imperatives necessary and sufficient for fitting within one's social milieu. They are like the flanges on the wheels of life. Morality is not just another rational concept which reason makes and breaks with equal finesse and flourish.

What feels good or bad is hardwired at birth for the senses, so that the baby (as with all sentient beings) feels hunger and satiation, pain and pleasure, light and dark, bitter and sweet, noise and silence. However, what is good or bad in the ethical sense can only be imprinted in the context of the human experience over time. Many professions have ethical standards which concern themselves less with the quality of goods and services provided and more with the conduct (and motives) of their members. Ethical standards can only apply among qualified equals, those who have the credentials to determine and judge any breach in conduct. First among equals implies that only those qualified can engage each other, whether in praise (recognition and acceptance) or condemnation (rejection and isolation).

But in most professional or non-professional lives that lack an explicit ethical code (which is the case for most people), judgements drown out everyday life with their drone and din. This is the reverse of get ready, take aim and shoot, which has become the normal practice with the passing of instantaneous judgements without qualification, justification or any attempt at understanding. It resembles a gun-happy attitude of instant justice, where everyone feels entitled to be the judge, jury and executioner in the flat-out pursuit of money and fair share or entitlement. This is an inescapable fact of life and part of human nature. The outcome of these judgements can range from relatively harmless to homicidal.

The need to belong may be hardwired, as it is in the survival interest of the baby to learn the language of the culture as quickly as possible and fit in, because once the child is capable of speech[18] and self-expression, he or she has the capacity to cause disharmony, which in the wrong quarters can prove more than just unpleasant. The means of this learning process is the mother tongue, which is aptly descriptive not only in that it is the language spoken by the mother, but in that it truly is the language which ensures and nourishes the well-being and survival of a human life. Without a language consisting of words and numbers, whose richness and applicability is only matched by its inexhaustibility and imagination, one would be limited to, at best, a three-dimensional format, or more likely, one of only two dimensions (representations on a flat surface), which translates to rigid mutual exclusivity (*I'm definitely and always right, you're not*). This can prevail even with language fluency. All languages are characterized by their multidimensionality, enabling and facilitating the probing of many realities, and revealing paradoxes and shades of grey as a result of these encounters and endeavours.

The concept of the gestation period in this context takes on a different meaning and implication for human being readiness (as well as for other social species), because while nine months ensures a sustainable life, it does not ensure its long-term survivability or flourishing. The complete gestational period therefore could conceivably range from nine months plus four years to nine months plus 18 years or more: quite a different and awesome slant on parental, societal and educational responsibilities and requirements. This relatively long gestational period can be compared to that of the various stages that a butterfly goes through for a great bulk of its lifetime in preparation for the final metamorphosis, dominated by a prolonged period of incubation and relative inactivity with a relatively short but significant final manifestation long enough to procreate, if it survives all the other stages.

The concept of morality, in terms of what is acceptable and good or unacceptable and bad, is thereby imprintable very quickly after speech capability develops because it is intricately tied to survival. A child at seven years of age [19] is deemed fully accountable for his or her actions in the Russian culture, when the practice of attending confessions can begin. This is also a practice of the Catholic faith. "Give me a child until he is seven and I will

18. "As soon as the child is able to talk, or when he attained the age of four years, four months and four days he is taught the Bis'illah, the first words of the Koran...." D.S. Roberts, op. cit., p. 118.
19. Islam also "...specified seven years as a general rule, at which age the child is considered to be able to discriminate and can choose with which parent it wishes to live." D.S. Roberts, op. cit., p. 120.

show you the man," was the profound Jesuit saying which resulted in the Granada Television documentary entitled, "7 UP."

While there may be physiological reasons (birth canal dimensions) why the human brain size is relatively smaller at birth compared to its eventual size than is the case in other species, it may be that it does not make biological sense to be born with a fully developed brain. The encoding of the cultural language can only make sense after birth because it is entirely subject to and a function of its environment, including family members and others already flourishing. To survive, a new life has to fit in, tune in, and connect with the existing family picture, and eventual social landscape. This is a lifelong process and endeavour, since the process of wiring and re-wiring does not cease throughout life (although for survival reasons it is most rapid and dramatic in the first few years of life, with its attendant 'psychological moment'). This non-completeness of the brain at birth probably accounts for the adaptability and flourishing of human beings in a wide spectrum of habitats, despite common physiological constraints. While there are many universal human values, each society has unique values which may be in conflict or inconsistent with those of others because in its setting and settlement, where they flourish, certain values would ensure their long-term survival while others could prove cataclysmic to the belongers.

The cultural language cannot be hardwired at birth because the environment (physical and social) is subject to change as family units and societies move, adapt and evolve within geographic boundaries which determine availability, utilization and sharing of resources. The cultural language in many countries has evolved over millennia of interaction with and among the habitat, inhabitants and habits. Woven into it are the human values and conduct that will ensure its flourishing. Biology is destiny; it is also location and personal history. Destiny is merely a metaphor for the cumulative result of individual choice-making—choices for which one is fully accountable because despite all that may appear to be fixed, there still remains an ineffable and ineffaceable domain of infinite permutation of possibilities and probabilities which are enabled and facilitated by one's cultural paradigm.

An individual's life is therefore the product of a combination of deterministic and existential variables which can influence each other in varying degrees. While the effects of deterministic variables can be mitigated, they cannot be denied or neutralized, so that cultural intelligence and attendant self-awareness are helpful in approximating an acceptable choice or outcome. There is no arbitrariness in living an encultured life because choices are made in the context of one's inherited cultural paradigm. Adopting and achieving great familiarity with many or most of the practices (spoken language, dress, mannerisms) and beliefs (work ethics, religion, intellectual heritage) of another culture cannot change one's ethnicity, just as gender roles have no bearing on the determination or manifestation of gender.

The desire to nurture and create transcends gender or other one-dimensional categorization by traditional cultural imperatives, ethnicity, media imagery and other attempts at constraining and stereotyping. To believe that men (in gender context) are not as delicate and warm in touch and feeling as women ignores the compassion, beauty, grace and delicateness that are revealed in the lives and creative output of men who embody these sensibilities in the extreme. Some of the renowned works and lives (Michelangelo, Bach, Coleridge, St. Francis) capture and convey far more than mere three-dimensionality, revealing many levels of perception or consciousness displaying a variety of perspectives. Their appeal transcends the senses, and one is transported and transformed in the experience, be it literature, music, painting, sculpture or architecture. There may be such men today, but perhaps they are just not sexy and young enough for box-office appeal to generate advertising revenue and flog consumer goods and services. Men as parents, teachers and mentors play as essential a role as women in nurturing and rearing the younger members of society. Power and significance are not merely reflected by scope and scale of size, strength or wealth.

One cannot enter or leave one's cultural paradigm like changing outfits, professions or religion. The inputs and influences that first gained entry and connected form the foundation for the cumulation of and interaction with subsequent ones. An individual, by definition, cannot be multicultural or multinational: there is one initialization point or perspective and all others are a sub-set of this supra-set. The eight situations listed at the beginning of this chapter cover all continents since people have always moved about. It seems like there is more movement in modernity, but it is more likely to be proportional to those of ages past. The key difference lies in the effect of the 24/7 global image circulation and dominance of English as the *lingua franca*. For the aforementioned situations, an individual falling into one of these categories would likely:

1. Develop a culture of one ('I-centrism' characterized by indeterminateness and indeterminableness), with a rigidly narrow, limited and shallow outlook, similar to someone locking himself up in a

room with one small peephole of light. When this is pervasive in the nation, one usually finds the term culture being associated with just about anything and (mis)used with great frequency. (The U.K. Sunday Times newspaper includes a magazine supplement boldly titled "CULTURE," containing popular entertainment and TV programme listings. This is a common practice found in many countries.) The culture of one is characterized by its a priori incapacity or curtailment of capacity to engage in dialogue (requiring an exchange and entertainment of ideas in various contexts and perspectives), since all are subsumed (materiality and content are irrelevant) in the context and perspective of the 'I' (what I think, feel, want), irrespective of a goal or purpose (if such even exists). The engagement and allure of omnipotence and omniscience with the 'I' is so intense that disengagement from the personal and subjective 'I' at any level, which is so essential to learning and getting along, becomes a non-starter. This is not narcissism, which at least has the distinction of love of self, a quality unfortunately lacking in the culture of one, but a singular and overriding need to prevail at any cost. Western countries seem to experience greater malaise because the braking forces of culture are disarmed by and insufficient against the tidal waves of change brought to bear upon it with the advent of rapid industrialization and economic expansion. Ancient cultures do not have an inexhaustible immune system as similar problems confront them, as they cave into looking backwards with restoration movements and consistent mis-planning, so that confusion more than anything else reigns, increasingly drawn into the same vortex of consumerism and capitalism. Learn, change and live does not seem to hold out as much appeal as lives clinging onto infallibility, immutability and preferred illusions of certainty.

2. Adopt a fundamentalistic approach to the traditional culture with great emphasis on its idiosyncrasies and differences with others. This is characterized by nostalgia, purification, jingoism, antagonism to outsiders, extreme patriotism and its attendant regression into the past, indicating a lack of appreciation for the concept of time-order.

3. Buy into the message or notion of superiority and perceive conversion into the colonialist's culture as a means of achieving and affirming higher social status or a means of entry into an improved

economic life. The colonial version of culture is a spectacularized, sanitized or bastardized representation of its home version, which by virtue of being applicable to all inhabitants equally, not exclusively for those with racial, political, social, economic and educational advantages wrenched by might, manifests very differently in these diametrically opposing contexts (content and subject differentiation). Thus, regardless of the reason for conversion, as opposed to being merely knowledgeable about another culture, the converted become neither fish nor fowl; cultural conversion is mostly an exercise in futility with not much upside, but with attendant and certain loss of a sense of belonging. The indigenous will view the conversion as rejection or betrayal or weakness of character. The host culture will not accept what is not indigenous, with its lack not only of the inner language and cues but also outer markings, i.e., the essential requirements of the 'look and feel' cannot be met satisfactorily. The extreme of this is equating one's cultural identity with one's passport as its validation and affirmation.

4. Retain an incomplete or vestigial cultural template which will continue to fade as it is supplemented and supplanted by membership and participation in one or more interest groups.

5. Find that the cultural paradigm is subsumed by the economic one, with pursuit of material wealth becoming the sole consideration for any decision.

6. Veer towards or adopt a supra-culture of humanity with its broadest and deepest sense of belonging and meaning. One simply identifies with all of humanity and humanist values, which can result in feeling natural and at ease everywhere.

These are some examples of the many degrees and forms of cultural castration whereby attempts at substitution, synthesis, reconstitution or reconstruction seem never quite satisfactory. Even the last category wobbles in the contexts of universal brotherhood, borderless patriotism and the Kingdom of All Life which demarcate the chasm between belief and practice. The sense of alienation expressed in the line, "I stood among them, but not of them"[20]

---

20. William H. Marshall, ed., *The Major English Romantic Poets* (Washington Square Press/ Simon & Schuster, 1963), p. 288.

(Childe Harold's Pilgrimage, Canto III by Lord Byron) can apply to anyone, born anywhere, at any time, because a sense of commonality and commonness with others or a sense of humanity with its shared history and experience is learned, not innate. Being human does not make one inclined to be humane

In the modern era, with ease of relocation and travel, non-dependence of habitat (almost non-awareness since it no longer is necessary to be aware), and the all-pervasive mass media, the cultural language and its transmission have been abandoned in preference for the culture of one, characterized by involution and a deluge of dogmatism and doctrinairism which create a feeling of living in a dog-eat-dog world. This manifestation shares the same degree of durability and impenetrability of all involuted creations; it is quite a formidable construct *in situ*, posing a great challenge to harmonious coexistence, whether it is a natural state or a reaction to causative factors as a means of self-defense and survival whereby egression results in confinement of self, not its liberation.

Our search for serenity and security can be achieved by focused and disciplined effort in engaging and understanding the tensions and pluralities around us and by making trade-offs and compromises, continually working on enabling skills for balancing on the tightrope with mindfulness. It can also be attained by becoming an object incapable of acting upon or being acted upon by complete disengagement, withdrawal and isolation so no light can penetrate it and there is neither comedy nor tragedy, but only numbness and ignorance. The latter scenario is well served by individualism and a host of dogmatisms which confine and suppress the senses; the former through moral cultivation, comprehensive education and organic nurturing which empower and liberate the self and the senses.

Such are the boundless possibilities in the interim of being versus the polarity of non-being, illusion versus reality, singularity versus infinity, all pivoting on appropriate attitude and orientation, oscillating between the resolution of the inner and the outer forces and the forces of polarization. The senses are tuned in, steadfast and malleable or tone deaf and petrified. Human beings are part of the organic world and as such need constant nurture, attention and maintenance to become progressively more mindful given the potential upsides and downsides. Liberty, equality, fraternity and the pursuit of happiness are cold, abstract, analytic, objective constructs of a select group of men[21] who, despite their many intellectual strengths, seem out of touch with the workings of an organic and progressive nature and culture or seem to excel in denial of reality. Judgements, moral or otherwise, are rarely rendered in purity or certainty but, rather, circumstantially and subjectively, sometimes scratching nobility. A reliable and consistent indicator of words and deeds lies in the seeing of purposes served from the outside-in perspective over time (longitudinal studies). Such perspective is increasingly unlikely when events, opinions and attitudes are increasingly warped and made uniform by the mass media as it creates and caters to ever shorter and more indiscriminate attention spans.

21. Author's Note: Perhaps the study of men who left cultural identity legacies may prove more illuminating for the disciplines of cultural anthropology, sociology and psychology than an inordinate amount of study about the Founding Fathers. For example, Talleyrand (1754-1838), Metternich (1773-1859) and Bismark (1815-1898) all lived during highly turbulent times, when status and birthright were no guarantee against downward mobility, folly of self-inflicted wounds or survival. Of their lives, we might seek to answer the following questions:
1.   What purposes did they serve and how did they deal with adversity and success?
2.   What qualities enabled them to live productive and fruitful lives well into their eighties?
3.   What were their legacies to the cultural identity of their respective countries (France, Austria, Germany) as well as Europe?
   Studies of their lives and times should demonstrate that lies and truth are merely servants of purpose and can only be evaluated in context, not against some absolute measure of good-ness or banalities such as 'honesty is the best policy', 'truths-good, lies-bad' or 'cleanliness is next to godliness'.

In a culture of one there is no responsibility because in behaving in accordance with *just the way I am*, there is an implied absence of choice. There is no need for praise or blame, nor for gratitude or sympathy—not only to oneself but to all others—since they also could not have behaved in ways that are other than what they are. This is a safe cocoon, not only in minimizing or eliminating any external intrusion, interference, judgement or acknowledgement, but best of all in blamelessness of the self, since the self is merely a victim of personality. There is no mental or inner picture of *who I am* nor *what I should be*, and in the absence of such a picture, no effort of any kind, consistent or otherwise, with an internal set of goals and values, since they are also subjective and arbitrary, being subsumed by *what I want*.

The corollary is that there is no desire even to understand oneself because, in the absence of any standards except those of *what I want*, there can be no strength or weakness, success or failure, acceptance or rejection, praise or sympathy, gratitude or remorse. What is just or unjust is simply *what is my way* and *what is not my way*. In the absence of any common denominator to balance against these individual tendencies to drift randomly, the social pattern unravels. However unique and different an individual becomes, an understanding or awareness of some common denominators (such as humanistic goals and values or kinship ties) would provide a safety net.

While one has the inalienable right to choose, this does not imply that this right should at all times be exercised. The power to choose does not give rise to any power; it merely creates a responsibility or burden for the outcome(s) of the choice that may not necessarily be right. The right to vote, the right to bear arms, the right to speak and the right to procreate are rights that are not always exercised; other people do not have to believe in or comply with what one person decides is right simply because of a communication of this fact without context or qualifications (to the position stated and of the speaker). What is the value, meaning or relevance of a position that one cannot be bothered to explain nor is able to defend, let alone argue convincingly?

What is even more disconcerting than the forfeiture of free will and curtailment of liberty as the result of being a slave to one's appetite, is the resulting willful indifference which forms an amplifying loop with the cocooned I. The heart and mind are increasingly conditioned to harden so that ultimately what results is far removed from and no longer resembles its natural state. To be so deprived of and disengaged from intellectual and emotional self-expression by injunctions such as *say nothing, do nothing,* and *don't interfere* leaves one to exist as something less than human. This is not fatalism, but indifference and apathy. It is ironic that increasing apathy is matched by an increasing clamour for justice (personal, racial, sexual, economic, political) and assertion of all manner of rights in ever narrower contexts. The operative word in "injustice prevails when good men remain silent" (Edmund Burke 1729-97) is not so much "silent" as "good," which can only prevail if it is not just a relative and subjective convenience du jour.

The right or freedom to choose only implies and is preceded by the willingness to accept responsibility for the consequences of choice whose multi-dimensional ripple-effect belies the seeming simplicity of choice. Thus to act upon an idea as well as to subscribe to one is a multi-edged sword. To be or not to be, to act or not to act, to do or not to do, pale in significance to un-be, un-act and un-do in a time/space continuum: *ergo* the Buddhist adage for mindfulness or to be ever present in the moment. There is no mention of justice as a goal in the Ten Commandments[22]—only a code of moral conduct for a virtuous life because "everything flows," said Heraclitus (540-480 BC), and therefore we "cannot step twice into the same river."[23]

With the inversion of all the cardinal vices and commercialization or devaluation of virtues, only the Ten Commandments seem to be left standing as a vestigial scaffold bereft of its foundation. Justice seems to have become a standalone, one-dimensional, catch-all virtue rather than in combination with its supporting cast of prudence, fortitude, temperance, faith, hope and charity, just as the vices (lust, envy, covetousness, sloth, gluttony, pride, anger) have been neutralized.

Sex and violence represent choices of compromise and conflict at the most intense and interactive juncture of relationships. Sexual relationships involve

22. "Do not take revenge but leave room for God's wrath, for it is written: 'It is mine to avenge; I will repay,' says the Lord." Romans 12:19.

Author's Note: The Ten Commandments delineate a code of conduct in relationships with the universal oneness and otherness that are important to honour in order to realize a virtuous life. The ordering of the commands are not necessarily temporal or priority sequenced and they are challenging because these relationships are all equally important, simultaneously, requiring thoughtful attitude and attention at all times. Thus a liberated and virtuous life abounds with hard choices.

23. Jostein Gaarder, op. cit., p. 34.

intimate communion with another and are not acts merely for the satisfaction of appetite by chance. Rather, they are an opportunity to cultivate and expand the depth and breadth of the mind, heart and body, simultaneously. The value of partnership is in the invitation and embrace of another, to see through a different window, developing skills of compromise and balance in order to prepare for the high-wire act of rearing and nurturing the next generation: the supra-goal of society. Violence, on the other hand, is the unilateral rejection of another's reality predisposed and tending towards the need to render it extinct. Neither celibacy nor procreation is compulsive, but they pivot upon whether one views the next generation as common inclusive stock or private exclusive property.

If one is unable to connect with one other world view with a sense of equanimity, what is the probability of negotiating the relationships with the weaker or stronger, the younger or older, let alone with another world-view brought forth through procreation, adoption or purchase? Relationships range from voluntary to involuntary and influence the available range of choices that are oftentimes made with great difficulty and discipline. But if relationships are not defined and understood in their ramifications of language, conduct and attitude, they are not only discarded with great ease but without the exercise of choice: all relationships are whims and likely to be whimsical and fleeting. While modernity has eliminated the many rites of passage into majority status, it is ill-prepared or unwilling to face the many fall-outs, since these tend to disproportionately impact the young and the impressionable in the planned view of those who proclaim rights of private property as the exclusive and supreme right.

The U.S. is unique because patriotism does not rest upon nationality, which is the strongest unifying force for most countries. The U.S. is not simply made up of 50 states, but of many ethnic groups. The final qualifying process for citizenship involves testing for some familiarity with the English language (which can be waived or substituted) and cursory knowledge of the Constitution and laws, followed by the formality of the oath of allegiance. The pledged allegiance is not to a way of life or a culture, but only to political and legal systems based on humanitarian principles. However, awareness and understanding of these principles are not an explicit requirement of citizenship.

While offering legal rights, citizenship in the U.S. does not require (nor should it require) relinquishing an individual's way of life as determined by their cultural heritage; an individual's own sense of honour and dignity merits preservation and protection. But this is not an absolute right because it is superseded by the human and legal rights already in place, which offer protection against child labour, child brides, child and spousal abuse, forced labour, and other instances of might over right. Because of the emphasis on liberty and equality, often without the responsibilities entailed by these political values (not virtues), many people feel that they have an inalienable right to practice and believe whatever they want, without any modification whatsoever, irrespective of the century of immigration or country of origin.

In the upper echelons of 18th-century society, life revolved not only around intellectualism but also an indisputable standard of morality that was neither arbitrary nor relative. Independence, coupled with rights to liberty and equality, is a status achieved and conferred through an understanding of the moral dimensions in all aspects of thought and action. Because independence applies universally to all, and universality means that liberty and equality are to be practiced in such a way as to ensure that all are unimpeded and undiminished in their pursuit of happiness or purpose, harmony of an individual co-exists and rests upon harmony with and among all. Did the authors of the Declaration of Independence intend for liberty and equality to be applied to each individual as a discrete element or was it their intent that the term individual serve as a metaphor for all human beings, given that these were values which could conflict in concept and practice between individuals? Or could it be that they were simply unaware that these values could collide? Citizenship in a democratic political system is much more challenging and demanding of individual responsibility than an autocratic or paternalistic one, in that an individual's liberty and equality must entail recognition of same for all others. This is a factor which may not be required or be inconsistent with certain cultures, or not so explicitly expressed. Therefore the qualifications for citizenship, regardless of where one is born geographically or culturally, must necessarily include an appreciation of the ethical dimension of liberty and equality.

The symbol of the U.S. for all Americans is the Statue of Liberty, since it is a land of mostly immigrants. The words on the plaque of the Statue of Liberty capture the spirit of the U.S. and the essence of humaneness like no other; they are more important and significant than those in the Declaration of Independence and the Constitution, which are political and legal documents, not moral texts.

What is the fundamental primordial picture or image of an American? If there is a picture, it is one fabricated and perpetuated by the entertainment industry: for example, the heroic and rugged individual prevailing against great odds and trials and succumbing to no one; the top dog or the underdog resentful of not being equal or equally treated. The American mind-set is shaped by a heritage of extreme non-conformity; many people set off for the U.S. because they could not bear to conform with what they perceived to be undesirable and inhospitable conditions for their temporal as well as spiritual well-being. Fortunately, for a time they had in common a Western European cultural[24] and religious tradition to which they could conform because their practices and beliefs were derivative of these, not a total repudiation or wholesale substitution thereof. However, at the heart of the founding of the

24. Author's Note: The blending of the various Western European traditions necessarily creates a somewhat blander version, without the ties to the specific land and landscape that characterize and define each of these cultures, along with a highly refined and developed ethnocentrism among them, which is only eclipsed by the internecine, esoteric and inter-locale aptitude and finesse in the same vein. They have character; putdowns are an appreciable art form, discerning certain class, status and taste. While there are many broadsides traded between the British and French, Dutch, Flemish and French, German and French, etc., there are regionally held views within these countries, giving each a distinctive colour, flavour and feel. Thomas Hardy's novels serve as good representations of such localness. Even in China, Korea and India, there seems to be a deeper sense of connection to the specific locale of ancestry that is organic and embedded in self-identity and proves more endearing than a political or propagandized construct to serve the power interests of the few.

U.S. is an inherited, non-conformist attitude with an aptitude for denial and rejection.

For most Americans, the motivation for emigration to, or the appeal of life in the U.S. (from the 17th century to today) has been largely due to economic and, to a lesser extent, political considerations. Culture is hardly ever a determining factor. Immigrants have been transplanted with their cultural identity intact, albeit without the defender of the faith tenacity of the Élites with their vested interests in time-honoured (sacred) traditions. There is, however, a pent-up frustration with oppression, and a need to better their betters through the most tangible means available for securing class and status—that is, money. This quest for money seems to eclipse many other accomplishments as well as compensate for many shortcoming, and when it is combined with the rigid convictions and heavy-handedness of the class converted, wielding power to protect and perpetuate their vested interest over those below who clamour for their share, so continues the Sisyphean cycle of oppression. As long as the purpose of power is to maintain the status quo in service of vested interests, to monopolize gain or benefit, then the cycle of oppressor and oppressed will self-perpetuate, trapped by the trappings of power safeguarded by capitalism and wealth, subsuming or overshadowing all other considerations and not in the public interest. The goal of public good, defined by various factors and implemented by various means, is replaced by money as the sole factor with capitalism as the only *modus operandi*, so that there is a complete reversal of goals and means, as well as an inversion of public and economic interests. The gatekeepers and rulemakers are in service to vested interests, with appropriation and abdication of public service and interest.

Subsumed in the pursuit of the material at all costs and in the absence of extended families, cultural identity has been eroded, helped along by the assimilation of the young through the mass media and through peer pressure in schools, reinforcing this new identity which no longer conforms to, let alone resembles, their original one. The only common denominator shared by all, therefore, is that of non-conformity, regardless of whether or not one can trace one's ancestry back to the Mayflower. So it really does not matter who has been here the longest, because all ethnic groups will eventually run into the same problem: youth alienation beyond that of the usual generation gap in a *de facto* culture of non-conformity, and in the absence of systematic cultural transmission, a prevalence of the culture of one.

There will be confrontations along the lines of who have been here the longest and contributed the most, and therefore have more of a right to determine national policy and have their interests take priority. But the concepts of first-come, first-served or first-in, first-out, as practiced at fast food counters and airline check-ins, or the criteria of superior wealth, power and talent, are all out of context on a sinking ship or in an emergency ward (which, in many ways, resembles the current social state) where human values prevail; the hallmark of the human species being that the weak and the infirm are, in large measure, cared for and valued.

Citizenship in the Context of a Culture of Money

An individual can be considered as an ever-changing permutation or a unique time matrix so that his/her perception and sense of reality is likely to be unique. The challenge of education is to instill enough shared knowledge and memories to balance those of the individual and, through enculturation, initialize the unbreakable and ever-constant ties and footings of blood and land. These ties are set in motion and place, in longitude and latitude, by a reverence for time along with a code of conduct and a matrix of nominations that capture the essence of relationships as encapsulated in shared language. This learning programme which is repeated from generation to generation preempts tendencies toward unilateralism. No one is born good or evil but only with a potential for becoming a sage or a killer with many shades in between as covered by the bell curve. There can be few finer goals for parents than to guide, enable and liberate their children toward the path of becoming genuine human beings. Such lives are characterized by benignity and dignity in the matrix of life, mounted upon their unique dharmas and perhaps attaining a state of homeostasis, happiness or enoughness. To grow old, ripen and mature through the gift of time and to droop with the weight and fullness of age is a goal to be pursued, because age is not just another concept or a choice, denied or made at will.

From such rooting in the Language of Relationships 101, in the context of a family, the vocabulary grows in many dimensions through each encounter with other unique beings, from shallow and fleeting to profound and enduring. The art and virtue of life is realized through specific performance at each point of contact, demonstrating conduct becoming or unbecoming of a human being which can honour or nullify one's name. Cultures centred upon the family cradle individuality because uniqueness is given recognition and expression in the specific terminologies and manners that define a position within a set. An individual is not valued by intelligence or some other test scores, the right looks, athletic prowess, professional achievement or wealth, but by the hat he/she wears as defined by traditional rites of capping that symbolize rank and status in the context of family and the operational cultural paradigm.

In America, where much of daily life is subsumed by the language of money (money talks), there are few other contexts for relationships as traditional ties dwindle and wither away. Almost everything seems to carry a price tag, and even the so-called democratically elected offices tend to fall into the laps of those with the biggest war chests. The scales of justice are also loaded to favour those with the most money. Since no one and nothing, including the practitioners and practices of medicine and law, are error-, fool-, deception-, negligence- and time-proof, money becomes the ever-called upon and reliable insurance policy as fiduciary, filial, personal, professional and honourable duties become extinct. Not only does the U.S. enjoy the highest per capita income along with one of the highest ratios of doctors to total population, it probably enjoys the highest ratio of lawyers and lawsuits to base population. These ratios correlate as much to the state of health and justice as much as income correlates to academic achievement in the general population. Such measurements seem to be better inverse indicators. These high-priced service providers tend to skew the distribution of services to serve those who can most pay them in money or some other *quid pro quo*. Justice is as well served as the lawyers are in standing up for those most able to defend themselves by footing open-ended bills. Money seems to inspire some pretty spectacular, reckless or ridiculous propositions, postures and positions, which result in getting all bent out of shape. When the probability of winning is this fixed, courage and its fellow cast members in the roster of virtues are rendered meaningless, helpless and irrelevant.

There is no corruption when its counterpart finds such meagre expression. The system is not morally bankrupt—morality is simply absent. The discourse is not about good and fair competition, but just a mass media onslaught of canned eye-candy coupled with the relentless and inescapable pounding in of the same simple messages of good versus bad, us versus them, and money versus everything else, by virtue of repetition. The mass media and the mega-industries are not going to spare any expense to ensure that their money pipelines remain free and clear by underwriting those who will best serve their interests. Words such as compassion, courage, trust, dignity, honour, integrity and humility, which are felt up-close and personal as a reflection of deeds, will be so often repeated for mass depersonalized consumption and illusion that they will be drained of any meaning, dissolving into more blah-blah, further ensuring that only money maintains its firm grip on power. This is not government of, by and for the people—it is totalitarianism of, by and for the moneyed. The sleight of hand and alchemy exemplified by these vested interests lies in the conversion of so much garbage into profit streams and creating such a mountain of garbage as to crowd out and drown dissent and diversity.

This is not pluralism, assimilation, counter-culture or even fragmentation. It is annihilation of the human culture by weapons of mass production and mass destruction. Is the Texan penchant for more, bigger and gaudier via a missile defense system that will feed and grow the military industrial complex ad nauseam while nauseating organic lives as critical to deploy as developing 'mind' defense systems? Does the future hold increased likelihood of physical assault against which a physical defense system must be built or of insults to the mind that must be equipped and immunized to withstand such take-over ploys? All that seems to count and be remembered is the media designated winner. There is virtually no search for what is wrong or missing with this picture because the tube always seems full, refreshed and complete as it depends upon image, volume and speed to promote forgetfulness, gullibility and ignorance by recycling and repackaging the old into the new, the same into the different and vice versa.

The mass media's bulimic binge and purge cycles leave the mass audience in an anorexic and helter-skelter mental state (reed-thin attenuation and short attention span) that is always hungry for and addicted to junk food for the mind. With technology at its disposal, all systems are increasing pumped up with greater efficiency and economy of scale, with hearts and minds unengaged on both sides of the screen. PhDs and specialists learn a great deal about ever narrower fields, but the mass audience learns virtually nothing about anything that counts for living well and the state of happiness for all lives. What is downloaded is what the vested interests want to see go down ably packaged, scripted and presented by talking heads who best serve, pre-serve, protect and defend their agenda. Details are increasingly fudged, smudged and glossed over, with the big picture bearing no resemblance and relationship to them as ethos becomes ad hoc, and bathos draped in artifice and charm with constant replay, overtakes pathos of the heart and mind. Why do con artists and freeloaders proliferate and thrive? Because there has never been a shortage of air-heads, suckers and quitters, and the industry of identity is going about its business of increasing this market size. Not only is the economic divide between those who have and have not becoming unbridgeable with the spoils being divided by the two-party system and the military industrial combines, there is an even more alarming divide between those who live, watch, believe and stand by their TV sets, web sites and other outputs of the identity deficit industries versus those who choose to hold on to their dear lives with critical and independent antennas and minds. Rather than a political divide, this represents a divide between those involved strictly in the pursuit of money and winning at any cost, versus those with a philosophy of life and humanity.

What kind of mind-sets are all these proliferating mass technologies in terms of size, ownership and penetration augmenting other than what has been formed and shaped by their previous versions of mass application by the few in charge? What distinguishes the U.S. is not only the many global economic clubs that it chooses to join as a dominant player, but the many international mandates that it opts out of, such as the ban on land mines, environmental protection treaties, war crimes tribunals, processing and punishing of minors as adults, and foot-dragging or non-participation in many UN-sponsored programmes on ideological rationalizations which seem distinctly inhumane, anti-choice and anti-diversity. On both these bandwagons, it keeps company with other select nations which share views that are stilted towards profits and inhumanity as a package deal. The stance of the U.S. seems consistent with the sacred right to own guns or a free license to kill anyone or anything that poses a threat to private and economic property or some unilateral fixation of some kind. These choices are well-defended by economic, military and numerous ism-cocked models, whose intricacy and construct they alone can appreciate with their superior intellect which turns a blind eye to humanity for the sake of hegemonic expansion and expediency. Humanity, like other coins of the same ilk, are cheapened and tossed aside, rendered valueless in the singular context of profits.

For the most part, money remains much misunderstood and maligned as well as taken too seriously and not seriously enough. It is under-appreciated in its potential for causing much unhappiness and conflict and over-appreciated in its potential for delivering happiness and co-existence. Money plays an important role in life, but when it is riddled and shot through with money, whereby only money seems to talk and remains an object of desire, even of worship—becoming a human being and developing a language of relationships are likely to continue to be bypassed, unmissed. How arid and one-dimensional life becomes when the mind is continually bombarded, snookered and bamboozled by up-to-the-minute stock market ticks and economic indices along with the nipped, tucked and gussied-up faces spouting their scripted, nonsensical and artificial language which serves to mask the improbable and implausible razzmatazz on cause and effect. The countless assumptions, theories, models and terminologies are as convoluted and forced as they are removed from clarity, relevance and wellness of organic existence. All the tricks of the trade are brought to bear to compensate for extreme one-dimensionality and flatness. Such clever ploys only tend to compound and exacerbate simpleton-ness, resulting in fool-prone products that ironically target, appeal and find their best, diehard and easiest consumers or the choicest prey without a prayer for escaping. This market segment can only pray within their immutable box in thrall of the aura and pomp of power that bind them to the office-holder, whose integrity in banality and *non-gravitas* is indisputable. They look up devotedly to those who could not care or spare a nano-second or nano-dollar for their well-being and interest, other than as mass contributors and body counts at rallies for mass media coverage but ponce and punt for money rather than serve and garner for the many. The inexhaustible come-ons and put-ons of technology have merely replaced crystal balls, snake oils and the likes, but the traditional art of yarn-spinning continues unabatedly to serve the purposes of power and profit growth, concentration and maintenance, versus the state of happiness of the many.

Money is only as powerful as the role one assigns to it: master or slave. Reverence, coupled with an appreciation for the essential inter-relatedness in symbiosis between all that is, remains obfuscated, untaught and undiscovered in this money-laden milieu. Such skewed renditions of life make a mockery of equality between various parties, which presumes symmetry and reciprocity not only in attitude and intent but in greater regard to specific manner, deed and performance. Nobody is perfect or infallible and sometimes lies are better than truths if they serve to prevent harm and to protect the weak and the innocent. To believe in something so simplistic as an absolute truth or one amalgamated book, along with those who claim to possess it, and ceaselessly bandy it above all other heads in order to lord over the masses, rather than those who seek to release and illuminate it in some context, will more likely lead to a path of repression and enslavement than progress and liberty.

Since we can be our own worst enemy and no wounds hurt as much as those we inflict upon ourselves, self-knowledge will serve us well in teaching us to heal ourselves and to break through our own comforting illusions of being unilaterally right. Can anyone truly know another let alone one's own self? One can only appreciate and judge processes, deeds and what has third party verifiability and witness which can attest to the innumerable permutations and manifestations of truth as we strive to become benign, transparent and human. No one individual or single-axis group can create, own, sell or destroy truth; two can equalize, neutralize or destroy each other's truth; three independent points can attest and relate to or nullify and disjoint a truth. How little time, effort and money is spent in the formal study and understanding of the role of money, the ultimate constructed illusion of ownership and omnipotence, beguiling its greatest amassers with delusions of their grandeur, god-like status and power of creation, destruction and immortality. In a culture of money, it behooves one to appreciate, not deign, the earn-rate versus the burn-rate of money, or the long-anticipated hello versus the instant-messaged goodbye and send-off. How much time and money do we invest in readiness for work to which we devote 45 years of our lives versus our non-work times and relationships as well as retirement? Hope, trust and life can seem to fit into this paradigm with the proviso that nothing can bring back and restore the unique moment or life that is the sublime and *sui generis*. *Logos* (meaning) and *veritas* (beauty) do not intersect without the light, life and vitality that illuminate, inter-relate and warm all, equally.

With the ascendancy of individualism and nanoism, it seems to have been a downhill roll to the lowest common denominator from the pinnacles of understanding of the Oneness reached during the 6th century BC, in tandem with man as a servant of God to man as God. Moral principles and principles of relationships have moved from being vested and deeply-held in our hearts outwards in lock-step with increasing submission to private property, profits and marketing propaganda, both secular and non-secular. Principles that carried necessary and sufficient weight to promote and promulgate harmony amongst the few and the many are increasingly etched and codified in ever greater detail and volume in statutes, safeguarded by legal institutions, high priests and acolytes that serve the interests of those with property. Principles seem to oxidize in their journey from the inside to the outside and as they proliferate from a memorable handful to an overkill of terminologies that are rendered as meaningless as they are purchasable. Instead of growth and evolution through integration, the result is just a trade-off or displacement of service to the Good at the apex for goods and services of the base. This is accompanied by the rationale of—where there is no heart, there can be no pain—that promotes mindless consumption which is best served by being stoned out of one's mind or being as hard as stone for maximum denial and suppression of change and compassion.

Illusions and dogmas of democracy, capitalism and Christianity are valuable as marketable commodities to render profits that serve to strengthen the hierarchy of money and property. All three of these isms serve equally well in usurping and undermining family structures and values. In societies subsumed by capitalism, it is essential to maintain the notion that moral principles are necessary in tandem with legal statutes to carry the burden of sufficiency in penalty to maintain peace and order in the public sphere. But neither moral principles nor laws are as necessary and sufficient as money in order to prevail as what is right is infinitely debatable in a culture of nanoism where resorting to might of money or gun settles the score and secures the desired outcome, sooner than later, a desirable trait in and of itself when delayed gratification is gratification denied.

Meaning, imagination and courage are irrelevant when money and might define and rule hierarchy so that individual possession, understanding and appreciation of money become necessary but not sufficient for individual state of happiness. Life that is entirely focused and driven by money, ownership and physical consumption without a satiation register becomes increasingly lopsided. The three aspects of body, mind and spirit increasingly merge as they are converted into marketable and purchasable goods and services so that rather than understanding their inter-relationships, they become interchangeable. The industry of identity excels in culling, creating and expanding needs that can be catered to by efficient consumption delivery that generates their very own feedback loops for revenue systems. Greater dependency on easy external solutions that are as pervasive as credit cards and cash registers to complex internal imbalances increases demand as long as attention spans herd within the box of the familiar. A good example of this can be found in the perrenial hit parade brought to us by the industries of enlightenment, ever-lasting hope and one-size fits all solutions. By incessantly substituting the word 'culture' for industry or business, the attention of the transient, uncounted and expendable are detracted as well as subdued and pacified by illusions of aspirations and lucky breaks versus perspiration and inspiration, from the security-blanketed and -detailed few who gorge on profit troughs. The slippage of culture is accompanied by the disappearance of fair and square which has ben replaced by free, as in free trade, free market, free press, free speech and freeload. The inverted sensibility of the talking mugs and hired mouthpieces increasingly desensitize monetized subscribers through repetition, so that few find it odd that only criminals are deferentially referred to as Mister Fullname while heads of state do not merit such treatment. These practices serve to obstruct change and other possibilities in order to lock-in profit streams by eliminating moral sentiment, sense of the flow time, and compilations of long-term memory in favour of increasing volume of transactions through information, products and services that only has value in obsolescence and replaceability by the latest versions as in yesterday's news. We live with the reality that money serves our purpose for the purchase of shelter, food, necessities and niceties, but must not become slaves to money through consumption maximization, since this displaces, alienates and blinds us from the vitality, sublimeness and poignancy of life that can safeguard our hearts from becoming hard, bitter, deaf, mute and blind. Money snips the nexus of cause and effect, pleasure and morality, and happiness and balance, as what is bought without delay substitutes what is earned with effort.

Nanoism in a culture of money feeds litigation, litigants, lawyers and their supporting institutions and industries. To litigate requires financial fortitude not blind faith in the legal principles or being in the right whereby confidence in moral principles may be necessary but not sufficient for certainty. To litigate is to merely pay for the privilege of entertaining uncertainly by the principals with the guarantee of certain benefits to those who risk nothing. To litigate is to crap-shoot in that doing what is right (moral duty) versus being right (deceptive and dirty but legal, special, limited and thoroughly rationalized and protected), has a negligible bearing on outcome. Winning in the court of law or public opinion does not guarantee collecting on the judgement or recovering sunk costs in time and money in a process designed to dull the edges, deplete defendant's resources willy-nilly, and drag standards into irrelevance. Legal challenges and victories are unrelated to and over time and tend to undermine and displace moral sentiments and principles in their wake since bought legality and felt morality part ways in fine, unreadable and con-voluted print. The conflicts in Korea, Vietnam and many other countries demonstrate that bodycount and score-keeping are irrelevant to the spirit of enduring cultures that revere life. Triumph of moral principles result in joyous public celebration, whereas legal wins result in backroom payoffs and paybacks that deface and degrade trust since in a milieu of contracts and *quid pro quo*, trust does not merit consideration. The principals end up in service to the service providers who nod, wink and spit at the open-ended expense of principals and principles, independent of outcome, as reflected in the writings of Swift and Dickens. Lawyers like any other commission-nibbling agents make their living by not having to live with the consequences of their actions or inactions. If medical malpractice suits represent a fraction of the errors, incompetences or purposes that did not serve the interest of the patients, it is likely that legal malpractice suits represent even a smaller fraction of clients left holding the short straws as other interests are served. The benefit of a compromise contains elements of timeliness, amicability, mutual satisfaction and certainty versus the lack of any such attributes entailed in litigation. It is in this context that to litigate is to lose since the outcome or rendering of justice is latched onto money and power of the principals. These principals include a host of hooligans, thugs and ponces who enjoy equal and demo-cratic rights and access to buy, sell or intimidate an assortment of certified and credentialed service providers, entirely at their disposal and always ready, willing and able to provide specific performance to defend their client's meritorious rights, confidentially, legally and profitably. The principle of justice is sold to the highest bidder, more often than not, with what is just or unjust being solely in the eye of the beholder in contempt and obfuscation rather than content of law, moral principles, edification or happiness of the many.

In a culture of money and litigation, justice becomes increasingly meaningless as virtue and vice are interchangeable in service of profit with lip-service to the all important concept of equal justice under the law—the *sine qua non* and most worthwhile illusion to be maintained for the masses for the dear lives, lifestyles and livelihood of the few. The robustness of the pliers and institutions of law inversely correlates to the understanding and practice of justice, compromise and compassion by the individuals of all levels and types that constitute, intersect and criss-cross a society. It is convenient to forget that even God favoured Abel, who pleased him more, and moreover displayed his favour for Cain to see and feel. Favouritism may be unavoidable but not its display once the consequence of such is appreciated. The art of law is as predicated upon a sense of fair play as in any other field of artistic endeavor that merits accolade by valuing both social harmony and visceral humours versus legal practices and policies that accord the highest priority to revenue maximization and bad-debt elimination.

Do con-artists exploit naïveté and innocence, and are people too trusting, or is it simply laziness, greed, aversion to detail and illusions of familiarity with the big picture that have lined the pockets of these enterprising exploiters, giving them a winning edge, time and time again? Children like hearing the same stories over and over again, taking pleasure in their own knowingness. But this sense of familiarity and the pleasure and security imparted can oftentimes lead to the need to stay within what is known as 'my world'. This can be seen in adults who revel and are engrossed in television or other mass media programmes with familiar plots and characters. What these law and justice shows have in common is their failure to indicate how such competent and concerned lawyers were found and retained. It seems that lawyers just take up walk-in clients and work flat out on their behalf before minimum retainer cheques have been cleared through their banks. In the mass-media productions, the high burn rate of the money metre in minute clicking increments that churns out uniform invoices irrespective of the quality, completeness or timeliness in representation or outcome, is non-existent. The contextual library of other worlds becomes increasingly limited as the imagination is tightly bound, so that the exclusive 'my way or no way' becomes the only way. The airtight tautology of my way as the absolutely right way needs no explanation, and is as meaningless as the limited vocabulary accessible from the lack of any such practice. This exemplifies fear of the unknown, not just of the unknowable, and the fear of thinking which might just lead to change and growth. This fear is passed off as pride or originality and is so great that sticking with my way and staying within my world at any cost is preferable even when it is self-destructive and has no bearing on being right or wrong in any context. But of course the damage extends beyond the self, since there is a web of relationships and since hatred and violence accompany fear with the need to take it out on anyone and everyone, since the self is merely a victim and therefore entirely blameless. The possibility of being wrong cannot and will not be entertained, and the fear of failure is so absolute and petrifying that there can not be an iota of budging or a mustard seed of doubt. There are no mind games, no placing of puts or calls, no going short or long, no hedging or any play whatsoever based upon what is—only the hermetically sealed tautology of the one worldview.

How many make their livelihood by being full-time professional liars, only seeing from one absolute point-of-view, ensuring that no other perspective sees the light of day, staging spectacles to showcase temporal power and glory as mass media events, distorting the truths and lies of others, focusing with increasing intensity through decreasing aperture and spreading their lies as far and wide as possible, aimed at those least able, likely or willing to engage their minds? Who can kill, cause pain and inflict harm upon those without speaking roles or who cannot speak for themselves and do not strut on stage or have a stage to strut upon, while remaining stone-faced with tight and drawn lips or with a signature smirk? Lies are packaged and sold to maximize profits and minimize losses. Lies that consume the most time, effort and money are self-deceptions (willingness to be taken in, to be in) which are well-served by the industries of identity. Truths do not need to carry a price-tag and are freely available to those free enough to seek and see them. There are as many truths as lies to serve the purpose of anyone, so that processes for telling them apart, to weigh their merit and materiality within appropriate contexts, are likely to bear more fruit and be more significant for learning than binary categorizations.

While it may be unnecessary to prove the infallibility and invincibility of God, it may be possible that God presides over, participates in or is Change as represented by the Greek symbol for Delta, wherein lies the moment, light or seed of truth. The infinite overlapping of even and uneven triangles approximates a sphere whose centre comes into being as long as there is a seeding and a way of seeing. Each additional triangle (e.g. between thought, word and deed) reconfigures the reach while creating openings at the perimeter that, like the stomata, sense and respond to change. Where is such a sense of integrity between thought, word and deed when chickens are pumped full of stimulants and with razor blades tied to their legs for mortal combat in the interest of legalized gambling and to provide wholesome family entertainment backed up by absolute state rights? The centre is compounded with each iteration of change and like the nucleus, held together by the strong force which is the strongest force operating at such infinitesimal distances for the purpose of maintaining integrity and unity while processing and incorporating change in concordant sychronicity. This is the seed that is transplanted from mentor to disciple and from the one to the many, generation to generation, transcending time and space as the learning curves shift, grow and overlap incrementally transformed versus identical duplication and repetition of the same. When the initial seeding and sense of centre is incorrectly positioned, deformed or absent and the way of seeing warped or blinded, or any other combination of these factors, the resulting spheres can be just as strong in destructiveness aligned with *Ahriman* versus benignity of *Ormuzd* (Zoroastrian spirits of evil and good). The parable of the mustard seed in Matthew 17:20 shows that both a little faith and little doubt goes a long way when there is clarity of purpose in service to the revealed truths of the centred heart of Oneness (*monad*) versus illusions, desire and appetite of one (*nanod*[25]). The chasm that exists between a little faith or doubt to no faith or doubt is as large as a mountain.

Cultures defined and driven by the dogmas, rights and isms of commerce, politics, science and religion are separate and distinct from organic human cultures which embrace the following 3 P's:

1. Principles whose primary objective is to minimize harm and

25. Author's Note: Nanod is the author's term for one who subscribes to nanoism or individualism representing the interest and worldview of one in a billion with a chronic inability to see any other point of view, compromise or apologize with the corollary ineptness in gratitude and humility. With no superimposition or juxtaposition of any other parallel universes, the picture remains as partial as possible without a key to unlock the door to the vista of the infinite Oneness. This often extends to a lack of integrity within an individual as thought, word, and deed are dissected into separate categories. Since we cannot literally get into someone (human and non-human) else's skin and know his/her/its feelings and thoughts, all we have to work with are the words and deeds that we perceive and permutate through our senses and sensibilities to clue us in on the internal third point. This in turn colours and flavours our response so that dialogues can range from non-happening and meaningless to some sense of coherence and reflection. Interconnections involving the totality of organic inlets and outlets for intimate gender or species independent communion with others dwarf those limited to the five senses and the sexual organs to the chagrin of the mass media that relentlessly plugs, curtails, perverts, and inverts such capacity and capability to feel. Relationships and incorporation of the other reside in a continuum that is unobsessed with bipedal and binary categorizations. The mass media empires thrive as the world of the factual is crowded out by factitious loops that lull and dull acuity while reinforcing sloth, procrastination, maximum wastage, unfamiliarity with integrity and aversion to complexity, process and detail.

maximize harmony. These principles operate relative to positions while simultaneously defining positions in the multiple overlapping spheres of life from private to public, which are embedded in language, manners and traditions or social ideology.

2. Processes for decision-making which cannot exist or be operational under the fixation of 'I want' and 'my way or no way' which pre-empts and bypasses any choice. Such singularity creates an illusory equivalency to right or wrong and winning or losing when such contexts are essentially missing. Pride and vanity worthy of shallowness or vice versa in self-assertion, self-validation and self-authentication do not even step up to the binary plate of mutual exclusivity.

3. Precepts and precedents of relationships that have withstood the test of time (real-time trials and errors) to preserve the many, and have been passed down by the predecessors. They provide minimum safety nets and insurance against absences, deficiencies and defects in the language of relationships, principles and processes. With fullness of time, experience and thinking, many reach the same conclusions tending to reaffirm the wisdom of the ages ensuring that they are passed down for the benefit of future generations. They illuminate a path when incommensurable lives (not concepts, values or rights) are in conflict requiring asymmetric trade-offs based on principles and precedents of relationships that are equally binding and reinforced for the benefit of the many over time in meaning and Oneness. Such practices render a sense of acceptability rather than some absolute or relative notion of justice or the right of the might. These are not some esoteric and trendy concepts of values and rights requiring swearing of oaths, discovery, trial and testimonials of absolute ends, proofs and truths by individuals with deep-pockets to keep up a retinue of hired help. They also serve by providing a default path towards least harm or minimum acceptability since many may not be inclined or afforded the benefit of time to think or tend to believe in the existence of fool-proof, simple and absolute right or wrong.

When the 3 P's are absent, singularity of individualism thrives and diminution of the language of relationships prevails, so that the idea of the other (the bridge to one or innumerable worlds or wonders) which is so essential for feeling and intuiting the path to Oneness, cannot come into being. In a world of no other, no relationship, no language, no purpose, no becoming and no fitness or finesse, life becomes increasingly dulled into non-existence as it finds consolation in the mass media and mass consumption. The mind flees or flips as it is entertained and captivated by endless looping of the known, superficial and disposable in a world of uniformly answerable questions and familiar stories with predictable ends. The sensation of treading faster and harder to relentlessly stay ahead and to forge on without a backward glance or remorse but with eyes riveted to what's in front, creates an illusion of progressing while all the time staying unchanged or regressing as time marches on by marking change.

That there is a common problem faced by all ethnic groups is fortunate, because it allows for effort to be unified and focused in teaching adequate choice-making skills to the young. Mastery of maths and sciences may be useful as career prerequisites, but good choice-making skills will be useful throughout life. The primary role of cultural imperatives is to help develop choice-making skills; this not only ensures consistency with the cultural goals and values, but their very survival. Culture is not the rule of man or rule of law; it is the rule of doing what is consistent with who one is as a human being within a specific cultural identity and heritage. One's consistency and integrity is a reflection of how well an individual is acquainted with his or her cultural heritage and paradigm.

Every culture educates its young in choice-making skills; in every culture parents scold the young about what is bad or unacceptable in terms of their own unique cultural paradigm. The prevailing dominance of economic pursuits, accompanied by vestigial remains of cultural identities, afflicted and superseded by pervasive media images and messages, has resulted in parents who are not only unsure as to what and how to teach, but who are both physically and mentally absent from the children's framework. *What would my parents think or feel about what I'm doing* does not merit consideration when doing my own thing takes centre stage, even in parenthood. Being a full-time mother or father is oftentimes seen as someone who needs to get a life and is derided by those who seem to believe that raising children is not a full-time job or should be done by those for whom it is a livelihood. For

26. "Commands or imperatives are not factual statements; they are not descriptions; they are not true or false... they order, they direct, they terrify, they generate action...values are commands, and that they are created, not discovered." Isaiah Berlin, *The Sense of Reality* (Pimlico, 1997), p. 178.

27. "If the will were unaffected by inclinations it would be what Kant calls a 'holy will'. But human beings are not like that; hence the force of moral principles is that they are felt as imperatives—demands upon the will, possibly against inclination." D.W. Hamlyn, op. cit., p. 236.

28. "... the Islamic concept of allowed and forbidden...The rules of Islamic laws are valid by virtue of their existence and not because of their rationality." D.S. Roberts, op, cit., p. 57.

parents and teachers to shirk this responsibility with *que sera sera, laissez-faire* (non-interference) or *who-am-I-to-judge* attitudes is to dismiss the sense of duty and honour permeating kinship and social relationships in most cultures that try to impart belonging and meaning.

'To teach or not to teach' is not a proposition usually entertained by most parents because the need to communicate and be understood is an inherent human trait, as are the needs to be recognized and accepted by others. The cultural paradigm provides the template of materiality, perspective and context to enable human co-existence with the others, and provides these considerations for sound choice-making. The soundness of choice is relative, but choice itself is not relative or arbitrary. To deny the existence or relevance of others is to render language and its evolution irrelevant and meaningless, because language only exists in the context of the other. If a tree falls in the forest and nobody is around, is there sound? If you know something but cannot communicate it to others, is there any knowing or knowledge? There are exceptional individuals who impart their illumination without words by embodying a philosophy of life in compassion and benignity whose mere presence, or having once been, facilitates sharing and communion with others. Sometimes silence can speak volumes that no words can. The beauty of knowledge is in its sharing. Knowledge is like love, in that the more it is hoarded, the more it shrinks and withers, and the more it is given and shared, the more it grows and thrives. The diffusiveness and velocity of knowledge affect cultural development as much as diffusiveness and velocity of capital determine the quality and quantity of economic growth. This is the potential empowerment enabled by the Internet—if it is used with discipline and purpose.

It is rare to encounter a professional (or for that matter, anyone) who imparts sufficient and adequate information, with the benefit of his/her training and knowledge, rather than the meager minimum, even with remuneration. The onus is on the consumer, customer, client, patient or electorate to prompt, probe and prod the product or service provider, accountant, lawyer, nurse, doctor or politician to output adequate (let alone full) information without being intimidated into apathy, complaisance or dumbfounded silence.

The need to be superior and right, to engage in one-upmanship, to ridicule, to humiliate, to be snide or clever in a milieu of I-centricism, often overrides, obfuscates and obviates custodial, fiduciary, filial or other humanistic considerations. Examples of this type of behaviour can be seen between parent/child, teacher/student, boss/subordinate, and in other instances where there is inequality beyond the context of just information retention and knowledge. The subterfuge may be veiled but no less significant than physical cruelty, subjugation and oppression of the weak or the weaker.

The resulting level of frustration and animosity in dealing with these providers of specific knowledge is akin to dealing with computers which will only respond if the questions are specifically posed in correct sequence, syntax and structure. At least the computer does respond with correct prompting, even though it may prove tedious. The marketing jargon *fuzzy logic* used to sell appliances was quickly replaced by *user friendly*. The interest of economy, efficiency or expediency reaches a state of diminishing return in the context of the well-being of the one and the many, when information is not only commoditized but hoarded to serve a narrow and obscured interest. This is also evident in the proliferation of internal company and profession-specific dictionaries and reference manuals, where paper shuffling becomes an art form, creating a safe and secure domain of the intangible and the obscure. This is modern alchemy: the transformation of the immaterial into the material. It does not bode well for the electorate that an increasing proportion of the elected are lawyers.

While it may be comforting to espouse the rule of law over the rule of man, the rule of law is created and administered by men whose interest may not be consistent with public interest and whose sense of justice may not resemble that of the society's. What is legal is not synonymous with what is right, and the flagrancy and smugness with which politicians state that their actions are perfectly legal is not only symptomatic of their loopy moral compass but also of their disdain for the electorate and presumption of its gullibility.

The commoditization of knowledge, with the incessant nickel-and-diming at all levels of interaction, results in a situation whereby one feels quite fortunate to remain relatively unscammed and unsullied. Incivility is so widespread and common that it becomes the norm. It still registers as undesirable, unacceptable and unattractive with some, but it is so pervasive that many feel a sense of futility, just as most tend to look and veer away from beggars. It is a testament to human resiliency that more people do not withdraw into isolation, given the constant state of alertness and vigilance required in grappling with modernity.[29] DEFCON 5 (maximum defense condition) is not an exception but rather the norm, in order to maintain one's sense of honour and dignity, if not one's sanity.

Meeting the needs of enculturation is more demanding, time-consuming and complex for humans than for other species because no other species has such a capacity or propensity for destruction (capacity for destruction being directly related to the amount of instructions or programming required to preserve the species). All cultures recognize that human beings are neither benign and benevolent nor simply beasts of burden, to be directed and coerced. Cultural imperatives tend to be proscriptive, almost admonishing in tone, because they are insuring against the downside of human nature: the upside can take flight on its own. One only needs insurance for potential losses, not gains. Ethics is not a subject to be confined to the Department of Philosophy; it should be introduced throughout the early years of education.

Regardless of how rigidly respect for elders and filial piety are defined by culturally mandated codes of conduct, relentless inconsistencies by elders with their own conduct will render this respect incoherent and irrelevant. These inconsistencies need to be minimized and only be exceptions to the rule, because absolute compliance and consistency in conduct to maintain self honour and dignity at all times is an impossibility for most people. Whether the effort by the elders to be consistent is sincere or not, absence of such effort will ensure that these values fade away from the cultural landscape and become irretrievably lost. Being older means that one has experienced and survived more adversity in life; the experience is beyond the comprehension of one who has not made the same journey. In addition, all cultural imperatives are exercised in the context of a kind heart or compassion, which renders the act of evaluating and judging of the older as to worthiness of respect from the younger, not only inappropriate, unsound and without merit, but immoral, since the concept of duty excludes preferences and judgements.

Therefore, while respect for elders and filial piety seem like self-serving rules which protect the vested interests of the elders, they impose a great

---

29. "...In this, Berlin's voice is akin to that of Job, in refusing with a passion the pretense that there is peace when our lives abound in deep conflicts and hard choices." John Gray, *Berlin* (Fontana Press, 1995), p.168.

obligation on the elders to work at compliance with their own code of conduct. There is symmetry between effort and reward. There is no free ride for anyone, because the power of cultural paradigms is based on the countless interrelationships of the participants in a holistic and synergistic sphere. If there is need for correction, it flows from the elder to the younger and in the context of first amongst equals (i.e., by one's peers or someone who is deemed to have qualified for authority by cultural mandate). It demands equality (symmetry) in effort by all belongers to enjoy the benefits bestowed in freeing the human endeavour and spirit from chaos, while at the same time it assuages the need to understand all things. The pursuit of knowledge is encouraged, but omniscience and omnipotence are not. This may explain the humbleness of the truly cultured person, and his or her inclination to preach with words, reason and patience, not to dictate with force, arbitrariness and intolerance.

The dissatisfaction resulting from extreme emphasis on liberty and equality (two potentially collidable values) has created an untenable situation in all walks of life that rely upon the cooperation, tolerance and compromise of pluralities within and amongst individuals. Co-opting and preempting of authority and authorship have come to symbolize liberty and equality. Authority and authorship are essential prerequisites to the value and function of liberty and equality in the context of the collective. There has been no substitution for hierarchy, which defines and imbues authority and authorship in individual and social contexts, but merely its denial, resulting in dysfunction and chaos, leading to more unhappiness.

There is much building-up of self-esteem, without the attendant effort or result and achievement, through such helpful rejoinders as: *you're as good as (better, more special than) anyone else / you're fine just as you are / just please yourself / it doesn't matter what anyone else says.* This conditioning or enculturation of self-indulgence, willfulness and narcissism in one individual merely results in a most unattractive and unpleasant encounter, but in the context of a society at large, it unravels the ties that bind and mend. While there is much ado as to whether self-esteem is a precursor or product of accomplishment, it is not a stand-alone concept. It rests best upon a foundation of self-knowledge or in discovering the dharma (purpose, principle), as the dharma of fire is to be hot, of light is to illuminate, and of life is to live.

When cultural evolution was location-bound and habitat-specific, the world seemed to be a much bigger place, but modern technology of transportation and information, combined with the development of global enterprises, have made it much less so. As elements of culture that are a function of geography recede in importance to the society within it, the remaining non-geographically derived elements will have much more in common, in terms of what it is to be a human being, with less antagonism and distinctness to all other cultures. One no longer even needs to physically move and be present elsewhere to become non-location specific, because the minimum requirements for sustaining life with economic development will have much more in common in terms of accessibility, availability and distribution of goods and services (similarity in habitat); the world can be experienced (seen and heard) within the confines of one's living quarters.

But cultural identities will still prevail for two reasons: (1) as a fountain of living, not merely being alive, by providing a sense of belonging, meaning and purpose;[30] and (2) for all of human existence, geography and a sense of place have been intricately and tightly bound with human evolution. While there is now a great deal more movement, a vast majority of people have always stayed in their homeland, virtual or otherwise. The sense of loyalty and belongingness to the land of one's birth is primordial and transcends ethnicity; it is the real estate of self-identity. The more established or ancient the culture, the more intense and deeper this bond with the land. With increasing incidence of one's place of birth or livelihood being different from one's origin, there is a greater need for a structured and systematic enculturation in humanizing values.

Paradoxically, what will be left of cultural differences will not be so much differences in ideologies and values but external distinctions of physical appearance and nostalgic manifestations of idiosyncrasies of times past. There are two paths for cultures in the modern world: to become increasingly nostalgic and amplify idiosyncrasies, uniqueness and distinctiveness, or to emphasize what is shared with all other cultures by contributing its heritage in the understanding of human experience, commonality of purpose and endeavour which will have much affinity and consistency with other cultures. The differences that remain, while endowing the belongers with a unique sense of identity and history, will neither be so vast nor confrontational as to justify the kind of antagonisms so prevalent in the past. After all, what makes an individual happy or sad, virtuous or corrupt, a belonger or an outcast, transcends, in its simplicity and reality, all the questions and debate as to why this is so.

At the core of every cultural template is the incorporation of a minimum set of values and guidelines for behaviour to promote and preserve social harmony while respecting and giving due recognition to the pluralities within an individual as well as amongst individuals. The same can be observed in all religions, distilled of ethnocentrism and non-secularism. Rules of social encounter and engagement range from basic table manners, forms of greeting

30. "... an increasing degree of industrialization and mechanization leads to the disintegration of society, to degradation of the deepest human values—affection, loyalty, fraternity, a sense of common purpose—all in the name of progress, identified with order, efficiency, production." Isaiah Berlin, *The Sense of Reality*, op. cit., p. 255.

and address, to a sense of hierarchy of values and of individual positions which counter and curb the rapacity of might over right (to protect the weak and the young, as well as respect for age and wisdom, irrespective of power and wealth).

These rules, encompassing tolerance and compromise, may at first glance appear constrictive, but the effect is quite the reverse: individuality and individual choice-making are maximized. Fitting in is important, but not as important as getting along, so that the degree of conformity is left to the individual, with social censure and isolation being the penalties. The twin goals of all cultures are promotion and preservation of social harmony and human dignity, not uniformity and repression.

Liberty and equality, as free-floating, stand-alone values, are impracticable, especially under the auspices (or inauspiciousness) of capitalism (in which these, in addition to justice, are not merely non-considerations but, more often than not, obstructions to be overcome).

Economic theories and models, like most business presentations, are process and result-driven, with only a cursory nod or a complete absence of attention to the explicit or implicit assumptions upon which the process and result rest. With the pervasiveness of the lexicon of capitalism (laissez-faire, free market, competition), debates, including those concerning social and political issues, are distilled into permutations of price and quantity: the two key concepts understood by most sellers and buyers. The nuance, subtlety or beauty of the language becomes subservient and subsumed by the crudity of the marketplace. Inevitably then, what is preferable, better or good becomes equated with more, bigger, newer, faster, different, younger and sexier—which are attributes having nothing to do with human virtues.

One needs to be pretty jaundiced to have the sense of humour much encouraged in the so-called convivial atmosphere of today's arenas of capitalism. The typical thinking, behaviour and lexicon, which are shaped, promoted and typified by it, are neither conducive nor salubrious to social harmony, let alone its sense of justice. Consider the terminology: back stabbing, the killer instinct, swimming with the sharks, eat or be eaten, one-upmanship, survival of the fittest, roadkill, take no prisoners, zero tolerance, master of the universe, moguls, kings, princes, warriors, knights, tsars, heroes, cannibalization rate, category killers, master and slave terminals, etc., in addition to its many insightful gender-specific references, including brown sugar, honey-pie and sweetie. In this environment, the successful person is one who can appreciate the opposition's point of view in order to overcome, neutralize or quell it and prevail; appreciation and understanding of different perspectives serve different ends, depending on one's set of values. Knowledge only has moral content in its application or when coupled with purpose. Without an overarching and encompassing cultural (humanizing) paradigm to give liberty, equality and capitalism appropriate ethical context—confrontations and differences will only multiply and escalate, resulting in less of each, to the detriment of the one and the many, accompanied by ever-increasing statutory censures and prohibitions, viz., the code of law.

To invest the time and resources to enculture a child during his or her presentation of the psychological moment is incommensurable with the need for ever-increasing legal codification, enforcement, supervision, medication, counseling, censorship, incarceration and punishment. The greater the bunker mentality, where even entertaining (let alone acknowledging) another point of view becomes intolerable and anything is preferable to admitting fallacy or fallibility—the greater the volume of legal statutes (the extreme codification of cultural imperatives) that tend to proscribe unacceptable behaviour in all its minuscule and minute details. Prudence, propriety and self-responsibility will fall by the wayside, along with liberty when 'to err is human' takes on the mantra of *I'm always right and in the right*.

A person who denies with all of his will and might what may be different, inconsistent or contradictory to his point of view, despite all evidence and reason to the contrary, is not just being dogmatic or doctrinaire, he is simply choosing to be stupid (whereby the degree of stupidity is only rivaled by its sheer arrogance or obduracy), a right that one is fully entitled to but nevertheless reflects badly on choice-making skills and enculturation. No form of legally enforced censorship can match that of self-imposed censorship—shutting out anything that is not to one's liking, regardless of consequences to oneself or others, thereby bypassing any choice-making, the hallmark of liberty, having so attenuated the decision tree that it consists of merely a thin hollow reed.

The objective of enculturation, as much as formal education, is to liberate the individual from the fear of the unknown and arbitrariness with intellectual discipline and rigours of discourse. Without an appreciation of the meaning of 'first amongst equals', equality becomes unqualified, arbitrary and non-contextual, i.e., meaningless.

Culture, by imparting a sense of belonging and teaching how to get along so that each individual does not have to figure it out for himself through the school of hard knocks, liberates the individual in the pursuit of individuality in a way that does not harm or impede another's pursuit. To be forewarned is to be forearmed, and foreknowledge or knowledge of the forefathers (predecessors) enables continuation and cumulation of learning, rather than repetition of the same predicaments and obstacles. This is epitomized, for example, in the Buddhist and Talmudic intellectual traditions where all questions and debates are facilitated and many times resolved, but not arbitrarily or without context of all that has already transpired.

The fundamental common purpose of all cultures, regardless of ethnicity or religion or geography, is to instill an awareness and acknowledgement of the others, whose worth is no less than that of self-worth and worthiness as a human being: *uniqueness is ubiquitous.* Even if one were able to remove ethnicity, gender, ability, religion and age as biases against equality and equal treatment, one is still left with much that is different and still needs to be accounted for and integrated; equality cannot make everyone the same but it seeks to treat people equally in a humanistic context, equally deserving of respect and equally capable of dignity. The Chinese characters for culture aptly symbolize knowledge and integration. To know is to get along in both senses (to be in harmony with others, as well as to be able to make progress).

The purpose of life may be to progress towards a sense of completeness through an understanding that one is never complete as a self, but that completion can be approximated in self-lessness with one other or all others in the context of either polygenism or monogenism, differentiation between which may be a matter of time-scale applied. This then moves into the realm of the mystics who are to be found in many ancient cultures, and who similarly describe the disappearance or joining of the self into the One or Circle. Interestingly, this is like the leading edge of scientific inquiry in its search for universality or a universal common denominator which resembles and reveals more that is innumerate, mysterious, unknowable (compared with knowable, but with great difficulty) or beyond human comprehension.

The paradox of a cultural paradigm, as with knowledge, is that by imposing boundaries (imperatives) and setting rules (through values and codes of conduct), it frees the individual for a journey of unlimited potential. A high degree of cultural intelligence (deep-rootedness) confers a greater sense of belonging and confidence of self-identity, enabling exploration into other cultures and various fields of knowledge in which one cannot have, or need, the quality or sense of belongingness: ties that bind (or bond) leave one freer. Just as a vector or array finds expression and meaning in reference to its point of origin regardless of the number of dimensions, the self finds the same from a centre point: what seems like a lot of rules can simply be distilled, as the dignity of the one rests upon dignity of all, and coordination rests upon the point of origin in all dimensions.

Judaism, Christianity, Islam; Buddhism, Taoism, and Confucianism: the first three and the latter three share common denominators of pedigree, geography and category, with the former being monotheistic religions and the latter being non-deistic philosophies of life and living. All, with the exception of Judaism,[31] have a very inclusive and expansive outlook and definition of their group constituency so that virtually none are excluded from their global footprints. All emphasize reading of the text or 'the word'

31. Author's Note: And yet, one would be hard-pressed to find an organic culture or a monotheistic religion that is more embracing, representative and inclusive of all the peoples of the Old World than Judaism, in its essence, heart and origin. There were twelve tribes before the Diaspora and there is as much or even greater diversity, after. Like many other ancient cultures, it transcends ethnicity and nationality which are modern constructs divorced from a cultural paradigm or *modus vivendi* to serve totalitarian and centralized power politics and interests. But it is a unique fusion of culture and religion that transcends even language and geography: its essence survives translation, transplantation and translocation. Not many other cultures can be said to have endured more, for as long, and yet prevail with its peoples, language (Hebrew-Aramaic), history, belief, integrity, honour, dignity, practice and civility largely intact, with unity and community. Judaism's chosen resource and recourse has been of life, by life and for life, with moral principles that have proven to be both necessary and sufficient for survival against overwhelming odds. Most Jews did not become slaves even in enslavement, because their own evolution continued without losing sight of, through detachment or betrayal, their centre point: the sacredness in and of life. This is a sentiment of a cultural paradigm and not necessarily of individuals within it, whereby adherence is largely a matter of individual attitude, aptitude, choice and inclination. None are lost to the extent that their sense of identity and their code of life are kept intact and whole, by the majority. The special pointer used to read the Torah focuses and paces the mind so that regardless of whether the reader is good or bad, the reading is good and complete. There is no single word missed, misconstrued or contaminated by the touch of one person: the sacred text transcends the individual.

Judaism has demonstrated its superpower and distinguishes itself by not insisting upon expansion, conversion and destruction of others. Israelites are no less capable of exterminating dissenters within or enemies without than any other peoples. It is not a belief in pacifism or liberalism but solely consistent with honoring the codes of conduct in life. Injustice has

above all else, transcending love and hate, power and property, liberty and equality, tax and religion, democracy and capitalism, even God and his prophets.

Islam can be viewed as the third way of co-existence that recognises and incorporates both Judaism and Christianity by building upon a common root for an Arab-ized outcome that fits and integrates with the heritage and tradition of a cultural language for a viable and enduring identity. Given the continuous fragmentation within monotheistic beliefs, Hinduism and other polytheistic outlooks with the notion of the infinite oneness and the one in the infinite seems to come increasingly to the forefront. The picture that comes into focus indicates that the individualistic godheads bear uncanny

not been answered with injustice or abandonment of identity, but with the practice of compassion and helping each other, including those who are different, which reflects their experience of what it means to be oppressed and persecuted. Many peoples have experienced oppression and enslavement, but few have burned into their memories the actions and attitudes of the oppressors, which have caused such unhappiness as to lead to their eventual downfall. If God does exist, it is unlikely that God fancies a master or a slave, just as an individual should not fancy being or identifying with one or the other. Judaism insists upon co-existence, even while surrounded by those who would rather die than to co-exist. As with all festering conflicts through the ages, mutual dissatisfaction and destruction are preferred and willed if complete vindication of willfulness is unattainable by the proponents of violence or extremists on both sides.

Pro-life, not temporal justice, has been at its centre, coupled with rituals and practices consistent with and supportive of this belief. Being "Chosen" to serve or rule requires the focusing of collective energy to generate sufficient trophic and negentropic factors to offset entropy, in order for life to flourish, not just exist, by maintaining a constant balance. This is encapsulated in a code of duty or reverence to life, along with a language whose built-in hierarchy matches those of human needs, as found in other ancient cultures with staying power, which equally nourish and inform their belongers at all times, places and occasions. Such a code circumvents the tendency towards judgement and justification associated with vanity or self-vindication, self-immolation and self-indulgence, by creating an awareness of the supra-set of the One and Oneness. This attitude attempts to reconcile the uniqueness of an individual with the universality of individuality. The singular windows are transformed into infinite mirrors, whereby barriers of vanity, or the ego as a construct of vanity, voluntarily and willingly surrender and dissolve into the Way of Life. In such a moment of awakening, all categories crumble, save that of being alive.

resemblance to their respective believers, just as those for cows, sheep, pigs and cockroaches would emulate these life-forms if they found it possible and necessary to conceive of their own godheads. Such tendencies seem to be well represented in the religions of antiquity, which not only revere many life-forms but those of hybrid permutations based upon nature versus the unidentifiable labels of various sects, such as the church of Urim and Thummin or other obscure and esoteric segmentations of modernity which would more aptly be served by identification with St. Jude, the patron saint of lost causes.

As religions are increasingly mounted and laminated onto political platforms of winning at all costs along with the speedy and nifty segmentation of ethnocentrism, conflicts explode in quantum leaps and bounds, aided by the weapons of mass destruction against all life-forms and habitats profiting and proliferating the industries of identity. The traditional hierarchy of the scholar, farmer, worker and merchant is inverted in favour of the simple measurability of denominations of money over the finer and immeasurable distinctions that value the wellness and fitness of the many, from generation to generation. The ancient cultures share in the high valuation of scholars since they have the greatest multiplier effect on the intellectual development of the respective societies by creating, preserving, re-interpreting and disseminating cumulative knowledge to the next generation of teachers. The lose/lose or nothing-to-gain scenario of individualism renders freedom, equality, justice and happiness null and void, versus joint and non-several, since none of the jargons of virtue are realizable without the other for existential relationships, compromise and continuity through time and space.

The main attraction and strength of enduring systems of belief lie in their integrative universality, which counterbalances the disintegrative pull and push of closed-mindedness amply sustained by individualism, ethnocentrism and geography (location or locale). Thus, the concept of a global village is an ancient one, not a recent phenomenon of the information age, which can be regarded more as its natural extension and facilitator. Similarly, if the concept of consanguinity is expanded to its broadest application, all human beings can be regarded as having originated from the same pool of life. It is bound by a common history of pain and gain, exploited and exploiter, enslavement (physical or spiritual) and dictatorship, and life, death and regeneration.

Just as the word individual (e.g., in the Declaration of Independence) takes on a different meaning depending on how inclusive and extensive the set definition is, so too do the nominations in the stories contained in religious texts. When Cain slew Abel, was the horror confined to the spilling a brother's blood or was it symbolic of the Brotherhood of men? In Buddhism, this censure extends to all sentient beings. Brotherhood extends across the ethnic, gender and age array of all individuals, and to cause harm (directly or indirectly) to one's brother is deemed immoral. This story is referenced in the three major religious texts as one of the first and essential lessons or rules of human existence, and much of the cultural text or subtext alludes to the same. All of these books and their interpretations are extremely lengthy, although the message is a simple one: love your brother.

Imperatives without context can be dangerous, and all much worked and pondered over texts go to great length to explain these contexts. These discourses caution against many of the human tendencies toward vices and indicate that an act, verbal or physical, which will cause harm (1) cannot be solely based on an individual's (one self) perception of inequality or injustice; (2) cannot be performed in an unstable or heightened emotional state, as this does not allow for clear thinking and appropriate choice-making; (3) cannot involve an irreversible act committed on another life of equal value to the one committing such an act; and (4) must minimize commission of such an act upon one who is not the cause for the perceived wrong, but merely the operative of choice-making by another, i.e., collateral damage.

It discourages a one-dimensional view of truth or justice or life, and emphasizes in-depth thinking. Violence will not go away without some intellectual connection as to why thinking and verbally communicating are better alternatives when one is calm and collected. The imperatives can be distilled into: don't engage in any activity that will pose or inflict potential or irreversible actual harm against the one or the many without first thinking about it a lot. This timeless, oft-repeated rejoinder proves to be the most difficult and challenging to impart and implement through all times and places.

All of the prophets and sages were not born as such, with a priori knowledge, but became wise through their own trials and tribulations. They were not advocates of capitalism, imperialism, nationalism or patriotism, nor did they condemn those who did not share their view. They did not have the benefit of a formal education, but possessed a certain cultural identity through enculturation and self-knowledge. They observed, thought, compared, experienced and generalized, not universalized. This last distinction is important: exceptions do not invalidate or nullify the generalization, but do quite the reverse, by their very nature in lying at the margins of the bell-curve. Their teachings have withstood the test of time because most people identified with them in varying degrees of understanding or adherence. They spent prolonged periods alone in the wilderness, doubting, questioning and struggling to understand their pluralistic nature and overcome their own heart of darkness, as the stories of Daniel illustrate through his encounters with the angel Gabriel and in the den of lions. The teachers wanted to share and communicate their understanding, in its most inclusive and expansive dimensions, in words and deeds to their fellow men. Universality is not sought in the understanding of human nature because its variation is infinite; the two tail ends of the distribution curve, regardless of its shape, are asymptotical (i.e., they never meet the x or y axis).

The importance of an ideal is not in its attainment so much as providing a reference point with which to align, so that the cumulative effect of choice-making tends towards it, much like the magnetic poles resulting in a tendency towards alignment, balance, parity, equilibrium and order. There are both deterministic and non-deterministic factors in life; one needs to understand and appreciate the distinction and make the best effort towards approximation of the goal desired, and not engage in mindless, undirected or random choice-making locked in the mind-set of a predatory zero-sum consumer/owner.

Every culture has its concept of the ideal, representing what it considers desirable in its members, not what it considers attainable. These ideals are prescribed and widely disseminated through the family circle, various social and academic institutions, and in all walks of life. Most members know these rules and yet live lives which vary in degree of deviation from them. There is an infinite variation and variety of family life and individual life; one only needs to appreciate that it takes just four variables and two two-way combinations to result in an infinite variety of DNA expressions while retaining a sense of sameness or similarity.

Transgressors and adherents know they are not going to be struck down by lightning for straying, but most still try to stay within the parameter of these prescriptions for acceptability so as to enjoy the benefits of belonging within a family and community. Unlike the legal system, there are no explicit forces applied for compliance, deterrence measures or defined penalties for various degrees of infractions: the operative force is only what is biologically hardwired as a basic need for recognition, acceptance, and their attendant sense of belongingness and to belong.

The black and white paradigm of correct or incorrect has its place and value in areas where numeration or a high degree of certainty or agreement are demonstrable, but become not only inappropriate or impractical (an individual cannot constantly be seeking affirmation, validation or taking polls) but dangerous, if carried over into all areas of choice-making. The cost/benefit paradigm in matters of ethics and choosing a path in life consists of innumerable variables that cannot be neatly categorized and prioritized. There are too many apples and oranges (abortion: right to choose, procreation, and termination of life; euthanasia: compassion, dignity and weighing what constitutes a life; death penalty: forgiveness, mercy and need to punish), which cannot be assigned probabilities on the same scale, as well as too many oil and water[32] points of view in the process of nation building or defining national identity in modernity but with no fewer challenges than in antiquity (Israel, Ireland, Canada, the Balkans).

These perspectives are mutually exclusive but must somehow be respected, integrated and considered. Rather than have each generation face and experience the same trials over and over again, the forebears have passed on their knowledge so that unnecessary and mitigable sufferings can be minimized, so that progress becomes cumulative rather than re-initialized for each generation. Suffering never ceases, but people in many countries seem to possess superhuman resilience and endurance that empowers them to overcome incredible odds against extinction, conversion or enslavement.

The limitations imposed by a specific degree of cultural intelligence and how well it is transmitted by one's parents are mitigated by the pervasiveness of its presence and influence as one progresses in life, as long as the society deems its cultural paradigm to be of value to the one and the many. The

32. "...the iron and clay in the toes of Nebucadnezzar's image; they may cleave, but they will not incorporate." Francis Bacon, *Essays* [1597, 1612, 1625] (Wordsworth Editions, 1997), p. 11.

Author's Note: But the feet still function.

forbears probably also appreciated the need to be prepared for uncertainty and ambiguity, and knew that the journey to fulfill one's purpose would benefit from cumulative knowledge. A cultural grid is expansive in many dimensions, accommodating layering of memories upon an initiated platform; assimilation and fusion do not circumvent or displace the point or direction of origin, i.e., the purpose of getting on and along.

A butterfly, depending on its sub-species, can spend over 90% of its existence in metamorphasizing into its final expression which lasts only briefly (but long enough to realize its purpose) until it expires. The importance is that it survives intact through its relatively long and perilous journey to reach this final outcome and that sufficient numbers ensure its continuation as a species with individual cumulative benefits passed on to the many, which for a butterfly is limited to its physical attributes in a specific locale, and therefore concentrated along this dimension. As much diversity and interaction as there are in final expressions in nature, not all men will have the same outcome but share the common purpose in promoting the well-being of the species; all have an equal opportunity and potential to contribute to or detract from it, albeit in different degrees and ways.

No cultural paradigm equates right with might (strength or wealth) or obduracy (rigid, inflexible and blind fixation in one dimension) because the forbears found that conflict was always rife and inevitable in any society of two or more people, and that it was preferable to settle differences through social discourse (intelligent dialogue of exchanging words and ideas) rather than physical violence capable of unleashing untold destruction, unlimited destructiveness, and collateral damage or abdication or abstinence from social life. (The former entails elimination of those and their affiliates who do not agree with the one, and the latter results in becoming a recluse, disengaged and disconnected from disorder or potential disorder, with both cases tending toward too much caring or its total absence.) As these two tail-ends of the bell-curve encroach into the realm of the normative, especially since the media tends to thrive upon these fringe stories, wastage and destruction seem to prevail as most seem unable or unwilling to specialize beyond that of being predators based upon some superficial categorizations for the sake of killing for its own sake and justifying consumption way beyond need. Lack of mental and physical self-discipline take a back seat to increasingly convoluted theories and excuses for destructive behaviours while physical interdiction, uniform sentencing and mass incarceration are rigidly enforced and funded.

Such approaches further disconnect cause from effect by the illusion of having the outcomes under control, masked or out-of-sight by locking up, doping and brain-washing *en masse* while the individual is shoved aside and devalued as he or she is increasingly sized up in economic terms.

No other species has demonstrated such an enormous intellectual capability or ability, in potentiality and actuality, to develop killer applications in such variety, quantity and degree. These users of technology not only cause harm physically, mentally and emotionally, but seem to possess a large built-in redundancy or reserve, for suppression of compassion. Such redundancy gives rise to a free pass and justification to disregard or look away in nonchalance from those whose interests and wellness they cannot categorically identify with or can categorically deny in expressions of common humanity, coupled with excess and excessiveness of appetite. The development of so many ways to take life from anything that moves and to destroy anything that exists is indeed an impressive demonstration of human ingenuity.

Because expertise and knowledge in the ways of the forbears, as well as knowledge itself in many other areas of discipline are so salutary and salubrious to social well-being and soundness of choice, scholars and scholarship (teachers and teachings) are highly valued. Entry into this special class has been relatively open, transcending the class structure; status and privilege are not purely based on birthright or material wealth. With intellectual attainment, one could overcome and cross barriers, even in traditional cultures, with a tightly regulated hierarchy of class and gender roles or other distinctions of non-equality or qualifiers of 'first amongst equals': credibility and its corollary, reputation, have meaning only in this context. Through the benefit of foreknowledge and ordering of the inner life, enculturation and education impart a reference point, creating an awareness or a sense of direction and a built-in alarm system or survival instinct to monitor or signal straying or unacceptability.

If one reads and studies the cultural subtext or religious stories in the context that any one of the characters depicted in it could simply and always be just you or me, since they are allegorical and metaphorical or symbolic and intellectual in nature, the lessons would convey a deeper meaning; they would become an internalized experience, not just a story or fictional event. Then each lesson would become a case study of *What would you do, think, or feel?* and *How does it apply to you?* to counter the tendency towards *It has nothing to do with me, I don't want to know or even consider it.* Rules without this personalization process, which reverberate and resonate internally (materiality, perspective and context along one dimension, humanizing values and the concept of dignity of the one and the many along the other dimensions), paradoxically become arbitrary and trivialized with the Almighty or the Authority being equated to and becoming equivalent to *because I say so.*

One's purpose in life might be only fleeting or momentary, or it could endure for many generations. Acts of kindness and generosity, whether consisting of helping an elderly lady cross the street, answering a passerby's request for directions, giving up a seat on the bus to a stranger, or discovering and communicating some truths about the physical world or the realities of human existence and all that it interacts with, mean a great deal for human existence and flourishing, just as all of the elements depicted on the periodic table play a role, whether stable and durable or unstable and non-durable. The biological or hardwired need to belong is only matched by the existential need to differentiate and be different: one needs to exercise choice-making with care, diligence and intelligence to navigate between these two conflicting needs so that their cumulative outcome approximates and is consistent with one's concept of dignity of the one and the many. As far as memory stretches back, man has never viewed his existence as a random and deterministic event with himself merely being operated upon, because all his thought and actions reflected choice-making, not simply tossing a coin, throwing a die or going as the wind blows.

One cannot be all to everyone, but does this mean that one needs to be so little to anyone? Or that one can be everything to one other? One cannot have, do or be everything that is desired;[33] however, this is no excuse or cause for *ressentiment* (a feeling of bitter anger or resentment, together with a sense of frustration at being powerless to express hostility overtly), if one prepares and plans to make one's best effort for each challenge that comes around the corner. A samurai sword is forged by skillful pounding and folding, consistently, uniformly and artfully, over and over again, resulting in its greater strength and flexibility, and most of all, resiliency. In a like manner, one develops and trains to overcome obstacles in life with propriety.[34,35] This is also

---

33. "No doubt to do entirely as one likes could destroy not only one's neighbours but oneself. Freedom is only one value among others, and cannot be realized without rules and limits. But in the hour of revolt this is inevitably forgotten." Isaiah Berlin, *The Crooked Timber of Humanity* (Vintage Books, 1992), p. 259.

represented by the bamboo as a symbol of flexibility and tenacity weathering the storm and stress of life with integrity in form and essence intact.

Each generation feels somehow that life was easier or simpler for its predecessor (without all the time-saving devices and conveniences of today, requiring both less and more specialization), as time heals, mends and dims memories. But for those who lived at the time, the obstacles probably were perceived and felt to be just as insurmountable, the time too limited, the demands too straining and the sacrifice too great, just as it seems that one's own situation is somehow always more difficult or unique than someone else's. Living is intellectual juggling to the best of one's ability, knowing when and which balls need to be dropped or added and why, as much as which ones must never be let go of, while balancing on a tightrope, all requiring guidance, diligence, knowledge, practice, experience, discipline and, most of all, resilience and grace, with an appreciation of one's cultural paradigm as a safety net or safe zone.

While there is great diligence and diversity in Nature in maximizing lives in co-existence while minimizing waste, it seems only humans minimize lives while maximizing wastage. Nature divaricates and man prevaricates most dangerously and destructively in self-knowledge, so that instead of understanding his position and pluralities to do his best within Nature, he tries his best to be above it as its master. The heat and thrill of pursuit of mastery overtakes purpose and careful considerations of costs and benefits of more than one viewpoint.

Choice Making and Set Theory in the Context of the Cycle of Wars

Throughout the millennia of world history that we are privileged to peruse at leisure, there are many records and monuments as legacies of the victors and

34. "The virtue of prosperity is temperance; the virtue of adversity is fortitude...Prosperity is not without many fears and dictates; and adversity is not without comforts and hope...certain virtues are like precious odours, most fragrant when they are incensed or crushed: for prosperity doth best discover vice, but adversity doth best discover virtue." Francis Bacon, op. cit., pp. 15-16.

35. "Whatsoever your hands find to do, do it with all your might, for in the grave where you are going, there is neither working nor planning nor knowledge nor wisdom." Ecclesiastes 9:10.

scant few of the destroyed. Empire building that crosses many borders, from ancient to modern times, destroys more than adds to collective knowledge, and euphemistically labels the carnage and mayhem as unintended consequences or collateral damage, as conflicts are seeded for generations to come. Some memorable examples range from the destruction of Zoroastrian texts in Persia by Alexander's expansionism, the destruction of the Library at Alexandria by the Romans, to the destruction of human cultures on every continent sparked by the Renaissance and fueled by Industrialization and scientism. The modern high priests of profit, speed and efficiency wield their weapons of mass destruction, literally and figuratively, marketing guns to isms with images that displace and devour lives and memories, ushering in cultures of no remorse. Much seems to have changed except our perception of what war is, as we are still bombarded with the same images and words of body counts and real estate as measures of success and failure. By examining cause and effect we can reach the conclusion that wars have always been about the enslavement of the mind, since the body then follows. A good modern day example of this is the success story of the gambling empire (and other addictive behaviour promotion) whose glitter and glitz draws visitors to spectacles as moths to flames versus bees to honey. Guests are converted to players and then treated like kings as all stops are pulled to keep the customer continuously parting with his cash to the *Customer is King* jingle and with a steady trickle of complimentary offers.

As with other addictions, the knowledge that the odds, no matter how infinitesimal, always favour the house has no effect on behaviour. Knowledge by itself seems to be ineffectual against the fervent belief that the jackpot is only one more throw away. Creating and feeding this belief is a comprehensive value-added cashflow chain system for producing an increasing flow of profits in which all other sectors of society are integrated. To understand the human toll, one can examine this value-added chain in terms of actual (physical) and virtual (packaged) manhours consumed at every stage and process. Virtual manhours would cover items liked the transportation, hotel and meals packages, game and monitoring product development, manufacturing, sales and distribution, electric and gas power generation down to the wager as the cash package. This, when combined with other Empires, put in perspective the amount of manhours diverted or subtracted from taking care of oneself and one's dependents. The cause of this as it has been through the ages is the adage that a slave who believes himself to be a king makes the best kind of slave to own. Thus repeat customers are successfully courted and wooed by the industries of identity as long as people don't truly see the next guy as an equal but choose the dichotomy of the master and slave.

With the roll out of the industrial age requiring economic expansionism and an insatiable appetite for actual manhours as fuels for growth, the technology age requiring continuous supply or depletion of non-renewable energy sources and the information age requiring more eyeballs and mind turfs, the magnitude of human enslavement which is required exceeds that of any previous Empire builder and visionary. We are still in the same input, process, output and feedback loop. Addition of the 24/7 news recycling technology makes no difference since it is largely an extension of propaganda or outside-in conditioning. Real news is boring and too long in a culture pre-set and wired for instant gratification and efficiently filtered out as noise or easily forgotten with the next round of picture refreshment. The theatre has not changed except for exponential growth in the viewing audience size. Box-office revenue has not increased as a result of improvements in product and service quality, but simply through sheer volume. And volume is moved by loss-leader marketing or variations on the illusory theme of something for nothing, which has proven to be a most enduring hook. Adults, just as much as children, seem to enjoy hearing the stories they know best, over and over again.

In the past, limited manhours and daylight availability meant that more people were directly involved in the production and preparation of making a life and eating to live. Now, when there seems to be an almost inexhaustible supply of manhours, ever greater amounts seem to be used up in producing goods that end up as piles of junk. People still gravitate to virtual political power and loyal party members cast (dummy) votes along party lines whether they are on screen or not. Since when did per capita income or its corollary tax expenditure (overhead) per capita become an indicator of the well-being of a nation? Just like the ideal weight for people, to keep adding bulk reaches a point of diminishing or negative returns with many unintended consequences beyond the health consequences for one person. Overhead for the entire society must increase both to pick up the slack and to provide support and assistance to those in need of more care and attention. This then leads to further growth in the already burgeoning health technology and services industry or 'human tinkering unlimited' enterprises. Commercial industries always sprout and thrive best when outcomes of poor individual choices are rationalized and justified as inevitable and the causes left fuzzy, untreated and uncauterized.

If weight is such a wonderful indicator for so many ailments, why are so many junk foods and sugar-laden drinks saturating the marketplace while people are led to believe that magic pills, silver bullets and genetic cures are just around the corner? These myths are most likely perpetuated by the same kind of people who are capable of turning cattle (herbivores) into cannibals by feeding them pulverized carcasses of their own kind [see Appendix 1.1]. This practice should be banned not on the ground of disease prevention, but because it is instinctively repulsive and reprehensible to life. It is more of a misnomer to label this mad cow disease rather than insanely greedy human disease. Was this idea propelled by sound ecology for waste minimization and recycling, or by profit maximization and greed run amuck? What is in the feed for all other farm stock and pets? Are child literacy, tax reduction and arms build-up really the *numero uno* issues? Is maintaining the divide of a two-party system and supporting hate-mongers for strictly binary splitting of the spoils so paramount? Are we once again going to swallow this deleterious balderdash or fall for the same smoke-screen put up by the predators and cannibals? Or does the real issue lie with the Department of Agriculture, FDA, EPA and all industries related to the food chain, in terms of their willingness to evolve toward co-existence with all that live rather than exploiting and treating organic beings as mass inorganic products to be measured and converted in dollars and cents, to be held in captivity, enslaved, turned into cannibals and slaughtered in such mass quantities as to maximize wastage or be promoted as loss leaders or sure baits for humans? What indigenous culture and people of the native soil throughout the history of world civilization have engaged in such mass destruction, promoted such mass cannibalism and produced so much non-biodegradable waste as well as such wastes of timelines or lives?

One way forward is to stop wasting so much time on both ends of making and spending money. It is very simple to observe that for most people, spending occurs in an eye-blink while making money does not. If making money seems like a lot of hard work, spending it should be just as difficult (if not more) since this too represents virtual (indirect) time plus activity (direct) time. We all know from early childhood that it always takes longer to make than break something and that something does not come from nothing.

Children need more than the same old 3R's plus religion—they need to be taught how to think through cause and effect and to take excellent care of their time because they are really worth every moment of it. (This is further described in Chapter 15). If there is a mountain of surplus, it should go into rebuilding the schools using the corporate designs of the last decade to enhance the look and feel of space for the children and to ensure that the food they eat is safe and not produced through cannibalism. Then an army of the best chefs should be assembled to bring the taste and nutrition of meals served to the standard established by our mothers. All the large schools should have fully staffed and equipped health and fitness centres installed. Instead of lawyers, accountants and frustrated parents forming school supervisory boards, they should be composed of three couples over 40 years of age who do not want or cannot have their own children, along with an ergonomics expert, architect, head chef, pediatrician, philosopher and librarian. If schools represent society's custodians for the future and centres for learning to serve all children, not subsidized daycare or a dumpsite, it is indicative of how much societies have progressed when centres to worship images and monuments to serve money and politicians (churches, corporate offices, banks, airports, resorts, war memorials, zoos, aquariums and museums with dead and living beings in captivity) are more beautifully built, better staffed, funded and maintained.

Profits, commercial or government, come at someone's expense of under-serviced or undervalued time. Profits will continue to grow as long as the mantra of profit maximization and its unit of measure holds its firm grip on the reins of power. This will be achieved, as before, through an increased rate of under-servicing, or under-valuation of human time, or by increased expansion in the base of such activities on a global scale. When the mass media invests equal time and passion on the state of humankind and all else that exists with equal attention to each stock and presentation of each minute change, up or down, as it invests with the state of the economy and the global financial markets, then the bridge to democracy will be made a bit more secure for crossing by the many.

Even without the ability to read, write and do sums along with blind faith in God, people have managed to live together happily for a very long time. In modernity, these formal communications are considered to be essential, but they should be preceded by and taught in conjunction with the new R's of:

1. Rest and Recreation

2. Reflection and Repose

3. Relationships and Responsibility

If labour for wage takes eight hours/day (or four hours/day) to meet basic living standards, and sleep takes on average eight, then eight are left as idle or downtime which can serve individual purpose. Since a third of the day is spent in idle gear, as much or more emphasis should be placed on teaching children how to use this time for their labour of love as for trading their time and labour for money. Most children used to learn how to spend time at home with families and were taught self-discipline for application to purpose. With an absence of extended family members, the slack in the teaching of the R's listed above needs to be picked up by formal educational and social service providers. One way to counter the forces of maximum consumption is to develop an appreciation for the feeling of contentment or state of happiness associated with 'just hits the spot' (*jok dang*) or 'sufficiently elegant, thank you' (*choong boon*) conditions.

The endless substitutions, repetitions and explanations for virtues, values and rights, like the reciting of the Ten Commandments and the Lord's Daily Prayer, do not result in much progress inside-out, when they simply remain in their category of words and concepts. Rather, these are destinations reached in inter-action for a common purpose of fitting-in and living well. To get there from here, the horse and cart, like cause and effect, needs to be represented in working order for children. Peace, harmony, gratitude, humility, charity, reverence and many other words representing virtue are outcomes or effects of a purposeful mind and heart in relationship with another being. Virtue is only realizable when purpose is not self-serving and unilateral but other-serving and co-lateral so that it will build into character in a lifetime of effort. Therefore, to help children towards a virtuous life is to teach them the purpose of life and the principle of relationships in his or her life which are constant. Then they are free from the syndrome of 'you can't get there from here'.

Whether time is spent in wage-making or otherwise, it should be spent in best effort to fulfill the duty of excellence to oneself, independent of the type of labour or recognition. This is to distinguish honesty and earnestness in labour versus the honour and accolade of labour. One can influence the other but not control or guarantee it, since cause and effect tend to be a circular flow in relationships, not discrete and linear dichotomy of the master and slave. Labour of love should be kept distinct from love of labour or vanity in what one has created. Time that is not valued by oneself is unlikely to be of value to anyone else.

Portraitures of how others see one continue to hold our fascination and attention more than idealized self-image. As these various projections come into alignment and focus, integrity begins to take shape. We cannot see ourselves without reflecting upon reflections. Reality is not static, and since each headset is a unique transceiver, we can only tune in ourselves by paying attention to cues and clues for direction. Taking the time to slow down and listen carefully at each step is likelier to be more fruitful than fidgeting about randomly and rapidly, with all the dials and switches at our disposal with speakers blaring away. Harmonic oscillation is a symphony of synchronized sounds, and it is up to each individual to discover how humans fit in, making sublime music or static noise, in the cosmic hallways.

Musicality is everywhere, unseen and unheard but felt in the movements, transpiration, heartbeats and brain-waves, all transmitting and registering unique signature scents, traces and trails in realization of its dharma or purpose. It carries the programme and programming of our lives for timelines (longitudes) and growth or change potentials (latitudes). Purpose is accessible in the peace and quiet of our idle times spent in reflecting and reposing. In the hustle and bustle of modernity, lives often expire without any trace of having heard or carried a tune, having remained unharmonized instruments that are both unplayed and unplayable. The collective lifelines of the gambling, Internet, television, and other industrial empires hinge upon the musical score or *dharma* of life being obscured by shutting down our sense of permeability and transience in time. They are fed when we stop minding or taking our time and lose our sense of time by stopping to look outside. Life is not lived in precision, but in an inexhaustible repertoire of scent sensations in which the nose is the lead indicator.

It is interesting to observe that in the few occasions when Chinese people do make declarative 'I' or 'you' statements in the context of true/not true, their right index finger is invariably pointing at a nose. Smell evokes images and sensations much as music does, and in *Hamlet* the allusion to a particular kind of smell sets the stage for what is to unfold. Ancient languages are rich in describing scent and taste sensations, and they include many such metaphors that are unmistakable and immediate for the belongers, unlike the voluminous and convoluted concoctions of the cork and pop beverage industries. These hyper-artificial terminologies are as unreal as the many which depict architectural styles (rococo, tromp l'oeil, art deco, post-modern, neoclassical, new age etc.), home furnishing, fashions and coutures. Much of cultural art conveys a flow of time in stillness versus non-art that cannibalizes time with the ringing of the cash till. The clock on the wall has no bearing on what time it really is or when the music will stop. We can only play with life as long as we are in the playground, reading the musical score or shutting ourselves off by being constantly bombarded by blinding and deafening sights and sounds as sincere lifetime devotees to illusions and their beneficiaries.

Human beings are born with the potential for both good and bad, as well as with an intellect capable of developing choice-making skills, free from the obstacles of blind prejudices, uncontrolled emotions, and delusions of omniscience and omnipotence of only one subjective perspective. Culture provides the bridge to acknowledgment of others, through enculturation, and imparts the necessary and sufficient sense of morality. Morality is not based upon some arbitrary construct of one individual, but on a coherent system of values and rules of engagement, through trial and error of billions of man-years. Enculturation can be viewed as the foundation for developing empathy: what the subjective 'I' feels can be held to apply to the other. A culture is the culmination and synthesis over the millennia of human case studies to regulate human relationships, especially within a family.

A cultural paradigm is not predictive or characterized by the search for certainty like maths, and sciences, which are precise within the confines of their man-made constructs. Maths and sciences are categories of knowledge whereby their specificity and certainty are equaled only by their emptiness and cluelessness about how to belong, conduct oneself or know oneself in relationship to others. Cultural intelligence is as non-precise and indeterminate, but provides richness and value for living as a human being, and forms the basis for the quality and quantity of other intelligences, be they emotional or intellectual. They are both valuable and relevant fields of study and endeavour. One can specialize in one or both, but one needs to be aware of their purposes and limits, as well as the potential of each area of knowledge, and not confuse the two.

Whether one believes that life is predictable and ordered or indeterminate and chaotic or nihilistic, cultural paradigms suggest a way of living with a sense of belonging and human dignity, perhaps even with grace. Even if everything appears random and unpredictable, an individual is not just a victim or an entity merely being operated upon. The more unpredictable life is or becomes (like the weather), the more one needs to be better prepared. That is the most one can do: making the best effort minimizes regrets after the fact.

Through the process of enculturation, the fear and apprehension of the unknown, unfamiliar and different are systematically checked from turning into hatred, rage and blind prejudice. If this process does not occur, society will face random acts of violence and convulsions. Enculturation is essential at the early stage of life when there is a better chance of successful integration than at a later stage, when instead of initializing enculturation, a different construct *in situ* needs to be changed and modified. In not providing children with the benefit of enculturation, transmitted in a systematic and structured way, society is engaging in pre-meditated neglect and wholesale abdication of responsibility to the future generation. The inner voice of the Good Samaritan urging one to help those in need is forgotten, and necessitates the substitution and institutionalization of parental and adult responsibilities through the creation of social service agencies and an increasing codification through civil and family laws governing adult and family life, as well as the shifting of responsibilities from family and private domain to the school systems and other public institutions. Liberty recedes as common sense decreases and rule of law increases.

Legal statutes are the extreme and explicit manifestation of cultural imperatives; interpretation of the law and sentencing are facilitated by and reflective of an understanding of its spirit derived from the cultural milieu within which the legal system operates. Cultural imperatives offer a zone of safety and a fallback position which will result in the least harm to the one and the many when there is doubt, uncertainty and inadequate knowledge, because the necessity of knowing all can be circumvented and an acceptable choice still made possible. In abandoning common sense for the supremacy of the sense of one, the result is that instead of a menu of choices popping up, the decision tree is so attenuated and truncated that it becomes just a stump. Knowledge and facility with choice-making cannot only transform the mulberry bush into a decision tree with many branches of possibilities, but also prevent the irreversible dead-ending of options.

The greatest evil that most people can recall occurred in the 20th century, much of it captured on video reels, so that it is not just some ancient history on paper. And yet what was learned from these events that can become part of the human heritage and lexicon? While history says that nothing can be exactly the same ever again, which gives some measure of relief, if one has not learned or gained any self-knowledge or insight from history then the experience of a similar nature can be re-lived and repeated: the lesson being that anyone and everyone has the potential to initiate and perpetuate evil whether directly, vicariously, or as spectators and bystanders. No one is exempt or has earned a free pass. While it may be tidy to assign all blame to

Nazis and Nazism (which can be metaphors for all evil or the greatest of evil), all of humankind shares equally in the potential for evil because no society anywhere is exempt from acts of Nazism. One should not picture oneself as a Nazi, with fear, horror and loathing, but make a determined resolve to be ever alert and vigilant in one's own conduct and engagement with those who are unknown, unfamiliar and different, and ask of oneself: *What can and should I do if I find myself in this situation?*

Evil has been part and parcel of human existence through all ages, as long as man felt justified to vindicate his position and point of view, and refused to acknowledge that his fellow man is equally capable of feeling pain and humiliation, equally entitled to be treated with respect, and is someone whose sense of honour and dignity is equal to that of his own. This is the essential meaning of equality: not sameness in look and outlook, but to be equally free of obstacles to pursue one's own purpose. The mission of all cultures is to free man from the concentration camp of his own mind through enculturation and education. The purpose of pro-life versus pro-temporal power is the thin end of the wedge that separates enculturation from indoctrination, just as purpose determines the outcome of knowledge application. Just as an idea or a book cannot be singularly judged on the basis of authorship but on the merit of its content, so too should all people regardless of how different they are in appearance. Truth can often turn out to be unpleasant, but life need not be so.

Before the advent of audio, video and information technology, evil did not have a worldwide audience, although it has occurred all the time in all places. Most people have witnessed evil through the mass media, and whether it was so compelling to watch due to the perverse fascination with the morbid or the morbid fascination of the perverse, most people retain a picture of evil and its atrocities. The mass media have provided one upside—depositing this picture in the minds of many, there is no longer the possibility of claiming lack of awareness or ignorance of evil and what it means. Rather than shying away from scenes of sharks writhing with their fins razored off, elephants with their tusks chain-sawed off, bears caged and milked as living donors for their bile, these crimes need to be in full view of all the direct and indirect perpetrators, bystanders and consumers so as to convey the ineffable pain caused for extracting profits by marketing propaganda that creates and feeds illusions to ensure over-consumption that does not nourish. Puppy and baby mills will thrive as long as greed is rewarding and lives are treated as commodities, not merely for survival, but for profit maximization.

The mass media and other economic entities operate under the quasi-rules of capitalism, accompanied by social Darwinism, where the strong and the fit thrive without regard for the weak and infirm, who have not earned and therefore are not entitled to wealth, comfort and security. Capital market theory rests upon some key assumptions, many of which vary in degree of realizability in practice; one of these is free and equal access and availability of all relevant information to all participants at the same time, a requirement which no advancement in information technology is likely ever to fulfill.

As with all other theories (manmade constructs), the importance is to appreciate their limitations (assumptions) and specific applicability. The two most absurd and frequently encountered assumptions being *ceteris paribus* (all else remaining the same), since virtually nothing does, and the a priori placement of man or his interests at the apex of all life on the planet. Looking up or being looked down upon requires effort and forbearance versus the ease of level, sidelong or downcast looks. These assumptions lead to treating an organic and sentient life as inorganic and insentient, and to oppression, degradation, and destruction of other lives, even of other men, through novel and interesting terminologies, definitions and assumptions. Such rationalizations with the self and self-interest at the apex serve as justification for petty and mean acts to the grand and horrific since the need to choose has been side-stepped. How free is a man who does not engage in choice-making?

Theories have great value, but not in universal application to categories or in context outside their parameters of operability and functionality. The economic entities thrive through satisfying the wants and needs of the consumer. They merely give them what they want by pumping out entertainment programmes and consumer products, just as the drug peddler or the pimp is in the business of 'want' satisfaction. This attitude of just 'giving them what they want' is also prevalent in parents indulging their children, as well as the school curriculum indulging the students. Competition, free market and capitalism are being bandied about across the board as the great American panacea for social and political ills, including those of the educational system, when it is abundantly clear that these approaches have many serious shortcomings even in the sphere of economics, due to their crude, narrow, loose and limited definitions of costs and benefits combined with a total absence of any ethical and ecological dimensions.

Who sets the rules of competition and does competition necessarily result in the showcasing of the best? Being the best is not even considered as a virtue in religious or cultural texts, and given that there are six billion people, the best may not even have participated. Capitalism is not an ideology that has been formally adopted or instituted, but is merely a practice that seeped into the socioeconomic sphere in the absence of a defining or definitive cultural paradigm. One need only appreciate the scope and magnitude of legal statutes and regulatory entities which attempt to curb and restrain the goal of competition: the complete domination of might over right, with rules of the mighty, by the mighty, for the almighty.

For all of the struggle and sacrifice over centuries since the founding of the U.S. (or millennia of human existence), democracy and its crowning achievements (the Declaration of Independence, the Universal Declaration of Human Rights and the Civil Rights Act) remain just withering parchments; the words remain etched on paper and not in the hearts and minds of many because image has prevailed and has been crowned the undisputed champion of competition. Illusion provides comfort, whereas reality promises only a never-ending struggle without any final resolution.

What separates and distinguishes man from the beasts, where the physical and sensory determine the survival of the strongest, where attributes can be measured, ranked, stacked and showcased, glorified by competition which can only evaluate and therefore value such attributions, is precisely all that resides outside the realm of the physical and the sensory. The senses require balancing with the sensibilities because sensory inputs (although immediate, direct and impactful) are by no means an accurate and reliable indicator of reality. Thus, democracy is a struggle of sensibility over the sensory in that it's a struggle not only *against* the visible tip of repression, but mostly *for* the invisible underlying humanistic principles. Capitalism is the antithesis of these principles with its all-out, 'take no prisoners', 'no holds barred', rampant competition for money representing the ultimate man-constructed illusion at the altar of Mammon.

What theory can explain man in such a limited scope and context as in his economic dimensions that, if not similarly and equally repudiated and rescinded, can simply be swept aside by his act? This is not to suggest that theories are irrelevant, but rather that knowledge of them must be accompanied by an appreciation of their limitations. Such appreciations are circumvented when teaching and testing focus on their subjective mechanics, not an understanding of all the assumptions they rest upon, and therefore impose limits on their applications. There is perhaps too much homage paid to the KISS principle (Keep It Simple, Stupid) in all facets of life. In seeking simple and easy answers, not only are the essence and purpose of the exercise lost, but problem-solving skills and character development are arrested or regressed. The inclination for the quick fix, along with the denial of the messy and complex, needs to be balanced with substance and substantiality.

Much of modern history is beset with calamities brought on by the propensity toward the simple and easy by the many, harnessed by the few, into a herd or mob mentality. In much the same way, a specific solution to a specific problem, which seemed to have worked once, is oftentimes called into service for all manner of problems. Yet the standard response remains much the same, with disdain and dismissal of the complex without final resolution or permanent solution. Modernity, rather than displacing or excluding traditions, has greater need to embrace and incorporate them just as age and experience tend to lead to greater acceptance and appreciation of the ambiguous and the uncertain.

The key difference for the mass media and other economic entities is that in addition to being in the business of satisfying wants, they are also instrumental in the creation of these wants. So the consumer can be regarded as a beast of burden who toils endlessly away, trying to satisfy an endless and escalating cycle of must-have's and must-do's, downloaded from the pervasive invasion of the senses by the want-creating machinery and machination. One cannot simply switch it off without becoming sensory deprived. This illusion of freedom to consume is very seductive, insidious, and powerful, being segued and main-lined in through the auditory and visual senses, with the underlying assumption that through these activities of consumption, *I'll be happy or happier*, rather than asking, *What will make me happy?* or *Do I need all these things to be happy?*—considerations requiring self-reflection, analysis and pruning.

But, as is the case with evil and other bad things that happen, any goal to eradicate these is neither plausible nor possible. It is futile because they are a fact of human existence and part of human nature. The dilemma of supervision is not only the severe curtailment of liberty, but the plausibility of ceaseless supervision and the question of who supervises the supervisor. Rather than more censorship, the goal must be to address how these encounters reverberate within the mind of the individual. Is it entering a free-for-all zone or is it entering a reception area for analysis-and-choice zone?

For any duel to be fair, even the loser, at the very least, is equipped with a probability of winning while not denying the role of providence or luck. In similar fashion, most people are capable of being readied and equipped for encounters with mass media inputs as well as with tragedy, loss, evil, and all others in the realm of the unknown, unfamiliar and different. So that unlike the beast—paralyzed by fear, frenzied into panic, beaten into submission, trapped into a corner, unable to settle differences except through mortal struggle, incapable of seeing a way out or forward—human beings are not mere beasts nor can they ever be, given the capacity for destruction which would run counter to the survival of the species.

Enculturation increases the probability that the human species will flourish over the long-term. Whether this is good or bad is beyond the realm of knowledge. By stepping through the door of culture, man frees himself from the fate of the beast and the obstacles to liberty, choice-making and action, lack of which cause the beast to merely suffer as a victim of its fate. The human ability to transcend impulse (including sexual, procreational and self-preservation drives) and impulsiveness is learned, not innate. Individuals have both the potential for good and evil, and where one ends up on this spectrum is determined by the cumulative effect of choice-making, whereby the quality of choice itself is relative in its goodness or badness.

However, the choice itself is rarely arbitrary and subjective, having reference to the values and imperatives of the cultural paradigm's value/cost/benefit matrix. This can be represented as (x/a, b, c - axis = compassion, tolerance, compromise), (y/a, b, c - axis = materiality, perspective, context) and (z/a, b, c - axis = dignity and honour of one, the family, the others).

Being imprinted with this cultural template for processing inputs can enhance the probability of making choices which may be poor and yet tend towards, or incrementally approximate, acceptability. This template, once burned in over time with effort, trial and error, will serve as an insurance policy against becoming unhinged from purpose and relevance. The probability of losing one's temper along with the mind and heart, resulting in drifting off from the centre and towards unqualified self-vindication at any cost, will be diminished. The insidiousness of self-vindication augers the apotheosis of rationalism in permutations of mutually assured destruction that represents the antithesis of pro-life traditions in context of pluralism or co-existence.

Thus, an adoption of this decision-making paradigm will serve to enhance the integrity of the self as the connectedness to the centre is maintained so that internal dissonance and occurrence of self-inflicted wounds are minimized.

Some people and some things are difficult to love, and yet they are loved. Some subjects and emotions (internal and external realities) are challenging to understand and master, and yet they can be mastered. The value of an idea, a person and all things that exist in the world should not rest upon the ease with which they can be accessed and assessed by arbitrary and subjective affinities and abilities, but rather through the attitude adopted, stance taken and attendant effort made to break through the limits of one's own constrained, biased and tainted imagination and intellect, to realities and existence beyond the one picture window.

When studying the periods before, after and especially during the Age of Renaissance (1400-1600) or the Periods of Rationalism, Empiricism and Enlightenment, completeness in learning is short-changed, -shrifted, and -sighted, unless balanced and comprehensive views are presented,[36] rather than asymmetric and selective ones of a nation. When the perspectives of the losers and their losses are equally represented with those of the winners and their spoils, then true learning and understanding come to fruition and converge. Rosy outlook and recall, fairy tales of the triumph of good over evil, and the preeminence of science and technology are infertile soils in which moral cultivation and virtue can only be sterile, shallow and incomplete.

The appealing labels of the Renaissance, Enlightenment and other ages or men, serve to mask the magnitude and depth of discord and disingenuousness unleashed by selective knowledge versus indiscriminate exploitation and destruction, patented private ownership of knowledge versus pluralism of knowing and inorganic imbalance versus organic growth. The intricate and infinite web of inter-relatedness and co-existence remains unpenetrable, while the illusions of free and freedom blind our vision. Much of human existence and survival has been a testament to overcoming obstacles, be they internal or external to man, with honesty and courage.

---

36. "But looking at the movement of the stars I am not able to picture to myself the rotation of the earth and I am right in saying that the stars move... And just as the conclusions of the astronomers would have been idle and precarious had they not been based on observations of the visible sky in relation to one meridian and one horizon, so would my conclusions be idle and precarious were they not based on that understanding of good and evil which was and will always be the same for all men...." Leo Tolstoy, op. cit., p. 806.

No individual is the same as or equivalent to or interchangeable with another. Equality is not quantifiable because it is not a quantitative concept; it is a moral concept or imperative. It can only be approached from a 'universal human goals and values' perspective which recognizes and respects a human being and his or her pursuit of happiness or purpose without obstacles and disincentives.

To understand one's own potential for good or bad in terms of moral outcomes (which only makes sense in the context of others) is to begin to approach others as being equal in value or worth as oneself. Appreciating and understanding morality and moral conduct are necessary prerequisites to choosing a good or bad path in the context of human encounters, and equality can only be measured in this ethical sense. Non-discrimination laws and their enforcement are a necessity as long as one-dimensional stereotypes, rather than humanness and character, remain an overarching input or variable in the judgement and assessment of others.

Some corporate executives who have worked for many years in a company with effective anti-discriminatory policies will revert back to type when these constraints no longer operate in their social or work environment, as is the case with overseas postings. Behaviour changes when there are no risks of legal recourses or loss of government contracts and no reward of promotions or awards. The attitude and behaviour transformation of expatriates and corporate compensation policies for supposed hardships in overseas postings would provide an illuminating study of class conversion and return on investment. The effect of expatriatism seems to be an extension of colonialism with its worst attribute: racism. Beauty is in the eye of the beholder just as human equality is in the eye of the beholder.

Equality can be safeguarded through strong laws accompanied by diligent monitoring and enforcement of equal opportunity and accessibility, but not through integration. People tend to congregate with those who are on the same or a similar cultural axis (wave-length) where they can be most themselves (tuned-in) in a congenial atmosphere that imparts a greater sense of belonging and confidence.

Education provides a passport to other cultural groups who may be different but who are similar in their humanistic values, just as work groups provide an opportunity for cooperation to achieve a supra-goal which cannot be achieved individually. These relationships require tolerance and compromise of individual differences, be they cultural, intellectual, emotional or physical. A functioning group is maintained as long as its integrative forces exceed the divisive ones. The decisive variables for integration are (a) the degree of inclusiveness and expansiveness conferred on the definition of the group or the set, in including only those who are familiar and similar in look and outlook; and (b) whether the goal or purpose is defined to be specific to a particular individual or group, or is general and universal.

It takes a great deal of effort to pull and push against recidivism or reverting back to type by not all, but perhaps a majority of belongers. Education, awareness building and reminders (maintenance) of non-discrimination against what is different (categories of ethnicity, gender, age, religion, lifestyle) are required continuously, so that these messages don't drop out of the picture, with so many other contentions for mind-space.

Each category of the different represents a different perspective of a shared culture as equal belongers (in the U.S., for example) but in the context of their distinct category and respective role fulfilled. These different perspectives and contexts enhance and serve the culture, just as they impart greater completeness and soundness (integrity) to knowledge. This is a formidable challenge for society; for example, when given all of the nationwide effort and laws to encourage and enforce 'buckling up', there is still less than 70% compliance even though the message leaves no uncertainty as to the fact that it would reduce the probability of injury in an accident, not only to the adults, but to their children. This is more so with cell phones and other distractions.

The field of medicine has the '50th percentile man', who serves as a representative of a human being. In administering treatment as if all people, regardless of gender, age and ethnicity, are equivalent to this model, equality has been achieved in the treatment of the disease but not of the patient. To the extent that gender, age and ethnicity can be determining variables for the presentation and progress of ailments, they need to be reflected in the nature and course of the treatment. The limitations of the 50th percentile man become more apparent as the science of medicine advances technologically, and an awareness and appreciation for the art side of medical practice emerges.

As with social attempts at equality via 'force-fitting' so many incompatibles and incompatibilities into one neat mould, the science of medicine, centred on a lowest common denominator of one gender (male), one age (somewhere in mid-life) and one ethnicity (Caucasian), results in a practice of detachment rather than engagement with the individual. There are monotheistic tendencies and aspects in many other fields which have led to advancements in one category of knowledge (certainty in facts and figures) but not in others (understanding the why's and how's). The field of medicine can have as many dimensions as there are pluralities of individuals. This may not be very practical, but incorporation of the ethnic, gender and age dimensions may be possible as the practitioners' profile broadens to represent these pluralities, along with research design inclusiveness facilitated by increasingly sophisticated, broadly distributed and efficient networking and computing capabilities.

Being human means having an information processing capability which is not only good in terms of efficiency, but also in a moral sense. Unfiltered, unprocessed or underprocessed inputs can translate into outputs characterized by amorphousness, randomness and arbitrariness. Sensory inputs connect with primordial or inherent processing capabilities, which are activated in a reactive and reflexive way as a survival array. But with evolution of a group or social life, this survival array is tempered to derive benefits that far exceed costs to the one or the many. Cultural array is engaged to balance or mitigate the survival array that is solely concerned with the self. The human intellect has evolved or been endowed with processing capabilities which do not necessarily output just what is natural, easy, expedient, convenient, self-satisfying, self-validating, or self-affirming in a transactional manner (where outputs are of the same order, magnitude and nature as inputs), but in a transformational way, where inputs can metamorphosize and result in outcomes of entirely different order, magnitude and nature.

The human intellect has the capability to transcend the sensory interface; its greatest feature and potential is its capacity for moral understanding. While many other social species are encultured for acceptability and unacceptability of behaviour in the group or pack to meet survival needs, the range and scope of human choice-making present no such boundaries in their potential for goodness or badness in moral terms, because morality transcends life as a unidimensionality of only survival and unliteralness of a singular life. Humans are the most adaptable and flexible, and therefore the most ubiquitous of terrestrial species; the evolutionary trade-offs have been simple and safe (relatively harmless to others) with limited potential or complex and dangerous (absolutely to itself and others) with unlimited potential. Whether this is a result of evolution or divine endowment, human beings have the capability for acts of selflessness, which is a unique trait. (Acts of heroism, courage, loyalty and selflessness by companion and trained animals as well as those in the wild are morally unjudgeable from a subjective perspective, only observable and appreciable by humans.)

The most awesome display of selflessness is when maternal instincts are fully awakened and unleashed. Philosophy, as espoused mostly by men, seems to be at a loggerhead with this force as patriarchal social structures which value static vertical order above dynamic lateral equilibrium have evolved in tandem with organized violence. As compassion is divorced from the giving and preserving of life, and a dichotomy between the male and female domains remains firmly entrenched, it becomes increasingly associated with unmanliness, pity and contempt. Compassion is summarily dismissed when viewed as a formidable impediment to killing without justification, when killing becomes the business of war that feeds the military industrial combines. The ascendancy of this outlook is exemplified in the success of converting women to this point-of-view with equal access to military careers within rigid structures and rules. It is great for the business of war when everyone joins in, in the arms race, including children.

A human being can sacrifice himself or act against what is in his best interest, or intervene and incur costs (beyond those of time and resources) transcending his own personal pain, suffering or need for an ideal, for the sake of his fellow man or for those who are weaker and less capable than himself: he makes a radical choice as an individual but not an unprecedented one. These are *not* motives and actions predicated upon reciprocity or remuneration or recognition arising out of considerations such as *What's in it for me?* or, even more ominously and apathetically, *Why should I help or intervene when no one has or will do likewise for me* or *I don't want to know* or *I don't care since it doesn't affect me or my way of life.*

These stances tend to stifle both intellectual and emotional development, with attendant reduction and attenuation of understanding of morality and imagination at the expense of entertaining any remote possibility of being wrong or foolish or incurring a setback or cost. Non-interference becomes a euphemism for staying uninvolved and not caring, which is just apathy with justification. It's the logic of *I don't bother you, therefore you have no right to bother me.* That such a law as the Good Samaritan law is required is evidence of the prevalence of the latter attitudes.

Teaching maths, sciences and vocations involves downloading precepts, conjectures and findings of their many predecessors. Students are not expected to rediscover and figure for themselves all of the cumulative and collective underpinnings of these supposedly essential subjects, which are in the process of being cropped and pruned to satisfy commercial requirements. However, lessons in the 'how and way to be', which have been passed generationally by re-booting the operating systems or cultural programmes within the context (heart and hearth) of the family structure, have largely disintegrated and the children are left to meander.

The why (purpose and meaning) of life may be desired to be imbued with profundity, but not to the exclusion, incompatibility or inconsistency with the how's and way's of living life found in the inexhaustible texts and memories of surviving cultures. These lessons intensely and intently transpire, inspire and imprint throughout and within the personal and organic nature of familial bonds which cannot be replaced or replicated in a classroom. The demands of and for teachers grow exponentially when parents view and bask in their role as subsidized financial backers and owners. In the chase of the material, recognition and non-exertion, they are increasingly abdicating, abstaining, disqualifying and opting out of minding, teaching and preparing their children for the classroom by imbuing them with a sense of duty, dignity, discipline, diligence and devotion, overarched by compassion.

As long as family structure (marriage, parenthood, filial piety) is not viewed as sacrosanct for itself, transcending the 'I' and forming the backbone of a cultural grid, the attempt to fix the resulting societal problems outside the family will continue. Money, technologies and bodies will be increasingly shoveled into the educational systems, labour training camps or remedial institutions, bypassing and dislocating the teachings of the 'how to be' and the 'way to be' of human existence or cultural grid. The purpose of enculturation and education is therefore primarily to increase the probability of a favourable outcome for the one and the many, through adequate equipping, training and exercising of the intellect of each individual. This is reflected in many of the 'coming of age' requirements and rituals of various cultures and religions, conferring status and signaling full membership as a belonger.

The educational system still retains much of the romantic tradition of individualism and the legacy of empiricism. It is no longer serving its primary mission: to prepare the young for adult responsibilities and obligations. This romantic outlook, combined with complete dominance of the empirical experiences, takes on a bigger-than-life picture in the mind, pumped and hyped by the mass media, especially the entertainment industry which sentimentalizes and simplifies the stories of the outcasts and the underdogs, all sensorally expressed and driven. An extremely distorted and incomplete picture is projected onto the national picture screen or mind-set.

Romanticism, an 18th-century idea representing a life dedicated to individuality, freedom of the human spirit, and pursuit of an ideal for which no sacrifice is too great, may on the surface sound pretty wonderful; but if one magnifies this onto the entire population, it no longer is a very tenable concept. It works for a few, but not for all, and not surprisingly, in any given generation only a handful of men at best are worthy enough to cut a figure as a romantic hero.

What did the great romantic thinkers in philosophy, art and politics have in common?

1. They were all cultured men with an extremely strong sense of their own cultural identities, and they drew much knowledge and strength from it (i.e., as is the case for most great achievers, regardless of their field). This centredness enabled them to traverse deeply into other dimensions.

2. They were all exceptionally erudite and strongly grounded in Greek and Latin languages and classics, displaying great reverence for nature and nostalgia for the past.

3. Behind the free spirit lay a highly disciplined mind and will. They were not bound by the material and the temporal, and were a counter force to empiricism and rationalism.

4. Most did not make it to middle or old age, a stage of life which tends to provide a different perspective on life, with the passage of time accompanied by a keener appreciation or apprehension of mortality. They may have developed a more balanced or mature outlook

from their extreme positions of younger and carefree days when they wandered "as lonely as a cloud" or *sans souci*. They may have been less prolific or else kept their thoughts private at these later stages. But even if it were otherwise, it is unlikely that their more matured and tempered outlooks would have garnered or enjoyed much public attention or that of posterity: radicalism and the cult of secular personalities having more 'oomph' and mileage with the disproportionately young and with those who wish to stay arrested at this stage of development.

5. None of them attempted or enjoyed a traditional family life, which would have been contradictory to their way of life as romantics, engaged in the singular and uncompromising pursuit of their ideal. They, and those who cared for them, all paid a price for their pursuit, and none sought to have it all ways or looked for a free ride or got it.

6. They left a profound body of work which pictured another view of the nature and potential of man, influencing all future generations in many dimensions, internally and externally.

If the U.S. educational system and parents are supposed to prepare children for adulthood, how are the following questions to be answered: What other country has such a variety of law enforcement agencies and sub-agencies? What other country has such a prominent ATF (alcohol, tobacco and firearms) agency, but no Department or Ministry of Culture? The ATF could represent the U.S. culture in its pervasive influence, along with the NRA (National Rifle Association)[37] and DEA (Drug Enforcement Agency) and both sides of the abortion polemics and diatribes. This may be the result of placing too great a focus on individuality, with the media amplifying and propelling its celebrity. Could there be a correlation between this over-emphasis and distortion of individuality with the proliferation of legal statutes and enforcement agencies?

37. Author's Note: NRA (no reply allowed) seems to be the above-the-ground ideological progeny of KKK (kill kill kill) to carry on the tradition of anti-change, anti-diversity, anti-learning, anti-compromise, anti-compassion and anti-intellectualism. The overwhelming need to prevail by skewing the odds in its favour, regardless of context, with certain and lethal force, masks its aversion to the fair-and-square duel format whereby equality and chance may just play out and reveal it to be less than omnnipotent or even necessary. The killer

The underlying principle of the educational system should be 'first among equals' (*primus inter pares*), not 'out of many, one' (*e pluribus unum*). What does 'out of many, one' mean in terms of an educational philosophy? This romantic notion, combined with a trigger-happy attitude of the culture of one and capitalism, is a unique recipe for a cauldron of seething and frothing brew without a temperature control panel or a safety release: there is no counter-balance. Enforcement by law of force after the fact is not engaging the enemy at the battle line; it is merely equivalent to stabbing the wounded in the aftermath of the struggle to tally up the score (body count) for performance (damage assessment) reporting.

The frontier of the battle is in the hearts and minds of the children who, as potential adults, potential parents and as those having a significant stake in making acceptable choices, should be adequately and sufficiently equipped with choice-making skills, together with a keen awareness of the society's 'Ethics 101'. The children must be readied in order to have a fair chance in engagements with the external world. This becomes ever more critical as avoiding or controlling the source, flavour and quantity of inputs decreases. It is akin to being battle-ready in order to ensure that children are not over-whelmed into withdrawal and isolation, not seduced into illusory freedom, and not deluded into a sense of omnipotence.

In an age when so much money and attention are spent on attiring children and sending them to pricey private schools so that they can get into prestige colleges, they have, in essence, been reduced to the status of acces-sories and symbols of status (a development noted and hyped, to great effect, by the advertising industry and the mass media). There is no correlation between the amount of money spent and the amount of learning received or, more importantly, on the increased sense of happiness and well-being in the children. To slosh money around in the hope that some good will come out of it for the children who look nice and are in nice surroundings is more than just wishful thinking—it is willful neglect and dereliction of duty. To suppose that the children will come through the end of this pipeline fully ready and

absolutely must be protected with freedom to spread its killing messages and absolutely must not be separated from its killing arsenal as the means to serve its purpose to kill, since killing delayed is killing denied, so that intellectual activity is not only a waste of time but entirely suspect. Is mastery of any language, discipline or skill necessary in a point-and-click milieu awash with over 200 million guns, where differences are inalienable, unbridgeable and intol-erable, to be eliminated with ease and finality, assured and supported by members of the club.

able to deal with the round-the-clock, non-stop pummeling of the mass media and the challenge of navigating through life's journey in this information age is like sending a soldier out into the heat of battle in a designer outfit, hoping that it won't come back requiring drycleaning. Material things, not life, have come to carry greater value.

As in any military or business exercise, a battle cannot be won (let alone the war) without an achievable and clearly defined objective, without clear demarcation of the lines of engagement, in-depth analysis of the strengths and weaknesses of the opposition and without strategic targeting for deployment of limited resources while ensuring minimum casualties by adequately train-ing, supplying and equipping the troops. All of these activities cannot be blinded by the presumption of certain victory, and a fallback position should always be incorporated as more than just a superficial or supercilious after-thought. Battle readiness for a child in the information age requires the development of a robust, vigourous and disciplined intellect built upon a firm foundation of kinship values and humanistic principles, so that he is less like-ly to flounder on a slippery slope or lose himself in the fray and quagmire of the crossfire, wherever and whenever they originate and occur.

It seems that children today have to do their best in a double bind. They are reaching physical maturity at an earlier age and the period of childhood is shortened in duration, while they are increasingly less prepared and equipped in the precise category of knowledge required for navigating in the structurally-altered world brought about by consumerism coupled with technological developments. Their odds for flourishing are diminished. Children are not only having to make a great many more choices but at an accelerated time-order pace (more input, less time) due to increased exposure to novelty, variety, and complexity (input quantity, intensity and category matrix) accompanied by decreasing time allocation for information processing and disposition.

This phenomenon can be compared to the ever-decreasing user adoption time for new technology products; i.e., market penetration of the general population and universal usage are achieved in shorter time periods. One need only gauge the time from initial introduction of new consumer products to everyday general usage: for example, landline phones, b/w TV sets, colour TV sets, cable TV, microwave ovens, facsimile machines, cellular phones, the Internet and e-mail. This accelerated adoption time by the general population is brought about and facilitated by the economies of scale and competition and the mass media of the information age, resulting in a change in both the pace and rhythm of life.

And yet children are taught as if they are still processing information in a sequential and one-dimensional manner rather than simultaneously and multidimensionally, viz. multitasking. While physical multitasking (riding a bicycle while playing a musical instrument, juggling while tightrope balancing, talking on the cellular phone while driving) can be impossible for many or most people, mental multitasking is not, because it is not constrained by the three- (or four-) dimensionality of the material world. Using the computer as an analogy, as the power of the CPU increases it can perform more functions faster as well as support more applications of greater complexity. It provides the platform upon which more sub-routines can reside and function, enabling greater amounts and complexities of input for processing.

The resulting performance improvements are of a higher-order magnitude, not just directly proportional, linear or one-dimensional. For the educational curriculum, this implies that set theory, probability theory and matrix algebra, under the global subject heading of choice-making skills, need to be packaged and allegorized for teaching children at an earlier age so that they can connect with the multidimensionality of choice-making parameters, while the cultural (ethical) values template provides the filter, context and priority assignment against ever-increasing information inputs, giving the user interface some means of controlling and sorting the amount and nature of inputs.

This values template, working in tandem with learned choice-making skills, can process and dispose of the inputs, tending towards acceptability or appropriateness within the cultural paradigm. Just as antibodies take on mass and shape to lock on to foreign invasive cells for neutralization and appropriate disposition, encultured receptors of the mind can slot and file processed inputs by category and context, building a library of allegories for referencing. Not unlike the training of the immune system, the intellect also needs to be trained and disciplined to progress from simple and concise to increasing complexity and decreasing concreteness throughout its lifespan.

An un-encultured or 'culture of one' mind is characterized by amorphousness and tends to be unable to connect and slot information. Every species (plant and animal) is endowed with a different degree of adaptability for flourishing, and the human species is no exception; it is merely endowed with the most, along with the unique opportunity to succeed or fail depending on how adequately or inadequately this endowment is utilized. Human life is much more about and of the 'grey matter' than mutual exclusivity of one correct or incorrect answer, as the popularity of game shows which test factual or topical knowledge would suggest. The more one wishes for simplicity and to think in simple terms of right or wrong, the more likely one is liable to be not only engaged in an exercise of futility or delusion, but of causing harm to the one and the many. One can only direct one's effort to veer (philosophy of calculus) towards a common goal and purpose of humanization (harmony), acting in a humanistic way, and be relieved and satisfied to be at least pointing in the path-of-least-harm direction.

The human brain is designed to be capable of processing the new and complex, but capability does not automatically translate into doability without adequate training during childhood, a time of great receptivity and flexibility. Just as muscle tissues retain memory, the brain will reference earlier training without explicit user command or even awareness. To use another analogy, many products today use rechargeable batteries which present a memory effect whereby the more fully the battery capacity is used up, the greater the remaining recharge capacity and extension of battery lifespan.

Unlike the battery, the brain does not lose absolute capacity nor cumulative and flow-through effects of learning. However, similar to the battery, its recharge capacity increases with greater usage. It operates like a CPU, able to call up an infinite supply of usable memory and workspace to be tacked on to that already *in situ*, as the task requires. The capability and capacity limits of the human brain reach far beyond the boundaries of its own direct observations and experiences, as reflected in and by all human inventions and constructs of ingenuity. None of these could have occurred by thinking in three-dimensional terms or only of the represented or representable: its only constraint is that of its own imagination.

Society protects children from potentially devastating illnesses through immunization programmes: a little pain now to avoid a lot of pain later. Teaching children how to think and how to behave in terms of humanistic values, along with parental responsibilities and skills during the compulsory years of school attendance, is to give them at least a fighting chance in flourishing as adults. This requires a radical paradigm shift for the educational system, which to a large extent operates today as if still in the 18th century or an even earlier social, economic, geopolitical and family milieu, when knowledge and facts were not readily available in such vast detail and quantity as through today's information technology. In the past, traditional values combined with strong family and community ties, as well as ties to the land itself, left no uncertainty as to the individual's cultural identity, thereby imparting to the belonger a clear set of values, a code of conduct and a personal sense of honour and dignity.

A child today has no such ties even to the land, with high-rise dwellings, concrete and tarmac surfaces, family reformulations or reconstitutions, and shifting communities. Information technology enables a child to look up fact-based information with great ease and speed. The need to memorize vast quantities of facts and the importance of testing for factual knowledge recedes as the need to reason and think (conceptual and problem-solving skills) advances. The educational curriculum needs to reflect this shifting of emphasis from one category of knowledge to another: from facts and figures to why's and how's. If the weighting is 90% facts and memorizing and 10% reasoning and explaining, it needs to shift radically to reflect the social, family, environmental, ecological, technological and geopolitical realities of today, in order to adequately prepare the child to have better than even odds of thriving in the 21st century.

An inanimate plastic box cannot teach debating skills nor the art of discourse and dialogue nor the rigours of intellectual discipline. What this means for the educational system is that to serve and function into the 21st century and beyond, it has to reach way, way, back to the original subject and teaching format, viz. Philosophy and Discourse. The result: instead of being mindless consumers succumbing to their impulses, the children will have an opportunity to become discerning, discrete and disciplined adults with greater freedom in exercising their choices and expressing themselves. To paraphrase the last stanza of Tennyson's poem, "The Charge of the Light Brigade," for encultured children of tomorrow:

> Mass media to the right, mass media to the left
> Messages from the right, messages from the left
> Inputs of all shapes, sizes and sorts everywhere.
> They are always to engage in discourse
> They are always to reason why and to ask how
> They are at all times to think through their options.
> Up to the peak of their potential they can climb

continued

With deep-rooted Decision trees sprouting strong branches.
They need never fear obsolescence;
Their *kaizen* ability for continuous learning and improvement will ensure
They are not just lowest common denominators
But each and every one, a unique intended human being.

There is no greater joy displayed by children than when they feel or sense that they have done the right thing and pleased their elders. The pleasure registered and expressed by the elder is mirrored back, amplified many-fold by the child. This is the pleasure and reward of teaching. There is no greater joy or satisfaction for a child than overcoming obstacles and being able and enabled to know and to do. While familiarity may breed contempt amongst people, more knowledge tends to lead to more curiosity and wonderment as displayed by those who specialize and pursue their specialty with great willpower, focus and dedication, fluidly and effortlessly in the flow, to the casual observer. That familiarity breeds contempt may highlight the profound difference between knowledge that impedes versus sufficient and enough knowledge that lubricates and expands the process of moving on and out. As more and greater obstacles are overcome, the capacity and capability of the intellect operates with greater efficiency and effectiveness, imparting to the child a greater sense of security and confidence.

This surely is the most heartfelt desire of every parent: not just the physical and economic independence associated with leaving the nest, but a sense of independence reached through a never-ending cycle of learning and overcoming difficulties. An education curriculum which extensively covers ethics, choice-making skills and parenting skills is designed to spare the children and future generations unnecessary and avoidable suffering, and at the same time empower them for the unavoidable and inevitable suffering which is in the nature of life. It improves their odds of flourishing and provides them with a fallback position so that they can withstand setbacks, regroup, recharge, re-engage and reconnect. Cultural intelligence transcends all other types of intelligence as a determining factor for increasing the odds of flourishing.

To incarcerate, medicate, supervise, coerce and censor is equal to input reduction and distortion; not only is liberty curtailed, but development of choice-making skills is circumvented. These approaches are counterproductive to learning and cause more irreparable and indelible harm to the one for temporary gain or benefit of others. One only can (and should) empathize with children who are frustrated in trying to cope as best as they can when their choice of tools is inadequate and inappropriate for the tasks and challenges they face in real life. Just as a handyman's job is facilitated with a well-stocked toolbox and familiarity with the nature of the problem to be fixed, so too should a child be equipped with a wide variety of analytical tools (how) and a hierarchy of values (why), as well as choice-making skills (what is the category of the problem). They cannot simply be given a straight-edged screwdriver when a Philips screwdriver (or another type or category of tool or combination of tools) is called for.

The nature of warfare has structurally changed in the information age, literally and symbolically. They cannot simply be told that 'honesty is the best policy' (arbitrarily and without any context whatsoever) when this does not seem to be the case, as they keenly observe from the behavior of their elders. There are more than adequate explanations to justify the practicality of being honest for the functioning of the one and the many in many different social settings: clear, undistorted communications facilitate the timely solving and disposition of problems as they arise, rather than having them pile as they are denied, distorted or put aside, thereby transforming into a permanent, messy and unresolvable entanglement which impairs the function and flourish of daily life.

One does not simply hope and pray for a better future and haphazardly try something or anything. One ensures that the probability of such an outcome is increased through adequate training and tooling of the children. It simply is inadequate and inappropriate to tell them to 'work harder, think smarter, sleep faster and be good' while the elders are not willing to do the same, even for the sake of the children. As a last resort there is the most illuminating and edifying of all lines (the frequency and tone of which is only matched by its counterproductiveness)—*This is my house* (or *classroom*) and *these are my rules*—which implies mutual exclusivity (not yours) rather than inclusiveness and belonging, and signifies and signals the sheer arbitrariness and capriciousness of rules, thereby perpetuating a culture of one.

Stories and pictures need completion or approximate completeness for proper internalization and integration of lessons and knowledge. Children are drawn to this type of learning, as evidenced by their eagerness in listening or watching the same stories over and over again, deriving greater pleasure from a sense of *déjà vu* and the certainty and security in their own knowledgeability more than from the stories themselves; the challenge for adults is to tell the complete story beyond the fairy-tale endings which only signify another cycle of trials and tribulations.[38]

It is unlikely that many parents would have read Bruno Bettelheim's book, *The Uses of Enchantment: The Meaning and Importance of Fairy Tales,*[39] which not only explains the many values of fairy tales but also their numerous downsides and major pitfalls. One also needs to differentiate the perspective of an adult reading lessons into the stories, from that of a child in whose photo album of the mind these tales may take hold with profound and significant anchoring when the mind is at the peak of receptivity. Such is the case with the term 'the noble savage', where the perspective is completely at odds with that of the indigenous people for whom it is at best risible and at worst ominous, as a consequence of how widely held the perspective becomes, transcending reality.

There is more than an adequate supply of stories, beyond Biblical sources, which can be repackaged and abridged for children of all ages, from ancient

38. Author's Note: While fairy tales (mass-produced and -consumed stories) can be captivating, instructive and entertaining for children (and many adults), many are characterized by two-dimensionality in the extreme, setting up an inconsistent or unrealistic picture of life: their clearly defined characters, who are either all good or all bad; gender differentiation and assignment; complete absence or irrelevance of adults or elders; non-presence of a family; complete absence of daily social, political and economic life; detachment from a sense of time and place; emphasis on physical appearance as an indicator of goodness; cartoon format (consistent with cartoon characters and settings); and unsavoury destruction of what is considered bad.

Cartoons and other forms of visual art are powerful communication media which can transcend their two-dimensionality by depicting concepts or stories which are multidimensional in scope and scale, as has been amply demonstrated by many artists of this genre. There are some happy and fortunate marriages of content, format, function and structure, and there are some that are not. Sometimes it is not as easy to discern the state of happiness when one dominates, overwhelms, mitigates or nullifies the expression or the necessity for expression of the other. With the benefit of more experience and age, certain fairy tales, like *Alice in Wonderland*, may reveal much more depth that many adults can appreciate.

There are three indications of how selectively and contextually many fairy tales are passed onto children as standard fare:

myths[40] to other works of literature, including poetry from the 18th and 19th centuries when social structural shifts and turbulence of seismic proportions occurred, largely defining the global terms and conditions of life to this day. There are many writers who have produced great works in every major European country during the last 250 years (with much of what defines life today having originated in this continent). The following writers are a limited sample, selected because their work emphasizes multidimensionality of life and humanistic values: John Milton, Goethe, Schiller, Coleridge, Shelley, Byron, George Eliot, Jane Austen, Victor Hugo, Emile Zola, Dostoevsky, Turgenev, Joseph Conrad and Theodore Dreiser.

While it is acknowledged that every country in each century has its share of works of great creativity, the criteria for selection is in the context of absolute and cumulative effect on posterity on social, political, economic and philosophical dimensions within the global set. From an educational point of view, ethnocentric tendencies need to be minimized in favour of the big picture; very few purchase decisions are made based on where a product or

1. Percentage of parents who review the pros and cons of a fairy tale or any printed material targeted at the children's market.

2. Percentage of popular adult best sellers that continue the traditional fairy tale endings, repackaged and spiced.

3. Number of books sold on the themes of Peter Pan and Cinderella syndromes suggesting the lasting hold and influence of these type of stories even well into adulthood.

They pose and set up a seriously *grim* (foreboding) outlook for a child developing sufficient and necessary choice-making skills and flourishing. Why would anyone want to limit a child to a work of two-dimensionality, mutual exclusivity or a zero sum game outlook unless curtailment of his liberty or attenuation of his potential are the desired outcomes? An indication of the timeless effect of fairy tales can be seen in their continued influence in the outlook on life and popularity as a genre well into adulthood. On balance, there may be bigger downside risks over any significant upsides.

39. Bruno Bettelheim, *The Uses of Enchantment: The Meaning and Importance of Fairy Tales* (Vintage Books, 1976).

40. Thomas Bulfinch [1796-1867], *Myths of Greece and Rome* (Penguin Books, 1981).

service originates, who made it, or how it is made (ethnicity, type of labour, level of compensation), and economic decisions based on completeness of merit (holistic) tend to prevail, rather than those based on ethnocentric leanings or on the exclusion of humanistic considerations (it is hoped). One does not usually weigh and judge the content or its merit, based upon authorship by country of origin, academic achievement, ethnicity or beliefs held, to appreciate its educational or practical value. While some authors may have left historical records, directly or indirectly, as to their personal life, thoughts, daily circumstances, beliefs and leanings, most have not. It is difficult enough to get to know a living person, let alone some individual who has been consigned to posterity a long time ago.

There is such a rich and abundant source of material that can replace fairy tales and appeal to children. Materials for children at this vulnerable stage should contain as few elements as possible for potential distortions and disengagements, especially since this is entirely mitigable, if not avoidable. Fairy tales can be enjoyed later, when they can be appreciated with a perspective gained from 18 years or more of experience and knowledge. Abridged stories need to be revisited as complete and original versions in later years of schooling, so that depth of understanding is encouraged and established. These are books that are not amenable to speed reading and one paragraph synopsis, but instead require careful reflective reading.

Distinctions between cursory and topical knowledge, characterized by referencibility and empirical certainty, requiring no personalization, compared to in-depth understanding gained through personal and individualized thinking (discipline, patience, effort, observation, comparison, generalization, applicability, materiality, exceptions), characterized by written and verbal communication skills, need to be established by the time the child completes 12 years of formal education. These latter characteristics cover both scientific and non-scientific endeavours where discipline and depth are prerequisites to getting along and on. There appears to be an inverse relationship between meaningful and organic learning versus the market valuation of degrees and market values which desire effective and efficient problem-solving for profit maximization. The need for meaning is thus a separate category of pursuit and should not seek validation in economic terms. The pursuit of one or the other, personal meaning and well-being, need not be mutually exclusive but, rather, prioritized and sequenced with demurrals and deferrals, since they are usually at cross-purposes but both attainable or catenatable with effort, balance and compromise over time.

A cultural grid serves to mediate and mitigate a wide range and depth of relationships through cultivating a reverence for life and the art of living. The trinity of life is being, non-being and inter-being; the intermediariness is the non-tangible relationships or bonds that exist in the in-between space and time, both transcending and bridging being and non-being. The relevance of brotherhood and unity is in the context and confines of attitude, not in meaning, purpose or judgement. Thus compassion, hospitality and balance among all that is unique and different are uniquely and individually challenging, pivoting around mindfulness, and not based on some absolute man-made construct, including religion and science. The journey of the spirit is initiated and cultivated with an appreciation of and for life, with caring for the well-being of the one and the many, beyond I-centrism, monism and homo-centrism, in ever-expanding circles.

The purpose of education is not uniformity or regimentation but, rather, to free the student from obstacles which may impair or impede his pursuit of purpose and potential. Instilling a sense of intellectual and personal discipline is of paramount importance in this regard, as it has such significant implications for flourishing or floundering. The more random, scattered, shallow (one-dimensional) and numerous the information and sensory exposure are outside the home and school environments, the more focused and in-depth the coverage of specific subjects needs to be during the enculturation and educational process, to attain some degree of understanding and appreciation. Thinking that is limited to one or two dimensions, mutual exclusivity and zero sum outlook need to progress to a multidimensional format with grey outcomes, resulting in no harm to others.

A wide variety of subjects is important, but trade-offs are a prerequisite given the limited time and resources, as well as the one-time window of opportunity for achieving the educational goal. Subjects such as political science, economics, anthropology, sociology, psychology or photography can be pursued at college or through personal interests and hobbies. After completion of Grade 12, students should be prepared to make life-defining or determining decisions of livelihood and lifestyle which are life-affirming; they must not just waste the four years of college, drifting and dabbling, but spend this time in focused learning and activities which will be consistent with and supportive of their choices.

The corollary of choice-making is problem-solving. Students need to be taught to compose problem statements and to structure problems to increase their probability of resolution, to take inventory of available resources and to assemble necessary resources not on hand, to monitor progress so as to know when to stop, re-think and re-direct, not to lose sight of or forget what is at stake (the object of the exercise), i.e., not to be blinded, sidetracked, or derailed into wasting time and effort in a futile or counterproductive manner. *I want and I can* must be in the context of why and how, emphasizing comprehensiveness of thinking. By encouraging contextual thinking, hopelessness and helplessness, expressed by anger and frustration, can be better managed and channeled into more focused, paced and disciplined efforts.

Eight Compulsory subjects are recommended, in addition to the six Core subjects to follow.

Compulsory Subjects: sciences (maths, physics, biology, chemistry) and the arts (English, literature, history, geography).

English (or the language spoken by the majority) is recommended as the primary educational language in a country of many nationalities, not as a replacement or substitute for the mother tongue, which may continue to be spoken at home or in other reference groups, but as a means of establishing common ground. Four reasons can be suggested:

1.   The burden of subsidizing so many languages is not sustainable or supportable because, in treating all languages as of equal value, all will need to be accommodated. Parents can ensure proficiency in the student's mother tongue or first language through its use at home and with private tutoring, if they deem it essential. Too many languages in the school will diminish teacher and teaching effectiveness in connecting with the students and with the course load required; mastery of the subject matter takes precedence over the specific language in which it is taught. What one knows and how well one thinks are of higher priority than which language one speaks; knowing one language, in depth and breadth, offers greater functionality than cursory familiarity with many languages. In addition, cliques will form on the language axis and the integrative effect of school life, which may be the only context for such exposure for many students, will become diluted.

2.   Almost all countries have one national language, and in a country with so many diverse nationalities, a common language becomes of greater importance as a common bond. The virtuous functioning of a democratic political system rests upon freedom of speech and uncensored information made widely available to and widely read by an educated electorate, which impose a greater burden on the role of one common language and critical thinking. Like local news stations, most mother tongue publications and TV channels tend to be narrowly focused, with a unique perspective, programming and agenda.

Understanding the mainstream perspective, in the context of and in conjunction with ethnic or interest group publications and media, will result in seeing the larger picture, providing a platform for national civic dialogue and engagement.

3.   On another level, the English language, already a *de facto* language of global commerce, has much to recommend it as a universal language, both in its simplicity and neutrality, as well as its wide usage. It does not entrench status distinction, in that there is an absence of high or common forms; there are fewer gender and age distinctions and fewer incorporations of specific values of a culture. While one's mother tongue is important to a sense of identity, belonging and functionality with a specific group, an understanding of the English language gives one a passport to traverse and experience a more expansive economic and intellectual landscape.

Ethnocentric tendencies around national languages need to be viewed in the context of co-existence with the English language and with the goal of broadening the global base of common factors across all cultural dimensions, as well as economic significance. There will always be a home (place of origin with ties of blood and land) for the mother tongue, as it is too intricately and intimately tied in and enmeshed with its respective culture. As long as the culture flourishes, so will its language. As long as people are curious about their roots and other cultures, and want to learn its languages, there will always be an incentive to study a foreign language.

4.   What language is spoken is less deterministic of long-term flourishing than one's degree of facility (depth and breadth) with it, in conjunction with the inner language of relationships, purpose and fitness, which impart a sense of service, meaning and belonging. A lot of the latter will already have been established before entering the school system and will enhance the learning process of the core curriculum in a language spoken by the majority, in addition to increasing the probability and degree of fitting in to the majority landscape and minimizing a sense of alienation and isolation.

Having more than one official national language carries multidimensional cost to the one and the many regardless of language preference; all the arguments for it are against it, and the benefit of the super-majority will need to weigh in. Very few countries adopt two official national languages and those that do will have had some traumatic or involuntary historical reason. As long as language is perceived to define ethnicity, and foster ethnocentrism, it will be much more of a divisive force than merely a barrier to communications.

In the teaching of compulsory subjects, by de-emphasizing memorization and the testing of factual knowledge, while increasing conceptual understanding, the teaching method for traditional subjects and the amount of classroom time consumed may be compressed and enhanced. The Internet can facilitate most of the fact-familiarization requirements, interactive learning and testing, refining skills of selecting (accept/reject criteria setting), sorting (establishing hierarchy along one or more dimensions) and communicating (labeling and formatting for comprehensiveness in reporting and filing). The direct human interface is critical in the teaching of the core subjects, and this valuable resource should be freed up as much as possible from the teaching of structured compulsory subjects.

Recreational activities, such as team sports and other track and field activities, along with music, drawing, crafts and home economics need to be spaced around the core and compulsory curriculum during the 12 years of school attendance. Children will usually make the time and effort for activities that interest them, but will still require supervision and guidance in the basics of these endeavours until they acquire sufficient familiarity and reach adequate maturity to pursue them on their own as hobbies or vocations.

Six Core Subjects: humanism, choice-making skills, parenting and budgeting skills, communication skills, ecology and the environment, health maintenance.

> 1. Humanism would include ethics, art of discourse, introduction to logic (how to think and communicate in complete sentences), values and conduct. Case studies in literature, history and current events would be presented from at least two but preferably three perspectives, to emphasize depth and understanding (rather than breadth and facts, as covered under compulsory subjects) and to illustrate compassion, tolerance, compromise, materiality, perspective, context, and dignity of the one and the many.

2. Choice-making Skills: Probability Theory and Statistics
Matrix Algebra
Set Theory
Checkers and Chess

3. Parenting, budgeting (financial) and time management (Appendix 2) skills would include physiological and psychological development and needs profile of the baby, from conception to four years of age, the time requiring direct and intense parental involvement, matched by daily physical care, nutritional, medical, emotional, financial, facility and time requirements. An essay entitled, 'Why I would choose someone like myself to be my mother or father if I could', would be part of the final exam for passing this course at each grade.

4. Communication skills would include basic theory and practice in listening, writing and speaking beyond unilateralism. Being able to articulate words is a different kettle of fish from reading in and for understanding recognition and incorporation. Video and other formats of presentation could be left for the college level.

5. Ecology and the environment would cover a basic introduction to how human beings fit into the ecological scheme and how they affect the environment.

6. Health maintenance would be covered in a course on nutrition and exercise (calisthenics, gym use and yoga), with the purpose of creating an awareness that the most important assets of the students' lives are time, time-order and mental/physical health. The students need to be taught   the proper or minimum maintenance required for optimal performance, as time and health progressions are irreversible, irreplaceable and finite. This programme needs to encourage constant or a minimum level of vigilance by being part of the educational process at every grade. Good eating, exercise, rest (sleep) and hygiene habits need to be encouraged and reinforced, giving greater benefits over their lifetime than when formed later, resulting in less cost to the one or society. Aging is universal and is not a concept confined to the elderly; the young change and age relatively faster than the old. Knowledge of preventive care at a young age can have the most long-term and significant positive effects, compared to the acquisition of such knowledge at the onset of deterioration or break down. The

students need to be taught that each body is different and that there is no ideal shape or size. The objective is to take good care of what one has and not succumb to media images.[41] Topics should cover preventive care: annual physicals, including eye and ear exams, oral hygiene and annual dental exams; sleep management; avoidance of potential sources of damage to vision and hearing such as UV rays, glare, prolonged 'screen' time (sun, PC and TV), noise pollution, etc. They should also be taught basic first aid and pharmacology, and introduced to home safety and ergonomics. School facilities should include various health care facilities adequately equipped and staffed by general practitioners, dentists, pharmacists, dietitians, physical trainers and nurses who practice their profession on campus, as well as participate in the teaching of this core subject.

41. Author's Note: Sex and violence have become a war zone and a showcase of moralizing, private property and entertainment devoid of the dual purposes of expressing fitness for procreation and of restraint for co-existence. With the peeling away from and off from purpose and means which is the Way of Nature, sex and violence are merely the untethered ends, removed from any consideration or understanding of relationships and inter-relatedness which are complex, dynamic and uncertain requiring constant vigilance, endless compromises and internal recalibrations. Since appetites rather than satisfactorily meeting the thresholds of relationships drive the impetus to engage in sex and violence, the right to procreate and to kill become inalienable absolute and equal entitlements when nothing could be further removed from or reflective of Nature. While the mass media displays sex and violence most of the time in selective nature shows, lives that dwell within Nature devote most of their time preoccupied in diligence and care for preparedness and fitness for procreation as well as much collaboration and compromise for co-existence. It is not the biggest and strongest that prevail, but co-existence from single-celled orders to complex hierarchical social communities. They all adumbrate a code of organic life that each being seems to embrace, and be embraced by that informs, relieves, reveals and releases through its entire life in its habitat. This is the whispering symphony of the inner voice that can be heard in the playing field of Nature. A child does not need to be taught sex or violence but, rather, discipline (restraint), fitness (fitting-in and -of, preparedness and readiness), relationships (ethics), purpose (co-existence) and the Ways of Nature (value of life and how to live well).

We see ourselves in relative relationship to others, be they below, equal or above in complexity, variety and numerity of contexts, as we journey over time and space. While the caveat that 'all men are created equal' is appealing,[42] even without its Divine context, it is silent on equality post creation or conception. Even at the stage of pre-conception there are numerous factors which would make for much inequality. As is the case of whether there is noise when a tree falls in the forest if no one is there to hear it, so too with the existence of self and the need for attention from others. The purpose of ethics as a field of infinite endeavour may be to provide the tools for engagement with the other(s) where the potential for conflict is unlimited since each self is a unique permutation, in order to reach or settle into a state of dynamic compromise; such ethical considerations being operational in viable and lasting cultures.

Programming binary formats of win/lose, along with willfulness and self-esteem building or unlimited freedom to do as I please, leaves a self with inadequate skills which results in the formation of its own negative amplifying loop and damming up of the self. This in turn unravels and tears the civic fibre of society by the inevitable rage unleashed by thwarted willfulness. It is through experience which comes with age and the widening and deepening contacts with others that these interfacing skills come into play and are honed and refined, as different projected and reflected perspectives are layered and meshed. Even in isolation, be it voluntary or involuntary, one has access to and memory of many versions of the own self and other selves in the continuum of time and space. Sartre wrote in *No Exit* that "hell is other people"; so too can it be said that heaven is other people and pursuit of happiness is not a solitary game or a singular gain.

The perception that hierarchy is static and rigid still persists in many minds and results in much resentment. But hierarchy is a dynamic structure in an open economy which facilitates upward or downward mobility. Traditional determinants of roles and obligations (age, gender and birth

---

42. Appealing as when, "Rousseau asks why it is that man, who was born free, is nevertheless everywhere in chains; ... 'It would be equally reasonable', adds the eminent critic Émile Faguet, 'to say that sheep are born carnivorous, and everywhere nibble grass.'" Isaiah Berlin, *The Proper Study of Mankind*, op. cit., pp. 266, 519.

order) may still apply in personal life, but in a professional or social context, status is a function of qualification and merit. It is not self-affirmed or validated, but can only be conferred by others through their recognition and acceptance as a 'first amongst equals'. They reflect on intellect, experience, effort and most importantly, achievement. Wealth may circumvent all of these other qualities, but it alone does not determine status. Because of the dominant role that economic activity occupies in many lives and the mass media portrayal of wealth as the ultimate in status, there is a schism created between status as traditionally conveyed in the cultural context where wealth is not an explicit or sole determinant thereof[43] and the power and influence wealth actually exerts that resembles and emulates status. Because wealth and capitalism can carry such potential for the destabilization of a society, as capitalism is globally adopted it becomes even more critical for cultural paradigms to be well understood and transmitted.

All social activities, including economic ones, can only flourish within the context of a cultural paradigm that ensures the long-term survival of the many; without this umbrella, a one-dimensional economic value will prevail and consume all other dimensions of pluralities and values: (1) social, family and political; (2) ethnicity, gender and age; (3) liberty, equality and justice; and (4) environmental and ecological. If there is no unified effort to reinforce the cultural bulwark, it is only a matter of time before a society finds itself back in the pre-democratic era, with power concentrated in the hands of a few which exerts control over the lives of the many.

It is extremely difficult to balance upward mobility and social stability, but the sense and sensibility of balance cannot be ignored.[44] Most cultures and history have weighed in on the latter (social stability), as evidenced by ancient cultures of millennia which favoured birth right and suppressed

---

43. "A sense of hierarchy is particularly strong in the family....The respect for knowledge is demonstrated by the power and authority of the ulemas (religious scholars)." "...it is the ancient desire to win prestige in other men's eyes, and to win a respected and important place in society. In Islam, it is people who regulate and dominate business, not business that dominate them." D.S. Roberts, op. cit., pp. 124, 161.

44. Author's note: Just as money acts as a powerful variable in a dynamic hierarchy, so too does it in the political system, especially in tandem with the mass media consolidation or religious fervour and fanaticism. One possible counter to the extreme outcomes that result from this concentration of power is for the electorate to be as encultured in its values as in its education and intellectual choice-making.

individualism, as well as the 18th century Western political developments for social equality and justice as a reaction against power concentration accompanied by the unleashing of individualism, which may have been an unintended consequence. How non-secular entities have dealt with their material and commercial dimensions and how extensive and pervasive this problem becomes, in both its past and present, reflect on the difficulty of this problem. The purpose of culture is to enable man to make choices and find his path beyond the one-dimensionality of economic considerations through enculturation and education.

Upward or downward mobility is a function of one's choices, as well as factors beyond one's control. One can only make the best of the choices available by being prepared as well as possible. Life does not need to be a zero sum game, unless one chooses to make it so; it involves making trade-offs and compromises which result in a sense of balance consistent with one's identity and the fulfillment of all duties and obligations to those whose well-being matters. Each organizational structure reflects the function and business nature of the entity. What is common among all these various types of structure is that each position is clearly defined in terms of its authority and responsibility. Whether the individual is qualified or accountable is not a subject of broad debate or consensus. If every decision is challenged and each position has to earn the respect of those below, the result would be utter chaos. The corporate man is to work towards the common stated goal and comply with procedures and policies, both implied as well as explicitly codified in various corporate manuals. In organizational theory, the culture of the corporation is also addressed and deemed essential to its well-being.

In a culture of equality everyone feels entitled to be #1, while not appreciating that one cannot become #1 without having been a successful #2. Also, while being #2 is a prerequisite to becoming #1, it is not a guarantee of being made #1, nor of being successful as #1. Finally, being #1 is not a guaranteed, permanent state. Hierarchy only works if everyone understands the concept of duty: to be of service and to provide service, without personal judgement or preference. Being a subordinate does not imply servility. It is only an indication of rank and order that must be acknowledged in discharging one's duties as a condition of employment. It is not necessary for a subordinate to like or respect the supervisor, but absence of positive regard must not prevail at the expense of civility and respect for the hierarchy (regardless of excellence of the work performed). Similarly, a good supervisor who appreciates the effect of bad feelings on productivity and effectiveness and more importantly, remembers his or her own tenure as a subordinate, will make an effort to minimize this source of wastefulness. In a meritocracy, many subordinates are eventually promoted to supervisory roles. But very few tend to bring their insight from their former positions, so there are many whom subordinates cannot bear to work for. They are instead inspired into departure if they value their time rather than endure such non-collaboration, insolence and repugnance that sums up borderline attitudes and behaviour. Those who remain tend to deliver less than their best, wait out or actively participate in removal of such ineptness.

Corporate cultures tend to be reflections of, as well as consistent with, the society-at-large and its cultural milieu: some corporate cultures are lead indicators and some, lagging indicators. These rules make up the *modus vivendi* of society. Even a family, which represents the smallest group unit of a society, is guided by the cultural values and practices to uphold the various positions within it and to foster their respective functionalities. If kinship positions and relationships, in terms of authority and responsibility, are not upheld, there is a multiplier effect, resulting in tears in the social fabric.

Islam means 'submission to' or 'humbleness before' God. This attitude is at the core of every religion, acknowledging that organic beings are pleomorphic and polymorphic, with change as the only constant, resulting in infinite manifestations of Nature. The purpose of submission is not servility and blind devotion, but to awaken and come to the realization that true liberation is only attainable in harmonious co-existence in Nature. Being in harmony requires total awareness and unawareness simultaneously, so that the strands of time are neither too flaccid nor too taut, in order to catch the ever-changing Cosmic winds and play true and full. The measure of beauty in poetic thought and expression is its ability to mind-share such ineffable moments with the others in whom each encounter differs, and is different each time.

Culture is like religion in many respects. There are many prescriptions with which most people are familiar in varying degrees and yet never fully, or even approximately, comply. At the fringe of all religion is fundamentalism, e.g., the Roman Catholic Church in Christianity and the Orthodox sects in others. These are essential because as people have differed or deviated in interpretation and splintered off in practice, and as this diffusion (over time and physical distances) continues, unless there is a standard or some origin to trace back to (etymology), eventually all meaning will be lost in dilution.

Similarly, in every culture there are different degrees of study and adherence to what is prescribed as the proper attitude and conduct. The significance and difference of culture is that, unlike religion, one is simply born into it—it is not an option. Of course, some people do not like rules of any kind, and in not wanting to acknowledge any, deny the existence or applicability of any rule to their way of life or profess not to know what and why they are. If they act consistently with this choice, the probability increases that they will eventually end up with deficits in identity, becoming voracious and vociferous consumers, outcasts or rejects of society. This population segment seems to be experiencing unprecedented growth.

The arc of life demands playing a wide range of roles,[45] and since both participants and the relationships are dynamic and pleochroic, role-playing cannot be simply reduced to a good or bad person or any other binary format. Goodness or badness can only be manifested in the outcome of the interactions with the other through an understanding of what is considered proper or harmonious in the practices of one's culture. These guidelines are taught, internalized and developed over a lifetime, as there can be no rigid or absolute rules, given the fluidity and flux of relationships. Such magnitude of unpredictability or uncertainty does not preclude but, rather, demands greater preparedness that is a function of comprehensiveness of cultural programming and identity, not some generic attribute or willful inclination.

45. "Whosoever of you would be the chiefest, shall be the servant of all. For even the Son of man came, not to be ministered unto but to minister, and to give his life a ransom of many." Mark 10: 44 and 45.

What ethical rules take hold first and how does the mind categorize them? Which are discarded and which are assimilated? The cultural imperatives taught from a very young age can be said to reside in the realm of the 'superego', the rules-keeper aspect of the subconscious, first described by Sigmund Freud. The interaction of the rules with the impulses of the 'id' determines how the 'ego' develops, as a navigator and balancer between these two pulling forces. What stays categorized as the rules depends very much on actual encounters with how they appear to operate. If too many of the rules are seen to be broken with impunity and without perceived or real consequences in all arenas of life, by parents, teachers, peers, churchgoers and public figures, and if all the rules take on an arbitrary or relative nature, the 'superego' simply disappears. Essentially, there are no rules (or what are considered rules are aptly subjective), and the rules which may take root usually equate to 'I' imperatives or some inspired dogmatism which has easily penetrated and germinated in such fertile soil *sans* steadfast gatekeepers and a well-developed risk processing unit. Age, test-scores, degrees, looks, church attendance and wealth do not provide immunity. This is then identical in function to the 'id'.

If there is no superego but only the id, then the ego, which referees between them, can be said not to functionally exist, because it is unnecessary. This is the paradox one observes in dealing with the self-constructed individual. Instead of an ego, which defines the individual in how he thinks, acts and talks, there is a blank. How he thinks, acts and talks consists of the id (e.g., monopoly of 'I' as sole subject of all conversation) saturated with the candy of the senses. How can anything else result but estrangement, isolation and disconnection? Even getting a connection is impossible without the sugar-coating. This is not a generational, racial, religious or intelligence gap. This is an ego gap, where there is no superego framework for rules to slot into. *Mea culpa* and moral agency are not concepts that can be entertained or applied in such a state.

If this were a benign state (*just me, left alone with my 'candy basket'*), it would not be cause for alarm. But to the extent that human beings have not evolved or may never evolve to a stage where the need to belong and the need for acceptance and recognition are not completely compensated for or overcome by all the sense needs being met (although sensory satiation itself may, ironically, exacerbate these other needs since they are not as easily satisfied), frustration is sure to follow. This will set the stage for some form of release, as these feelings of frustration are not likely to dissipate, given the built-in inadequacies of coping mechanisms or the absence of cultural imperatives. They may accumulate and find an outlet for release in anti-social behaviour, from simple faux pas to violent rage, suicide and/or homicide.

With some prompting, many people recall the brutality and hatred demonstrated by the torture and murder of James Byrd Jr. (age 49) on June 7, 1998, in Jasper, Texas and even more remember the violent death of Matthew Shepard (age 21) on October 12, 1998, in Laramie, Wyoming (see Appendix 1.2). But given how quickly these atrocities have disappeared from the public eye, one must wonder if it is because these individuals are not considered to be as valuable to society as, for example, James Dean and Marilyn Monroe, because their stories cannot be translated into countless hours of programmes that glamourize suicidal loner glitterati, resulting in enormous profits. This is most unfortunate, because the lives and deaths of James Byrd and Matthew Shepard are invaluable in teaching us profound lessons about ourselves and the incommensurability of each and every life. From them we can learn that each and every one must count, equally—or no one will. They are our precious children, no less beloved and beyond compare to all other lives, to whom we impart beingness, names and identities, our flesh and blood, whose lonely and cruel deaths send shrapnel of pain that pierce our hearts. These scar tissues and tears that mend and heal over time nevertheless leave permanent signatures and imprints for all times to come to serve us all well in recalling, honouring and remembering them. The incorruptible, incontestable and inviolable book of life has been written and remains open for all to read and learn from—without any *Index Expurgatorius* or *Index Librorum Prohibitorum*—to be good to each other and that goodness is not a unilateral happening or an inert state. Happiness need not be pursued, earned or destroyed as it is in the being and becoming but unhappiness is actively created by deliberate and wanton acts that deny humanity and are unfitting and unbecoming of it. We will be stronger and better as a people and as individuals when we insist that these two lives are never forgotten or allowed to be erased from however small a corner it may be that they indelibly occupy in the largesse and collectiveness of our minds and hearts.

If all that is left is impulse and action without thinking, without suffering, without belonging, without recognition and acceptance, do the remnants constitute a human being? Has the futility of Utopian realization by the self been replaced by the possibility of oblivion?

This tendency must be countered with a coherent counterforce of human (cultural) imperatives as a way of thinking and acting. Child rearing consists of civilizing instructions or *modus vivendi*; all human beings take the path from *I want* and *I can*, a realm concerned with the self only, to *Can I* and *Should I*, a realm of consideration and concern for others, as well as other's considerations in terms of acceptability or permissibility. Humanism is not about winning or losing; it is a set of values with a code of conduct which respects what it is to be human and acts as a buffer to the inhumanity of humans.

It has taken a lot of people and resources, working together across all walks of life, to build and perpetuate the 'candy of the mind and senses Colossus', and it will take just as much united effort to counter its pervasive and over-whelming effects. Only a national mandate can make available the people and resources required for this massive undertaking. To temper the influence of commercial globalization and mass media of the last few decades will require tackling the perplexing questions: *What do we learn from five millennia of experience as human beings?* and *Why don't we learn from our past?* The attributes of the learning curve from its initialization level, slope and turning points need to reflect the benefit of past memories and those of others so that it is not just a faithful rendering of a static curve, time and time again, destined for repetition of the same bends and twists.

To rely on Christianity or a particular religion as the sole cultural template, which in turn shapes family values, is tenuous, especially in an increasingly pluralistic and secular society. Instilling non-secular philosophic teachings which cultivate humanistic ethics is likelier to have greater staying power. These may one day lead to a religious faith rather than drilling in religious dogmas which can flounder even in seminary-like settings with rigourous theological discourses. The Divine can only be felt through enlightened not blind faith. The latter tends to result in its discard or replacement with ease at the slightest of doubt, slight of credibility or requirement of sacrifice, compromise and effort so that Bible stories and the like are categorized into just another genre of ho-hum fiction or non-fiction.

Dogmatic lessons are vulnerable and lead to extremes of fundamentalism or its wholesale abandonment: both cases displaying an excess of self-right-eousness or withdrawal, reflecting an absence of self which is subsumed, unformed or underdeveloped, lacking any sense of shame, balance or moderation. Unless religious belief is tightly interwoven into the fabric of daily life and anchored in a code of conduct, which is unlikely in a pluralistic society, it cannot propagate and sustain family and social or cultural values which become subservient to materialism and consumerism, habitually tossed aside and cast-off with passing trends.

Attendance and compliance to a religion can be compulsory at a young age, but with diminution and dissipation of moral capital and the waning of taboos, as well as the social, economic and political decline of religious influences in the context of increasingly global and pluralistic milieux, it is subject to rejection and repudiation at a later stage. Thus basing family values on a religious footing in a pluralistic society can be a rather sisyphean task: beliefs are discarded as the young reach their majority, and are increasingly unconvincingly and incompletely transmitted. The problem is compounded by the void created by a shriveling or absent non-secular tradition or duty-based philosophic foundation for daily living and virtuous life. One generation hoists the Ten Commandments up the pole; it is then lowered, trampled upon and disregarded, only to be again raised and lowered by each successive generation without ever reaffirming and reattaining its previous might or height.

There is no standardized test for attitude and self-knowledge: only the moment of truth. One can only attempt to instill a sense of duty and excellence and glimpse at manifestation of self-knowledge in the consideration, concern and care or degree of due diligence exercised in engagement with the other(s), including the natural world. This is not to confuse ignorance with innocence, indifference with tolerance, non-affiliation with independence, subservience with loyalty, civility with servility, knowledge for wisdom, spiritual journey for group therapy, blind faith for devotion and empowerment with enlightenment. Truth and its many manifestations germinate, compromise and emanate from within and flow in interaction with the other, depending upon the clarity of understanding of the relationship that is operational and the definition of the set. These relationships and definitions are taught and absorbed within the family and community through the transmission of the cultural code or language.

Good faith or goodness does not fall from above; it is not drummed in or innate; it is not bought off-the-shelf; it is not downloaded in modular bytes and snippets from some form of mass media; it is not given out for free from some external source. It is internally seeded and developed over a lifetime of learning and effort, finding reciprocity in kind as its sole and occasional reward. Even when it is not reciprocated, it does not sour and shrink but, rather, strengthens. It is an internal illumination that guides the way in shaping, strengthening and maturing the ego as it seeks harmony and completeness. Silence is not assent, consent or dissent, but it requires greater discipline and forbearance than to speak. It is preferable to incomplete sentences, linear sound bites, saying less than nothing, running around the bush and lying or beating a dead horse and wasting time. The portals to serenity, innocence and union are accessible through moral and intellectual cultivation for approaching and contributing to mindfulness and wisdom.

All that can interface or be represented by money are equally categorized, segmented, targetted and pickled to look for what's new and latest, what's the next big thing or illusion, and what's around the corner, and to be pre-occupied with what's in, what's edgy and on the cutting edge. Do the information highways open the portals of the individual or are they merely multi-channel, multi-platform and unblinking pipelines enabling the peddlers to hook, bait, gall, gull, and gut, neatly, efficiently, indiscriminately and profitably, whatever happens to be on the receiving end of the node or terminal, linked ubiquitously by a proliferation of personalized address devices and networks? The talk is about the edge or the thin end of the wedge and not much else so that what the wedge is, is irrelevant and immaterial, since it turns out to be and must necessarily be eminently replaceable and unworthwhile in order to feed, recycle and grow revenue systems. We get a lot of off-the-cuff riffraffs, cuts and openings (cosmetic markings, tattoos, holes and scars that signify nothing but more quid pro quo commercial transactions, entirely liberated from rites) without building up or remembering anything since they are uniformly short, shallow, threadbare and meaningless, or literally superficial and superfluous or indubitably forgettable. Hearts and minds remain untouched, unmoved and unchanged, becoming colder, slower and harder, as the seconds tick off and the clocks run out, unminded. Such a frenzy of activity or boredom creates pools of concentration with super-uppers and upper-hands for the winner-take-all machination of capitalism and super-downers, plugging and handicapping the free-flowing of diverse and divaricating organic energies. Like-sized and shaped, and equally loose and interchangeable nuts and bolts, gorge on debt or shortselling and leveraging off of time and relationships (selling their past, present and future), vertically, horizontally and democratically, supposedly for self-interest or some illusory and idealized future of no account.

If economics are all about self-interest, it behooves us to develop and invest in a self that can be differentiated, sustained and authenticated, along with an ability to clearly identify and articulate purpose, principle (standard), principal (organic system), and cumulative interest of our personal making, well-being and namesake, versus some mass illusions and labels of indeterminate prose, ethics and origin. Mass appeal and buy-in seem to suggest the greater affinity of bipedalism to bifurcating binarism of the reptilian brain rather than stepping up to the neocortical polymathic frontier of pluralism and informed decision-making to narrow and close the gaps between the evolving positive and the Mean. Such is the unease in the face of inevitable change and uncertainty, that doing nothing or donning rigid blinders for assured respite from suffering and refuge from learning to preserve the known and repeatable payoffs and scenarios, are increasingly desired and readily bought, against the slim and uncertain odds of success from incremental progress of gradualism and change. The marketplace of modernity abounds with user-friendly, tidy and disposable pacifiers, looks and killer-applications in astounding varieties and price ranges for every category of unintended consequences and inconsequential servers, clients, peepers and suckers, with democratization that levels off class, status and taste to usher in popularism or mass prejudice, perception, privilege and preference. Ladled on top of race, religion and real-estate, these open up and widen more cracks to serve those whose interests feast upon the drawing and quartering of the frenzied and fragmented many.

Spontaneity, originality and creativity are not what they are cut out to be by the masters of marketing jingoism but their reverse, as messages and images are carefully packaged to implant and elicit such reactions and notions. These happenings are designed to make people good consumers, believers and slaves to industries and doctrines. Why should lives be sacrificed for noble and utopian ideals that tend to clear-cut, objectify and mechanize lives? Surely, one should invest time and resources into areas where tutoring, mentorship and apprenticeship are necessary prequisites and not for what can be readily purchased, learned and observed on one's own time and steam. Money is not the sole measure nor motivator, but merely an impediment if one chooses to make it so or chooses an end which is entirely contingent upon it. The liberated, equalized and justified ego in a human form can buy, eat, rationalize, deny and replicate ad nauseum, but rarely does it get around to self-actualization or realization of its own potential, since such activities come without quantifiable costs and benefits or a clearly visible path and finish-line to a winners circle, economic or otherwise. Making something out of nothing has its rewards and making nothing out of something has its costs, but many highfaluting occupations and activities, oftentimes requiring credentials and membership in some fraternal and professional order to maximize income, deniability, insulation and protection, equally and consistently bypass what is, especially of individuality and of the times, for the sake of and as fodder for institutional precedents or hubris. Such orders and institutionalism are predisposed to not carry nor pull their own weight but predicated upon cornering benefits by yoking, befuddling, billing and burdening the many outside. When white-washing, hypocorism (pet names, kitschy monikers) and hypocrisy are the norm, does a culture, character or name exist other than as a marketing or academic concept, tool and term?

The more fundamental the political parties and their platforms become in harking back to the 'good old days' and the 'heritage of the founding fathers', the more they will continue to become marginalized, as the population base that can identify with this imagery will narrow. The political structure may allow for some disconnects between the will of the people and the will of those in power, but to the extent that politicians and political thinking become marginalized and not in sync with the electorate as a whole, they will become increasingly impotent to effect change. While current political struggle is internecine among established and entrenched Caucasian ethnic groups, changing population demographics will inevitably create ethnically defined political entities, exacerbated by the skewing of age profiles within these groups (a higher proportion of the young in non-Caucasian, compared to a higher proportion of the old in Caucasian groups), as well as the absolute increase in the over-sixty group overall (a generational divide). Struggles amongst people with similar ethnic and religious backgrounds pale in comparison with those between groups that have nothing in common, especially with regard to ethnicity and religion.

In a nation consisting mainly of culture of ones, the area and categories of overlapping interests between groups may become diminished or discrete, so that common cause becomes indefinable. In trying to appeal to an adequate cross-section of voters in order to formulate policies and effect change, or in trying to appeal to everyone, no one is appeased. The result is not merely the politics of difference but of disassociation, whereby there is no longer an exchange of views: the civil discourse and civic (as well as common) language disappears, and is replaced by unchallengeable, idiosyncratic dogmas. Even pluralism becomes untenable in this vortex of 'I-centrism'. One can be nostalgic for the past when times seemed simpler and when society seemed more uniform, but just like birth order, time-order is irreversible.

While there is much mention of family values and visual display of a model family (Caucasian) as a concept, there is an absence of specifics on what these values are. In cultures that have survived against great odds and retained much of their unique cultural identity in all the critical ways that matter to the belongers, there is a very strong sense of what a family is and how it functions. The ties that bind and the strength of the bond are determined by consanguinity in an expanding circle that originates with one's father and mother. The degree of these blood ties is well-defined, and appropriate behaviour, in both speech and manner to each member, is prescribed. It is ritualistic, inbred, and internally coherent within an individual and within the ever-widening circle of social relationships.

The social pressure exerted on non-conformity can be intense because the consequence can be expulsion and isolation from the group, a fate worse than death in many cultures. The family wants each of the members to respect his or her place, act accordingly and remain a belonger. No parents would wish their child to become an outcast and lead a life of exile. Without cultural imperatives of respect for the elder and filial piety, the young, who cannot appreciate the value of experience over knowledge nor their own mortality (life for many teenagers everywhere seems to be a never-ending series of do and dare), cannot grow up with a pro-social *modus vivendi*. Many prefer to park themselves at this stage of adolescence, way past the expiration of the meter. Adolescence is a stage in life representing a time of excess and excessiveness in self-indulgence and self-delusions. Traditional cultures discourage such obsessive preoccupation with the self, but in the U.S. it often ends up as a permanent state which is not disparaged or disdained but, rather, encouraged and celebrated.

All cultures seem to share this recognition of the family (kinship, tribe, clan) and the human need to belong to a group. While this has been the case for much of human existence, technology combined with a lack of cultural identity seems to be creating loners and outcasts (with arrested development at the stage of adolescence) at an unprecedented rate. There are severe social and political consequences of having such a large pool of loners. Who and how many are incarcerated? What does it say about a society that requires a Good Samaritan law when many cannot be bothered to help a stranger in need and prefer to turn a blind eye? Such hardening and shutting out of the heart can seep into one's attitude to family and friends in need. Is being a loner a desirable state for an individual? Would so many choose this path or just be simply allowed to drift into it if the consequences were known in advance or if there were adequate braking forces (cultural imperatives) which could prevent it from occurring—at least in the first 18 years?

How valid is the statement: *I am rich, therefore I am happy?* This is best demonstrated by comparing the baby boom (1946-1964) and the economic Depression generations. If anything demonstrates the relative non-importance of lots of money and the paramount importance of lots of extended family members and family time, this comparison should lay any doubts to rest. Ties of kinship and shared times (memories) are incommensurable with money; a society that drives the care givers to a pay cheque lifestyle needs to examine its priorities seriously, as it trades what is invaluable and irreplaceable for incremental monetary gain, all under the guise of equality.

If all relevant issues centre on the pocketbook, and voters are seen as only caring about their pocketbook, is this then to be the sole purview of the politician? That is, if an issue does not affect the pocketbook, it's not an issue. If it adversely affects it, fix it or ditch it. If it positively affects it, support it and expand it. To rely on the forces of capitalism as a means of social cohesion, with money as the glue, is precarious at the best of times, but positively delusional as the disparity between the rich and poor becomes ever wider, precisely due to the nature of capitalism. The fact that an increasing percentage of households now participate in the stock market still does not outweigh or balance this concentration of wealth and power. Most investors or speculators have no impact on corporate decision-making processes of any kind at any level, being structurally locked out of the system. Holding a tiny percentage of shares does not give rise to any economic power nor increase participation in the economy nor influence formulation of economic policies, all of which are cornered by vested interests. The liability to shareholders is subordinate to all other debts.

The goal of corporate decisions is not what one would expect (e.g., maximizing returns to shareholders, maximizing profits, increasing efficiency, or gaining market share), but is entirely in servitude and servility to the corporate power structure and its interests. If shareholders' interests are at best secondary, the very notions of public interest and doing the right thing (as opposed to a *do it right the first time* mantra) are vague concepts.

But the illusion of linkage between capitalism, as an efficient market theory, and its practice, as consistent with its theoretical underpinnings and goals, is created and maintained with increasing fervour and determination by both the perpetrators and victims, as illusion and reality part company. What feeds this need to believe that abstract theories, as complex, sophisticated, sexy and appealing as they are, can somehow mitigate, if not eliminate, the greed and avarice of sellers and buyers in practice?

Politics and politicians have become insipid and banal in a society whose cultural identity seems even more so. The debate centres on the same perpetual questions: How much centralization and decentralization? How much individual liberty and social stability? How much equality and plurality? But no one bothers to ask: What can we do about a lack of a national cultural identity?

Do children just provide political sound bites and tax deductions? Is a picture of a family a tried-and-true political tool, to be hauled out to humanize a politician with warm and fuzzy overtones of sentimentality and nostalgia that fade in and out during the time-outs between the overriding concerns around the economy, investment strategies, retirement planning and entertainment programming? Are the welfare of children, educational reform and family values just political chestnuts? The concerns are as superficial as the lack of specific cultural, social and family values, definitions and examples.

Since political sound bites keep quoting from the Declaration of Independence and Bill of Rights, as if they were a cultural standard bearers of some sort, their favourite words and documents can stand some scrutiny. How comprehensive or democratic is a document solely generated for and signed by 56 male Caucasian immigrants or their male descendants without any input or assent from the indigenous, imported and female representatives? The Declaration is a political manifesto, penned in haste, to forge a political alliance among 13 colonies that did not necessarily share the same goals or have any sense of brotherhood, a most un-WASPish sentiment in any case. It is not an in-depth scholarly work of the first water, and has more in common with the communist manifesto and ideals than capitalism. Was it based on a popular mandate with proportional representation among the 13 colonies/countries or was it forged in a heady atmosphere of revolution when quick resolve is all, and follow-up planning inconsequential and irrelevant? For a revolutionary, like a gambler, it is the act of throwing the die, not necessarily the outcome, that holds the greatest sway and thrill. It does not even reflect any *zeitgeist*, the popular sentiment or prevailing attitude of a people, since each state was a country unto itself. They certainly were not unaware of slavery and the daily transactions in human flesh. They certainly were aware of their individual stature and pecking order, showing reticence and deference of cooperation as well as displaying rivalry and enmity of competition with decorum and all the *de rigueur* of the times.

Confucianism may seem restrictive, but at least it recognizes the contribution and role of women in family and society. Buddhism is not gender-biased or driven, and Taoism is literally universal. These do not endow any inalienable rights or attributes to man, but only address the right ways to be human in the public, natural and metaphysical contexts. These non-deistic philosophies, in both their temporal and spiritual texts, are not concerned with rights, attributes or entitlements, but only with what is right in an ethical context and the many rites of passage required for achieving the status of an adult human being as well as for existence in a natural organic world.

A priori assertions are not self-evident truths and clash with not only empiricism, quite in vogue in the mid-18th century, but also with common sense. Where is reverence for God in determining specific attributes for the 'created', and are these so absolute and certain as to be 'inalienable' even by God? This seems to be an underhanded display of vanity, arrogance, hypocrisy and conceit on par with the motto of the British royalty: *Dieu et mon droit* (God and my right). Such references are hard to find in any texts of ancient cultures, even in their most sacred or radical books. When so many political goals are seen as inalienable rights, they quickly become equated with entitlements so that they are not only supposed to be gained without any effort whatsoever, but having these rights entail no gratitude or appreciation, becoming just so much gibberish.

There are also many broadsides traded between various factions engaged in the imbroglio of abortion and gun debates who like to bandy very selective and non-contextualized words from the Bible, Constitution, Bill of Rights and Declaration. Instead of resorting to retreads and recitations, they might be better served to consider what constitutes a genuine person or human being beyond 'life' as a standalone word. All cultures have reverence for life, but what constitutes becoming a human being meriting social acknowledgment requires meeting quite a list of specific qualifications without any entitlement to rights of any sort, except that of belonging.

Those Caucasians and others who prefer to remain unwaveringly infallible and close-minded should seriously reflect on both their historical and current attitudes and conducts with respect to exactly who they consider as their fellow human beings with all these inalienable rights, since few other groups have excelled at mass dehumanization as they have managed to thus far. The people of Caucasian descent are a part of humanity but the agenda, means and ends dictated by their power élites are increasingly at odds with the rest of the world and oftentimes decried as evil, bullyism and bulverism[46] or

46. "**Bulverism** A common phenomenon in argument, where an opponent's case is reduced to causes and therefore dismissed, as in 'You only say that because you are a woman.' Psychological interpretations are particularly prone to this fallacy—for instance, the view that

continued

in diplomatic terms, unilateral and isolationist. In what other country but the U.S. is there such an outcry and need for hate crimes legislation at the federal level? Do comparisons to a long list of countries such as Iraq, Tibet, Indonesia, the Middle East, the Balkans, Russia, China, numerous African states, with their unique histories, but many sharing a common historical perspective which points to the same group of non-indigenous culprits for having laid the careful foundation for the on-going slaughter and mayhem, provide any saving grace in equality or disparity in degrees? From the comfort and insularity of mental and physical distance, assuaged by collective amnesia and perfunctory mass media propaganda, this group continues to profit from the exploitation of natives (cheap labour) and debt-building to ensure poverty into posterity, while evangelizing and extolling the virtues of Christianity, Capitalism and Democracy to the poor and ignorant masses— and topping it all off, further profits by selling the technology for killing and torture. Why does one group represent such danger for all others? Are hate crimes discriminatory since they mostly target and victimize one group of perpetrators, the WASPs?

Few other groups seem to have been endowed with such lack of ties of land or a sense of origin, whether they are factually borne out or captured in traditions and rites, as this one heterogeneous group. Rare is a culture that seems to produce individuals with such a unique inability to manage relationships with the other, perpetuating myths of superiority and ethnocentrism based upon colour, money and terminating power or killer applications. The ability to eviscerate life is proportional to its tendencies to impose its unique categorizations and generalizations while bypassing individuality: individualism is valued but not individuals. While all religious texts convey

belief in God is wish-fullfillment. Naturalism, discussed in [C.S. Lewis's] *Miracles*, reduces all thinking and thus beliefs to causes, and in the process eliminates the validity of its own truth claims.

'Bulverism' is Lewis's name for this widespread view, a view that typically explains why a person is wrong before demonstrating that a person is wrong. This view marks the death of reason. Lewis points out, 'Either we can know nothing or thought has reasons only, and no causes.' Much of *Miracles* consists of a sophisticated rebuttal of this attitude. His essay, 'Bulverism, or, The Foundation of 20th Century Thought,' can be found in *God in the Dock, Undeceptions,* and *First and Second Things.*"
Collin Duriez, *The C.S. Lewis Encyclopedia*, (Crossing Books, 2000), p. 38.

the same messages of brotherhood and unity, with endless repetitions and admonitions, the complexity and difficulty of implementation and execution is proportional to and reflected by the massive volumes of text devoted to explanations, debates and examples, without much tangible result. This is largely due to loss of credibility and erosion of moral capital, both within and without, as more entertaining distractions compete for increasingly shorter attention spans. A human mind seems to come ill-equipped with a propensity towards mindfulness but, rather, with a propensity towards mindlessness. Life is hard and demanding and there is no room for falsity, especially that of false and qualified compassion.

The Declaration is appealing because it sounds so simple and reasonable, and well it should, being a product of the age of reason with a liberal dash of Romantic individualism combined with the cutting of the Gordion knot of the Church in a flourish of the pen. In considering this impressive document with the benefit of some hindsight (which more often than not is as good or bad as foresight):

1. Life does not unfold in the 'age of reason', but from the body to mind to heart and perhaps to spirit with priorities and precedents which may not be at all reasonable. Human beings, like all organisms, adapt, evolve, decay and regenerate, all through processes in which reason does not seem to have a starring role. People do not procreate, create, live, destroy, kill, die and bury for reason, with reason or reasonably. (A 'Pascal's Wager': The probability of satisfactorily reasoning out the why's of life is remote, but it is more likely to be approached by understanding how to live through mindfulness or the Way of least harm).

2. Romanticism was and remains a reaction against rationalism, empiricism, utilarianism and industrialism. It starts off with extreme individualism and progresses on to the destruction of individuals when its net is politically cast, and cast over nationalistic ethnocentrism. So, combining these elements is rather like a brew of water and oil, whichever of the two rises to the top at suitable occasions.

3. The Church has been separated from the State on paper, but all signatories being proper WASPs, they could not but make reference to God. In Western cultures, the moral and ethical contexts flow from the Church, and however fine a document the Declaration may be,

without these contexts it cannot be conscripted to serve as a cultural template. Since religion has been excluded, wisely, due to its totalitarian tendencies and cult of personalities, along with an astoundingly cruel and bloody track record, once jettisoned, it cannot be allowed to seep back in.

But where to find and locate this ethical and moral context (or heart)? This is the dilemma and the reason for the Declaration of Independence, Bill of Rights and the Constitution, all taking on inviolable, sacred and holy mantles or non-secularity. People from all walks of life having walked in from different cultures and centuries, without these simple political words and taking all sides of all kinds of issues, invoke and chant the same snippy, snappy and empty words. No wonder the courts are backlogged when there are no fallback positions or alternatives, where all rights are absolute entitlements and people are equally endowed and armed with an ability to shout, scream, rant, rave and shoot. This is the 'shoot, take aim, get ready' mentality in all its glory.

These documents do not constitute and do not have the constituents for or pedigrees of moral and ethical heart because the political is more often than not a corruption, betrayal and inversion of the ways of the heart whereby means justify the end, as Machiavelli and the ancient book of war by the Chinese General Sun Tzu attest and allude to with some real experience, credibility and insight. Many such books are naturally adopted by the modern masters of the universe. Just as a saintly prostitute with a heart of gold is a fantasy, such a politician would be equally as unlikely but also undesirable in reality. Seeking ideals, ethics or morality in the realm of politics where means mean nothing and the end is all (say and do anything, just win at any cost) is to choose illusion over reality or mindlessness over mindfulness. Being perfect is not a human manifestation otherwise we would no longer be here. We seek a leader who will hold the centre and provide balance against polarization

But politicians, entertainers and prostitutes, in an age of the visual, need to package and peddle 'face' and 'face time' with measurable market value. The meaning of face in terms of virtue or virtuosity, which is independent of and transcends the visual form or one dimensional sensation, is forgotten and discarded. Many on both sides of the media divide become like Babbitt, Dorian Gray, Faust or Narcissus, obsessed with face as public physical presentation but without public virtue or inner beauty which degenerate and deform as the schism between the inner and outer face become unbridgeable until dismissed or leveled by the remote control or death. Vanity has been the subject of many epic stories as cautionary tales through the ages, but in vain.

Instead of an inner explosion of sensation in response to distilled and composed delivery of the complex and the many or the single and the simple, modern technology attempts at the same effect through one-dimensional excess with more digitized and louder sound systems and bigger and more pixilated pictures, along with faster play and discard mechanisms. In this impressive battery of sight and sound, the absence of content becomes not only imperceptible but irrelevant. Such a jetsam of audio and visual assault annihilates mindfulness. The pioneers, captains, leaders and visionaries of commerce mounted on mass media readily respond with a mount of choreographed standard sound bites accompanied by cued music and fuzzy visuals, mouthing: *oops, unintended consequences, old mate* or *we are benevolent entities satisfying consumer demand to the best of our abilities* or *there has been no definitive direct causal link or absolutely irrefutable proof scientifically established to warrant any cause for public concern.* In other words: don't even think about, let alone try to dam up any of our revenue streams.

The crowning achievement of commerce has been in the shaping of popular taste (expectations and standards) or the cult of the lowest common denominator which is therefore satisfied with the consumer products and services duly provided. The consumer is always in play in the box of positive capabilities which do not require any time or effort to cultivate and maintain, and thus are highly desirable attributes. This forms a nice, tight loop of self-satisfaction consisting of *what I like is easy to satisfy because what I like is the simple, quick and easy.* This gives much credence to the view that the evolutionary timeline of humans is a mere blink of an eye when compared to the age of the universe, making us essentially cave dwellers, still.

The declaration *I have a right to my life, liberty and equality* sounds like something an uncouth and rebellious teenager might fling at his parents. Indeed, Romanticism can be seen as a manifestation of the cult of testosterone-spiked and ignescent youth rebelling against death and decay. The combustibility of youth represented by all passion all the time, with no time for reasoning and reasonableness, is ignited and fanned to keep the fervour of any *ignis fatuus* (false light) movement going, which otherwise would fizzle and extinguish with a whimpering hiss under the dawning light of day or with common sense and stoic calm of experience and age.

The cult of youth can be found in many glorified, idealistic, dogmatic or extreme movements where death comes all too soon and inevitably, whether in combat, duel or suicide, without ever developing the ability or having an opportunity to know and understand the perspective of the many over an average life span. An uninformed and immature choice is made for certain 'noble' death over the uncertain ignoble life when the value and meaning of life itself is under-appreciated and undiscovered.

Romanticism did not invent the cult of youth. It merely gave an appealing label to a practice exploited by numerous polarized political and religious factions, tyrants, fanatics and zealots throughout the ages. They mobilized and converted the blind adolescent passions into blind allegiance by imparting an illusion of identity, acceptance and belonging to an exclusive and righteous group. None are as easy to propagandize as the young. Such a salient point is not lost on the captains of commerce, especially those within the mass media, who have commandeered this bandwagon, squeezing the religious and political factions into a corner, to carry on this traditional practice of dehumanization, exploitation and indefinite extension of youth and adolescence so that no one escapes its net. Beauty, a subject of numerous philosophic discourse in so many cultures, has become as one-dimensional as the word itself.

While revolutionaries, revolutions and political manifestos have come and gone through Korea's long and turbulent history, many of them dwarfing the American Revolution in egotism, heroism, sacrifice, ideas and bloodshed in lives and duration, the cultural context has always remained, before, during and after the storms. The American Revolution remains an *idée fixe* because political detachment from Britain also severed any cultural context of which there were but a few straws to clutch given a pluralistic immigrant population consisting of mostly economic refugees from their respective home cultures, especially those inundated by totalitarian religious persecutions, but with an equally firm grip on their own totalitarian dogmas.

Political identity is all that remains, polarizing at one extreme and ephemeral at the other as isms, causes, ideas and issues come and go. Some seek to bolster their political identity in the refuge of religious dogmas, resulting in even greater polarization and cultural void, further severing the ties that bind as if that were possible. There is still no *zeitgeist*—only apathy, zealotry and a lot of questions looking for closure subsumed in the world of appetite and the material. It is not a case of the tail wagging the dog, it is all tails without a body, or the tale of the five blind mice, or the game of pin-the-tail on the donkey when no one knows what a donkey is let alone where it is.

Politics becomes not only dysfunctional but obsolete in this milieu, void of cultural context, common sense and sensibility. The purpose of Mao's cultural revolution was to create a cultural vacuum in which totalitarian Might (be it political, religious or economic) could suck up all the oxygen, ensuring that no further revolutions could ever take hold in the literal and symbolic absence of the heart and soul of a people. Monistic cults and movements harness the industry of the masses by enslaving, exploiting and sustaining their ignorance, insecurity, injunctions (dogmas), ineluctability, ineptitude and intolerance of the others in terms of peoples, texts and questions i.e., other realities. These are distinct and separate from illiteracy that does not impede or correlate with cultural or other types of intelligence or illumination. They suppress and impede venturing beyond the absolute infallibility of the nanod outlook and the singular book: they represent totalitarian and undemocratic state and stasis of the mind, or mind block and lock typical of blockheads. Much the same can be said for various totalitarian waves which aim to cultivate an atmosphere of amorality where family bonds and moral compasses are rendered irrelevant and disarrayed, resulting in a sense of aloneness and powerlessness of the individual.

Money and degrees, unfortunately, are not the panacea for these shortcomings. They can open doors if one is prone to rigorously make certain choices in a milieu where liberty involves context, effort, discipline, study and compromise. Otherwise and oftentimes, money and degrees merely compound and entrench these obstacles, which are equally amplified by vanity (a virulent form of self-esteem), feeding and fed by a need for a sense of superiority, enslaved by pride and desire, ensuring no dissipation of appetite, but rather the reverse. In lieu of emancipation, the field of vision narrows thereby attenuating the range of choices, tilting towards fatalism or impotence of self-knowledge, -formation, -development or -identity.

How do we come to terms with what is equal, equivalent and identical? In the answer lies the key to co-existence that begins and ends with categorizations and set definitions which runs the gamut as great as the physical and non-physical spectrum of human and non-human beings, ultimately reducible to one. The need to differentiate by individuals is fed by the vices that metastasize into apathy as the pursuit of knowledge is displaced by preservation of ignorance by the aficionado of relativism and bulverism. With much practice these isms render self-knowledge, self-interest and self-identity moot in a tightening noose of tautologies. The transition from 'I don't care about anything' to 'nothing matters' is effortless whereas learning or exploration of the unknown begins with self-knowledge and liberty from the self. Our skin is only a border bounded by our own illusion and imagination in solvency and diffusion wherein matter and principle can become light that eludes binary categorization.

Thus the nurturing and the education of the young takes on greater urgency and importance, requiring a curriculum that emphasizes the development of mindfulness along with philosophy lessons to open the mind to a range of ideas and a diversity of relationships that serve to illuminate the process of unfolding and becoming human. With globalization and mass media consolidation, this applies to all individuals in all places, since very few can be said to be exempt from these twin influences of cultural destruction or homogenization.

To the extent that culture is a way of life and an intrinsic part of one's identity, (who I am, in the context of ancestry) and that diversity of ethnicity brings its own version of ethics, a wide variety of lifestyles and languages for communications and entertainment, the formal effort to inculcate common goals and values will necessarily be limited but, at the same time, even more critical. Without commonality along at least one dimension of what being an American (or citizen in an ethnically diverse country) means, there can be no common identification and belonging. Even if only fractional overlap of goals and values can be achieved, this is still a most worthwhile endeavour. It only needs to be sufficient to maintain civic discourse in a common civic language, to impart a sense of civic duty.

Fear and apprehension of the unknown imply some degree of respect or awe, but disdain and denigration imply an a priori judgement of superiority of what is known. The latter reaction is associated with blind prejudice, as a judgement has been rendered without any basis for comparison. It is simply an affirmation of a fixed position: *What I know must be superior to what I don't know or understand.* The primary purpose of education is not simply to increase knowledge of facts and knowledge of the topical, but to instill an attitude of open-mindedness, intellectual discipline, patience towards the unfamiliar, either intuitively (an immediate or innate understanding) or empirically (demonstrable to the five senses), in order to reduce judgements without merit. The secondary but equally important purpose of education is to teach choice-making skills: that not all needs can be satisfied and that appropriate trade-offs need to be made. The needs of people may be different, so that satisfying one may mean denial of another; one cannot satisfy all of one's desires; there are limitations to liberty, equality and justice.

The ultimate moment of truth and test of character is in the encounter with the unknown; the outcome will be determined by the attitude which has been shaped by previous such encounters in training. Gaining some control over one's emotions is in no way equivalent to denial or suppression but, rather, quite the reverse: it increases the freedom of choice as well as the range of choices. Whether life, work or study is a drag or not is largely a function of attitude and intellect which can picture consequences and outcomes. What is required is not a mindless, sunny disposition, but an engaging mind which can engage in transformational activity when pried loose from transactional preoccupation with the 'I'.

Cultural identity, even in traditional cultures where extended families live together, tends to be transmitted to the young in an unsystematic and unstructured method in tandem with cultural pride and superiority. Cultural identity is such an intrinsic and yet pervasive part of one's being in terms of ancestry, heritage, language, values, food, dress and mannerisms, that it is taken for granted and not questioned or thought about a lot. How it is transmitted is just a 'way of life' and happens without much volition or design by those who are engaged in its transmission. In modern cultures, with a variety of definitions of family unit and family life, there is even more randomness in how and what cultural values are transmitted by talks and examples of model behaviour. The dominant information input is from the entertainment media and peers. No matter how incompletely or haphazardly a cultural identity is formed, the sense of pride and superiority is still very much attached, with *my way* or *our way* evidenced in behaviour.

In the U.S. there are many fuses for igniting and exciting divisiveness because of its innumerable ethnic groups and types of households, each with its own language, customs and manners. Additional fuel is provided by a proliferation of ethnically targeted and market segmented TV channels (even from the home country, via satellite), web sites, videos, CDs and publications in many languages. Thus it is natural that people cluster around what is familiar and shared, including English-speaking Caucasian groups. These internally created borders of the mind spill over into society when vested interests and inalienable rights collide. Ethnic pride, regardless of association with a traditional, modern or self-constructed culture, exacerbates the divisiveness when wide economic disparity and racial prejudice are thrown in. The consequences for the mind, body and spirit can be equally alienating and attenuating from diversity.

These fault lines in U.S. society will always exist, and unless some shared goals and values are instilled in the 12 compulsory years of schooling, there are no other opportunities available to counter fractious fractionalization. The formal effort will be limited by the time (hours per week of study devoted to human goals, values, conduct), but this effort will be critical in defining at least one common axis of what being an American means at the widest common denominator.

The older generation, instead of being isolated into retirement homes and communities as if they were another species, need to be integrated back into the daily life of the young, thereby remaining in view and familiar. Current trends have resulted in creating not only cultural fault lines, but also age fault lines; because the elders look, talk and act differently, or are rarely seen, they seem of another culture or 'alien'. This too is sustained by the mass media, populated by youth and beauty. The elders of society have always played an essential role in the transmission of cultural identity through their great wealth of experience and knowledge, especially that of the family history. Society needs to assess the role of the elderly beyond viewing them as unattractive, unwanted and unwarranted burdens, because ultimately respect of the elder is not only self-serving, but in the interest of social wellness. Consumerism, which dictates 'out with the old, in with the new', has crossed over into commoditization of people: how much progress has really been made since slavery was politically corrected?

The elderly and retired have also been conditioned by the media in their pursuit of youth, beauty and leisure activities. Rather than living up to their own standards, they have grouped through voluntary segregation to compete in their own beauty pageants and scoring events (score with the opposite sex, keep score of who is ahead or behind, who is a winner or loser), or just to hang out and do their own thing. While pursuit of their own interests after a lifetime of dedication to those of their family's is unquestionable, their survival into old age is a testament to their choice-making and parenting skills, which they can teach the young by sharing their own experiences.

Working part-time or volunteering at a daycare centre, kindergarten or after-school activities can be as rewarding for the elders as it is enriching for the younger generation. The recent trend is to build senior and retirement communities in proximity to a college campus to fulfill the desire for continuing education and safety concerns of the elders. By locating facilities for children in proximity as well, the elders can not only continue with their learning but also tend and teach the younger members of society.

What is missing in the educational curriculum is subjective or possessive cultural studies as a subject. There is literature, history, language, etc., specific to a country, but no subject of 'my culture' on its own. Such a course would help in explaining what the values, beliefs and practices are, together with the ethical implications and rationale. In countries with a Ministry or Department of Culture, the task is not simply to preserve the relics of the past, but to ensure that all aspects of culture are systematically and comprehensively transmitted through the education system. With homogenization of the mass media (economic and content consolidation) and increased relocation, reassignment and reconstitution challenging indigenousness (e.g., moving into another neighbourhood or country, from homemaker to pay cheque earner, or to a new family structure or composition), the process of enculturation has fundamentally changed, or in many instances, become extinct. The time when one's cultural paradigm was all around in the environment and used to be unnoticeable, like breathing in and out, is passé.

What makes the effort to combat and counter the destruction of the planet and other species seem so futile? This can be easily demonstrated by listening to a group debate on hunting. It usually ends in a stalemate because of value differences and disinterest or disdain impeding any consensus. The common mantras bandied about are: *My opinion is the only valid one and of value to me/Compromise signifies defeat/The conflict is always me against you.* There is no interest in a meeting of the minds and there is no counter to moving beyond fixed positions because values are held to be totally subjective and equally valid. It is an endless loop of conflict since self-serving purpose justifies the volleys of : *I'm right and you have no right to deny me my pleasure/I going to starve and die if I don't hunt/The thrill of the hunt justifies killing/These animals need culling as they are a social nuisance or economic threat to my way of life.* If the mind-set cannot move, there is no way forward. A transactional mind is a digital mind composed of binary evaluations, and anything that cannot be force-fitted into this tidy scheme is refused entry or denied or destroyed.

If individuals are not educated about how they fit into the social fabric and are not taught compassion, tolerance and compromise from an early age, but are instead left literally alone and to their own devices, to fill up and grow up under random influences and self-constructs with unique neurological wiring, is the end result (anti-social behaviour, suicide and/or homicide) so surprising and unpredictable? Not only are the results of such self-constructed individuals dysfunctional in the broad social context, but the true insidiousness and danger lie with the self-perpetuating and self-affirming features associated with pride of creation and ownership.

The only sure answer to this problem is that there is no universal panacea, and effort should not be directed at a total solution of some kind. The answer is not uniformity and indoctrination: it is to educate and foster an understanding of what it is to be a human being, what human values are, and why they are essential by making full use of available knowledge to teach all of the essential requirements for bearing and rearing of the young. To the extent that human beings are not totally wired-up at birth, with substantial increase in brain mass and new neurological connections made after birth, with the greatest gain up to four years of age but continuing throughout life, the greater the burden as well as opportunity of a cultural identity to mini-mize the randomness and arbitrariness of the wiring process. How one is taught to behave, through feedback and by example, affects how one thinks and feels.

The debate cannot carry on endlessly, with fragmented sound bites tossing around the word 'culture' (e.g. consumer culture, disposable culture, gun culture, culture of violence, clique culture, teen culture, music culture, culture of blame, media culture, etc.) without appreciating what culture usually means in the context of the entire country. This term defines a people by their common history and heritage, language, customs, values and behaviours. How does this term apply to the U.S. where none of these are held in common, especially in the context of its population profile of the next millennium? The U.S. can define for itself a culture of humanity because this is the only platform on which any consensus is possible. This can be the focus of a truly collective effort to counter the growing cultural vacuum or at least can have the chance of succeeding against the permanent occupation by the culture of one and the mass media, characterized by randomness and arbitrariness.

To insist that parents can and should cope with their children, with the help of their community and church groups (i.e. keep the status quo), invites serious questioning as to the vested interests and sanity of the proponents of this basically do-nothing approach. What chance do even the most caring and diligent of parents stand against the armed-to-the-teeth onslaught of the media juggernaut, juxtaposed with the modern phenomena of fragmentation of the extended family and community?

This Acquired Identity Deficiency Syndrome needs to be countered with practical guidelines for parents and dynamic involvement by the educational system; the custodian and the depository of all the hopes and dreams of the society. Surely, the purpose of philosophy is to make people think; there is no shortage of philosophy teachers who are uniquely qualified and yet unem-ployed, under-employed or under-appreciated in all the universities and communities throughout the country. Teaching a classroom of children a course in Ethics could become a philosophy student's graduation requirement. Philosophy professors could supplement their income, gain experience in real life, and contribute to the community in a practical manner by teaching in Grades 1 to 12 or even at kindergartens and daycare centres. What could be more enriching and give more job satisfaction than to teach the skill of thinking to the choice-makers of tomorrow—those who will be making more life-altering and life-significant decisions than any other segment of the population?

There is no cure-all, only a consensus that a united effort is required, with the attendant trade-offs by individuals to let go of some of their individuality (or rather the reverse) for that of being human and to counter the seductive pull of some clichéd individuality which cannot be legislated away. Resources need to be pooled and directed back to the individual because this is the frontier of all cultural engagement, where life is not a level playing field, but where the outcome is determined by the skill with which one navigates, endowed by the power of choice and the possibility of choosing wisely.

No society is free of aberration and no society can eradicate it. A society can only try to minimize aberration through checks and balances to minimize the fall-out of collateral or peripheral damage. There is no room for copping out, with exhaustive listing of the unintended consequences, in search of the perfect solution. There appears to be a correlation between the misery index and prevalence of unconstrained and non-contextual individuality.

Without discipline (not of the regimental, coercive and repressive sort, but of self-control, understanding of one's nature, and acknowledgement of perspectives other than one's own), there can be no patience. Without patience, learning becomes an insurmountable challenge. Discipline and patience enable greater effort, as well as tenacity. Cultural imperatives imply a higher authority and set up a mentorship model to calibrate in the young an attentive and respectful mind-set towards one's elders and teachers.

Discipline of any nature, but especially of the mind, cannot be fostered without respect for authority. A young mind is tuned into one type of learning until about four years of age, in order to establish the 'I'. A transition to a different type of learning is required, from just *I want* to having to explain *why*, which is a substantial jump into the realm of rationalization requiring contextual thinking before and beyond the 'I'. This is what happens through the process of increasing socialization and education beyond the confines of the family and the security of unconditional love. Not only is a great deal of relevant information input and a logical way of thinking necessary, but so is recognition of others who may have different opinions or be different. This jump is similar to traversing the gaps between knowing what to do, committing to do and actually doing. 'Walking the talk' is a formidable challenge of integrity.

The tragedy of being human is that human beings, while endowed with so much intellectual capacity and capability, for the most part do not really want to think much beyond just *doing as I please* and *getting what I want*. Therefore, cultural imperatives become ever more important in guiding behaviour, which in turn shapes the attitudes formed in the mind toward minimizing the friction that is inevitable if everyone insists on exerting his or her will. It is *I want, therefore I am*, compared to *I think, therefore I am*. The goal of the cultural imperative is to establish and satisfy *I communicate and belong, therefore I am*.

Ancient cultures (e.g., Egyptian, Persian, Greek, Jewish, Indian, Chinese, Nordic, Celtic, Teutonic) which have endured through millennia of strife, slaughter and enslavement with their extended family structure and values largely intact, share similarities. They include reverence, rites, registers and rituals to: (1) record and integrate cumulative and collective knowledge in text; (2) observe birth, marriage and death; (3) mark passage into majority status; (4) confer special status on teachers and elders; and (5) commemorate ancestors, preserve and honour lineage and Nature. Each culture's (non-Gregorian) calendar regulates and regularizes the timing, type and duration of offerings and homages with specific accoutrement, texts, foods, accessories, symbols and sounds within the home as well as in public settings. The clothes, foods, music and text are not the latest and greatest in fashion, but reflections of dynamic private and public history. The practices are bound and embedded upon duty ethics, humility and self-cultivation for the purpose of identity substantiation and sustenance through recognition, affirmation and understanding of interminable relationships with the family, tribe and Nature.

This is in contrast to the work ethics (where ethics exist at all) of modernity related to the purpose of making money. As family structures devolve or evolve, the rites of culture or the enculturation process fall through the cracks of the shattered vessel, uncaught and unnoticed, in a milieu of I-centrism. The social conscience and consensus fractures widen, deepen and extend the fault lines. Through these amplifying faults fall the young and the old as the pool of retiring teachers and elders grows while the pool of graduating parents shrinks. Compromise, collaboration and complementarity are cloaked in negativity as the cult of the idiolect dissects, neuters, perverts, converts and inverts the seven virtues and seven vices as listed on page 86. Instead of self-exertion, all that remains is self-assertion.

There are only two critical time periods when education by parents and teachers is mandatory: birth to preschool and then kindergarten through Grade 12. From a public policy standpoint, the only forum in which the state can effectively operate is the school system. It is the only opportunity to teach what it means to be human, with humanizing values. These 12 years offer the one chance to influence how a life will be lived, with twenty-five to thirty hours a week of formal education counterbalancing a lifetime of countless hours spent watching TV or engaged in other forms of entertainment.

This means that minimum and sufficient choice-making and parenting skills, humanizing values and behaviour must first be determined at their widest common denominator and taught in the 18-year window of maximum opportunity, when a 'captive' audience is available (the same captive audience that is courted by commercial and media interests, and prized as much as it is priced). It is not so much a case of who is minding the children, as what is first taking hold of their minds and therefore affecting all that follows. Since all children are potential parents and will make potentially significant choices, it only makes sense to instruct them in these essential learned skills in a systematic manner, until they reach 18 years of age.

Parents must be educated to value all children and not just their own, because all life is equally valuable. There can be peace when parents love their children more than they love themselves or hate their enemies. Parents cannot parent properly if children are viewed only from the parents' perspective and as a means of fulfilling their own needs. Children need to be respected as unique individuals with their own destinies; it needs to be clear that parents are not owners, buddies or friends, but custodians of the future.

It is not uncommon to see parents reliving their childhood through their children, pining with nostalgia for those innocent and carefree days or rediscovering their joy of living. How many parents wish they could be kids again or that their children could remain kids always? How many parents act like kids and refuse to grow up? How many parents assuage their own sense of loneliness by living vicariously through their children or treating them as friends? What kind of adult examples are being set and what effect do messages like *just be natural* or *just be yourself* or *just please yourself* convey? Is letting it all hang out such a good alternative to natural inhibitions, which may be a way of the mind hinting at a need for caution and discretion? Is reticence (not repression or suppression) so undesirable a trait to foster? Which of these characteristics are pro-social and address the needs of the young and prepare them for adulthood? Does liberty translate into libertine?

All babies and children appear adorable, but this does not excuse complacency in their educational needs. One only needs to walk through any major city or look at pictures of those who are incarcerated and remember that all of these people were, at one time, adorable babies. Love really is not enough. Children also need rules, discipline, consistency and stability; most importantly, they must see and feel consistency between what they are taught and what they experience, and they must feel that they are never alone. In this regard, every adult has a responsibility to set a good example. The term *in loco parentis* suggests that there are many other members of society who have parental obligations and responsibilities towards the young, and that this function is by no means the sole prerogative and exclusive domain of those who bear direct responsibility. Children represent the future of society and the world at large, with implications for the many not just the one and the family unit. One teaches a child by explanation, persuasion and most of all, by example (children excel at mimicry). One does not teach by the exercise of non-contextual authority and power, unless one is aiming to teach how arbitrary their uses are.

The most powerful transmitter of cultural identity is the family, and therefore the parents themselves need to have a clear and consistent understanding of their own cultural identity (inter-marriages or adoption require a selection and conformity to one, at least for four to 18 years; if the child is interested, he will explore more on his own when he is old enough, with initialization and deep roots in one paradigm). The greatest lesson and challenge of life is to know that you can't have, do and be everything you want. To keep searching for unconditional love is not being able to admit the uniqueness and preciousness of parental (biological and adoptive) love.

This is challenging since the three paramount concerns of life in modern societies are sex, love and marriage, in the individualistic and economic contexts of equality (i.e. score keeping: how to make the least effort to get the most benefit), instead of duty, responsibility and commitment, in the context of family (i.e. child-rearing: making the best effort for family wellness). There is a delusion maintained that equality and marriage can exist in tandem when in fact equality, with its implied quantifications in dollars, timesheets, various forms of score keeping and to-do lists, etc., represents the antithesis of coupling into infrangible unity. To try and measure commitment is an exercise in futility, and the very attempt reflects a society in the grip of unbridled capitalism where everything needs to be quantified, equalized, commoditized, dollarized and given proper valuation for trading and trade-offs. How many ways can prostitution be redefined? This is simply trying to force a piece of the puzzle to fit into a space of incompatible dimension. Any relationship, whether personal or professional, simply requires one to try one's best to progress and move forward in development, without keeping score of how much is enough, deserved or owed, or whether there is a fair exchange, from a subjective and arbitrary point of view. By holding back from making the best effort in favour of just enough or as little as possible, potential gains, material or otherwise, cannot ever be realized. This is clearly evident in studying promotions within organizations which reflect less merit than effort made to get along and ahead.

Sex has become an overriding end as a recreational and vocational function rather than a procreational one. Love is laminated with sex and vice versa in the consumer marketing blitz, and increasingly viewed by those who buy into the message from the perspective of, and in the form of, fairy tales ending with 'they lived happily ever after', with almost a deliberate avoidance of the continuous diligence required (hard work and effort), the seemingly endless cycles of ups and downs, or any attempt to delve into or explain daily life with its endless challenges and lessons to be learned. A good example of this is the endless recycling of the Hollywood version of *Romeo and Juliet*, which lifts and peddles the sexy parts played by sexy stars as some kind of glorification of sex and death for the sake of true love. Love is portrayed as the be all and end all, when real life informs partners and parents that love is not enough, and that although it is necessary, it is by no means sufficient against the test of time. By lopping off the beginning and end, squaring the circle, and diminishing or deleting other parts, the comprehensiveness of context which would suggest otherwise is skipped over. This is a story of willful, much indulged adolescents who cannot take no for an answer, but must have what they want at all costs. As a result, they cause irreparable and irreversible harm not only to themselves, but to those who care for and about them, with the unleashing of sexual and violent forces. The key line to recall and remember is at the end of this fiction: "All are punished." Truth appears mundane and dull, compared to the iridescence of illusions.

Finally, marriage is viewed by many as a means to achieving personal goals of independence, security and happiness within a legal commitment. Parents and elders may sometimes be invited, involved or informed, but rarely for the purpose of seeking, earning and securing their blessing and approval of the union symbolizing eternity. A marriage ceremony is now notable for its personalization, with incorporation of individualized show elements. It no longer is a commitment of honour and an affirmation of lifetime belonging to the clan. Kinship no longer matters or counts for much. It is merely a matter of self-satisfaction, divorced from the rearing of the young and intimate incorporation of the other's perspective as an ultimate affirmation of the maturity of the self into selflessness. What kind of person, after all, would place his/her interest above that of his or her spouse and offspring or make less than his or her best effort in the interest of the family?

As sex in the mass media becomes ever more pervasive, sex and sexuality are being driven down further into childhood, with the education curriculum including these subjects at an ever younger age. The way to counter inappropriate sex is not through sex education as a stand-alone. If the sex drive is a biological drive to procreate, then sex education without the attendant teaching of the value of life and the responsibilities and skills needed for nurturing and rearing the young is incomplete and meaningless for both genders. The more complex, demanding, and time-consuming the process of nurturing and rearing the newborn to maturity—the fewer the inherent or inborn parental skills and the greater the need for an extended family or group for the child's proper or adequate social and physical maturation.

As human babies need such intensive care, both physically and emotionally, and since they are not born with an innate sense of ethics and parenting skills, the need for teaching these skills as a survival imperative is in direct inverse correlation with the demise of the extended family and diminution of the cultural paradigm: what it takes to survive and what constitutes quality of life in the modern world involve more than scavenging and foraging for food. The ability to have sex is not a milestone of passage into adulthood, but procreating *is* an irreversible departure from childhood. There must be a minimum prerequisite of an emotional, financial and physical nest, if not an understanding of ethics, parental skills and obligations. Even if emotional nesting cannot be taught convincingly, the complete breakdown of the physical and financial nest, inventoried in terms of time and money, can be taught.

Unlike many other disciplines, on-the-job training and experience are not possible for parenthood, even though the need for these far exceeds those in the factual categories of knowledge. But just as an education in many irrelevant subjects helps the young become familiar with the intuitively unfamiliar and different (*this may well be their greater purpose*), so too can an education in parenthood provide enough knowledge in better preparation for this lifetime responsibility. Great leaders may be born, not made, but even minimally adequate parents are trained, not born.

As with all teachings, the objective is not compliance, so much as the transmission of an awareness of consequences. Many people act irresponsibly for different reasons, but most people will not deliberately choose to do so when familiar with the consequences. People may engage in casual sex, but their attitude to sex should not ever be superficial, casual or lacking in awareness of its potential to create—and terminate—life. Cultures that value duty and responsibility to oneself and the family, and equate commitment with dignity and honour, would necessarily have a very different concept of family where consanguinity plays a critical role in determining the membership within the family. If the family dynamics are not structured with rules, stability and consistency, to enable transmission of cultural identity in which gender roles also play an essential part and are clearly defined and valued, then the time from birth to preschool will not have been effectively deployed, thus placing greater burden on the educational system, as well as all adults outside the family unit. A child who spends much of his or her time in front of the TV set[47] and is constantly indulged is not likely to appreciate or understand the concepts of delayed gratification or even gratitude.

What does the ability to choose mean, and how are choice-making skills developed if a child is indulged and always gets his or her way? What does freedom mean as an absolute right or entitlement, without an appreciation of what it is in context of relationships? What does equality mean if it just applies to getting one's way at all costs or without an appreciation of where and when one is in the continuum of relationships and time? What does

---

47. Sixty-five percent of children eight and older have a TV in their bedroom and say that the set is usually on at mealtime. Sixty-one percent say their parents have no rules about TV watching. Source: Kaiser Family Foundation, as cited in *Newsweek*, November 28, 1999.

justice mean without a sense of what is right and wrong (ethics) and without an appreciation of the pluralities amongst and within individual(s)? Empiricism and science which attempt to dissect, demystify and eviscerate beauty and Nature cannot transcend the time and space continuum because they are tautological constructs in which inputs, processes and outputs are a function of and bounded by time and space. All analyses are constrained and contingent but useful in understanding redundancy and its necessity and importance to release essentiality. The human mind, like the Bible and other significant texts, has necessary and sufficient redundancies (99.9%) to enable, cushion and guide the essence (0.1%) into the Way. No study is independent of the limits of the student.

Paradoxically, with the advent of the information and the technological age, man is literally going back into the cave; sensibility has given way to the sensory. There is no dialect, only 'idiolect'. It is inverse monotheism, with the self as the omniscient and omnipotent. One just wants to be left alone physically, intellectually and emotionally. One is overwhelmed with exposure to sex and violence, so that these acts of ultimate intimacy and ultimate finality, which share the common distinction of having more proscriptions than any other acts in all religions and cultures, have become not only impersonal but dehumanized.

Attaining majority or reaching a stage of full legal age with rights and responsibilities used to be an indicator of some level of maturity, with attendant understanding of social and civic lives so that one could get married (engage in procreation) as well as sign up for military duty (potential to kill or be killed). While sex and violence were by no means totally restrained before, with the loss of meaning associated with attainment of majority today there is an absence of both personal and social braking forces for pause and reflection.

Sex and violence are coupled as potential forces of creation and destruction of life and as an affirmation of the self's position in the perpetuation and termination of this linkage. In the realization that the self is but the result of these self-same potential forces and that while coming into being is not subject to choice, as with exit to nothingness, the moment between these two events is the only opportunity for choice to influence how finality or death can be met: with fear and apprehension or with dignity and grace.

This, then, is to acknowledge the decreasing significance and relevance of self over time as new links are formed and it diffuses and dilutes, approaching nothingness but not absolutely nothing. This can be viewed not only as a physiological progression, but also as intellectual or spiritual in that one influences the many, as many influence the one, in physical and limited as well as non-physical and unlimited dimensions.

Since family members and teachers have the early and intensive interactions with profound significance over time, they have the greatest opportunity and responsibility towards the young in their path towards maturity. What is taught is as important as what is signaled or left unsaid.

Contemplation of and/or engagement in these two forces and activities results in a profound and irreversible transformation of a self that is readied and prepared over time. This is not a quick and easy process with immediate results. The process of maturation primes the self for such encounters and its consequences in its journey towards death or nothingness. This self-knowledge and awareness allows for compassion to develop for all others engaged in the same journey, as there are no exceptions or escapes. The explicitness and pervasiveness of acts and images of sex and violence blow the fuse of this maturation process, disconnecting them from life and meaning by inversion and distortion of their implicit and explicit roles and contexts.

Crimes of passion (perverse coupling of sex and violence) or temporary insanity are both crimes with extenuating or excruciating or inexplicable reasons, representing the apotheosis of rationalization, where the uncontrolled domination of emotions is consigned to a realm completely devoid of personal responsibility. Since all are endowed with the benefits of both the intellectual and emotional, and these develop in tandem and are equally subject to self-discipline and restraint, crimes of passion could just as easily be called crimes of reason. It is a paradox of rationalization to consign such powers to emotions by dismissing them outside the person to non-temporal or supernatural forces beyond one's control. Those with mental disabilities do not need these types of protection by reason, as they are designed for those who would otherwise be culpable, if not for reasons provided. It follows then that these types of rationalization would suggest that emotional developments and discipline take precedence over rational ones, as immaturity and missteps in the former could negate the need or annihilate any achievements of the latter in one fell swoop. Attitude tends to prevail over aptitude.

For the vast majority who do not choose the path of renouncing the material world in service of the Divine or in pursuit of Enlightenment, the cultural paradigm serves to red-flag sex and violence and urges that it is better to err on the side of caution: if in doubt, think a lot first and proceed with caution in these two areas. There is much association of a state of grace or innocence with babies and childhood, but they also necessarily possess the inherited implicit human potentials for sex and violence which have not yet found expression. The least that could be done is to prepare them for their eventual encounters with these forces so that they can choose wisely in order to maintain their sense of balance and not stumble badly or sink permanently.

Violence has always accompanied men, and it ranges in type (physical, mental, spiritual) and magnitude (slight and temporary to significant and permanent) of scope and duration, affecting all ages throughout history. What has changed is that violence used to be committed in the contexts of survival, honour, religious convictions or national defense and expansion. There were goals stated and attempts to justify the carnage. Now there is just carnage without a declared fight for a purpose that is acceptable to the majority. It's unilateral violence for the sake of total and immediate satisfaction of the one and engagement in sexual activities because it is possible, without compassion or commitment or preparation for consequences. Decisions badly made are unlikely to result in positive outcomes when even good or well-prepared decisions do not guarantee desired outcomes.

At the very least, engagement in these activities should be discouraged until attainment of majority or later when there are more shock absorbers in reserve with greater intellectual and emotional maturity, allowing for absorption and integration of the new without disruption to the rest of the system. Such disruptions can have a cumulative impact when cessation in learning or regression occurs, with ramifications beyond just a lack of coping skills for sex and violence. If some degree of self-control and restraint are not achieved over the primal instincts or urges for procreation and survival, then it would be a challenge to overcome other urges, let alone progress onto human virtues of justice, prudence, fortitude, temperance and compassion. Life is a balancing act and tends towards equilibrium, and as much as one would like to believe otherwise, it is not a free ride or a toss of a coin, but requires constant effort, preparedness and discipline to live and exit with dignity and grace.

The commitment to and respect for the past, and then to the present and knowable, takes precedence over (but does not exclude) the future and the unknowable which need to be carefully considered in the context of precedents. Culture is the living legacy of history, not pristinely preserved relics of antiquity.

Man slips into the virtual life with great ease, in the absence of and in lieu of a real life, unencumbered by an organic culture; there is no effort required for benefit and no feeling of remorse or regret and pain or loss; there is no social stigma or ostracization because there are no standards, only a universe of deviations. If deviation exceeds the boundary of law, one is locked up by society; otherwise one is locked voluntarily into one's own very specialized and individualized cave. The expression, 'get a life', which seems to enjoy great mileage nowadays, is ironic; people whose lives revolve around some enter-tainment or SciFi construct or other secular or non-secular cults, are engaged precisely in 'getting a life'. Just about anything qualifies as being iconoclastic (in the traditional sense, this once meant opposition to icons or anti-imagery and worship of image), which becomes interchangeable with celebrity ('what's in' or just 'what I like'). Vicariousness supersedes visceral experience. Withdrawal equals safety and security. Many are well-equipped to reject and deny what is complex or unfamiliar, which is the antithesis of education and the liberated mind but well-traversed by dictators and their propaganda machinery.

Other than venturing out for money, food and fuel (which can be elimi-nated with electronic banking and delivery services), only work or the 12 years of compulsory education compel human contact outside the home, which has become the new 'old cave'. However, even this latter interaction is curtailed by the home schooling movement, although when the school curriculum is followed, it does not result in a different prognosis. But what is formally taught in schools has nothing to do with what it is to be human, with some inkling of ethics and custodial responsibility towards other humans and the environment, the ultimate home of man.

Reduction in the student/teacher ratio and increase in computer avail-ability and Internet access may increase the school budget in head count and capital expenditures (the traditional areas of corporate politicking for fiefdom expansion), resulting in the bureaucrats who own these budgets increasing their power, increasing employment and increasing revenue for equipment and service providers; however, it is highly dubious that these structural measures will result in increased academic standards or achievements. The result will be endless rationalizations and gyrations of statistics to obscure the view and reality. Most of the educational problems are philosophical in nature, a field of study that has taken on many negative connotations in modern times, deservedly and undeservedly. Its practitioners have been most notable for their silence, with philosophers taking the Hamletian[48] path towards disengagement, insulation and involution (like everyone else), unlike their predecessors who were an active, integral and leading-edge part of their society. Hamlet could be regarded as Shakespeare's take on wasted youth and lives that do not survive to fulfill their potential due to a mis- or missed step.

All the formal subjects are of another world, another time, another place. There is no cultural or human context for the child; he is not taught what it is to be human. It is revealing to look at the calendars of the U.S. and China to see what special days are commemorated and how time is valued. The latter celebrates man's observance and appreciation of nature and its cycles, as well as respect and remembrance of predecessors: how he lives and is affected by these. There is no such reference to nature or ancestry in the U.S. calendar; it's all about man and 'the Man'. What does this say about the inclusiveness of these respective cultures in what is deemed important and meaningful enough to qualify as statutory holidays? Even these individuals as well as historically significant events and ideas are increasingly associated, anticipated and memorable for shopping (sales and promotional events) and whether they result in closure of financial markets and institutions. Disproportionate time, money and space are given over to communicating sales and financial activities than to commemorating their meaning and the lives dedicated and sacrificed. If capitalism is the driving force behind how lives are lived and valued, why not just memorialize economic milestones and birthdays of the greatest commercial tycoons? We have Professional Secretaries Day, National Boss Day and Bank Holiday, rather than Culture Day, Respect for the Aged Day, Children's Day, Winter Solstice Day and Spring Equinox Day, all of which would unite the people of the land in a common purpose at recurring points in time.

Driven by the economic imperative, in the absence of cultural imperative more time is spent by parents away from the children. Even in cultures with strong cultural identities, cultural education is haphazard and random at best, not comprehensive, consistent or structured. In the U.S. does any cultural education take place or are the TV set and the mass media doing the job of cultural assimilation? The rule of law and its coercive enforcement pale in comparison to cultural imperatives, with their built-in checks and balances at every stage of life. In this context, knowing and understanding the legal system or even its existence is not as relevant, because adhering to and

---

48. Author's Note: Perhaps it is no coincidence that Hamlet is an adolescent male of rank with each one of these three attributes making him what he is: all thought, no action. Firstly, adolescence is the most self-obsessed stage of life preoccupied with much discursive conversation with the self as the sole audience; secondly, a female would be too busy getting on with the business of daily life geared towards bearing and rearing of the young, caring for other family members as well as the running of the household; and thirdly, a worker would be engaged from sunrise to sunset in eking out a living in productive service. Thus philosophy tends to be the preserve of privileged males.

complying with cultural imperatives requires an understanding of self—and self *vis-à-vis* others—which inherently implies recognition and consideration beyond just the self.

What are the media doing? Merely perpetuating themselves by conditioning homogeneity and promulgating, without even having to bother with proselytizing, their key messages, *viz.*:

1. Obsession with the 'look' and looks, especially youthfulness and sexuality. What matters is the superficial and temporal.

2. Creation of demand and feeding the impetus for immediate gratification. Emphasis on satisfaction as a right, requiring no waiting time and no personal effort.

3. Supreme role of individuality. Individuality reigns supreme and is not only unchallenged, but unchallengeable.

There is no recognition or respect for any authority or discipline of any kind. There is no distinction made between authoritative and authoritarian. What matters is only self-satisfaction. The mind is conditioned to seek the quick, easy and simple or tune-out and turn-off. There is some vague reference or lip service to equality to justify why one's right to pleasure and what is pleasurable are inviolable. *Caveat emptor* (let the buyer beware) has become *sauve qui peut* (escape if you can).

Sexuality and sex have been distorted and the distortions, amplified, politicized and propelled into prominence by the mass media, divorced or disengaged from the individual and sex as gender, of which it is but a minor or non-dominant characteristic. To be defined and judged by sexuality is to imply that the act of sex is the all-pervasive and primary occupation of an individual, when that individual is also and to a large extent formed, shaped and defined by ethnicity, gender and age, coupled with character, personality and abilities under the overarching value as a human being. Lifestyle choices and external manifestations of ethnicity, gender (both sexes being 'tarted up' by the media and as a matter of personal choice) and age, none of which requires effort and achievement or implies or conveys status (except perhaps age in some cultures, because to have grown old gracefully is to have overcome life's obstacles with dignity), recede into insignificance when weighed against the dignity of a genuine human being and the intrinsic value of a human life, which reflect universal human values and transcend individual choice regarding lifestyles or unilateral judgements.

It is ironic that the concept of tagging, badging or branding of groups considered to be undesirable is perpetrated by these groups themselves; these badges are now waved as symbols of differences rather than being waived in favour of human commonality and common cause. The window of perception has not changed and the picture still remains the same, just perpetuated by the 'differents'. What should remain in the private domain of the individual and the group is being pushed and spilled over into the public domain and, not belonging there or having any business there, is creating a frenzy, like a fish out of water. The commonality, rather than differences, should be accentuated in the public domain and potentials for divisiveness minimized because the differences can be celebrated and practiced in the private domain, protected by laws without recourse.

One does not need to brandish one's differences, only to be branded by them. What is of a higher priority: to be recognized and treated as a human being or to be identified by one's belief or lifestyle choices which are protected by the sanctity and privacy of one's home? The spiritual traditions that endure with meaning remain largely in the private domain of the family. This is evident in Indian homes with a shrine for the Hindu Trinity of Brahma, Vishnu and Shiva as well as other deities; in Chinese homes with shrines for ancestors and various deities and worthies; in Jewish homes where the Sabbath and many other rituals and symbols are observed by the family. The demarcation of the inner from outer spheres is quite literal and symbolic in the design and layout of traditional Chinese and Korean homes with the outer and inner gates and residences. The mezuzah at the entryway of a Jewish home not only blesses this sanctuary, but serves as a reminder to all who enter that they are entering into a way of life with inviolable relationships and obligations that are not subject to individual judgements or whims. In these traditions, the spiritual dimensions reside in the home in the hearts, minds and memories of family members throughout the year and are interwoven into the daily fabric of life, irrespective of lifestyles or personalities. What is sacred is not displayed on the sleeve, but constitutes an inner attitude, preserve and reflection. Personal information and details are revealed through the course of personal relationship development, not as an introduction card. If one values privacy, then one has to understand and practice the concept of private domain and why there is a differentiation with the public domain.

Resources and effort need to be directed at the broader front of crimes against humanity, not on personal preferences and practices. In each instance, when certain groups of people were targeted, persecuted, enslaved, interned or annihilated, the perpetrators identified and distinguished victims along one dimension only (religion, gender, ethnicity or some manifestation perceived as unacceptable). A picture was formed on this singular dimension which prevented them from simply being viewed as human beings but as something less, inferior, alien or inhuman.

The female gender has been the subject of extreme efforts at this type of one-dimensional categorization throughout much of history, especially in the age of the mass media. For example, a woman is characterized as either a saint or a slut. There is a tendency to judge an individual by a single act and/or on one axis, either smart and bitchy or dumb and blonde; or a number is assigned to quantify sex appeal, a practice unmatched in its perniciousness by any such linkage regarding the male gender. This practice still continues but with equal fervour by both sides; the symbols created by the instigators and perpetrators of hate have been given new and broader license with coverage by the mass media. If a symbol is deemed necessary, then a new one which is more representative of the totality of the individual and the group could be created.

In the fight for equal rights, what needs to be at the forefront are similarities with the majority in humanity and humanistic goals, not amplified displays of differences which will only serve to alienate further and thereby create a sense of discomfort, with the attendant divisiveness and confrontations. The probability of a larger support base is decreased more than in a policy of inaction. There now exist many groups that are defined much more broadly in fighting for values that are inclusive of many minority group interests and overlap them. One must remember whether the fight is about the right to be recognized as different, which is a function of the group and its members to perpetuate, or to be treated as equal human beings with equal access and opportunity, without obstacles and disincentives.

The U.S. media have so finely ground and polished the tug-of-war between individual rights (to liberty and equality) and the infringement of these (especially in the last 10 years with the concept of political correctness) that most debates have dissipated into banality. This, combined with cultural vacuity and diversity, has created a social milieu in which a person is not only uncertain as to his position (status, authority, opinion), often drowned out by endless chat by all and anyone, but he is uncertain whether he should even speak at all. There is a sense of powerlessness, helplessness and even futility, especially with the parents. So, those who end up speaking and dominating the field of talk and media space appear to be a bunch of talking heads, whose qualifications appear to be that they are capable of speaking in English, and are for the most part Caucasian male or a WASP-equivalent, and have extreme views. There are no debates or qualifications, only incomplete, non-contextual, unreferenced linear sound bites and media-cycle loops. What is the end result?

1. You're right and I'm also right. ↔ paralysis in equality
2. I'm right and you're wrong. ↔ isolation in mutual exclusivity
3. I'm wrong and you're wrong. ↔ equality in fallibility
4. Who knows? God only knows. ↔ equality in unaccountability

The first scenario is most frequent, without any sign of concession, compromise or understanding, but only relentless unilateral assertion of a singular position. Under the twin banner of I-centrism and winning at any cost, compromise becomes an anathema, a dirty word or un-American as these two needs crowd out materiality, perspective and context which contradict the third need: the quick, easy and simple fix. When any intention towards compromise is not only absent but takes on such negative connotations, resolution of conflicts and reconciliation amongst the perceived differents are not only no-brainers but also non-starters, which are conveniently complementary. The underlying principles for liberty, equality and justice are common and shared in theory, but their application in practice results in their opposites when people are categorized along a singular, simple and superficial dimension. As long as labels, not names, takes precedence, conflicts are unlikely to diminish and de-escalate.

There is no denial or discounting of the other side's prerogative to do likewise, thereby safeguarding equality, but serving no purpose since there is no communications strategy or strategic purpose, but only noise. Might prevails as in the other scenarios, with varying degrees of cost and benefit, incurred or conferred, unrelated to an individual or social sense of justice or reasonableness.

The second scenario is interesting, since there is as much or more gained from proving the other wrong as there is in proving oneself right and prevailing. This sense of *schadenfreude* is unexceptional and even when masked, not too difficult to discern.

The third scenario is the most infrequent and fleeting. Being right, with its seemingly everlasting display of ownership and vindication, is one of the most noteworthy aspects of (mass media amplified and recycled) American public discourse, mirrored by the abhorrence of being wrong with absence of admission, contrition or humility. Bragging rights appear to be a matter of course since what is known, discernible and recorded for posterity is the final result or outcome, not the exhaustive prerequisite for success in any field. Even the victorious is short-changed when information becomes just another momentary eye candy or sound bite.

The fourth and final scenario then, tends to be the conclusion or confusion left with the audience after such an edifying dose of non-contextual, unqualified and immaterial banter.

Endeavours in artistic, scientific, political, academic and even economic domains remain only as visually demonstrable highlights of the end result which are remembered and studied rather than accompanied with some appreciation of all the trials and errors, investment of time and effort, and discipline and drive. The end product, with severe compression of timelines and distillation of events, seems seamless and effortless; exceptional virtuosity imparts an abundance of these qualities, which both adds and detracts from the result depending on one's perspective and sensibility, irrespective of one-dimensional measures of intelligence. The mass media, in distilling and concentrating what can be easily packaged and shown, takes this disconnect between effort and outcome to new heights. Even when one appreciates the unknown and the unknowable, both within and without the border of one's skin through sensory perceptions (e.g. visible light and audible sounds, sense of smell, taste and touch), these are but a small representation of the entire spectrum of human existence and experience. Yet the appeal to these senses seems infinite and the possibilities are still endless for discovery and experience: this is the power of audio-visual media.

As technology allows and makes available ever increasing exposure to other cultures, ways of life and fantasies, especially those generated by the U.S. entertainment industry, it becomes ever more important to include a dominant and common cultural identity in the educational curriculum so that there is the possibility of making a conscientious choice of what will be allowed into an individual's personal space. The trade-offs being made are incommensurable and too important to be determined by random and passive absorption of inputs and mindless and capricious outputs. A deep understanding of one culture and cultural intelligence will lead to an ability to discern and evaluate these outside influences as to their consistency with the value hierarchy *in situ*.

The tremendous appeal of *Star Wars*, *Star Trek* and other entertainment products or phenomena in the U.S., and less so in other countries, indicates flip sides of the same coin. On the one side, the cultural vacuum in the U.S. facilitates such fervour, especially with the disproportionately young audience whose cultural identity has not yet rooted in depth and breadth, and who seem to find the greatest appeal from these. Conversely, this type of massive and immediate 'grab' and 'take-up' seems to indicate an inherent need of people, especially the young, for a cultural paradigm of some kind. There are media, religious and business heroes who take up mind space (the ultimate real estate or turf), but where is the source for a kind heart?

The child tax credit should be replaced by a resource renewal and rehabilitation tax to be calculated and collected on a per head count basis per household, and it should be revised from time to time, as with any other tax policies. To have a whiff of financial incentive in procreation is anti-family values. The state needs to be largely neutral or laissez-faire in order to foster self-responsibility in matters of marriage and procreation. While a social safety net benefits both those who are poor, unable or unwilling as well as those on the other side, it should not create an illusion of someone else taking care of the fallout of the consequences of individual behaviour reflecting inability or unwillingness to make hard choices. There are elements of social conformity in every culture to balance individualism and social order, and understanding social norms along with cultivating self-knowledge creates a path to manifestation of virtue that is a function and product or domain of relationships. In a world where so many children are born into violence, poverty, hunger, ignorance and illiteracy, and where so many die slow and lingering deaths in such a spiral, it seems unseemly to perpetuate the notion of replacement birth rate in context of perpetuating the illusion of ethnicity and superior genes. Children are not ego trips, satisfaction of appetite, ornaments of vanity or private property. Young lives are cannibalized when they are viewed as means for objectifying and realizing another's need for purpose and meaning.

Does an American Culture Exist in the Context of an Ideology?

While the Founding Fathers of America have left political (18th-century liberalism) and economic (capitalism) doctrines which place structures of law and order as well as profits before man, there is a gap in the individual and cultural (relationships) principles placing man as their paramount and central concerns. Political and economic doctrines regard men as a conglomeration (the people) to serve ends other than those of their own. Even though people, as consumers, stockholders or voters, may feel they have a say in who presides over them, the interest of the rulers are primarily to maintain the structure of authority and an aura of legitimacy. The Supreme Court or laws as interpreted by nine heads, whose purpose may or may not reflect the will of the majority, is a pro-authoritarian construct. Democracy is only a label for a movement with a wide range of purposes, and oftentimes it is used to achieve and secure dictatorships. These ends are usually defined by a select few and sometimes discovered by the indiscriminate and inattentive many, asynchronously or too late.

Democracy is not a structure of government or anything else structural, but is simply a process for changing unsatisfactory structures and safeguarding the mechanisms for change. The purpose of democracy is not the balance of power between the three nodes and their nodules, but to preserve the principles of permeability and transience so that change can be effected when and how, as determined by the informed majority. Thus, the foundation and development process of the individuals who constitute the majority in various political bodies are indispensable for democracy's proper maintenance and functioning. Following are some considerations of individual character development from various perspectives of time and region.

1. Many of the philosophies of German origin in the Romantic Age emphasize the individual and the process for realization of the potentials of unique individuality (dharma). Such a realization process does not take any less time or effort but, rather, much more than in the training for a life as a wage-earner through mass-produced and mass-downloaded information arrays. One of the key distinctions is in the difference in the time horizon and purpose or way of life which is a life-long project versus the mechanics of daily feeding and maintenance requirements. Most people may not find enjoyment in

employment but are still taught to work hard and serve at their best, which is the least they can do for honouring their own time. But employment should not detract from living life well or crowd out enjoyment of life independent of money chasing, squandering and piling activities. Children need to be taught as much or more about the R's for living well over the 3 R's for making a wage, since more of their lives will be spent outside of service to others and more in service to themselves and their families.

2. Confucianism takes man one step further by dealing with the principles and protocols requiring much self-discipline or self-cultivation for becoming fit for the social matrix, beginning with filial piety (duty to parents). Self-cultivation for expanding concentricity of human relationships s the antithesis of self-absorption, self-love and self-esteem that causes their collapse into a black hole. Confucianism and other ancient rites that revere time are not focused on rights and entitlements, but duties and ethics—a code of conduct befitting a human being.

The outcomes of thwarted wills tend to be as disproportionate in scope and scale as they are in doggedly assigning blame to anyone and anything but the self, regardless of initial cause but tending to be disconnected and reversed from it. Oftentimes, when an individual is denied a desire (love, acceptance, recognition, emotional or material consumption), it flips, pirouettes and turns on a dime into anger, spewing out to others whom the one deems must likewise be deprived. Or, the anger folds back in on the self. One who is not taught to reflect and repose tends to resort to this destructive model because there is no other recourse or menu popping up suggesting that an unsatisfactory or not-working-out-well path be abandoned for another way.

Terrorism does not go away with counter-terrorism and hyper-vigilence, but only seems to grow in its frustration as its grievances go unaddressed. To grow the arsenal of technology to repel and retaliate seems cheap when compared to sharing an iota of the god-given wealth and entitlements to feed, house and educate the many who do not belong in the carefully constructed definitions of a set who see themselves as divinely ordained to oppress. Approval for spending billions and trillions on national defense flies through with pork-barrelling all around, while 0.1% of such amount for the succour of the many results in much foot-dragging and screeching.

Quality of relationships slide on degrees of mutability (permeability and transience), so that as permanent bans, censorship or restrictions are placed upon it, it naturally decays as differences are increasingly non-integrated and hairline fractures become breaks. Appearances, gestures and words are the signals, cues and variables that qualify, govern and determine the nature of human relationships as we process, assess and exchange information mostly along these parameters. Agreeing to disagree (mutual immutability or preserving the status quo) can only favour might over the long-run, and tends to be peddled by such whose purpose, more often than not, does not coincide with doing what is right versus what is self-serving. Assessing relationships within an affiliation framework through internalization and reflection of self-origin and -composition are the hallmarks of enculturation, as going beyond the 2nd or 3rd deviation is to end up in an area of the infinite unrestricted, uncontainable and unlimited realm that is directionless and disconnected from timelines. The last home-stretch determines the outcome of almost-having-made-it versus passing with flying colours or almost-having-lost-it versus saved by a hair's breadth. Once we get a feel for people in the context of occasion, time and place, it is not perfection that is given or expected, with all the i's dotted and t's crossed in an overkill delivery, but merely what is adequate, appropriate and acceptable for safeguarding and maintaining peace and order for the many. One can only judge lies and truths by the purpose being served, and without an understanding of the principles governing harmfulness and harm-lessness, we all are likely to be at sea.

3.   In Hinduism, which places great importance on the possibilities of self-improvement, many levels of reality or existence are envisioned in the continuous approximation with an individual's dharma. Staying afloat and abreast is one level of skill attainment, but skimming the water by balancing and working with the surface cohesive tension is another wholly different level. When one's dharma unfolds, it express-es a sublime freedom that is neither excessive nor strained (unnatural)

but imparts a feeling of just-rightness which is ephemeral and yet lasting. This is a state of coherence and synchronicity for approaching 1 or 0 of pitch-perfect harmonic oscillation or call and response that leaves behind virtually no mark or trail, but just a whisper or scent of having been. It is the state of ultimate benignity or having been well borne. Perhaps this is the parable of Jesus walking on water in the calm stillness.

Descartes's statement, *I think, therefore I am*, can be extended to, *I learn and change in the context of belonging to the living world, therefore I am*. Tolstoy suggests that once we synchronize our sense of time and point of origin (centre), our unique perspectives seem to focus on one picture and we lean towards the same Way of Life. Hegel goes to great lengths to illuminate the learning process rather than what is taught as a subject or an absolute end. Heizenberg's Uncertainty Principle is another way of stating the Tao of Change. The many rituals and rites of various indigenous cultures honour the immutability of linkage with the predecessors through time. By revering and maintaining a sense of connection to past timelines or lives, the links of continuity and belonging can evolve and grow rather than decouple and wander into oblivion and decay. The challenge in life is to continuously maintain the just-right degree or philosophy of enoughness in mutability to remain fit for life.

For much of time, mind has tentatively edged over the body as principles have tempered force with the odds favouring such a tilt, with the slightest of margins or thinness of spread. Such outcomes are subtly and finely changed in ever-smaller details that are not measurable and localizable but appreciable and pleasing to our senses. The creative process pushes the envelope towards the Way of The Mean (life on the leading edge), suggesting movement even in stillness. The tender, fragile and delicate undulating waves of the cilia-lined membranes are strangers to inertness and inertia (boredom), being constantly delighted in their ability to probe, process and change. The surfeit of cilia serve as suprasensory or supraliminal tips of unlimited volume and area for change. They tantalizingly reach, touch and connect to the many into the space of Oneness at our ultimate frontiers or fringes of being. Perhaps this is why the prayer shawl (*tallit*) has fringes (*zizit*) on each corner. Thus our sense of smell and of taste (the 'breath of it') serve as irreplaceable leading indicators for learning and growth which we tune out and turn off, becoming supercilious, insufferable and priggish at our own peril, dulling and dimming these tips for change. Yes, there is nothing quite as exquisite and delightful as the real thing or any substitute for experience.

The ancient cultural codex and codicils have the reaches of an aquifer or root system that can be tapped into after straying far and wide, showing the way back home in order to reconstitutionalize. These prescriptions for the body, mind and soul seem to rely (intuitively) on the law of large numbers whereby the short-term outcomes for a small sample size (micro) may be chaotic, but the long-term prognosis for a very large sample size (macro) can approach certainty.

Korea's history is one of continuous reflection and reposing or practical philosophizing, a contradiction in terms in much of modernity where the spheres of philosophers seem inactive and non-interactive with those of the personal and public. Many leading Korean scholars engaged in these domains, serving as social and political agents of change as the reins of power shifted from dynasty to dynasty. They maintained a clarity of purpose to help lift and educate the many, not just self-serving interests. Their ideas were not only well thought out, but were established through time-tested trials and errors in the human social context. They chose not to be marginalized or peripheral to the fray, kept as exotic birds with fine unruffled plumages, on exclusive diets in their golden cages. They chose to serve their purpose rather than being trotted out to lend their voice and be put on display in service to political interests from time to time. Being anchored in real lives and times, their prescriptions tended to be convincing and compelling, having put people first, rather than coercive and compulsive as when structure is first fixed. This distinction can be observed in the works of architects who prioritize their design more than the people they serve and vice versa, indicating their alignment, or lack thereof, with the dharma of architecture for creating space for minds to live, learn and change.

No matter how infinitesimal, the present is more pregnant with the past than the future, even as it pitches ever so slightly and tentatively forwards. This is exemplified in the intellectual or mind traditions of many cultures that continue to evolve in the chains of thought from mentor to disciple, from father to son, from generation to generation. These are linking, layering and creative processes, rather than discrediting, defrocking and dismissing of the old and in-with-the-new mind-set shaped by the zero-sum, mutually exclusive and winner-take-all destructive ones arising from militarism, terrorism and bullyism. In former traditions, the past is given concrete recognition in the present and flows through the filters of generations. The predecessors' works are not denied, cut-off and left in disarray to decay. It is not restoration, reformation or revival, but incremental regeneration, rehabilitation and reprovisioning, i.e., organically evolved.The micro-changes in the centre increase in significance and effect exponentially as the distance from it increases and corollarily, macro-changes in the perimeter do not perturb and faze the centre. Nevertheless, it is moved and effected because it remains permeable and compassionate. Thus the words of the ancients (true and centred hearts and minds) still resonate loudly and clearly over time and space, constantly reminding us that we are not alone but of the One. It is not modern or traditional mindsets that are important, but that there be critical contextual thinking happening. The contextual library can most readily be built up through active and mindful engagement, so as to maximize lessons from encounters with the others who orbit around oneself. Since many people tilt toward impermeability and unilateralism with their own code of integrity that is unrelenting, unremorseful and unreflective, with a chronic inability to apologize and atone, they tend to get into a rut rather than becoming increasingly open and thereby increasing their depth and field of vision or possible options. The sheer amount and variety of secular and non-secular works addressing the Way and reverence of life seem to attest to the need for these topics to be taught and addressed continuously throughout life, as the inclination seems to be otherwise directed. Hate and intolerance appear to be natural, whereas compassion and acceptance seem to require constant and inordinate diligence and vigilance to disengage from the platform of the self and self-interest onto the non-self and service to the *dharma* of life, in order to realize and attain selfhood.

These are traditions based upon consensus, not on the flippancy of a coin-toss or 'because I say so'. They rest upon conclusions reached through many thousands of human lives dedicated to improving the human condition with true learning, arising from the integration of the inside-out process with outside-in reality checks. In capitalism, the marketplace rules; in democracy, the mob rules; but in the hearts and minds of men, the principles of human living rules. Organic systems develop in a just-enough and just-in-time incremental manner to fully live in a time/space continuum, not overwhelming the odds by winning at all costs. The dual purposes of system efficiency and acuity are jointly observed. The resources available and availability of resources are minimally expended and maximally calibrated with the system's probing proboscis so as to not forfeit its edge and sharpness for change and risk processing, whose receptors are so fine as to be able to distinguish changes in molecular structures. What is virtue but pretextual, contextual and subtextual thinking, just as fastidiousness changes from individual and private to social and public domains, from considerations of organic balance to total eradication of anything harmful or potentially harmful, at all costs. It is not surprising that morality and virtue, like the texts representing them, are relative interplays as a function of the trinity of pretext, context and subtext that permutate to impart to the reader sensations, sentiments and wafts of the subtlest nuances miraculously encoded within. It is only surprising to those who insist upon immutability and infallibility or are not widely read, as this may just lead to opening and broadening the mind, leading to non-sustainability of their pristinely preserved puerile, pusillanimous, purulent and pugnacious states. There is no growth or change in mind sharing and absolute mind-space. The immune system that has been weaned on the inorganic, inhuman and anti-life diet continues to build on its own integrity, and vigorously and violently rejects what it perceives as foreign matter by secreting compassion-suppressants. It results in a culture of rejection rather than acceptance—one that is Sisyphean, dismissive and destructive, rather than progressive, concrescent and conciliatory.

Being needy beings, we are prone to consume or over-do, oftentimes way beyond our need or own good. Thus it behooves us and is concomitant upon us to teach our young what these needs are along with developing a keen awareness of their satiation indicators, without which there cannot be any. These needs are whipped unto a frenzy by being bombarded with propaganda or brain-washings that place too much emphasis on having and doing it all and that winning is all that is important. The importance of tuning-in and knowing the unique satiation point so as to pull away or withdraw from the table of life's daily problems and struggles after a certain point, and not always push for total victory or overwhelming vindication are lost in the mad hurly-burly of sights and sounds. There are no permanent fixes in personal or working lives because there will always be new crops of challenges to be dealt with and to stay afloat and abreast of. Not to be towed under is work enough. To stay in touch with the satiation point and to maintain it just at this level of optimal contentment is the test and taste of life. We all suffer the loss of loved ones whose memories bring both a smile and a tear in out hearts. No matter how hard we want to hold on, by letting go freely we are left with memories that are much more than enough. There are no compensations for such losses, except in the way we individually choose to honour the loss that we feel by finding the strength inside to endure the loss and to overcome, in order to move forward with new resolve and purpose in life. To know the meaning of 'enough is enough' which helps to locate our unique and dynamic level of contentment and to be always mindful over it so that it is not irretrievably lost, is work enough in tipping the balance to favour enjoyment of life over employment for wage.

Many in modernity are convinced that knowing less gives rise to greater certainty over what little they do know. What is safeguarded is ignorance in airtight fixed positions with a dedication and fervour that would answer the prayers of many teachers and parents for such attitudes toward endeavours in learning. This type of conditioning towards information is similar to the uniformly unquestioning and unadventurous attitudes towards foods (products and services), which finds mass-acceptability because they are sold by trustworthy big businesses (they must know what they are doing) in big stores (designed to maximize and rationalize impulsive buys) bearing appropriate labels (manufactures and government likes to inform and protect us). The sterile supermarkets that maximize packaging and uniformity while minimizing both content as well as relationship with the seller, is the bane of cultures where wet-markets still thrive. The promotion, price and place consistently outweigh product or content in purchasing activities whereby individual choice-making is rendered non-essential through establishment of blind trust. The consumer has bought the message that some external, benign and unknown entity or the ubiquitous *they* know what is good for him or her as well as what it is he or she wants.

Trust, that is such a rare and uncommon characteristic of even the most intimate and long-lasting relationships, is rendered easily into externally defined and expressed attributes of trustworthiness which is layered on and pounded in by messages and images everywhere, all the time, from a mass media that is controlled by the few and the faceless. Thus, trust is equated to bigness, simplicity, repeatability and apparitions or appearances of familiarity creating the ever-pleasant addictive consumer experiences. *Who do you trust in your heart of hearts?* has been transformed into *What defines trustworthiness?* This marketing alchemy converts the intangible and invaluable into

a uniformly defined commodity, which in an honest quid pro quo or reciprocal exchange would be unnecessary, as would be considerations of ethnicity, gender, age or degrees held. So trust, which is the corollary of love, like
love, becomes just another debasable and convertible coinage for transactional purposes rather than investments of time and effort from the true heart
wherein reciprocity is immaterial when cultural languages cradle the
nature of the bonds and duties within relationships. When there is an
absence of a cultural framework for relationships, the industries of identity eagerly target and fill the void by promoting security in ignorance or
perpetuating the no-need-to-know syndrome since critical thinking is an
anathema to mindless consumption of time. Preservation of ignorance in
individualism replaces the pursuit and purpose of knowledge and wisdom by
the individual. What is not familiar or consistent with fixed positions is
automatically rejected and meets with a formidable system weaned upon mass
media and mass education that defends little and destroys much. When
Acquired Identity Deficit Syndrome becomes chronic and pervasive, it
becomes the norm, to the delight and profit of big government and big business with their bling-bling and blink-blink words and images.

In conclusion, there does not seem to be much of individualism in the
context of a cultural ideology except by default. Political and economic
sciences are not concerned with social or family issues, let alone the well-being
of an individual child. They are absorbed in power, money and structures for
their concentration and perpetuation. Individualism is rudderless, pointless
and directionless, being closer to purgatory than either heaven or hell. Such an
ideology is not found in any culture which has a mother's heart that cares so
very much for the future well-being of her child and therefore tries her very
best to ready him or her towards a favourable outcome. Mothers impart their
unique ways through habits of gestures, tones and words to serve the communication needs of their children. They are taught how to take care of
themselves physically and how to do well in life, which is a largely a function
of the learning process that settles their state of intellectual lot or cultural
aptitude. Each child is uniquely attended to since each has unique traits and
needs with the desire of a mother's heart being in individuality and indivisi-
bility, not replicable and replaceable product of a mass market or the people
at large.

A mother teaches her child a (not just any) language along with self-
control, -restraint and -discipline or mastery over inclination and will

versus self-love, -assertion and -esteem or enslavement to appetite and vanity. The former approach is an expression of an unending love for ensuring the long-term integrity and viability of the vessel of the mind and heart, so that they can enjoy the endless freedom and growth potential in life. The latter approach is fundamentally flawed and inhuman because a child's time is subordinate rather than paramount. This is not mind and principle over appetite and matter or putting the horse before the cart, but disconnection, disengagement and unmooring. These suggest an attitude of resignation as in the expressions 'whatever', 'so what', 'what can I do' and 'who cares' which characterize and distinguish adolescence, a stage of extremely unstable permeability and transience in search for dharma. As with all things, this too must pass and transit through time. The endless cycles of bloodbath, carnage and slaughter will only stop when the insatiable cannibals and predators, in whatever colour, bent and form, are no more.

Children do not need to be told repeatedly how special they are because all have been given unique names and places. These enable them to look to the left and right of paternal and maternal relationships which exist in the same time/space continuum as they do, as well as above to predecessors and below to future generations. When they are constantly treated as unique individuals, they will feel their individuality as being invaluable and irreplaceable, just as they are. If they are merely recipients of depersonalized mass-produced stories, products and services shared in the millions, the probability of individual blossoming is attenuated so that only physical differences tend to remain as the sole defining trait to benefit from disproportionate attention. This is what the industries of identity market very effectively as individualism and handsomely profit by.

One way to describe the Korean character is by comparison to the sweet rice cakes that are prepared after much pounding, beating and steaming, resulting in chewy, sticky and elastic but silky soft, delicate and flexible morsels, rather than rock-hard chips when dried up and not well tended to continuously. Such a tending and attitude transcend all measures and categories, except of absolute love and acceptance without any suppression, qualification or quantification of compassion. There seems to be a direct correlation between release of compassion suppressants to the nature and degree of consumption or what and how much is to be eaten in order to live. Thus the virtues of austerity, frugality and conservation serve the one and the many in many ways, by being able to feel without breaking and to be permeable and transient without disappearing. It is to be alive while all the time dying, so that to live well is to die well, as a tribute to time.

People seem to need a seminal event to rally around, to define their generation, and as a unifying call for change. The World Wars and the era of Depression served this role for a few generations, Woodstock, Vietnam and Watergate for another, and there is felt to be an absence for the current one. The impeachment proceedings involving President Bill Clinton and the outcome fit this bill in satisfying the various elements for a seminal event in their stupefying and stupendous ramifications for reform of the educational curriculum. The impeachment process needs to be studied from a non-political, non-media-hyped and non-personal perspective, using choice-making skills and humanistic values dimensions.

The call for impeachment was symptomatic of the prevalence of the 'culture of one': inadequate decision analysis and deficiencies in categorization. This event illustrated that a lot of education does not produce a lot of understanding and that academic intelligence does not translate into common sense or decency, which are purviews of cultural intelligence.

One can view politics as a spectrum which represents many of the characteristics of people since it is comprised of their collective abilities for governing and its formulation of public policies. The function of politics can range from a method of government to a means for personal validation or vindication; its effect can range from unifying to polarizing.

On either side of the political function is a spectrum of the manifestations of human behaviour in pursuit of political ends: from crude, cowardly, unscrupulous, unprincipled, rigid, narrow and hypocritical, to suave, prudent, courageous, diplomatic, visionary, flexible and practical. These descriptions can apply to all people at different times and situations. In terms of the participants in the impeachment process, extremes of these behaviours were prominently and abundantly displayed, with pride in place of dignity. It was not a case of loss of innocence so much as a loss of dignity all around, and demonstrated what can result when the sense of dignity recedes or disappears along with the cultural paradigm.

While standing up or fighting for one's principles with passion is unexceptional, to do so at all costs and blindly will not be salutary to the desired outcome. The impeachment debate did not involve a principle of such major proportions or significance that normal people could use it to rally around the flag. Whether it was justice or truth that was sought, neither justice nor truth operates in a vacuum or in absolute terms but, rather, in the context of other values such as mercy, compassion, tolerance, an understanding of circumstances and an appreciation of their significance. The act committed did not break any new ground in morality, and most people understand that perfection is not a possibility but only an ideal. No person is free of weakness or fallibility, as was more than adequately demonstrated during the proceedings. The new ground breached was by the politicians and the media who appeared to have lost sight of materiality and propriety, or common sense and common decency, in an all-out pursuit of their quarry or goal and audience market share (revenue) with its attendant celebrity.

There was no in-depth decision analysis to examine the goal in all of its dimensions, probability of winning and the collateral damage that could be incurred which might outweigh goal achievement, let alone the consequences of losing. No fallback position was determined. It was attenuation at its extreme, where there was no room left for even exploration and consideration of other paths. This seemed no different from someone with a gun killing another simply because he could; the numbers added up, therefore there must be an impeachment. What was this but an example of the culture of one at its extreme, to just have it *my way* and *I'm right* at all costs?

An example of incorrect categorization was in presenting the opinion of children as benchmarks, as if these carried serious weight and merit. Does the leadership of any other organization in any country solicit children's opinions for these types of decision? If they don't, does this then imply that they don't care about their opinions or welfare? Since when did children become models for behaviour, pundits of truth and justice, and opinion shapers? Is this another example of equality being applied across the board so that all opinions carry equal weight, regardless of qualification based on knowledge and experience? All that was demonstrated was an intolerance for opinion which differed, regardless of the category of its origin. Child labour laws protect children from exploitation for their cheap and easy labour, but not from unscrupulous and opportunistic media and politicians with the prosecutors carrying this ball towards their goal post, signifying their lack of appreciation for materiality and category of information and reflecting their unique interpretation of equality as a function of their agenda.

The State of the Union and the State of the State speeches seem largely to bypass the state of the children, with an abundance of examples and statistics cited covering inorganic matters. There should at least be an indication and indicators of the following issues concerning the state of the children 18 years of age and younger: standard of living, quality of life, health care, education, nutrition, poverty rate, mortality rate, crime rate and pregnancy rate. Many of these are at the bottom when compared with other industrialized nations[49] and should be cause for great concern, not swept aside by all of the inorganic good news. It says much about a nation that exults and glorifies in its billionaires, Treasury Secretary and Federal Reserve Chairman, as well as having a Drug Tsar (cultural term for Drug Control Policy Director), while the Department of Education and Human Services are pressed for existence. This seems quite consistent with a country founded upon 'religious freedom' and armed insurrections and sacrifice of its people for economic gain and tax avoidance, and calculates war and peace (life) or compassion and charity (virtue) as business ventures and political sound bites predicated upon certainty of winning, tangible results, payoffs, paybacks and naming rights. Those who disagree can study just how much life, liberty, equality, brotherhood, justice or happiness there has been for the peoples who have inhabited this land since 1776.

From the very beginning, the 'act' was an ethical issue that, by its very nature, belonged in the private domain of the individual; whether it took place on private or public property was insignificant. Because every bit of information which seemed to support the merit of the case was dragged in unfiltered, equally treated and similarly amplified—significance, categorization and ranking of the facts were obfuscated. Instead of opinion-building from the bottom up, there was a top-down force-fitting and up-sizing of an ethical and private issue into a great big mould of Constitutional, legal, political and public issues, resulting in it being spread very thin, as well as becoming quite a stretch of the imagination. All four domains into which the issue was propelled were not only out of context but were equally demoted in stature and demeaned by this upscaling exercise. This was like trying to force an object through an opening of unequal dimensions in breadth, depth and shape: even a four-year-old child knows the futility of this exercise in short order.

49. For a comparison of educational achievement and per capita income see the table on the following page.

Comparison of Educational Achievement and Per Capita Income

Country	Per Capita GDP (PPP*)	Savings % of GDP	People per doctor	Math** Score and Rank			Science Score and Rank		
				Grade 4	Grade 8	Grade 12	Grade 4	Grade 8	Grade 12
U.S.	$30,025	17%	387	545/12	500/28	461/19	565/03	534/17	480/16
Singapore	28,235	50	667	625/01	643/01		547/10	607/01	
Hong Kong	24,550	31	772	587/04	588/04		533/14	522/24	
Japan	23,105	30	545	597/03	605/03		574/02	571/03	
Canada	22,585	21	446	532/13	527/18	519/10	549/09	531/19	532/05
Germany	21,930	23	333		509/23	496/13		531/18	497/12
France	21,830	21	320		538/13	523/07			487/13
Australia	20,830	21	400	546/11	530/16	522/09	562/05	545/12	527/07
Italy	20,275	22	195			476/15			475/17
Britain	20,210	15	581	513/17	506/25		551/08	552/10	
S. Korea	13,660	35	855	611/02	607/02		597/01	565/04	
Russia	4,310	25	220		535/15	471/16		538/14	481/15
China	3,650	43	1,034						
India	1,680	26	2,165						
Grade Average				529	513	500	524	516	500

* PPP Purchasing Power Parity based on World Bank ratios takes into account price differences between countries, for a more accurate measure of national wealth. Source: Asiaweek April 16,1999

** Third International Mathematics and Science Study 1999 (TIMSS) [see Appendix 1.3] for additional excerpts.
  Some countries did not participate in Grade 12 study as standard of testing was deemed inadequate.

Grade 12 Top Students (from 16 countries)**

Rank	Advanced Math		Advanced Science	
	Nation	Score	Nation	Score
1	France	557	Norway	581
2	Russia	542	Sweden	573
3	Switzerland	533	Russia	545
4	Australia	525	Denmark	534
5	Denmark	522	Slovenia	523
6	Cyprus	518	Germany	522
7	Lithuania	516	Australia	518
15	U.S.	442	Austria	435
16	Austria	436	U.S.	423
	Grade Average	501	Grade Average	501

If inappropriate use of public space was an issue, it paled in comparison to the colossal amount of public space and time wasted, both physically and mentally, as well as the amount of public funds consumed toward an end that did not benefit, nor was sought by, the majority in the public domain. Even if a majority of the people wanted an end consistent with that pursued by the prosecutors, elected individuals should have done the right thing and reached independent decisions based solely on the facts and merits of the case, not blind party loyalty, as if this superseded all else, thereby circumventing the necessity for decision analysis. Is this the kind of example they want to set for the young? To be loyal to their group, no matter what? Isn't this like the old-style communism where children spied on their parents and elders as a sign of party loyalty?

With so many lawyers making up the team, it was unusual that there was an absence of application of cultural imperatives (ethics), jurisprudence, or *corpus delicti* underpinnings or philosophy of the law. There may be absolute Justice or Truth in concept for some people, but in practice these cannot operate as independent absolutes. The notion of 'innocent until proven guilty' and the necessity to err, in favour of letting a guilty man walk (false positive), versus convicting an innocent man (false negative), are important reflections of this and make clear a distinction between the ideal and the practical. The legal system, reflecting its underlying cultural values, aims to protect the majority and acts largely in a preventive manner to minimize harm to the many; it does not actively seek out individuals for punishment for non-compliance, creating a nation of snitches, as in totalitarian states where the rule of law is subsumed under the rule of (one) man with a mind-set of your pain, my gain.

Observing the proceedings and the attitudes raised more questions about why these people entered politics in the first place: To serve the public agenda in formulation of policies and enactments of programmes to achieve maximum benefit for the most? Or to fulfill their personal agenda in seeking a vendetta and expressing personal dislikes by publicly humiliating and invading the private lives of their enemies, with someone else footing the bill? Presidents are not elected for their degree of stoicism but for a balanced combination of the many human attributes which reflect the values prevailing at the time. Elected officials are not assumed to be omniscient and not given omnipotent powers. They are prized for their intellect and experience, intertwined with charismatic leadership qualities as perceived by each voter. No realistic person expects perfection but rightly expects a proximate adherence to acceptable ethical conduct.

The penalty for perceived unethical conduct cannot be without any other consideration of human weakness and strength as well as materiality, because to do so is to obliterate individual pluralism or multidimensionality of both sides. If the President has publicly and profusely apologized, who is to judge his sincerity or motives (unless one is endowed with the ability to read minds). This sort of judgement is merely a reflection of a priori belief, as it cannot be based on factual or empirical evidence. Why isn't there an apology forthcoming from the other side, sincere or otherwise, to the President and the public with the outcome of the decision proving them to have been in the wrong in so many ways?

This exercise was not very well thought out or executed, even in a two-dimensional format of win/lose, cost/benefit, cause/effect, guilt/innocence, honesty/dishonesty, none of which was clearly definable or achievable. The basis for such clarity in distinctions, as to approach certainty, did not exist. It represented the blind pursuit of a goal whose cost or harm exceeded any benefit or good. That this was not a search for truth and justice was amply demonstrated through attitudes displayed, achievement of which were not accommodated by, or in the design of, the Constitution or the law. It was fortunate that this was not a military exercise where, before even engaging in diplomatic dialogue, building consensus, formulating a defined mission objective and planning strategies—the nuclear arsenal was launched simply because it was doable, expedient and available.

The elected officials were elected to represent the interests of their respective constituencies, not for the purpose of creating a voting block along party lines, as in totalitarian states. After studying and analyzing all of the evidence, independently and in appropriate context, they would not have come to one uniform conclusion but would have had to choose amongst: (1) doing what was right, based on their own sense of morality or belief, independent of evidence and context; (2) reaching as objective a decision as possible, based purely on the evidence and context, showing independence of thinking and understanding of human nature; (3) deciding that despite personal thinking, which may not be consistent with the desire of the party leadership, blind party loyalty takes precedence; and (4) abdicating or bypassing any personal thinking or accountability by following party leadership. The prevalence of the last option and its reflection on an extreme need to conform was un-American, and nullified the democratic process in which people are elected to vote with their intellect and conscience, not simply be overridden by party loyalty. Do elected officials serve the party leadership, their own vanities and the interest of the few, or their constituents and the benefit of the many?

The process and its outcome were a betrayal of the public interest and trust, reflecting choice-making skills that were as poor as the extremes of their solidarity. Their determination to win at all costs was aptly matched by the insincerity, insubstantiality and immateriality of the case as a means to achieve their end, equally characterized by these same qualities. It must have been challenging to try and convince the audience that something small, insignificant and grey was, without any doubt whatsoever, large, significant and black. If one has the number of votes to make the rules of engagement and to table the motion, and the case is still lost, this speaks loudly about not only the merit of the case but also the quality (or lack thereof) in the thinking process behind it, beyond just bad luck.

The President's antagonists' supposed search for truth and justice rang as hollow as their need to assign blame by pointing to the counterculture of the 60's for the social ills of today, accompanied by their nostalgia for the past, skipping back one generation, reflecting no better on a mind-set set in reverse gear without appreciation of irreversibility of time-order and the epic damage that such attempts have wreaked on humanity. The study of history suggests 'Restoration' tends to be disastrous for the many. Putting this in the context of family values[50] (which is, ironically, the extremists' favourite sound bite): what kind of family value says that one's need to seek justice and truth justifies publicly humiliating a family member by using some fine point of the law? Is the benefit so significant and necessary for the well-being of the party as to

---

50. Author's Note: It is ironic that a fellow well into his middle-age representing the party of family values and compassionate conservatism can be so inarticulate in talking about his own family. What he does say seems to only demonstrate his lack of deference and respect for fatherhood and the elderly with repeated references to his father as 'the guy' in a equalizing manner depicted as mostly means to a political end. This also seems to apply equally to his utilitarian approach to other relationships with the singular use of the adjective 'good', presumably, in contrast to 'bad'. Thus is integrity displayed since this is consistent with the American practice of calling parents, teachers and other older relatives or strangers by their first names, nicknames or terms of endearment such as my old man, the old lady, sweetie, sugar, honey-pie. Such nonchalance is absent in non-English speaking cultures from Ethiopia,

continued

justify making the nation a global laughing stock and fodder for the mass media? It is ironic that a party so derisive of the breakdown in social values should show such a lack of common sense and common decency.

The President did not lose his intellectual credibility; it probably was enhanced by his ability to out-think his opponents and his display of mental toughness and resiliency; all worthy traits of leadership. He was elected because most Americans appreciate his multidimensionality in both intellect and personality. Character judgements of the President are often made which are not put into context or substantiated, i.e., an overabundance of incomplete and unqualified sentences. These snappy sound bites or columns which try to pass as some profound insight into character are ludicrous.

Character judgement often requires as much focus, discipline and time as it takes to develop one (e.g. *Life of Samuel Johnson* by James Boswell), and even intimate knowledge may not result in an accurate assessment; at the very least, it should not be a paper-thin fictional creation. These considerations were not cause for a moment of reflection but, rather, an impetus to mount ceaseless attempts at character assassination in all haste before the media heat dissipated. This provided an opportunity for media personalities to shed their impotence by assisting in a political death, and thereby achieve a bloodless political *coup d'état*, which somehow seems more intellectually acceptable than the other kind. The machinery of the mass media both served and circumvented their process and goal in that these verbal caricaturists in words operate in a triple bind: trying to function in an image-driven and time-constrained medium in a world where a picture is worth a thousand words when all they had was the word 'sex'. The President's ethical problem was confined to his personal life and for most people, was not such an exceptional or intolerable violation of the trust placed in him as a political leader as to justify political assassination.

The opposition sustained heavy damage, not only to their political credibility but also to their intellectual and ethical credibility, since they

---

Iran, Lithuania to other ancient civilizations. His appeal exemplifies the notion that a man is to be considered an infant whose bills are to be footed by other people's money until he is well into the mid-40s. The culture of anti-intellectualism is sustained by no-brainers. The nature of the crime or sin defines legal age via social conventions that completely bypass biological age and parental moral agency, converging tidily with trying and punishing children who commit adult-type crimes as adults. At least the term 'is' has a long and traditional philosophic pedigree.

chose to amplify and enact this whole affair through the mass media, dumping out so much porn (in unnecessarily graphic detail and volume) onto the public while professing puritanical sexual values and protracting it as long as possible for the benefit of their one-time opportunity at celebrity or 'face time' in the public domain. They abandoned the exercise of self-restraint and -control which distinguishes the private domain in favour of publicity and vanity. They have caused more damage to the Presidency and the image of the U.S. in the world through the means they chose to achieve their objective, and have amply demonstrated their one-dimensional set-in-stone mentality and their intolerant and uncompromising attitude. Credibility is difficult to establish but easy to lose, and that much harder to regain and sustain. If anyone else had to put up with this sort of sortie, it would not be unexpected that a public apology be demanded; it is to the President's credit that he has always maintained a high degree of public finesse, control, perspective and a willingness to move forward.

If people thought that it was wrong to impeach President Nixon because it served no other purpose other than to fill the coffers of the self-serving media and hypocrites of all colours masked as representatives of many, then it was even more inappropriate to impeach President Clinton, given the prolonged media feeding frenzy and hypocrisy that resulted. When whistle blowers and snitches are protected, rewarded and even celebrated, there is a much deeper problem at the top. It suggests a leadership style that tends to equate delegation with 'I don't want to see, hear or speak about problems because I am too exalted and lofty to deal with the details and the mechanics of the little people, be they employees or customers'.

A culture of honour is very mindful of its language because words are loaded with and by social meaning and propriety. In ancient languages, the meaning of honour is not just a matter of individual opinion but flows from an ingrained and shared code of conduct that reflects upon and determines the definition of relationships. Not only is there a sense of honour between relationships, but also in the delineation of personal and public spheres. Social structures transcend the individual not vice versa, because the former is usually designed by the many to subsume or mitigate the latter in acknowledgment of individual folly, fickleness and frailty. In the politics of personal destruction, the first and last resort is to attack the person regardless of the issue at hand or of the consequences. The purpose is not for clarity or benefit to the many, but only for vindication. This is similar to dealing with a person who takes every criticism personally, disassociating himself from the nature of the relationship and the work or service rendered. A person who does not value his time tends not to make his best effort in whatever task may be involved, not being too selective as to the selection of the task in the first place. When so much venom is released into the public domain, over and over again, it does not just dissipate but feeds into the industry of identity that thrives in such a milieu. As long as there is no prescribed atonement rites for any negative consequences, but apparent reward and renown—self-vindication, hatred and intolerance will propagate and literally consume the many, irrespective of their stand or non-stand on either side of the divide.

All of these shortcomings suggest a need to reform the educational curriculum to promote choice-making and communication skills. Lessons come in many cloaks and guises, and the political unsavouriness of the impeachment process should not detract from its value as an early warning indicator of what is to come. The right to vote should be a reflection of the content and merits of issues and elected individuals, not just some scripted kitsch generated by a marketing programme or media blitz. Domains of extremism will always exist, if for no other reason than to define all the other realities in between, so that the negative impacts of fundamentalism and apathy can be mitigated and diffused by the middle ground which cannot be sufficient if occupied by a culture of ones. If everyone or every group insists on amplifying their differences along one dimension or axis, the result will be the exact opposite of what their objective is: they will only be pictured, categorized and treated as different and thereby provoke extreme reactions. Instead of being recognized and accepted as equals, the different will be perceived as threats. Isn't one's name adequate and sufficient enough to serve the purpose of nomination for social purposes, in tandem with one's unique human attributes?

The impeachment process and its outcome left one with an uneasy feeling, in that a country founded on balancing rationalism and humanitarianism came so close to the brink of their antithesis. A lot of intellect without discipline is not going to progress very far, particularly in the absence of appreciation of other perspectives or consideration of materiality. Even an average intellect can go quite a distance with these attributes. The conservatives find choice-making to be a rather straight forward exercise, as determined by their black and white definition of intolerances and hatreds; the simpler, easier and less choice, the better. They do not face the dilemma of conscience of liberals, whose principles include tolerance and diversity. The impeachment process has yet again demonstrated that not only is the pursuit of unilaterally driven justice a function of money and power as it always has been, but that no amount of these can transform what are fundamentally unjust means and ends into ones that are just. There is no absolute and perfect justice except of the true heart aligned to non-self-serving purposes and like much else in life, is not free from the investment of time and effort.

This is one of the challenges of modernity as demonstrated by increasing adoption of international laws that are promulgated by few countries for lofty objectives which mask and rationalize economic and political interests. Since they are neither equally applied nor enforced, except to uniformly sweep away traditions whether embraced or disdained by the indigenous peoples, they are viewed as intrusive and exploitative rather than instructive and instrumental because they set a pace and tone outside their control. International laws are not bundled with resource and educational commitments which would nourish and educate as many people as possible, nor do they provide a context for their applicability and benefit within their own traditions and humanitarian values of brotherhood among all. International child labour laws are unlikely to have any affect on the deplorable and exploitative practices of enslavement of over 250 million children without such bundling. There has been virtually no change over the centuries in the ascendancy of might over right of capitalistic imperialism for the expansion and retention of spheres of vested interests. The only progress has been in the success of its increased subscriber base through globalization. Rather than overcoming our fear of change which engenders extreme actions and reaction against the strange, unfamiliar and different, the over-riding need for economic and political domination fuels the industry of hate which, in turn, is fueled by an insatiable appetite for measurable and displayable growth without a full accounting of all costs.

One need not be concerned with too much discipline or too many rules, because human ingenuity and plurality have always prevailed even under the harshest confinement or the strictest traditional cultural paradigms; the human ability for adaptation and infinite dimensionality and compensability is in its very design, ensuring resilience and preserving individuality. To see this, one only need study history and the many attempts at denying or destroying a man and his group's sense of dignity and identity, as well as exploitation of those perceived as weaker or inferior. The cultures which have endured are those that integrate the ties of blood in their broadest context among all belongers (brotherhood), recognize the ties of the land, value human life for its own sake, and incorporate the heritage of their forbears (all characteristics of ancient cultures). Strengthened by these tests, they live on, their sense of dignity and identity intact.

If democracy rests upon four pillars or assumptions, consisting of (1) free press and free speech, (2) an educated electorate, (3) an open economy and (4) the rule of law, then the pillar representative of greatest individuality and individual expression resides with being an encultured, educated and thinking voter with an appreciation that all four are not independent and attainable absolutes, but are contextual, dynamic, inseparable and interactive tendencies worth balancing and preserving for the benefit of the one and the many. The three forces of cultural influence in U.S. are Capitalism, Democracy and Christianity. These do not combine to form an equilateral triangle whereby the centre is independent of whichever side it rests upon. They do not deliver such an integrity of relationships since they are at cross-purposes of economic wealth concentration, theoretical equal distribution of political capital and specialization of spiritual salvation or monotheistic totalitarianism with secular interests. Democracy is the weak link and cannot generate sufficient force to counter the collapse of the triangle, resulting in the joining of Capitalism with Christianity towards evangelical expansionism and domination. These two systems have great affinity towards each other in their shared purpose of temporal governance with lots of slaves and are of equally anti-democratic with both liking to quote from their book of choice for a rich source of justifications: the secular law books and the Bible. The practical workings of democracy as a modulating force against totalitarianism is not equal distribution of education so much as initializing and motivating self-cultivation for propriety in relationships throughout a lifetime.

President Clinton's Legacy in the Context of the Global Culture of Life

Individuals tend to link up with a generic identity for group cohesion and order. The generic (inclusive) identity does not displace individuality (exclusivity) but works with a self-identity formation process which is resilient, versatile and robust enough to stand shoulder to shoulder with the generic one. But for a generic identity to last and evolve, it must have an advantage over individuality, no matter how infinitesimal this may be. This small difference is the drawing power and universal appeal of the One, which is the thin edge of a wedge to a world of compassion and the circularity of life, not individual vindication and cutting down of life. Enculturation differs from indoctrination, not in the means but the purpose served. While many ancient cultures survive and continue to evolve, dogmas and isms come and go. They share a language and practice of relationships and for gratitude and remorse that are equally exuberant. The pleasure or displeasure resulting from a service well rendered or a misdeed cannot be adequately conveyed by simple nominations of 'I' and 'you' or utterances of 'thank you' and 'sorry'.

For many, the Clinton doctrine will be that of indefatigable and relentless compassion that will bring much honour to the American people even as pundits parse his many deeds and misdeeds. But most people don't need PhDs, law degrees or even familiarity with English to grasp this quality. He was not a mere politician, but a leader who tried his best to be of service to all over servitude to political ideologies. His universal appeal will remain timeless to the citizens of the world who are instinctively drawn to a genuine or generic identity of inclusiveness. It is his true heart, aligned to the Centre, along with attention to detail, ability to focus, ability to self-mend and highly developed risk-processing intellect, that will endure, rather than the many venal, venomous and inveigled outside-in assessments and measures over character, morality and personality. All these analyzed traits miss the immediate appeal of his sincere devotion to the enjoyment and celebration of life and an ever-present sense of play. This is similar to an observation that anyone can make in that enjoyment of a meal served is sufficient in itself to have earned it: a familiar feeling for mothers when they watch their children eat heartily.

Another example of a sense of play can be found in the vocal poetry of Billie Holiday and Bobby Darin, whose singing styles and tastes are so natural and free as to belie the discipline, focus and subtle shading and detailing that fully dimensionalize each word, as well as the concordant collaboration with the other musicians. These characteristics are rare, precious, and very American. As Jimi Hendrix said, "If I'm free, it's because I'm always running." One thing these individuals have in common is that they all appear to be in touch with their unique holy grail or dharma, wholeheartedly and in fidelity. They display sublime beauty and power in their musicality and make each song their very own time signatures.

President Clinton has demonstrated filial piety and lends much credence to an old saying that suggests that behind every wonderful human being is a formidable force of nature—the mother, who does not seek acknowledgment or asserts ideologies requiring vindication. Those who are too enthralled in extremisms miss the Truth for their own self-serving truths and lies that shift and shuffle as the wind blows. Strength of a relationship lies in its longitude and latitude pointed to a true Centre of common purpose. Physical abuse, straying and separation are not determinants of its infrangibility. Lasting relationships tend to place much greater importance on unity that can overcome human frailty but not self-serving unilateralism.

The strong force within the atom may be the strongest of the four fundamental forces of nature, but it only operates at a distance of 10^{-13} cm. The conceptual unity resulting from coupling is as tightly bound but in practice endures even through the separation of time and distance. The belief that the union matters more than the individuals within it separately, even if the edge in favour is infinitesimal, sustains the unity for the purpose it serves for the well-being of existing (parents) and new lives (children). There are no perfect unions since no one is perfect: only those that last through life's ups and downs, with no one playing a slave or a master but instead both collaborating towards a shared purpose beyond that of self-service. The strength of the commitment lies in our word of honour—a human being's most invaluable asset—reflecting fidelity or integrity, for which many have given their lives in many places and times.

It may be no coincidence that we feel that we are confronting our nemesis or *doppelgänger* on a daily basis since, through incorporation in relationships, our minds and hearts open and expand into the essence of diversity and co-existence, especially in the rearing of the young and the caring of the weak and old. Durability of a relationship (equalization of unique temperaments in shades of harmonic union) weighs more heavily upon intimate acceptance of an individual's imperfections and less with external measurements of perfection or public doctrines. The considerations of a particular relationship, like the breaking of a heart, cannot be reduced by the banalities of average constructs or the fact that everyone inevitably experiences the loss of a loved one or a cause. There is a Korean saying that squabbles between a couple are like cutting up water, and most people prefer a single bite from a well-ripened fruit to eating many unripened ones. Partaking from the same vessels and plates consummates and validates many kinds of relationships, and a couple may choose to seal their unity by merely sharing water from the same cup.

Whether leaders are elected or imposed, the end result is a hierarchical authority structure of lineal descent. This, more often than not, reflects the lineage of the leader, independent of the means employed for ascension into leadership. Or, nepotism tends to be broadly practiced—'he or she is one of our own'. While much blood, sweat and tear have been expended for territorial expansion and physical security, as well as for economic and military supremacy, the need for generic identity building that can ring true, both inside-out and outside-in, requiring as much if not more effort than in economic, military and political expansionism, has lagged far behind. Rather than being perfunctory or condescending of the UN leadership, the transient custodians of the U.S. will benefit the country as a whole by more closely understanding the broad appeal and nature of such leader, past and present.

Studying the past and present Presidents in the context of domestic versus international perceptions will increasingly illuminate whether a generic identity is in the process of unfolding or the opposite is occurring leading to greater fragmentation. What great white men the Presidents were or are for the country recedes in significance over time for Americans and non-Americans alike. Any tendency towards isolationism, protectionism or other types of bunker mentality will only postpone the inevitable eruption, which will be greater and longer than could otherwise have been. Generic identity formation, in tandem with nation building, was implemented by many ancient cultures thousands of years ago, and this challenge to the U.S., like so many before it, is surmountable when its purpose or dharma becomes clear. Americans will find much that is helpful for their well-being in renewed study of their own heritage, alongside those of the ancients of India and China. The much abbreviated, rationalized, justified, romanticized and sanitized history of the white men is not a godsend of permanence that must forever be enshrined. The search of a generic identity will lead to the recovery or re-discovery of the human heart that is not blinded by the colours and forms of life, but simply joins in the Oneness that links all life. These are shortcomings faced by many other countries, even those with a strong sense of generic or national identities, but no other country carries the potential for negative or positive multiplier effect as much as the U.S.

Pro-life cannot be about overturning a legal statute or refusing to hear the cries for help from so many in despair and hunger, both at home and abroad. Can rationalization get any more surreal than this? Pro-life is a life-long dedication to the well-being of the many in becoming more human in the timeless journey towards identifying with the Oneness and Sacredness of all Life. If procreation is just a means to increasing population size, how different are humans from ants and who is keeping the score? The abortion issue encapsulates the issue of control over a means of production and is only interesting in how the principles of communal ownership (communism) and private property (capitalism) seem to be on the wrong sides of each other as they battle it out at the fringes of extremism.

In their fervent struggle, both are equally blind as to purpose, save that of winning at all costs, while the means of production is increasingly being hijacked by science and technology against which they can stand on common ground. Perhaps neither are interested in battling a common threat and composing a new song sheet, preferring the familiar chants and variations strictly on this theme. By transcending the organic and personal self-regulation, we are becoming increasingly at odds with Oneness and causing irreversible harm to so many others, and ultimately to ourselves. The equation always balances or cancels out, settling at 1 or 0, independent of our personal, cultural, national, religious, colour, weight, shape, sexual or political preferences.

Identity Industries in the Context of President Clinton

The U.S. mass media appears to be uniquely sycophantic to and symbiotic with parties that best protect and serve its vested interests. The fluidity and virtuosity demonstrated by the talking heads in consistently equating a sense of integrity as being a pitch-perfect calibration of unctuous smarm appropriately teed up with a snort, sneer or smirk or 'great personal charm' characterize their unique brand of disingenuousness. This seems to be the adopted script mouthed by talking WASP, WASP'tized and WASP'ish heads. WASP, like other generic terms that represent a bundle of attitudes and sentiments, can be instilled and held by anyone, independent of the human form that represents them.

The mass media, like assassins, terrorists, rumour mongers, smearers and gossipers through the ages, thrive on one-sidedness, binary-ness and destructiveness. The constricted choice seems to canonize or vilify some other, rather than to foster personal growth through reflecting, reposing, renewing and reconstitutionalizing versus mass mobilization through propaganda and regressive restoration. This is nicely supported and compounded by the tendency of the WASP'ish bend of mind which has a uniquely uniform stance and drone towards that which does not conform or serve its purpose of promoting insatiable intolerance. The tunnel-visioning viewers, who tend to like what is familiar, watch and listen to the same repetitive and biased messages in 24/7 cycles, nodding their heads while nodding off into mindlessness. The politics and coverage of personal destruction is consistent with the cannibalistic practices that the industries of identity have spawned and nurtured in those who are least endowed with self-identity, by maximizing the destruction of those who are richly imbued with their own.

The only saving grace of these WASP'ish minds is their lack of subtlety. Their overwhelmingly negative coverage of those they don't like, care for or agree with is so blatant and consistent as to not escape the least discerning of minds that can ask, Where is the other side's point-of-view? Truth is a distant second if it registers at all on these constricted radar screens, compared to winning at all costs and maximizing revenues for these talking heads and politicians who are cannibals and predators or work for such paymasters and taskmasters. These are people who are as equally incapable of gratitude and humility as they are inept in apologizing and compromising. The World Wars are the apotheosis of cannibalistic orgies favoured by these true believers' predilection for total wars and whose appetites thrive by gorging upon actual or virtual lives with a hunger that is never assuaged, but only grows as its fill increases. Their goal is not merely to win, but to annihilate those who are different. What is profit or surplus but the efficient rendering of fat from cannibalization of the strands of time or living beings. It is this tendency for cannibalism in human nature that the many teachings of compassion try to balance through the process of becoming human beings who do not tear-up and destroy the others, but co-exist, at a minimum, in relative freedom to be.

What job category or pursuit requires a fixed and permanent artful artifice of 'great personal charm' and language deficit as a pre-requisite or means for denial, deception, evasion, escape or rationalization to serve indefensible, hidden and self-serving ends? It seems that the presence of charm serves to excuse and qualify many deficiencies as in 'charming liar', 'charming addict', 'charming crook', 'charming pretender' and 'charming idiot'. At least or at best, with President Clinton one could see and sense in his posture and mannerism, great unease and unnaturalness when he is not being sincere to himself and others, even when he knows that he is mostly in the right, when trying to put one over with illusions and spins. Even with all his intellect and political skills, he cannot unnaturalize, obfuscate or overpower his own sense of personal integrity and convictions which colour and beat in his heart. Because he is such a natural, his odd moments of awkwardness seem to catch the media spotlight, not vice versa. His glaring fault appears to be an absence of disingenuousness in a milieu of mostly such. His family name is not just a means to an end, but represents his unique life which acknowledges those who have helped to shape his character—the true heart of a true son who can never do less than his personal best or lie to his mother.

He has made his name his own and is no master or slave to anyone, nor is anyone to him. Today, just as in ancient cultures, the name of a king is the equivalent of his mandate. President Clinton's inside-out projection of his own image cannot be enslaved by the superficiality of the mass media. He spent a great deal of effort trying to decipher and understand the feelings and thoughts of the people because he trusted them in the final analysis. A leader or father tries to understand his children so as to explain, reason and show them the Way forward in safety and security. After he has done his part, he trusts his children to make their own minds up. None or very few fathers follow the way of their children.

Bill Clinton is an Authentic American or a Genuine Human Being whose appeal is timeless and borderless from East to West and North to South. He seems to find lying to be extremely difficult and unnatural and it does not wear or sit well with him, being at great odds with his genuineness and authenticity. Lying does not bear true witness, signature and marking of time whereby reality only exists in time stamps and trails, i.e., the forensics of writing and dating which release a sense of chronology, synchronicity and *veritas*. People of culture who remember and revere their predecessors, wisdom and life do not compromise or forget the principle and sacredness of time which was, is and will be. The lasting effect of enculturation is that it stirs memories and sets off internal alarms which make lying difficult but also condition intolerance for lies and liars, especially when realized so consistently and with such great ease, impunity and smugness. This category of people are not bothered by defiling and desecrating themselves or anyone else because honour, dignity and principles all carry a price tag and a for sale sign. If one's own self is not held sacred, what meaning can there be in such morally bankrupt lives? The investment of time by a mother is an expression of pure compassion that is *sui generis* and ill-served by such disrespect for the self. He does not look down at or up to anyone, but only looks straight out, as an equal. How representative of the global human spirit the Americans truly are in having elected President Clinton to serve the many as an intermediary or a bridge to the future. It is not the height and might of office that makes the man, but the man who makes the office high and mighty in serving the many over the self-serving interest of the few.

The mass media are not in the education business. First and foremost, their primary business is to render profits with all else being by-products and secondary, accomplished through creating and satisfying demand for their products by entertaining as large an audience share as possible, defined by the lowest or broadest common denominator. A programme or product is formulated, packaged and formatted based on market segmentation studies to target specific market categories; to be successful and to succeed, it must capture a sufficient size within each category or across categories. To appeal to the lowest common denominator the interface must necessarily reflect its characteristics, therefore the mass media are populated by many individuals whose degree of objectivity is directly proportional to the degree of intellectual illumination or content required and thereby displayed.

The appeal of entertainment is in its extreme attenuation of one-dimensionality, and those who are successful at it could be considered experts or connoisseurs in a form of constricted, single planar intellectual exercise, formatted with the x-axis representing the degree of one-dimensionality or single-mindedness and the y-axis representing revenue. The basic thrust of successful products demonstrates these highly refined skills at transforming what is simple into the complex and what is complex into the simple, which is best exemplified by the envelope pushing and pulsating treatment of (in priority of importance): (1) sex and violence at the top of the billboard, (2) supported by the illuminating and insightful treatment of emotions and relationships, with (3) occasional guest appearances by liberty, equality and justice, for crossover appeal.

The shows featuring middle-aged WASP fellows commiserating with each other about their hard struggle up the socioeconomic ladder are the most pathetic and tragi-comedic indicators of their limited visual range and much qualified compassion. Such pristine absurdity comes into focus as they choose to take potshots and obsess over the likes of Maria Shriver or when another WASP fellow producing a series on dying is too busy to keep vigil at his mother's deathbed. It is a disturbing phenomenon to observe the ease with which people are brain-washed into intense dislike, hatred and rejection of individuals whom they have never met or know at all through regularly tuning into daily talk shows and infotainment. These shows are equally branded with dependable, regular and reliable airtime slots chiming unchanging, manufactured or artificial beat, tune and 'tude. They are equally characterized by an absence of lull, loll and languor that punctuate and score real time, imparting a sense of benignity and poignancy to its universal flow. The intensity and incontinence of emotion seems inversely related to degrees of first-hand knowledge and completeness of stories with arrogance fitting ignorance like a well-stitched glove.

Innuendo or passionately trite trashing takes on the guise of fact with repetition as what is virtually and scantily known seems actually true for the avid consumers of these shows. It would be interesting to correlate literacy levels with viewing habits and susceptibility to virtual suggestions since "Compared to other countries that have tested literacy, the U.S. has a higher concentration of adults who score at the lowest literacy levels" compared to Canada and Germany [see Appendix 3.1]. This daily downloading of attitudes that are designed to consistently feed hate seems to maximize suppression of compassion while minimizing pursuit of knowledge outside the box, literally. Such picayunish practices invert a language characterized by its anti-metaphoric or deictic (capable of proof and words such as *this, that, there, you* coupled with specific context) leanings towards irrelevance and denial of findings of fact or culpability in proof. If the intensity of such negativity was equally matched by intensity of compassion for the handful of familial and blood relations, there may just be greater harmony. But who can be bothered to waste time unless there is a financial payoff, promise or potential that compensates effort even within the scope of the labour of love. The prevalent and uniform common denominator of these programmes and their viewers seems to be the virtue of unfettered venality with the virtuosity of transforming the banal into bombshells so that substantive issues rarely see the light of day. The impulse for simple perfection and the absolute feeds the fetish for deification and demonization, equally. These are not attributes ascribable to, much less desirable of or attainable by human beings and their experiences within the bell-curve of our shared history littered with destruction and death, lit up by unshakable infallibility and dogma, in the absence of apologia and acknowledgment of any wrong-doing, petition for pardon or heartfelt plea for forgiveness.

As materiality, perspective and content recede, hearts are increasingly and passionately engaged with public entities and inorganic systems over personal interests and organic relationships. The always present whisper campaigns have been replaced by a new crop of irresponsible, vicious and unaccountable talking heads and sound bites, but now digitized and equipped with the trappings of celebrity bestowed upon them by the mass media, still serving the same old purpose—to destroy, at other people's expense, in time and money. It costs the perpetuators and perpetrators nothing as freedom of speech, free expression and press freedom along with asymmetrical or absence of critical thinking of the mass audience allows them to stake nothing or gives them a free-ride and -reign as notoriety of anything, from a snitch to a killer, becomes rewarding. And what is to stop them from hurling insults at anyone, even the President, since anyone can be targeted by the viewfinder and shot in the free-for-all open range, polished off and profited from. The elderly, parents and teachers are certainly not immune to being at the receiving end of this spiteful, hurtful and hateful unfurling fury and tongue-lashing venom, since all are equally disrespected, disposable and subject to personal, unilateral and equally valid judgements.

The hate-mongers are in an enviable position of realizing an infinite rate of return since there is virtually no initial investment required for being handsomely rewarded by the advertisers as well as developing loyal subscriber bases who feed upon hate and intolerance. It forms an enclosed system that feeds upon itself by horizontal and vertical integration and expansion, as its primary food source of human population grows exponentially while non-paying and non-human ones are decimated.

Can anyone, especially children, feel loved and nestled in this milieu or will they simply shut down unless drawn into the vortex of the predator and prey paradigm? How can organic beings reconcile and build bridges to each other if what divides them is overwhelmingly inorganic, except by becoming increasingly inorganic and non-human, just spinning their wheels as a cog in a large machine of mass destruction and unlimited appetite? Is it possible for a world of diversity and unique beings to thrive, let alone survive, in a culture of ubiquitous intolerance for the different? As the answer to the question of 'who am I and my kind?' becomes increasingly narrowly constructed, it does not take much to conclude that my set seems to be shrinking down to a membership of one while the non-my set seems to be growing alarmingly. This perception of threat and creation of fear, which are the corollary of hate, result in the need to destroy the other so that rather than strength in numbers, there is greater reliance on weapons of mass destruction in their many guises. This is a culture of loners who will do anything at any cost to make sure they don't become losers in the only way they have been conditioned—to win at all costs and to revere nothing, not their individuality nor the oneness in the universality of all lives. The ego remains inchoate and cannot come into being when it is this alone. Being ill-equipped and ill-at-ease to link up in any direction or dimension, it backs into nothing and remains a nothing. Like an infusorian, it dries up and dies when it does not find a pool of life to swim in, free to roam and explore, towards its dharma in harmony with oneness that is ever-present as long as time is revered.

Everyone is judged as an equal with all judgements carrying equal weight and equal validity. The robustness of a culture can be viewed through durability of relationships, especially within family units or the ease with which all and any kind of relationships can be discarded with impunity. While the concept of democracy has tried to define traditional class structures out of existence so that all are equally classless, individualism seems to have resulted in everyone having the equal opportunity to classify themselves so that the result seems to be a chaotic proliferation of classes.

Since the class of one proves unsatisfactory and meaningless, class distinctions seem to have clustered around superficial markings of physical traits, economic might and political banners without any of the drawbacks and drags of traditional values and attributes of class and status such as *noblesse oblige*, honouring bonds, duties and loyalties by upholding the family name and heritage as the torch is passed on from one generation to the next. Thus, American society seems simultaneously classless and yet preoccupied with endless classification. Integrity rarely comes into focus as the inside-out categorization tends to upscale and exceed any outside-in perception or reality check. This fuzziness or fudging tends to be prevalent since pumping up self-esteem, forgetfulness and avoidance of self-knowledge appear to tip the scale into uncharted territories. Since there are no uniform indicators or standards under the doctrine of individualism, most individuals without the right physical branding, economic means and political clout, are rendered largely impotent.

This results in a frenzy along the axes of looks, money and power over any traditional values which have largely been jettisoned. The masses are held together by their faith in the elusive equal treatment under the law, presumably since judges are supposed to be independent enough to serve the cause of justice and not below or above biting the hands that feed them. The challenge is to assimilate while preserving individuality, holding reverence for the Oneness of all that live rather than insisting upon the annihilation of the different. The impression moves from Jewish-American, Afro-American or *blank-blank*-American to American-Jew, American-African or American-*bleep-bleep*, and the always appealing heroic of the stand-alone-American or various other constructed categories towards a unique individual on the path to becoming a genuine human being.

But the viewer or consumer only sees the x-axis-driven output; the detrimental effect of TV (or other mass media) is not that it creates an alpha-wave state of mind or that its content is too sexual or violent, but that it shapes the mind into a one-dimensional, mutually exclusive and time-blind or time-independent format. If one were a risk-taker, a TV set could be allowed to flourish in the home if one is confident enough with one's diligence and intelligence to censor and monitor what is viewed by the children. But how about all the other manifestations of the mass media, such as the Internet? And what about the times when adults are not around to supervise, or the fact that the time spent at home with children is diminishing while their preference to spend time with peer groups is increasing?

The solution does not lie in censorship or supervision or getting rid of the TV and computer screens. It lies in instilling a time-awareness discipline with prioritizing, scheduling and rationing weekly time for a variety of activities. Understanding the value of time and how to value it are essential because it is irretrievable and irreplaceable; such understanding determines how one sells and spends time in balancing livelihood, lifestyle and quality of life. The total number of hours per week engaged with these media needs to be assigned and limited to ensure that study and other activities which encourage and promote development of a multidimensional framework are sufficiently maintained to more than offset or counterbalance the mass media's downside impacts. For those who are not risk-takers in matters concerning the welfare of their children, the answer lies in themselves, in how they prioritize their time and in their concerted effort to reform the educational curriculum and its institutions.

From the mid-'70s through the early '80s, when the impact of globalization and technology could be recognized, most business entities have assessed these implications of change and incorporated them into their long-range plans, earnestly initiating restructuring, re-alignment, reformulating, re-sizing, redeployment and re-constitutionalizing in order to survive and prevail in the new world order of economic realities. Even the look and feel of the corporate environment have changed with renovations, as innovative décor including artwork, architecture and landscaping emphasize user-friendliness for intellectual as well as physical work, compared to the sterile and institutional atmosphere of the past which still characterizes many schools. Although the corporate uniform has changed, uniformity in attire is kept largely intact, along with the requirement of a badge and number for security, administrative and social purposes. Compliance and hierarchy are still very much operational.

The educational template is way overdue for a similar magnitude of overhaul in a paradigm shift involving as many dimensions as those of the corporate entity. Corporations have undergone an organic transformation because they enjoy the benefit of, and are well served by, their defined and uniform monitoring systems, cost/benefit models (profit and loss, operational and cash flow statements and numerous decision analysis models), expressible in a common denomination independent of the specific category of business or activity. The educational, social and political monoliths have not metamorphosed in this way to serve their function and constituencies in satisfying the needs of the many. They have wasted a lot of time and resources in patch jobs and Band-Aid exercises to perpetuate existing structures, in resistance to or denial of changes. Ironically, this is diametrically opposite to what their attitude should epitomize. Rather than formulating and developing an equally radical and broad spectrum immune response to the relentless poisoning of the public weal and the minds of the young and impressionable, the various institutions have not only lagged behind but at an increasing rate.

This gap has been compounded by easy and ready resort to material, mechanical, pharmaceutical, and commercial solutions and inclinations, over the complex and time-consuming organic nurturing and development of the mind. Cast aside is guidance for developing and understanding the multifaceted language skills, above and beyond speech and text, of unlimited arrays and realities of relationships predicated upon priorities, precedents and goodwill, decision-analysis and set theory. Instead, the quick and easy banter of non-contextualized absolute rights and equal entitlements along with doses of religion lite, intolerant and righteous, breeds equally disconnected, short and unstable fuses. This fosters a culture of belief systems of static and exclusive absolutisms in lieu of dynamic learning systems to integrate memories and relationships through effort, thinking and conduct. The purpose of education—to instill discipline and open doors—is dimmed, perverted and inverted, swept along and aside by consumerism and disposalism. This is like preparing for a nuclear fallout by evangelizing that not only is radiation not toxic but beneficial. Whether an illusion is comforting, appealing or easy is irrelevant versus the manifest reality (rate of change of mass, distance, age and alignment) and sacredness of relationships. A reverence for the sacred leads to and reveals the realm of inter-beingness, the non-corporeal and non-temporal medium where compromise is the dynamic means of existence, not simply a static mean. Compromise of the mind, heart and body strives for focus and integrity between the ever-changing internal and external realities through the medium of relationships where virtue is constantly at play and solely realizable and thereby, manifested. Virtue is the fulcrum upon which relationships rest and balance.

What has fundamentally changed since the '50s and '60s is the absolute number of hours spent not only in physical inactivity but in mental inactivity or disengagement, resulting in extreme one-dimensionality and dormancy in both these contexts, viz. watching and eating. This need not be a terminal case of *rigor mortis* as long as parents care for their children more than for themselves, and as long as society deems its humanizing goals and values worth safeguarding and transmitting.

The obsession with body weight involving a tremendous investment of time and resources by both sellers and buyers is uniquely an American phenomenon where thinness passes as virtue, rather than an expression of vanity, victimology at the feet of fashion, or anorexia at the extreme. What drives this North American obsession with weight? Gluttony appears to be a stubborn religious relic of a sin that does not lend itself to the rationalization and image treatment or spinning into virtues, as do the other vices such as greed, avarice and vanity. This is precisely because of its measurability and visibility, two necessary attributes of modernity and the media which ironically make this vice incredibly difficult, if not impossible, to flip. The other distinct feature of this vice is that it poses no dire and direct harm to anyone else and is essentially harmless, except and maybe to the one.

With its attributes of visibility and measurability, one would imagine that gluttony would be a top-selling virtue. It seems to ricochet between a great way to indulge and pamper oneself to the opposite with all manners of diet products and services. The marketing of food with all of its related merchandise and merchandising is only matched by the same with weight-loss and other dietary goods and services generating a self-normalizing and self-perpetuating revenue stream for the peddlers. Junk food is a $50 billion growth industry in the U.S., with a rosy and robust outlook.

But it seems that flipping vices into virtues needs to meet some threshold: an old Puritanical streak of going for all or nothing, or intellectual plausibility of transformation or some kind of association with wealth and status as justification or mitigation. Perhaps it's just an attachment to keep at least one vice on its symbolic pedestal and now it carries the burden associated with all other vices combined, which have been made to vanish through conversion under the aegis of capitalism. Where piling on of its excess seems to render the other vices quite harmless and saleable, with something so real and tangible as weight, the opposite happens. There is no let up in the war against fat at all costs, since all other vices have been conquered and polished off. The amount of time and money devoted to this exercise towards thinness could eradicate hunger on the planet many times over. The danger of persisting in placing so much value and focus on looks appears unlearned to the point of being unlearnable, even after so much of history which bears witness to its social undermining. The lesson that everyone looks different and that what really carries weight is the individual's character, as Dr. King pointed out many decades ago, still reverberates to this day. But this message seems to have been drowned out by commercials and images in too many minds, or conscripted and snipped for political eye-candy and sound bite.

The Department of Education needs to create not only a Division of Humanizing Studies but also a Division of Mass Media to work in partnership with the State Boards of Education and with the Public Broadcasting System to create national multiple channels for age 4–18 sub-groups and core subject categories in order to maximize multidimensional thinking in these formative years (no inorganic interface until 4 years of age). All of the various mass media platforms need to be secured from TV, the Internet and radio to all forms of publication and offer a viable alternative to parents, so that they are supported in their desire and effort to do their very best for their children. Educational programming has sufficiently demonstrated its amenability to creative packaging and formatting which is conducive to the formation of good learning habits over a lifetime. There must be a very high degree of quality assurance in all of these endeavours through adequate monitoring and feedback systems and by maximal deployment of all higher educational resources, such as college and university professionals.

There are pools of highly trained talent and expertise from which the Department of Education could draw. The mass media as well business, legal and other disciplines all include people whose primary interest is not restricted to the pursuit of money and fame. These expansions could be financed by charging all commercial media operators airwave or licensing fees based on what the market will bear: competitive pricing with annual reviews to reflect current valuations consistent with capitalism, while government retains ownership of the airwaves, a public asset. These fee streams, combined with education royalty fees (1% to 5% of gross revenue on a sliding scale, starting at 10% and maxing out at 50% market share) on all businesses that enjoy greater than 10% national market share could provide the funding required. Such levels of market share can only be facilitated and achieved by a sufficient degree of homogeneity and stability of the marketplace, created by and sustained through all other political, legal, medical, economic, environmental (natural resources and ecological impacts) and social activities and programmes, including enculturation, education and research. These other activities also provide a structural framework, a pool of qualified labour, and other resources on the supply side of the business enterprise.

Diversified corporation's market share in each segment would be cumulative and cross-holdings would be pro-rated by percentage ownership and cumulative. Overseas revenue would be included since it is also a beneficiary of the homegrown talent pool and support structures. The implementation of such a collection programme can be facilitated by massive and adequate (SIC-coded) statistical and information databases, through audited business report filings within business entities, as well as various governmental agencies, especially the Security and Exchange Commission. The concept could naturally be extended: for example, the top 10% bracket of total compensation packages of a firm or top 10% earners in any market segment that can be defined. This dovetails neatly with the highly developed skills of segmentation and quantification by corporate marketing information systems.

There needs to be a symmetry (balance or justification) between all that a business entity draws from and depends on for its incorporation and its thriving (i.e., total benefits enjoyed with the total costs side of the equation). The expense statements of business enterprises are inadequate in this regard because all true costs are not defined and captured over time; until such time as this discipline is refined, approved, implemented and monitorable, a top-down education royalty fee can be considered a reasonable alternative, with the burden of proof for anything less residing in the business realm. After all, free rides or charity are not concepts amenable for entertainment nor tolerated well by the capitalistic system as it has been and continues to be practiced (although not necessarily as envisaged by its philosophical and theoretical underpinnings). An educational royalty fee is a form of expense recovery on a federal (not state) level since beneficiaries are mobile. It is not additional taxation.

While corporate focus on the revenue side has been forward-looking, multidimensional, expansive, inclusive and imaginative in its efforts at maximizing and capturing it at every possible source and transactional level, the efforts in expense categorization and capture have been singularly restricted to the simple, one-dimensional perspective of minimization and confined within its own impenetrable four walls. Not all experience in economic life, as in any other aspect of life, is so capturable, reducible, numerable and predictable, but still experienceable, evidenceable, occurrable and appreciable. The uniqueness of human perception and intellect is that it sees and thinks not only about what is represented and representable, but also about what is not, in its search for what is missing and what is possible in many dimensions.[51]

51. Author's Note: The simplified yin/yang symbol of Taoism (Appendix 3) can be seen as representation of this. Rather than being a flat, black and white symbol of dualism, it can be seen as innumerable spheres with infinite degrees of permeability, opaqueness and translucency and volume, with innumerable contact surfaces which expand and contract in a state of flux, consisting of dynamic infinite pluralism of innumerable opposites within and without, resulting in tendencies or integrativeness towards a synergistic and coherent synthesis, i.e., innumerable shades of grey, perhaps guided by the 'third eye', sixth sense, or some other homing beacon beyond the sensory field, for approximating equilibrium, alignment and direction. The way of Tao, sometimes referred to as the Middle Way, is no simple challenge: to be aware of, to appreciate and acknowledge the flip-side and to navigate a path through many alternatives usually requires experience and knowledge accumulated through more than just one or one's lifetime. It symbolizes the interminableness of intermediaries, tensions and pluralities. Since many texts on mysticism are available, this topic shall be left up to the reader for further consideration.

For much of its existence Western civilization has been constrained by the pervasiveness and constrictiveness of religion, as reflected in the large and impressive body of visual arts and literature which, regardless of magnificence, cannot but reference religion. Many of the common elements that exist in various Western countries can be traced back to their ancient Greek and Roman roots. Even after the 1500s when individualization via name signatures surfaced and great shifts occurred in many dimensions, including on the social, economic and political fronts, references to religion still continued to play a vital role. The Western tradition emphasizes the individual and tends to be direct and exhibitionistic, with much artwork consisting of portraits and depictions of individual character.

Eastern civilization, with many roots traceable to China, does not have non-secular constraints and probes nature and man with greater freedom and depth. But due to its rigid class system for maximum social order and stability, and the assignment of low value or status on business endeavours or individual achievements (except in scholarship), it suffers by limiting individual potential in exhibitionistic expressions. The potential destabilizing impact of capitalism is implicitly recognized because it throws a wrench into traditional hierarchical structure and subsumes many of its precepts of rights: right of the first born, right by blood, right by land; therefore, it is very much kept in check. The Eastern traditions tend to emphasize the universal and are characterized by their introspective and symbolic nature. Depictions of the human form tend to be stylized and other-worldly, and focus primarily on nature as subject; portraitures are few.

Much of Western philosophy is about facts and figures, man-made constructs, categorization, dissection, digressive, dichotomous, either/or, mutual exclusivity, and other binary formats. There is much homage to man's intellect and ability to reason. It is all very cerebral and detached from day-to-day living, characterized as much by hair-splitting and self-absorption as its absence of practical application for daily living. There is so much wishful, optimistic thinking about man, with much appeal to his reason as if this alone could withstand the forces of passion and greed. Likewise, the Western religions suppress and deny human nature and humanity in dichotomizing it into good and evil, as well as polarizing believers and non-believers just as (a) rationalism separates reason from emotion, (b) empiricism, science from non-science and (c) romanticism, the individual from the collective. It tends to prescribe a *modus vivendi* based on the ideal man and ideals of man, with emphasis on values such as liberty and equality without universal or group contextual goals, other than individual pursuit of happiness.

Much of Eastern philosophy is holistic, integral to day-to-day living, and addresses the nature of man and his position in and interaction with nature. It tries to see man as he is, not how the author wishes or envisions him to be. It recognizes the positive and negative aspects of human nature as a spectrum; the potential for good exists alongside the potential for evil. Many of these teachings are to be found in Eastern cultures and because a traditional cultural paradigm is so ingrained, it does not appeal directly to reason, let alone ask one to think about its tenets; it puts the individual face-to-face with 'what is' and 'what goes' in the living of one's daily life.

It tends to prescribe a *modus vivendi* based on what a man is and 'can be', with emphasis on the goal of social harmony and propriety, and with guidelines for the means (*viz.* values and code of conduct consistent with these goals). What is esteemed is not a wealthy or clever person who knows a lot of facts, but one with an ability to intuit the path to social harmony through a deep and profound understanding of the self, the innumerable interactions and inter-reactions within and without the workings of a society and the nature and potential of human beings.

The Western and Eastern traditions provide the linkage and integration of *I think, therefore I am* and *I belong, therefore I am.* The former contains much knowledge pertaining to individualism, and the latter provides the context and texture so that there is linkage between the one and the many over time. In the connecting and binding of such differing perspectives, beliefs, principles or practices, one learns to identify and appreciate internal inconsistencies of such coalescence, which also characterize many religious beliefs and yet do not detract from their purpose nor shake the faith of believers.

The metaphysical or mystical realm of knowledge is not some category of knowledge that man can master or force-fit unlike numerous man-made constructs representing the physical world that turns out also to have limits and inconsistencies. This is demonstrated by the search for a unification theory which attempts to unify four fundamental forces—(1) gravitational force (keeps all planets and galaxies in place), (2) electromagnetic force (binds electrons to nuclei and ties atoms together into molecules), (3) weak force (causes slow disintegration of atomic nuclei), (4) strong force (holds atomic nuclei together)—as covered by gravity, relativity and quantum theories, resulting in many strange phenomena, conjectures and koan-like language in trying to describe the big-bang, black holes, worm holes, particles, waves, speed/momentum, position, mass and spin, quintessence, challenging our imagination and comprehensibility of unity and infinity. Thus, Heizenberg's Uncertainty Principle states the impossibility of measuring at the same time two attributes which are different and yet connected, like momentum and position. The greater the effort exerted to dominate the natural world, the stronger the reminder that while we don't make the rules, we still need to respect and pay attention to them or ignore them at our own peril.

It is not surprising then that people experiencing the natural world differently around the world have differing senses of spiritual reality which cannot be, or perhaps should not be, subject to such complete and certain resolution or quenching, so that rather than synthesis or absolute unity, whereby all contradictions are eliminated, only syndesis retaining syncretic anomalies but nevertheless synergistic in effect is reachable. Such a state preserves and demands a sense of wonder, reverence and humbleness or a willing suspension of disbelief in the face of the sublime[52] when comparison is suspended,[53] and transcending our entire structure and scope of perception which compel comparison and judgement. Even cultures arising from shared time and space contain anomalies and quirks within them, reflecting the non-viability of absolute synthesis but more than satisfactorily imparting a sense of harmonic resonance, meaning and belonging. Coexistence of irreconcilables occurs in many dimensions which, while not subject to differentiation and integration or dissection and synthesis, still remain viable, vital and holistic, independent of our predicament or comprehension.

We can all laugh and cry at the same time for diametrically opposing reasons but are common in our sense of inappropriateness and ineffableness.

52. "...the main point of the sublime is that it takes us towards a recognition of the super-sensible." D.W. Hamlyn, op. cit., p. 241.

53. "...Many were the fruitless attempts made to define sublimity satisfactorily, when Coleridge, at length, pronounced it to consist in a suspension of the powers of comparison.... 'there are sounds more sublime than any sight can be, more absolutely suspending the power of comparison, and more utterly absorbing the mind's self consciousness, in its total attention to the object working upon it.'" Richard Holmes, *Coleridge: Early Visions*, op. cit., p. 230.

continued

As in theatre, the arc of tragedy best releases intense moments of the comedic and vice versa when poignancy collides with the ridiculous and incredulous. (e.g., Hamlet talking to and holding the skull of Yorick, the jester, in his hands; Romeo avowing his love and honour by betraying another to his family). We remember and forget as we want to stay, but know that we must move on. We laugh at and despair over our spouses, then remember that they were chosen over all others for a lifetime, and can only laugh at ourselves. We toil on without any guarantee of outcome except that of our own mortality, clinging onto our individual notion of the human spirit or the Divine. This sense is even more acute when one laughs while another cries from the same cause. It is borderline when the suffering, loss or pain of others become pleasure, right or gain; it is venal when distress and humiliation of others become entertainment and profit; it is terminal when defeat and death of others become victory and life; finally, it is non-human when laissez-faire, non-interference or silence becomes policy and justification for abdication of duty.

All are instances of extreme polarization within and without, mirroring the strength and benefit of a cultural identity as a function of an organic and timeless endeavour versus the weakness and cost of its absence, top-down mechanical projection or aberration. Personal identity is not what can be categorized, rationalized and elaborated but is always felt at such moments of unease or truth when internal alarms ring, as we forget, lose or are beside ourselves, but only can act, demonstrate or remonstrate.

There is no shortage of examples to draw upon around the world as cultural identities buckle and collapse in the West or are end-runned and gnawed away in the East by globalization and consolidation trumpeting

Author's Note: This sense of the sublime can be felt in our encounters with art in its many forms as in listening to music of composers who transcend the cacophony of daily life, like Beethoven piercing through his ringing deafness with resounding clarity and power. There is no wavering or wobbling of intent but clear display of masterly control over himself in disciplining and channeling his creative impulses via focused and concentrated beams hitting their marks, imploding and exploding in many directions and dimensions. The sense of symmetry and resolution conveyed by Bach, the suspension and anticipation by Chopin and the serenity and completeness by Brahms are quite nonpareil as are the works of many 18th and 19th-century composers. They seem to share a sense of time independent of any watch and to compress the essence of experience into a seamless and timeless whole that speaks to every man.

indiscriminate consumerism and its twin, rampant runaway disposalism. Television sets take up residency in every home and become the centre of attention for packaged and projected reality, while shopping malls crop up and creep into daily life as each day becomes increasingly transactional.

Instances of rage spewing forth from thwarted willfulness seem more frequent and intense in recent years, especially in the West, which perhaps has its root in its language. The English language seems unembedded or unencumbered with a cultural code of ethics based on relationship definitions or cultural imperatives and implications, but is geared more towards expressions of the individual, suggesting a need for both a greater formal study and approach to relationships. Although the Eastern cultures are more infused in daily life and language with ethical dimensions, this by no means translates into compliance and conformity, as there are numerous degrees of understanding, application and enforcement.

To be literate in the Chinese context requires familiarity and understanding of the vast and expansive philosophic underpinnings of the language, not merely in the speaking, reading and writing of it.[54] But to the extent that there is one common traditional language, no one is exempt from its social sphere: preserving and controlling the evolution of language preserves a way of life when it embodies its cultural grid, its *élan vital* or heart.[55] Mastery of Chinese calligraphy is an art of the spirit rather than just skill: it is a cultural matrix of ethics, beliefs, traditions echoing and reflecting nature and the past. The ideograms can be set up vertically or horizontally and in either direction

---

54. Three hundred and five terms are explained in the following book: Boye Lafayette De Mente, *China's Cultural Code Words* (National Textbook Co., 1996).

55. Author's Note: An explanation of forty fundamental Chinese characters may be found in the book by Barbara Aria with Russell Eng Gon, titled *The Spirit of the Chinese Character* (Running Heads Inc., 1992). Therein, the authors point out, "The word normally translated as 'heart' for instance—a word that forms the basis for many characters in this book—really means both the heart itself, the seat of emotions, and also the mind, for the 'heart' governs all human thought and action. The pictogrammatic image of the 'heart' (which in its ancient form showed the chambers and aorta) form the basis for many Chinese characters connected with spirit. In Chinese, 'heart' means the higher human feelings and attributes, including the mind and moral character." pp. 13, 48.

Examples of characters that include the symbol for the 'heart' in this book are: virtue, grace, compassion, forgiveness, ambition, love, patience, loyalty, melancholy.

(perhaps symbolizing many paths to the same goal), unlike English which lacks such flexibility and fusion of cultural values, but is more receptive and susceptible to change with associated costs and benefits. Chinese is an organic, metabolic and idiosyncratic language reflecting continuity, whereas English, being an amalgamation, tends to be disenfranchising and normalizing as well as a normalization of its many, many roots or sources, jockeying in jerks and jolts like a ronin, in fits and starts on indistinguishable and indiscriminate mount.

The Chinese language and its distinctive derivatives are laden with ethical values and judgements in social contexts.[56] It seems that Wittgenstein's 'picture theory of meaning' and 'private language argument' reflect the compressed, complex and compound pictogrammatic and ideogrammatic Chinese written language which draws upon physical, emotional, intellectual and spiritual concepts in private and public spheres through metaphors and analogies of nature. In this context, the mountain of Western philosophic branches from epistemology, linguistics, etymology, ethics, and metaphysics (Christianity) and numerous isms (rationalism, empiricism, determinism, utilitarianism, nihilism, existentialism) can be seen as valid pieces of an overall puzzle representing the search for a holistic picture in available and newly coined words, all similarly amalgamated and staying within the vernacular and patois, especially as population densities reached critical mass in concentration, conflict, transience and diversity in many European centres of commerce. Such comings and goings, as well as convergence and divergence, create a sense of discord, dissonance or 'bad vibes' causing disruptions and disturbance in the sphere of harmonic oscillation.

The Chinese language (possibly as well as other ancient and organic tongues) fuses language and meaning (see Appendix 4) in no uncertain terms, deeply rooted with the land (nature), its people and their experiences

---

56. This is expressed by Wittgenstein who emphasizes, "'the extent to which knowledge of how to follow a rule is embedded in behavioural and practical contexts and situations. Our understanding of the use of expressions in language presupposes such knowledge...the necessity for a public context if the idea of an inner process is to be intelligible...If language is to be a means of communications there must be agreement not only in definitions but also in judgement'...human beings are biological entities embedded in a public world." D.W. Hamlyn, op. cit., pp. 311-313.

and insights in physical, intellectual, emotional and spiritual dimensions. In contrast, English, being a polyglot, tends to be incomplete as a cultural grid transmission vehicle. The former is like walking on two legs with direction and purpose, whereas the omnifarious latter, with its different origins of place, time, peoples, design and purpose, results in disproportion and disparity of weight, length and strength, and therefore stumbles along on numerous legs, engulfed in the bog of its own making and unmaking, but nevertheless still remarkably functional and serviceable. Thus, both languages are complex, having different strengths and weaknesses, and require great effort for the mastery of clarity in construction and purpose or simplicity in deconstruction and obfuscation, for establishing or fudging personal identity and meaning but also for upholding and preserving or reversing and undoing democratic principles.

English is mechanical, functional and practical, but requires a poetic heart to address and serve emotional and spiritual needs. It tends to normalize, equalize, disenfranchise and flatten; it is ideally suited for commerce, science and technology. Television and other forms of mass media increasingly define and direct the language whereby words are castrated of the value, culture and heart of a people. They do a fine and efficient job of furthering generic, homogenous and acronymic terminologies, for fast, snappy, simple and punchy delivery as the visual and sound effects take over. They are experts at lopping, leveling, clipping and chopping, so that when a word, English or non-English, is appropriated by the mass media, it is mounted onto a scaffold for conversion, inversion or hanging.

Nuances, shadings and subtleties are not easily picked up and denuded of emotional, sensual and spiritual contexts and relationships, distanced and divorced from the source of origin resulting in the most inorganic of languages, which can be frustrating and limiting. Its true fluidity and flow can only be rarely glimpsed through poetry, an art form that is spiritually charged and moving, yet disciplined and centred. English is at one end of the spectrum in organic and holistic content. Language gives meaning and vitality to life through an organic creative process which retains the original spark and intent at its core, radiated and bathed in ethos and pathos. English can penetrate this level of consciousness, sensuality and organicity but with greater effort and study. A diamond in the rough contains the same potentiality as one that has been well-crafted through the flourish and finesse of workmanship to release its realizable balance between carat, cut and clarity. This is much like Michelangelo describing his creative process as releasing, wresting and realizing the potential form and beauty from within a block of marble.

Without penetrating the veil of illusion, the West, from an Eastern perspective seems cold and artificial, and the East, from the Western viewpoint appears murky and mysterious. Within these different traditions are intentions of integrating knowledge for the purpose of understanding the infinite zones of integration and differentiation. There have been in all cultures many explorers into the unknown and unknowable who were unique permutations in time, embodying the scientist, artist, poet and philosopher with centred convictions, who left their work for posterity in the medium of their virtuosity, demonstrating their human sensibilities and humanity in sharing their findings.

The ancient writings and patterns follow the east to west direction of the sun and the anti-clockwise rotation of the earth, with rich spiritual and visceral content. The modern, follows the west to east and clockwise patterns, rich in physical and vicarious content. Our languages, irrespective of underlying patterns, try to serve as a constant reminder that not only are we human, but we are organic beings and, as such, an integral part of the natural world, with physical and non-physical intentions and ties.

Writing Chinese reflects and links a way of feeling, thinking and living in an associative manner. Chinese ideograms, especially those that include 'heart', are poetic creations, and writing them with brush strokes is an attempt to capture and recreate the poetic heart and intent. Many commonly used words are tonal (Cantonese has six, seven or nine tones, depending on the Western system used) and zonal (Korean has ten vowels), similar to the striking or playing of a chord whereby the sound sets up and conveys the intensity and mood internally, externally and in-between in a visceral, organic and sensory manner. These intensities and moods are linked literally and symbolically, creating a harmonic resolution among multiple platforms and arrays, all bundled up at one go. It is a language of the mind, heart and body insistent upon placing man in the context of inner and outer realities, without separateness and disengagement. The person is an organic entity making an organic sound or symbol to represent an organic experience.

The art of Chinese calligraphy is the apotheosis of fusion of language and art for the purpose of holistic expression of the human experience, encapsulating both sensation and sentiment simultaneously and spontaneously.

Witnessing a master calligrapher is to see virtuosity at play. The flow and rhythm of writing or creating belies the simultaneous and spontaneous convergence of mental, physical, emotional and spiritual disciplines in fluidity, finesse and economy of motion. It is calmness at the centre of a storm, perfectly captured in the three Chinese characters depicting 'rest amidst motion' or 'perpetually unmoved in the mind while constantly moving with the word'. It seems like nothing, yet it is everything that matters. While many people can write Chinese, only a few approach or attain the sublimity and fidelity of calligraphy, invoking the sublime clarity in the birthing and releasing of meaning. This is the most potent, poetic, portable and transmittable component of the Chinese culture; the spirit of writing and the language of relationships orient and align the cultural heart and soul to the centre.

In Korean, one does not have to be so context-specific because the nuance of feeling or sense in emotional, intellectual and spiritual terms is already contained within the words, encompassing the totality of human perceptions and sensations in everyday words with symbolic and literal references to the five major organs: heart, lung, liver, stomach and pancreas. The vernacular ranges from visceral, literal and organic to metaphorical and metaphysical. In English, there is a denial, diminution and dismissal of the organic and emotional which circumvents understanding, controlling or disciplining these aspects of the self which is reflected in the aversion to family rites, wet-nursing and communal bathing.

Chinese writing captures organic form, state and condition (literally or metaphorically), conveying simultaneously the subjective self, the perceived non-self and the shared universal sensation. The perceived discrete individual parts are important, but the whole intention cannot be realized without the joining of the joints and the spacing of intermediary space. The mind progresses from what it sees to what it does not see, to what it cannot see, with the unseen and unseeable being as important as the seen and seeable in their interactions with and influences on the mind. The language includes numerous references to internal organs and systems (respiratory, nervous, circulatory), as well as natural and supernatural phenomena such as *chi* (life-force).

This ancient language seems organic and zonal in capturing the essence of being by true synthesis, transcending the Uncertainty Theory in conveying a sense of the position, hierarchy, category, materiality, locality and humoral all at once, for the one and the many. Words set off not a chain reaction but instantaneous arrays of sensation which engage the whole being, including its internal systems, sensors and humors. What seem like built-in redundancies become essential. With so many systems fired up, shifting gears, channeling in many dimensions of various forms, matter and non-matter, an overall order and balance still persists without overloading and crashing. The most miraculous aspect is that it all happens without on-line initiation, booting or start-up requiring active participation, will or effort, since processing of inputs is organically integrated. Nevertheless these organic systems, while most tolerant, require downtime, maintenance and repair as well as research and development to serve their receptive and perceptive functions.

If art is complementary to language, it says a lot about the essence or lack thereof, of everyday words and their meanings within a specific culture. Eastern art has an ephemeral quality with symbols associated with essence more than form as harmonious relationships between various elements are depicted in landscapes. At the other extreme is art that seems garish, bizarre and fantastic. These two extremes inspire feelings and impressions of peace and tranquility to terror and turbulence. The same comments can also apply to much of Western art, but they draw upon different sources and tend to be coupled and intertwined with Christianity and homocentric philosophies. Man is represented as distinct, separate and above nature, not merely a part of and participant in the landscape. In Eastern art, the artist seems to step back, receding into anonymity or oneness, taking in and projecting the whole view and spectrum, whereas in Western art the artist takes over and dominates so that his presence is unmistakable and cannot be missed. Perhaps all art forms, music, dance, song, literature or religion, be they Eastern or Western, are attempts to fill the void or the empty spaces in the language—reflecting, inferring and defining the shortcomings. They try to connect the senses to deeper planes, transcending and becoming an experience independent of language or ineffable sensations, many times invoking memories of ancient times, places, myths, legends and gods.

For Westerners, 'who said what' takes precedence over 'what was said' and the cult of personality or iconoclasm (old term, new meaning, indicating preference for ism' not available in iconolatry) prevails, completely disconnected from cultural conference of class and taste based upon knowledge, wisdom and age. The mass media, a communications format springing up from western technology, is naturally consistent with this, and since bigger is better, it amplifies and maximizes the processing of life into a flattened and stretched two-dimensional or binary format and mould. Content and meaning are efficiently wrung out, squeezed and flushed down the tube for the lowest common denominator appeal as the mass media inverts and reverses the sources and forces of culture, bypassing completely its purpose to humanize and harmonize. This represents subliminal conditioning and immunization against the sublime. There is no hypocrisy, bigotry, cowardice or lack of integrity when vice and virtue are so seamlessly and indistinguishably merged and flip-flopped in service of image, with might and profit bleating the banality of *it's only entertainment, we are only satisfying demand,* and *it's all and only human nature.*

There may be written and spoken English-English, American-, Canadian-, Australian-, Indian-, Caribbean-, Black-, etc., with insistence of distinct and unique identity in language based on some Freudian 'narcissism of minor differences', but there is only one root and source of the written Chinese ideogram while the numerous spoken dialects bear little similarity to each other. New words are continually minted in the English vernacular with an increasing abundance of acronyms of commerce, technology and institutions, further divorcing, diffusing and mechanizing a language that is already challenged in conveying organic meanings, sensations and impressions fused with public contexts of morality and ethics encompassing duty, obligation, integrity, honour and dignity, reflecting the human spirit and endeavour through the ages. The English language creates an illusion of being accepting of change with new words and terms, but in reality it is very resistant to change, remaining rough, hard, cold and inorganic in the impressions and sensations of non-English speakers as well as some English speakers. A heart can change, but first there must there be a heart.

Ancient and Eastern cultures locate the family unit and relationships at their very centre with rites, practices, values and language to sustain and support this essence, root or kernel. Through all the internecine and inter-border mayhem and slaughter, the culture of the family remains largely intact and firmly lodged. The American politicians have rightly identified family and family values as issues, but their attempts at addressing these have been superficial and rhetorical because to really delve into and talk about these results in wobbly, flaky and shaky unease in the medium of the English language. It is not a family-friendly language because there is no built-in hierarchy of sensibility and sentiment incorporating reverence or deference to age or wisdom. There is no shortage of desperate people in Korea, as well as extremes of polarity. Just as there is no perfect person, there is no perfect system, only daily work which takes care of most of the individual needs while also serving the need of the greater whole. The sacredness of duty and sense of honour and dignity are set in the context of others to a larger degree with stricter definitions of relative positions. This is not based on one opinion or some belief in a deity. It provides imperatives to attitudes and behaviours without exemption. Escape from or avoidance and evasion of duty is equivalent to trying to escape from the self, with deep and wide implications tending towards exile, isolation and rejection.

What is meant by happiness as in 'pursuit of happiness'? Is it a happening in the context of one? The American way is to be your own man, never mind the opinion of others, just pack up and move on—the individual is free and absolved from responsibility and commitment. But what purpose is served in decoupling generational, family, social and public relationships? It is not a difference in human nature between East and West, but the former makes being human a much more demanding and challenging proposition. There is no shortage of creative and uncreative attempts to circumvent the burden and avoid detection, as innuendo as much as actual discovery of deviation can have definite and swift consequences of equal severity. The young are not as afraid of apprehension by the police[57] as they are apprehensive of parental disapproval. The question that looms large is: can I live with myself if I visit shame and disgrace upon the family? In the West, once religion goes not much remains to provide a moral and ethical compass for daily life. Taoism, Confucianism and Buddhism cover both the natural and spiritual, as well as the public and temporal realities of life. Yet they are not a panacea for protecting and preventing fallout of human folly and fallacy. The only insurance against this slide is continuous effort and striving by the individual towards a sense of completeness and content through the cultivation of mindfulness.

English as a transactional medium is very efficient and forgiving; it can be spoken and written in an abbreviated, mispronounced and mis-spelled manner with the message remaining still passable and deliverable. In contrast, non-English languages are rigorously unforgiving. They must be spot-on in tone, inflection, rhythm and flow, and demand observance of all their

---

57. "Their young men are more afraid of what the family will do or say than they are of the police." D.S. Roberts, op. cit., p. 123.

anomalies, ticks and quirks, including the head shaking, body swaying, arms gesticulating, hand movements and facial expressions. The conformity must meet some organic threshold which is very elusive from an Americanized perspective. Therefore to access and grasp some semblance of the heart in English requires poetic sensibilities, capable of a *cri de coeur* versus *dernier cri*, which can recapture the folklores and folk songs or the emotional and spiritual roots of the language.

Such a poetic heart needs to be coupled with an appreciation of its intellectual evolution in the Western philosophies with their tireless (but tiresome) quest for completeness in trying to explain and understand man *vis-à-vis* himself, each strand aiming to solve the riddle of life. These philosophic endeavours are not so discrete and black and white, but their patterns are discernible in attempting comprehensiveness and balance: some of their patterns are pointilistic, mosaic or moiré-like. They represent a search for pieces of the same overall puzzle. The shape, form and size of each piece may not precisely interlock and snap into place, but they are still interdependent, inseparable and purposeful in looking at and seeing or reading into the nature and mind, of existence and man.

These can be humbling experiences because they often lead to the notion that man may not be the measure of all things or that he may not be at the top of the food chain or anything else. Our sense of self is most reachable and powerful when we are in a compassionate state or beyond the one self; it is at these moments when the answer to the question *Who am I?* becomes most apparent and transparent. One steps through the veil of illusion or through the other to find one-self on the other side in the hall of infinite mirrors.

The wither, thither and hither of nature and the universe is beyond our ken, but we are keen to it for keeping our own keep, kith and kin on an even keel. If one is too busy feeding the insatiable appetite, one may complete the round of life without sensing that anything was amiss or missing, and so end up as a complete stranger to oneself. Thus, the answer to whether you are with me or against me is moot and tautological in both context of self-denial and self-fulfillment, eternally perplexing and perplexingly circular.

Since words are the preferred or the only endowed means of communication, (humans lacking the grace, elegance, power, speed, ultra-senses and vocal-range hard-wired for non-humans), English speakers can resort to and find relief in acquiring greater depth and breadth through its poetic expressions, especially of the Romantic period, beginning at the age when a child can speak in complete sentences or by learning a non-amalgamated organic language which can be taught in a comparative if not in a comprehensive manner. This is preferable to learning or resorting to kicking and punching, screaming and ranting, hysteria and mania, splashing colours about, or less frequently but equally undesirably, withdrawing into silence and inactivity— all symptomatic of apoplectic undercurrents. Artistic expressions, creations and achievements are prized and admired because such concentration, convergence and fusion or virtuosity of poetry, vision, beauty and power are rare, but universally appealing and understood, transcending language, culture, religion and other a priori inclinations.

As populations centres grew in concentration, diversity and transiency, impregnating local customs with externally derived ideas, goods and gods,

- England went empirical with empire building, industrialization, commercial and colonial plunder and exploitation, a leader in the valuation of the tangible, bullyism and the process of homogenization for hegemonization until eclipsed by its former colony;

- France went rational, transfixed and bedazzled with itself into cycles of revolution, fratricide and terror;

- America combined the best or the worst of English and French excesses, many of which tend to reflect and distill their long tradition of mutual displeasure, intolerance and disdain, producing its own revolution and fratricidal slaughters, reprieved from one blood-letting to another by Mammon;

- Italy had the past glories of *Pax Romana*, the pope, the arts and artifacts as well as the credit for seeding and seeping Romecentricism, Romanism and Romanization into many diverse languages, arts, cultures, laws, religions and ideas, which still drive and colour the globalization impetus and appetite for duplication, efficiency, uniformity and over-the-top consumption; and

- Germany, post-Luther, dazed, reeling and confused in the aftermath resulting from the duration and magnitude of blood-letting and gore of religious fervour and rife, with fractured and fragmented lives, and lorded over by hundreds of absolute despots, delved further inwards into the mind. The sensitive and cultured souls and minds gave rise to

Romanticism in order to bring back and intensify the sense of being human with dignity and belonging in the natural and spiritual worlds via individual identity, self-knowledge and integrity, to withstand the calamities of life's *sturm und drang*.

Art is not so much an invocation of the past but an awakening call to the spirit with much of the debate regarding taste having to do with the nature of the call. It can be jolting and jarring, splashing and scattering, or calming, soothing, balmy, sublime and centering—or all of the aforementioned in a bundle. A picture, like specific performance, is worth a thousand words, but even with Chinese ideograms a completeness of expression may not be entirely satisfactory. It can still leave much aside, unsaid or unsayable, defining a space of silence and emptiness which propels and necessitates its opposite and vice versa. In Chinese, as in Korean art, many works are created by individual artists who integrate drawing with calligraphy and poetry, with each representing an integral part of the whole.

Speaking a language is a distinct and separate experience from entering one, which cannot be divorced from its unique perspective and experience of and within time and space. The process of learning a language is endless. It is like finding an oyster and figuring out what is inside without killing it. Knowing that a grain of sand is in the kernel of the pearl does not diminish or detract from its beauty, but renders it even more wondrous. What would be the point of proving that there is a pearl by killing all the oysters, or that there is a grain of sand by grinding up all the pearls? If the oyster is just gobbled up whole, one does not know if there ever was a pearl or not; only that it satisfied a hunger or taste.

Art is an attempt to satisfy a desire or longing for completeness of expression, encapsulating the infinite states, gradations or aura of happiness and unhappiness, ease and unease, tension and release, contraction and dilation, natural and supernatural, internal, external and intermediary, and finally the meaning of home and family in their numerous contexts. Language is an organic work of art in the way it looks, sounds and feels. Art and language are inexorably linked and inseparable. The written word is perhaps the greatest participatory work of art, a creation and testament of a people, reflecting and demonstrating their creative power, spirit and longing. It is an expression of the desire and need to live together and co-exist, accepting tearing someone apart literately, not literally, which tends to be an act of rare and final resort by the true literati and in itself is an appreciable art form developed dialectically. Vanity and illusion of the mind are no less challenging to break through and overcome as those in physical dimensions throughout our existence in a world of images as we try to capture glimpses of the elusive and ever-changing realities and Means.

There are many terms in the Chinese language depicting impressions, a sensation or state of the aura inside, outside and in-between the spheres of all that exists, particularly in the context of public relationships. We, like all other sensorily endowed beings, experience this art-like quality and impression of life in the infinite permutations and filtration of our senses, physically, emotionally, intellectually and spiritually, in a unique moment of time and space. This experience can leave us in a suprasensorial, spirit-like state of wonder, reverence and humility or in a temporal and fixed state of vanity, arrogance, ignominy, impudence and ignorance. How strange we must seem to each other given such an infinite variation of perception. It is a miracle that we can agree on anything and share so much in common as to create and agree upon a common language which serves not only as a means of expression, but also as the organic and evolving glue that keeps us from sliding into chaos.

Individuals are so distinct, even amongst family members, that to insist that we are all the same is a non-starter in any viable culture. This is quite evident in the intensity and duration of conflicts and purges in countries supposedly of one race, as well as in the internecine tribal and family feuds and factionalism enshrined from generation to generation, from ancient to modern times, with dire consequences for all. This fixation on apparent and superficial differences as well as those that run deeper cannot be resolved without even more deeply held shared values of life and the value of living as a starting point. The emphasis is upon individual cultivation of mindfulness, not universality.

Virtue, grace and compassion need to be cultivated along with a code of ethical conduct from childhood and throughout life because these, much less than their counterparts, are not natural inclinations, divinely inspired or otherwise. These words are found in virtually all languages which have been created and given specific meanings, similar and alike, having been passed on

58. "... tradition which holds that man cannot attain the right path through his own unaided efforts, and the inference is that individual fulfillment is more likely to lead to vice and evil than anything else." D.S. Roberts, op. cit., p. 79.

and taught through the generations since their opposites were more likely to prevail,[58] being less unavoidable and inevitable in life. These words and concepts, including those of sacredness and divineness, were around long before the advent of top-down religious institutions and will remain long after their obsolescence. Sexuality, gender, ethnicity, age, class and religious beliefs are just the tip of the iceberg of all our infinite differences, and education that leads to the heart and soul of a language, initiates and liberates the mind.

Compassion or parental love would not be such a challenge if we indeed were all the same. To insist that we are all the same when even these few apparent differences are so amplified by the mass media as well as in experience of daily life is to feed the desire to express unmistakable and distinct differences and be so recognized. Intolerance will only increase as the chasm between what is drilled and propagandized and what is, widens and deepens, with loss of credibility.

Religions are a result of and preceded by a language and a culture, and to the extent that new knowledge is integrated and values evolve around the central theme of a better understanding of man, his relationship to others and to the natural world, they serve their purpose. Religions that remain stagnant and static, frozen and petrified in time, fixated on dogmas, force fitting a straight-jacket on diversity may sprout tentative branches, but wither and shrivel away at the root and trunk, losing purpose and relevance. Christianity, a homocentric religion, seems to have lost touch with and interest in man and has become not only counter-cultural but culture destructive with its polarizing tendencies.

Where would Christianity be without the might of the sword in the past and nowadays, with its consumer-oriented economic, mass media and marketing arms appealing to those who like their beliefs neatly and tidily packaged and spoon-fed along with brand images, souvenirs and a book as an indicator of some kind of status or achievement? It is a religion that is not only nauseatingly self-righteous but insists upon conversion or punishment for non-subscribers in its tenets, history and practice. It seems to exist on a separate plane of existence from the daily lives of its subscribers, with periodic billings and reminders.

For some, as in many countries with entrenched class structures, being identified with the religion of the only remaining superpower may represent upward class mobility or a sense of equality and liberty. It may serve to signal their difference, modernity or trendiness in being identified with a new and different entity on the local scene. It could be a symptom of insecurity in search for a pacifier or warm and fuzzy blanket that holds out a promise of protection in the next cycle of war or catastrophe. It may be that their temporal lives are so overwhelming and fraught with insurmountable difficulties and trials that they find the chimera of paradise or heaven after death, consoling.

That Western countries tend to proclaim themselves to be Christian seems to go hand-in-hand with their inclination toward capitalism and materialism, coupled with military might representing the expediency of the sword in lieu of text in their dealings with the others. In this regard, Eastern traditions, Judaism and Islam seem closer allies in their faith based on text, in their strong code of conduct pivoting around family unit and unity, and the concept of brotherhood. These, combined with reverence and respect for scholarship for its own sake and for the elderly, incorporate the precedence of virtue and learning over the material and profit which are kept in check from their tidal sweep over the core values in the heart, mind and spirit of their community which breathes life into the culture. As all elements of society are involved in the observance and reverence for cultural or religious practices there is less of a reliance on a police state with its exclusive and labyrinthine and leviathan criminal and civil justice systems. Such systems are detached from any sense of a personal code of conduct or ethics, governing honour and dignity, so enmeshed in the social fabric of ancient and Eastern traditions focused on prevention. Within these traditions, all members pay a premium by concession or curtailment of individual liberty, will or inclination in favour of the privilege of continuity and belonging. There is greater investment and focus on prevention, rather than the payback and payoff orientation whereby justice comes into play only after commission, detection, irrefutable proof, trials and appeals, and sentencing, culminating in confinement or execution of the perpetrator, without any sense of justice having been served or achieved. All that the paper shuffling serves to generate is an abundance of billable hours, tabs and mountains of garbage.

Any concessions of will are an anathema to Americanism or are un-American, giving up an iota of what are considered sacred and absolute rights is inconceivable and moreover immoral. Such is the outcome in a milieu where absolutely nothing is forbidden, prohibited and censored whereby all rights are absolute, resulting in an inversion and perversion of culture without a common and unifying kernel of truth or beauty that can endure, nourish and guide through the *sturm und drang* that is life. It is literally shoot first, aim maybe, and perhaps get ready where life is meaningless, mean and has no value. This is perhaps best evidenced in the amount of readiness and preparedness with investment in organic time, material, knowledge and effort prior to conception of new life. This seems a uniquely human attribute, unlike the birds and the bees with all their nests, hives, vigilance and team-work.

This bleak scenario is not new or unique to America; we have seen this in many places and times throughout our shared history. But like much else in America, it is greatly magnified, spilling out onto the largest and most spectacular consumer canvass for all to behold. The picture painted and projected around the world, over and over, results in disdainful shrugging-off of anything American, retaliating in anger and despair, or joining in on the fray in avarice and envy. Is this why 95% of the Old World people and their way of life were displaced—to make way for the new owners with naming rights to the New World?

Are Americans so evolved that what is sacred is the right to bear all manner of arms in order to terminate and cannibalize life indiscriminately, with unlimited absolute rights of technology, liberty and abandonment? This is accommodated by re-labeling appetite and mindlessness as progress and efficiency, lubricated and band-aided by money and entertainment, in place of organic humors or the soup of life. So what results is the alphabet soup and reduction into A, T, G and C strings versus *chi*-charged strands of time. It is a world where an overkill of microscopic fine print with economic and legal mumbo-jumbo segregates pain from gain, control from ownership, and responsibility from authority. These separations and transformations of the organic to inorganic are executed with laparoscopic precision, causing minimum distress and disruption to the inorganic systems, and maximum insult and rupture to the organic beings, duly anesthetized and conditioned into mindlessness. The kitchen knife used by our mother to prepare the meals for her family symbolizes work that honours life with honourable services rendered, day-in and day-out, above that of the surgical scalpel. The well-being of the family nestles in the hands of our mothers who transform the labour for wage outside into a labour of love inside. It is only when rights are balanced with rites that democracy will fulfill its potential as the culture of the highest denominator—instead of the cult of the lowest, lost and lonely.

One way to appreciate cultural identity is to examine the effect on people who have been deprived of their cultural identity or have had severe trauma inflicted upon it. There are many historical and present day examples of the effect of colonialism, forced relocation and forced assimilation, as well as characteristics of societies with a clear cultural identity transcending borders and sovereignties. In the former category are people who were transported en masse for slave labour and for political assertion, such as African-Americans and Korean-Japanese, as well as those throughout outlying areas of Russia and China. In the latter category are dispersed and dispossessed peoples such as Armenians, (Russia, Turkey, Iran), Kurds (Turkey, Iran, Iraq), Jews and Gypsies. One can also study those cultures which have survived, in spite of great odds, withstanding the military might used by other cultures to obliterate them. Such study enables one to appreciate the infrangibility, durability and resilience certain cultures impart to the belongers.

To appreciate the concept of what passes as relative and therefore is purely subjective, consider the likeness in *you like coffee, I don't/you believe in God, I don't/you believe in killing, I don't.* The line crossed from what is relative to what is not, is quite clear. There is a bridge to be crossed, from having the power to exercising that power. This is the bridge of ethics which is primed by cultural imperatives. The encounters and outcomes of crossing this bridge between *what I can do* and *what I should do* both test and shape the ego in its preferences or choice-making skills. This is the rubicon of the mind: to deny, to flee, to succumb, to accept, to repel, to destroy, to annihilate, or to navigate skillfully and negotiate from the familiar to the unfamiliar, unknown or different. How can anyone be anything but a product of his culture and his times?

To appreciate the kinds of behaviour that relativism promotes and the kind of reaction it inspires, the following examples can be considered:

1. People who take such tremendous pride in their own ignorance and limitations *viz., that's all I know and care to know* and *that's the way I am, take it or leave it.*

2. People who are impressive in their possessive attachment to their own garbage and vice with enormous investment in time, money and effort, but quick with dismissive contempt for those characteristics in

others, particularly visible in the attitude, *it's not my litter* and *it's not in my space.*

3.   People who make such an all-out effort to insulate and preserve in stasis their own status of knowing and knowledge with built-in auto-deflect defense mechanisms. They seem to be clinging on for dear life in desperation and fear, unwilling and unable to let go.

4.   People who believe that it is their inalienable and inviolable right not to be challenged and therefore not to be made to explain, justify, qualify or defend their positions. Dialogue is impossible and trialogue, unimaginable.

5.   People who don't grow (up) and change, who have absolutely no regret or remorse and are tremendously proud of never having changed their *rigor mortis* positions at all costs or for any reason.

These examples typify extreme insulation and fortification, designed not only to protect but to deny or repel anything remotely disagreeable or different.

The American parents are trapped in a cultural no-win box where their opinion carries the same weight as their children's, since everyone is entitled to an opinion and since everyone is equal. They have an inherent inability to exert authority. To say *my house, my rules* simply is not addressing the issue, in that once the child leaves home he has no impetus to follow what he has been taught. That is why, if people in general, including parents, opt for arbitrariness (*because I say so/just do as you are told*) the result is an outcome that benefits neither the one nor the many. To say *because I'm older than you* or *because I'm your parent* would not go very far in a society where age is viewed with irreverence, bordering on derision or disdain, and where the joint, non-severable and lifelong moral responsibility of parenthood is not held in any great esteem compared to material wealth.

This attitude also has profound implications for teacher/student rela-tionships. What do parents who have it out with teachers prove? That they are actively involved and are smarter than teachers? They have merely demonstrated their own lack of respect for teachers as mentors and figures of authority, and for teaching as a profession. This lack of reverence then becomes the attitude of the children, who also feel equally entitled to judge and disparage their teachers. Like other people in supervisory and custodial positions, teachers serve a keystone function with both immediate and direct as well as long-term and indirect implications for the one and the many. Individual teachers, as in all other professional bodies, may have short-comings, but teaching and teachers as a critical social function and group need to have their roles and status respected and safeguarded. The 19th-century and lingering American tradition of relegating minding and teaching to those whose economic liberty is severely curtailed or restrict-ed and thereby default into the role of teachers needs radical revision if children and their education are truly of paramount concern today. Unionization of teachers, while answering economic and political equaliza-tion with any other group of non-white collar workers does not address nor uplift the social and cultural status of the teachers but quite the reverse, as they are measured and yoked to the same levelling monetization systems.

In light of the tendency towards expediency and arbitrariness, isn't it preferable to have a cultural imperative which has withstood the test of time and has been thoroughly vetted by scholars through the ages, which states that everyone must have respect for the elders, and is supported and reinforced by all other imperatives as well as by all members of society? The Western cultures and their associated values are fundamentally inconsistent and contradictory to this way of thinking. The traditional culture is internally consistent and coherent; the prescribed code of conduct for all permutations of social interactions fulfills its intended goal to promote social harmony and propriety by encouraging prudent behaviour without denying or suppressing individuality or divorcing the individual from human nature.

One has to be either incredibly arrogant or ignorant to believe that one can construct one's own cultural identity if one truly appreciates and understands all the separate and yet consistent elements required in its make-up. Even if such a self-construct is possible, a cultural identity of one is in practice meaningless, just as is a religion with only one believer. One is caught up in fighting a losing war, without any understanding of what one is fighting for or gaining, merely that my struggle (*mein kampf*) must con-tinue to preserve my own way. In most societies, individuals with this type of outlook are incarcerated or diagnosed as dysfunctional. If you listen to what these individuals say and how they try to justify themselves, the dan-gers of unimpeded self-construct are apparent: *It's not my fault, it's the fault of society/Nobody understands me/So what/Who cares.* This is the corollary of juvenile and unconstrained individuality: alienation and isolation which manifest in danger to others.

The paradox of individualism is in its plurality: its deceptive liberty or enslavement with respective pulldown menus of options, profound limits, complexity and universality resulting in infinite permutations and possibilities of the one and the many, in varying degrees of harmony or conflict thereby manifested. The scale of destruction and slaughter, unintended and benign or deliberate and malignant, were not lost on the past thinkers, as these were very much in evidence both in their own times as in times past. Those with an optimistic outlook reverted back to the individual, appealing to the best in human nature and advocating the cultivation of mindfulness, while those pessimistic, resorted to tyranny or suppression, recognizing the worst of it. Both sides' prescriptions were characterized by no shortage of rules and conditions of engagement and disengagement reflecting: In People We Distrust.

Schools are increasingly depending on and intersecting with commercial interests and morphing into institutions of dogma and commerce, disseminating and graduating singularities and price tags, rather than of erudition for discerning shades of truths and lies. They indulge and cater to economic demands, measures and results that preclude balance between the arts and sciences as well as positive and negative capabilities. Positive capabilities are amenable to leisurely pursuit at one's own time and expense for self-examination, whereas negative capabilities require greater exertion in order to qualify and produce services worth examination and consideration by others. Both capabilities help fill in the blanks as one aims for a sense of completeness between the bookends of life. The cultural grid provides for a sense of integrity between what one lives on and off, with by and for, sustaining and stabilizing the body and the mind, linking material with materiality.

In a culture that reveres scholarship, there is no intent or need to suppress or eradicate challenges of the cultural construct or to brainwash and indoctrinate the populace into absolute compliance. The cultural imperatives clearly define the end or the goal: to promote social harmony and propriety (dignity and honour of one and all). The means are prescribed but are by no means exhaustive, restrictive or even enforced by law. Scholarship is given such prominence because questioning and challenging the cultural construct without intellectual maturity, discipline, rigour and integrity are not only futile and meaningless, but unworthy. It is said that civilizations are judged by how their weakest members are treated, and much can be said for a culture in how it esteems teaching and teachers.

Similarly, the Talmudic, Buddhist and other traditions encourage debate by those qualified through study of the text, with an in-depth appreciation of all that has been debated before by the best trained minds. Much of the practice of law requires an understanding and knowledge of precedents for legal arguments and formulations of laws which are precedent-setting, precedent-consistent, or precedent-breaking. A scholar may be most tolerant of fools in the wider context of the society, but in the specific discipline and tradition of debating the text, most intolerant. Livelihood depends much on knowing the new and latest, superseding the old and the outdated. But life is served by timeless, cumulative and collective knowledge which enables an individual to gain perspectives which are not limited nor defined by a single lifespan of experience in time and space.

Departing, deserting or denying one's cultural identity, in toto, signifies preference for delusions of freedom and giving in to becoming merely a victim of personality. To decide that a sense of belonging is replaceable or can be superseded by a belief in self-determination is to have traded one's essence as a human being for a fool's paradise. Such an escape from one's cultural identity is not possible without a toll on one's well-being nor without dimunition in immunity to loneliness and alienation. Can respect for the elder (age and experience), filial piety (honour, duty, dignity, responsibility), reverence for scholarship ("the only freedom to which knowledge contributes is freedom from illusion"[59]) simply be replaced or superseded by the singular and

---

59. Isaiah Berlin, *The Proper Study of Mankind: An Anthology of Essays*, op. cit., p.107.

simple 'I want'? Are human beings born with awareness of equality and liberty or even happiness, and do they make sense in the context of the one 'I'?

The attraction of religion may reside in imparting an illusion of absolute and great knowingness bordering on smugness, with the added benefit of imbuing life with meaning and importance which flatter and console the vain and wandering ego, shrouding it from reality: *ergo*, ignorance is bliss. The non-deniability and non-necessity for proof of such beliefs provide the basis for both its intransigence and durability. Whether one is a cult follower or an enlightened believer pivots upon: (a) attitude towards the other in inclusivity or exclusivity, (b) reconciliation with uncertainty at the moment of truth juncture, (c) understanding paradoxes which can energize and liberate rather than paralyze and un-nerve, and (d) integrity or consistency of beliefs held (internal reality) with words and deeds (external manifestations).

The paradox of an open system of beliefs which encompasses most cultural constructs is that the greater the latitude and tolerance for compliance and the easier it seems simply to leave the circle, the greater its cohesive influence and sense of belonging. There exists a coherent and consistent internal logic that may not always be so readily discernible, but rather sensed and felt. Choice-making implies trade-offs in terms of cost/benefit and risk/reward. How these parameters are assessed is largely a function of an individual's state of mind and degree of intellectual rigour and discipline. Insofar as a society is a collection of individuals, its ends cannot be allowed to careen in a sea of opinions deemed equally valid. The means may be many, but the goals cannot be as arbitrary as that of any one individual's. Is the process of enculturation breaking the spirit and destroying the nobility of the wild beast, or is it facilitating the full potential of the human being as a choice-maker and endowing the individual with a sense of place and purpose? Rather than limit human endeavour and development, enculturation liberates it to its fullest expression.[60]

60. "... true poetry was never a formal game...but always an imaginative expression of inward knowledge; 'nor would it be otherwise until the idea were exploded that knowledge can be easily taught, and until we learnt the first great truth that to conquer ourselves is the only true knowledge.' ...He observed of poetry that it united passion with order, and he very beautifully illustrated the nature of the human mind, which seeks to gratify contrary properties (as sloth and the horror of vacancy) at the same time...." Richard Holmes, *Coleridge: Darker Reflections*, op. cit., p. 269.

Philosophy, or the way of the reflective and reflecting mind that endures, tends to be process descriptive and dynamic rather than single-mindedly static and single goal-oriented. In this context, the Hegelian philosophy describes the processes of (1) becoming and transforming, (2) learning and remembering incrementally through gradation and graduation, and (3) relationships in the spheres of self, family, community and State. Woven throughout these processes are the roles of negative capability and the master/slave metaphor whereby wealth does not necessarily release the master from enslavement to money, image and the material or from the grip of Mammon, illusions and marketing machinations. Wealth does not liberate but oftentimes warps and distorts perceptions from inside-out and outside-in, both driven and consumed by greed, mean-spiritedness, *schadenfreude*, the overwhelming need to win and get away with murder by playing fast and loose with rules. More often than not, both the perpetrators and victims implicitly

Author's Note: In the absence of love, discipline and reverence—hate, willfulness and disdain too quickly fill the void to provide a platform for identity formation, emulating authenticity. This is unworthy of the dimensions of parental or compassionate love for the many who are blessed by such, directly and biologically, as well as indirectly and socially, via adoption, guardianship and mentorship, irrespective and independent of material, status and intellectual endowments, bestowals or entitlements. Sloth, sloppiness and slights kill more people and cause more harm than all the body count of wars of this and past centuries. These range from traffic accidents, road rages, defective O rings and artificial body parts to the numerous unintended consequences of toxic chemical releases and the improper and insane production, processing and preparation of foods. *Mea culpa*, truth and justice, are too little and too late compared to preventive and cautionary measures through attention to detail and greater care and concern for others over just oneself as life flashes by in what seems like seconds. Each life that comes into being as a result of countless generations of blood, sweat and tears is no more in a split second of mind disengagement. Contritions and retributions and trite expressions such as *I'm so sorry, I couldn't help it, it was beyond my control, it was such a trivial detail* are an insult and affront to humanity as statistics are finitely tuned and compiled to justify failure- and error-rates. How comforting it is to live in a world of acceptable margins or error, accidents, mistakes, oversights and no-fault disclaimers. How disconcerting it is that these tend to compound and amplify over time, gathering mass, force and momentum under such care, explanation and protection, resulting in grand and glorious recycling of mistakes. What passes for normal in the absence of a centred heart is merely the prevalence of aberrations which represent the norm, but increasingly less the Mean.

and explicitly sign-on to these practices which impart a sense of superiority to others at every level of fine status differentiation or categorization, perpetuating the master/slave role-playing traditions of non-symmetry. Being of service is not predicated upon inequality but quite the reverse, in the manifestations of compassion and dharma that link and serve both parties equally. Relationships can be considered to reside in the continuum of the master/slave metaphor that serves to illustrate the dynamics of compromise, self-knowledge and conflict resolution in the switching of roles throughout life, as in parent/child, mentor/student, elder/younger, boss/subordinate, buyer/seller, client/server, meal ticket/parasite or I/you. Then, there are numerous symbiotic relationships where, despite dramatic differences, the parties contribute towards mutual benefit, co-existence and harmony versus profit maximization and greed at the expense, destruction and enslavement of the other. These relationships provide the contexts for service, served and server: the rendering of service forms and provisions the critical platform for linkage and realization between the server and served.

Identity is formed, shaped and developed as the middle zone of the continuum is increasingly criss-crossed over time, with retention and flow-through of memories of trial and error within a specific cultural or relational framework, giving rise to a sense of centre, fitness and balance. To consistently ignore and trivialize the other is to ensure that one becomes ignorant and trivial: this is the insidiousness of self-censorship and willfulness associated with constricted and immature individualism versus a liberated and ripened individual. One cultivates negative capability by being mindful of one's relative position in the interactions with the other, which shapes, forms, develops and defines identity. It is the relationship itself which defines what hat is being or to be worn. There are hats that are immutable and interminable as well as changeable and temporal, but there is no self or identity without the other.

The master/slave metaphor also represents a continuum where values of the mind and minds reside in a state of dynamic equilibrium. The tensions between might and right, freedom and duty, equality and hierarchy, order and chaos, etc., are resolved through extraction of price and prize, whose significance is sometimes but not always recognized after the impasse. The quantities and qualities of the strands of the mind are in constant flux, adjusting, accommodating and resulting in various states of harmonic oscillation and fidelity, within and without. Virtues are on trial and realized at

junctures of simultaneous convergence and divergence or linkage and separateness that define and characterize relationships. The East tends to give
greater weight to linkage and the West to separateness. The rites and rituals
of a culture are attempts to pass on these virtues, whose veracity has been
verified by trials of conflicting interests through the ages. They recreate and
recognize the thresholds in the many stages of becoming, along with the
priority, numerity and variety of relationships that suggest and lead to
harmony with Nature. What one individual considers to be natural is distinct
and separate from Nature, and is more likely to be at odds with it or be its
antithesis. Rites, for the belongers, are unavoidable and inescapable
reminders and guards embedded in a specific culture against the inclination
towards separateness, mindlessness and heartlessness by discard, bypass or
non-formation of relationships with attendant filters and rules of engagement.

The trinity of Christianity, Democracy and Capitalism is a modern
utopian concoction. The religious template is a derivative and amalgamated
book whose precepts are seldom reflected in the daily lives of those who
classify themselves as Christians. The Ten Commandments are like a house of
cards; if you remove, bend or break one, the whole is no more. But it is not
just a house of cards, because those who break it will find themselves unable
to repair it or themselves, and recourse is unlikely to be sought by transgressors in any case. For those who keep it whole in their daily actions as well as
in their hearts and minds, it will remain a source of solace and strength,
imparting their lives with fullness and meaning. One's root is not to be found
in genealogy, but in one's heart and mind or conscience and attitude towards
oneself and therefore others. The political template without a cultural one is
likely to result in the dominance of power and might, a plutocracy or mob
rule. Finally, the economic template, operating in such a religious and
political cauldron, creates a milieu of mindlessness and heartlessness glued
together by money and technology. It is the triumph of the inorganic over
the organic. There is no truth or beauty to be beheld or beloved at its centre
because its nature is inhuman and inhumane.

The Internet bypasses relationship building and maintenance. In fact,
it must neglect it in operating as a facilitator of the unilateral 'I' of linear
assertions by incubating infallible unilateralism. The Internet is full of
dot.coms, but the dots are rarely connected by the users who are conditioned
into instant scanning and disposal versus reflective reading and comprehension. It does away with the master/slave continuum by converting all of its

users into equally tethered slaves hooked on speed and novelty, believing themselves to be masters. It draws upon its illusion of free and instant power, authority, opinion and choice coupled with illusions of freedom from costs, consequences, qualifications, judgement and identity. There is no adjudication, commission, omission, repentance, recrimination, retraction or recanting. It is a free-for-all for, of and by pseudo-identities floating in amorality and anonymity without the capstan of relationships. Just like the structure and function of the PCs that preceded it, the Internet can be most non-ergonomic. What enables the cosmic sounds generated by a great orchestra goes unappreciated.

There is goodness to be realized in both the roles of master and slave, with results that do not denigrate and exploit the other as means, but which can only be achieved with collaborative effort predicated upon recognition of the other. Not only is there an illusion of the end of the master/slave continuum in the Internet age, but the very notion of goodness is missing and unmissed. It is a world of premises without a platform of conclusions. It creates a sense of connectedness with the power to instantly disconnect or dispose at will, invalidating and nullifying the value and purpose of relationships—such relationships being the godhead and the truth of cultures.

The chicken and the egg are oneness preserved and linked through time, undismembered by space. One is unlikely to realize goodness as a parent without realizing it as a child through filial piety. Can one be in harmony with Nature without being a part of it? It is this symmetry in relationships that enculturation imprints. While most are adamantly and vehemently vocal about their own children, too few appreciate the concept of liberty and duty in parking both the young and the old in their charge, in institutional or inorganic settings to be literally and figuratively fed inorganic matter.

Fulfilling the role of a parent ostensibly gives rise to a greater sense of power and control over the future through one's progeny, whereas the relationships with one's predecessors do not. The latter tend to give rise to a sense of resentment as they are seen to represent obstacles, restraints and infringements upon self-autonomy. Filial piety or honouring the past is not very appealing versus 'being the master of my own brood' or fixing for the future, until and unless the flow of time is understood. The current is free to flow in only one direction at a time and only when there is no breakage or damming up in the circuitry. Reaching adulthood or parenthood is not a signal for flipping a binary switch shutting off on-going relationships with the past, parents, mentors and elders. Instead, it results in a greater demand upon mindfulness and expansion of mind-space as the fulcrum or centre of the master/slave continuum is increasingly traversed and encountered in the to and fro of conducting human life, humanely.

There are no longer any values that transcend the I. What is good is solely a function of what I deem it to be, interestingly juxtaposed with the mantra of *I must not be judgemental.* Such self-neutralization accompanied by an absence of negative capability for compassion or parental love also mark parents who:

1. feel that their progeny will accord them better treatment than they have theirs, recycling the myth that they are indubitably better parents than theirs have been;

2. believe that filial piety and respect for elders are irrelevant for commercial success, so that children are just means to be valued, developed or exploited for consideration; and

3. conceive and consume their children for their purpose, appetite and vanity which can only be uniquely satisfied by their own flesh and blood.

The images of children as come-ons for commercial transactions increasingly proliferate as do images of those, dead or alive, who are easy to exploit, manipulate and cannibalize permeate the landscape, so that the master/slave metaphor is no more. Rather than savouring the whole fruit, only the discardable and dismemberable peel and pit are flashed, flushed of flesh or substance and the seed within, with increasing efficiency.

The flaccid strings of value relativism cleave and cling onto isms as they float by, grafting, skimming and surfing sounds over which they no longer exert and exercise any will, becoming increasingly disconnected, out-of-synch and unable to recognize, read and sing the music of Being. Such is the venal nature of the twisted pseudo-relationships in modern utopia where everything becomes salable and purchasable for a price. Self-knowledge is not only not cultivated, but is avoided since it can only be an impediment to the venal bargaining process for a lifestyle of the quick, easy and simple. The liberty pursued is freedom from self-knowledge for the totalitarian cult of self. In such inhospitable soil, culture does not take root, and cultures that have existed for over thousands of years simply wither away. Reading becomes a mechanical process of speed, ease and entertainment, rather than reflective and reflecting integration and impregnation of knowledge, of the self and the other, locating attitude and informing conduct in pursuit of completeness.

The purpose of the special status assigned to scholarship and knowledge within the cultural framework serves:

1.   To act as a negentropic factor against stasis and stagnation of closed systems by elevating and exempting scholars and teachers from traditional definers of status: right of the first born, right of blood and right of land. Even in ancient slave-based societies, barriers to upward mobility were not insurmountable. Modern barriers proliferate as rights of private property escalate with ever finer superficial categorizations and even finer prints.

2.   To act as the invisible hand of restraint, reserve and recovery or healing against extremes. They serve as another vessel for safeguarding in perpetuity the cultural codes embedded in language and practice of relationships since qualified scholarship includes in-depth mastery of the cultural 'classics' covering ethics, literature and poetry as a compulsory prerequisite.

3.   To work in partnership with parents who prepare and ready their children by instilling proper attitudes toward teachers and teachings. The scope, depth and nature of study for adulthood requires a team of teachers over twelve-plus years. This is the most intensive period devoted to building redundancy or reserve capacity. No one mind is expected to retain all and act as custodian for all knowledge. There are qualified centres of knowledge within a distributed and distributive network.

In the absence of a cultural backdrop, the modern utilitarian, consumer and commerce-friendly education is the antithesis of the above purposes. The market demand for specialization, recognition and consideration conscripts and subsumes scholarship, so that there can be no effective invisible hand of moderation as alluded to by Adam Smith in *The Wealth of Nations* [1776]. The study and development of classic texts, ethics and poetry go out the window, since they elude binary or multiple choice testing as well as financial payoffs when money rather than character becomes the measure of all values. Since there are no longer any rites of passage or qualifications into majority status other than chronological age or commission of sexual activities or crimes that confer instant adulthood, the pool of graduating adults shrinks for both parental and teaching positions.

Prizes, awards and PhDs of modernity grow exponentially along with unhappiness. These recognitions tend to be more symptomatic and emblematic of extremes of singularity and exclusivity rather than diversity and inclusivity. Such products are more vulnerable to attacks, inconsistencies and breakdowns and tend to come with formidable and airtight defensive systems. These taut and rigid strings are unlikely to play true and full and are more likely to either snap or transform. There are virtually no PhDs with years of research, study and dissertations on freedom, equality, fraternity, unity, happiness, truth or justice in the context of a cultural or relational framework. They remain abstract and conceptual in their determination to be neutral, objective, rigorously rational and empirical—or in a word, unreal. There are vociferous and numerous advocates, reformers and champions of these terms, but rarely do they impart or increase knowledge of them or their practices or practice them in their daily lives, but quite the reverse. Knowledge is now only valued for its ability to make a reply: only answers are valued and valuable, so questions are similarly constructed to meet this market requirement.

For these reasons, most people tend to gravitate more to fiction, and fictional works retain their timeless resonance as they illuminate the workings of relationships in a cultural context. Opinions are subjectively driven, passionate and often controversial. An example is Mary Shelley's *The Modern Prometheus*, which conveys the potential and process of becoming human or inhuman as an affair of the heart rather than of form, which is often used as a sole indicator of what is good or bad as it lies in the eyes of the beholder. Such excitement and channeling of nervous energy which sparks the imagination and inflames the heart are not what generally characterize the modern corridors of learning. How difficult it is to retain one's sense of play and how easily it is extinguished by mass-produced, universalized and homogenized formal education and the mass media as idiosyncratic enculturation within one's home diminishes as a counter-force in favour of a self-identity.

The seduction of certainty of illusions and man-construed order triumphs over the uncertainty of reality and unknowable order of Nature, conveniently labeled as chaos. This is the *prima facie* cause of denial of self and self-knowledge that leads to non-discipline and non-development of skills for navigating life through infinite transformations. Absolute suppression, segregation and denial of negative emotions as well as opposite tendencies lead to infantilization, imbalance, imbecility and non-preparedness. This is the scenario of *I don't know and I don't care* or *I care only about what I know* versus I *don't know but I do care*. I don't care is not an attitude but a non-attitude or complete absence of sentiment. The fields of math and science are subsets of philosophy in expressing constant changes or transformations and of inter-relatedness and relationships under controlled experimental designs, with absolute and artificial constrictions and constraints over the range of variables and variabilities.

The purpose and design of Nature are not under our control because we are merely a link in its infinite chain. But we certainly try our utmost to subsume and destroy this linkage and consume as much as possible, as if engaged in a zero-sum game with all else, way beyond our sustenance or fair share. But the study of these fields of knowledge serves to prepare us for encounters with the uncertain and unknown as we gradually move out from the comfort and security of home and family to that of increasing variables and variability and decreasing control. This is accompanied by decreasing need to control as well as fear, over time. Through the journey of life comes an appreciation and reverence for the exuberance, exhilaration, exertion, diversity and transformation of Being.

Thus, science continuously affirms the unknowable by exploring and exposing the knowable, or it is as much about the physical as the metaphysical. Many great thinkers of the past have been categorized as metaphysicians and philosophers, but these professions have now been so marginalized with the advent of specialization and revenue potential, that they have largely disappeared. Who nowadays reads *The Monadology* by Leibniz (1646-1716), a work that explains individuality and co-existence, and was written by the man who discovered calculus, developed binary numbers, gave expression to coordinate geometry, and named Cartesian coordinates in honour of Descartes? The modern approach to nominations in manner and type tends to be vain and shallow, driven by considerations of coolness, hip-ness, political hegemony and rights via mass recognition and royalty or usage fees. Many critical thinkers of the past ages were individuals who seem to have found and remained faithful to their dharma as teachers, working from compassionate hearts rather than in search of fame and fortune, whose sweet and magnanimous natures can still be discerned in their works as preserved for posterity. The amœba may be single celled, but it contains all the necessary and sufficient organic virtues to live to its potential of life and to give life. Instead of distributive knowledge, there is a proliferation of patents and intellectual property rights to secure, hoard and lock-in the revenue streams.

The mind possesses dual reflective properties similar to the combined attributes of an ellipse and hyperbola, with the ability to change the location of the focus, the structure of the curve and the amount and direction of energy release. At its optimal focus, it maximizes convergence and dispersion, to and from the other focus, external or internal to it. The inner illumination or spark is formed and positioned through infinite permutations of trial and error, hits and misses, and gain and pain or redundancies. These encounters with the uncertain and unknown form, develop and shape the bent of the mind. The limits and boundaries of the mind are pushed and pulled by uncertainty and unknowability. The mind cannot pulsate, throb and excite with life unless it comprehends these frontiers upon which liberation and enslavement hinge. A mind that cannot value uncertainty and unknowability is unmoved by the marvels and wonders, not only of Nature but of anything else. With a supercilious, smug, superior and self-righteous bent, it clings onto comforting ignorance, confinement and non-exertion rather than meet the challenges and tensions of sobering reality.

The sublime ceases to exist when all values are relative to the sole 'I' and paradoxically at the same time, all values are absolute. In this state there is nothing that urges the mind onward to put out feelers for the way of truth by balancing along the beams of plurality. On either side of these beams reside too much or too little and over-valuation or under-valuation. By rigidly staying within the box of the known and certain, the essence is paralyzed or snuffed out by fear of the unknown. The cannibalization of time is fed by the sacrifice of minds reflecting the synchronicity, efficiency and symmetry of Man. Without a sense of centre to locate its own, the seed, with its potential for life and life-giving potential, does not germinate but rots to give life to another which may or may not locate its centre, and so on.

The kernel of truth finds its origin and proper alignment by building upon a reservoir of redundancies, discovering its power of convergence and divergence within the dynamic parallax of the magnetic rotating field. Its physical attributes do not matter; only its asymptotic attitude contributes to the intensity and radiance of the halo, being in tune with the One. Then fear is no more, energy is free to flow, and there is harmony and clarity. To ignore and dispose of redundancies is to close the portals of the essential spark so that no light shines in or out. The mathematical fascination with conical structure and their practical applications transcends their boundaries. The probability of realization of any truth approaches zero when all endeavours presuppose purpose and demand reward, rather than seeking the way of co-existence in pluralism and knowledge valued and pursued for its own satisfaction. The jackpot, crackpot and smart-ass mentalities flourish in a fool's paradise that cherishes fictional creations or illusions rather than engaging the enemies of self-identity in the battlefield of the mind. How challenging is it to address the problem of shredding tires for certain payoffs and paybacks versus the shredding of innocent lives?

To teach ethics and behavioural modes which sustain and support the goals of society is distinct from making judgements over the goodness or badness of an individual's choice or conduct (moralizing). This is a distinction of cause and effect, of prevention and punishment, of the role of guardian of family values and enforcers of legal statutes. Religions are very clear about the way to salvation and the just and good life, just as each culture has a model of a virtuous man and life. Cultural paradigms, like religion, recognize the foibles of man and have prescriptions for repentance and redemption. The importance is that there is awareness of a standard and a developed sense of when a *faux pas* has been committed and the line crossed beyond the pale. This minimizes the need for a mountain of legal statutes and the associated high cost of enforcement, which cannot effectively reduce or contain nor have any significant effect on criminal behaviour.

This also gives context to knowledge and its applications, because it too can be put to good or bad use as well as increase or decrease potential of the one or the many. Knowledge sometimes can be an impediment to liberty and progress, and one needs to appreciate the limitations of the various one-dimensional measures of intelligence, such as an IQ score, as well as the effect that awareness of this type of one-dimensional number can have on parents and children. The parents feel that because the child is so intelligent, he does not need to be pushed or disciplined, and the child, knowing that he is considered 'above average', stops making any effort. To inform or to tell the truth as one perceives it, without thinking multidimensionally, is not only without merit, but potentially harmful.

Ethics can educate the man but cannot force him to act in any other way than what he himself perceives to be in his best interest, which at best includes personal dignity and honour as well as a sense of duty and responsibility. You can lead a horse to water but you cannot make it drink: is the intellect of a human being equivalent to that of a horse or is it just horse-sense that's better? Just as an individual is capable of choosing a less desirable path despite all indications to the contrary and in spite of his own better judgement (Pascal: "...the heart has its own reasons that reason knows not of...."), cultural imperatives try to mitigate this dilemma to achieve an outcome that is least harmful to the one and the many. Morality (distinct from moralizing) can only operate in the context of conscientiousness and tries to prevent or minimize the harmfulness of the inevitable moments of unreasonableness in outcome. What is the point of scolding a child and screaming *What a bad boy you are!* if there is no understanding of why something is good or bad. There is a tendency to draw back from moralizing because there is an overabundance of arbitrary moralizing without any context, where standards have ceased to exist and their replacement is just an unqualified individual opinion.

It seems as though there are more TV programmes addressing the caring for and training of pets (with a host of interpretations of liberty) than for children. There is no shortage of programmes on financial investment, retirement planning, home improvement, gardening, cooking, travel, health and beauty tips; all revolve around money and are as purchasable as they are transitory. Tucked around this mountain of material how-to's, to-do's, and must-have's is a small, barely registerable blip on duty ethics, humanism and parenting skills. Whether one is conservative or liberal or somewhere in between, one has to question whether there is harm in relieving children from the awesome burden of having to figure out for themselves what no other generation had to do on its own, particularly since a comprehensive body of knowledge already exists regarding: (1) what it means to be a human being and what humanizing values are, (2) how to get along with others, (3) what the basic rules of acceptable behaviour are, (4) why certain values are important, (5) how choice-making involves trade-offs in the multidimensional framework of materiality, perspective and context, as well as compassion, tolerance and compromise.

Every child needs to be taught ethics and humanism through case study methods designed for appropriate age groups at every year of school attendance. Promotion to the next grade and graduation should require a pass in these critical core subjects. No other subject will contribute as much to the child's well-being and flourishing throughout his or her life. All children from the age of four, when control over their bodies is complete and their mastery of language is adequate to express themselves, should be treated as potential adults; acceptable and unacceptable speech and behaviour should be clearly taught. This, more than indulgence at this stage of life, will perhaps circumvent the need for subduing children with medication (which may carry on throughout life), the endless rounds of counseling and psychotherapy, temper tantrums or other emotional outbursts leading to rage, violence and feelings of alienation and loneliness resulting in withdrawal and isolation. These outcomes are all the more tragic because they are, in most cases, both mitigable and preventable.

Perhaps this focused and targeted educational effort will result in less explicit need for ethical guidelines in various professional bodies where common sense is in short supply, as in all other areas of society where aimlessness, arbitrariness and instant animosity seem to rule. Every young child from early infancy looks to and tests the adults for clues and cues as feedback for acceptance or rejection. A child may not understand ethics and yet be able to completely appreciate what he or she wants and needs to learn in order to find acceptance and livelihood within and beyond the unconditional love of the family. In this regard, an extended family life plays an important role for enculturation and socialization of a child, as he or she learns to appreciate pluralities within and without, as the circle of kinship and unconditional love expands and diffuses. The child has greater opportunity to observe and learn its relative position, how to behave, handle conflicts, not always be the centre of attention, not always get his or her way, as the degree of consanguinity diminishes, relative to the child, while still within the safety zone of the family circle.

This is the true source of personal confidence and strength; mastery of the art of getting along and discipline over the self builds confidence like no other subject can. It is not education with degrees and diplomas that is the great equalizer, but mastery of the language of relationships representing the heart and spirit of a people, sharing common time and space with self-knowledge. Even if this cultural paradigm is abandoned or rejected through different stages and circumstances in life, it can always be returned to, just as one can return to one's home for safe harbour rather than the alternatives of having nothing at all, an artificial self-construct, or a by-product of an entertainment phenomenon.

In the East Asian continent, there has been no equivalent to a pope, papal see or religion-based empires of the likes of the Holy Roman Empire or the Ottoman Empire. While there certainly has been no lack of epic wars, religious fervour and crusades of slaughter and mayhem in divine dimensions whereby the name of God is invoked to justify such campaigns instigated, organized, financed and propelled by religious orders, have largely been avoided or prevented. Some well-known examples are the numerous Holy Crusades, the Spanish Inquisition, Salem witch trials and ceaseless pogroms.

Being virtuous and keeping one's good name is not a function of a religious label, but requires a life-long effort at self-reflection and self-knowledge aimed at understanding the plurality in the one and the universal. It involves spending time wisely; if not in and of service to others, then at least ensuring that no harm is caused. The home of cultural identity is not to be found in absolute and narrow isms or religions, but within the self and society where values are unlikely to be simple, quick and easy to master but worthwhile in the long haul for many generations to follow. There is no one path or answer but, rather, as many as there are different individuals willing to make the journey. This approach is less likely to end in regret, and the test is only of and for the self. Overcoming one's vanity, prejudice, hate and fear are as difficult as achieving self-knowledge because they are one and the same. There is no reward or recognition at the journey's end; only the clarity and gentleness of the heart and mind, bathed in the serenity of happiness.

The religious orders have effectively exploited the dualistic tendency of human nature and weaknesses to swell their base, the main achievement being the extensive and almost monopolistic employment of terms such as soul, heaven and hell, and the commission and redemption of sin. Although the ancient Greek philosophers studied and passed on what virtuous life meant for human beings, philosophy was not then, nor has it ever been a hot item with potential for mass market revenue.

Religion seems to have realized the market potential in appealing to the downtrodden and the ignorant, trapped in poverty and class structures, unable or unwilling to make the journey of self-knowledge without recognition and reward, but preferring further extension and development of their prejudices against those who will not indulge their vanity or willful wants. The notion of Keats's 'negative capability',[61] which opens the door to many other realities[62] as well as to the many, has no role to play in such a scenario; only the reverse is practiced and cultivated. While oppressive states have imposed

---

61. "Turgenev possessed in a highly developed form what Keats called negative capability, an ability to enter into beliefs, feelings, and attitudes alien and at times acutely antipathetic to his own...." Isaiah Berlin, 'Fathers and Children, the Romanes Lecture' [1970] in Ivan Turgenev, *Fathers and Sons* [1862] (Penguin Classics, 1975), p. 9.

Author's Note: The extreme case of this capability is when people are defined by what they hate or you are what you hate or 'be you see', as in stepping into the shoes of the other in order to connect or being a victim of solely sensory inputs.

62. He invoked the Pythagorean maxim, "until you understand a writer's ignorance, presume yourself ignorant of his understanding." Richard Holmes, *Coleridge: Darker Reflections*, op. cit., p. 407.

continued

merely a lifetime worth of physical strictures, religious dictates have been very comprehensively devised to preside over not only these dimensions, but also the heart and mind with their most successfully and creatively deployed term 'soul'. This enables governing not only this temporal life, but reaching all the way through eternity with the reward of heaven or unending agony in hell.

Judaism is a belief system that resulted from an organically developed culture over thousands of years. It has survived and will continue to do so because of this organic and holistic character of its people and their cultural paradigm regardless of place. Christianity is an amalgamation on many influences including Aramaic, Greek and Latin languages, as well as Hellenism and Paganism, and although it contains many similarity to Judaism, it is largely a reactionary movement away from it because the former demands much more and is much more demanding than the effort and sacrifice that most people are willing to make. Christianity is born of an evangelical impulse or zealous propagandizing fervour, marching to *Onward Christian Soldiers*.

Islam is also an amalgamation originating in a place of active trade and commerce. It is perhaps a reaction against non-indigenous ideas and divisive economic influences as well as the fickle, vain and fleeting individualistic memories that posed not only a political but a cultural threat in undermining and displacing an ancient Arabic culture. Although, like Judaism, it inter-

Author's Note: Similar sentiments are also expressed by Socrates: "He who knows not and knows not that he knows not is a fool. He who knows not and knows he knows not is wise." The Pythagorean virtue of triangles (triangulation, trinity) derive resilience and endurance from mutually illuminating, verifying and validating each point through the integrity, realization and release of truths or *veritas*. *Veritas* does not shy away from light, go AWOL, resort to any gall, guise or guile, and give or take any quarter, but binds, heals and nourishes, all the while showing that truth is beauty and beauty, truth. The third rail of our way versus my way or the highway, transcends the limited binary outlook, and points both parties towards the Way, imparting a sense of direction towards harmony through compromise and common purpose, transcending the limits of self-service. One of the oldest revealed truths to Zarathustra (628-551 B.C.), the Persian prophet and founder of Zoroastrianism, is the trinity of good thoughts, good words and good deeds as reflections and affirmations of each other, illuminated by light, within and without, existing in non-severable and infrangible unity, i.e. not as separate and independent elements to be categorized. This is in stark contrast to the unreal, static and negative bling-bling of 'see no evil, hear no evil, speak no evil'.

twines with daily life, the concept of universal brotherhood and unity cannot have appealed deeply, rooted profoundly or held great sway with the many. This is the case with most nomadic and tribal cultures with a clear idea of belongers and the others, reinforced through millennia of rituals and practices of shared, recorded and recollectable memories, as well as ties of blood and land. Religions in current form and practice, as captive monotheisms, represent extreme static codification, exclusive to a time and place, and are not dynamic and organic in their essence, which seems to be a radical departure from their original intent and design to educate and liberate the human spirit.

Where would Christianity, Islam and other dogmatic beliefs be without the ignorance and poverty of the masses and without their use of military and political capital or intense and active engagement in temporal affairs for maintaining totalitarian control? How many more organic and holistic cultures and languages would have survived without these hegemonic forces? Rather than good news for men they have caused ineffable grief and destruction under the banner of absolutism in creating an illusion of certainty. The fear and suppression of truth is implicit in belief systems so at odds with the reality of daily life, human nature, the natural world and most of all with its own teachings of brotherhood and unity. They do not connect the polarities with a bridge or intermediary space, but insist upon separation and separateness so that life is no longer holistic but schizophrenic, with deep and festering wounds or insults that do not heal.

The potential of globalization in reducing poverty and ignorance is appealing, but carried forward in tandem with the message of capitalism, greed and excess, it cannot produce such results. Rather, the reverse will occur with greater efficiency, producing a further decline in happiness where it is already in short supply. The remedy is that most viable and perpetual cultures contain counter-forces and brakes against material excess and mindlessness so that integration of the new with the old ways ensures preservation of the cultural heart and its beat for those who are enlightened enough or fortunate enough to have one. These evolved and designed rituals and codes incorporated the ties and bonds of a people with their land, reflected and internalized in the language and their expressions, so that what flows from within as a result of enculturation seems habitual, second-nature, dyed and embedded into daily life.

The traditions of the Old World that criss-crossed the four cardinal points in the seven continents, represent formidable creations of magnanimous hearts and minds who saw much that needed preservation, protection and perpetuation from and for man, especially man from himself. They are acts of compassion which impart a sense of belonging, of home, of centredness, and a kernel of truth, enabling the people to flourish as they moved or were moved, coming into contact, intermingling and integrating the new and the unfamiliar. The cultural paradigm enables incorporation of new knowledge into an expansive framework radiating out and expanding from the kernel and radiated by it throughout. The centre will hold amidst the swells and swirls and is meant to hold as the structure and content grow and change like all organic creations. It can sustain anomalies, paradoxes, and tolerate differences because these by definition are exceptions and give greater meaning to the overall coherence, symmetry and pattern. Through distance of time and dispersion over many lands and generations, the centre remains, its heart unmoved and untouched, calm and steadfast, a lighthouse that broadcasts its beacon of light to give a sense of hope and home, guidance and solace for all travelers, all similarly at sea and in the dark.

The Jewish culture, like other ancient cultures that place high value on wisdom (knowledge and experience), the learning process and the elderly will live into the future. People who badge, blazen and bleat their identity as true believers, strict constructionists and fundamentalists destroy and displace human culture while emulating it, and their superficial disdain of capitalism, while hoarding and enjoying its spoils, masks their intent for political hegemony and deception. Their leaders promote totalitarianism and isolationism while espousing brotherhood and unity, instigate hate and fear while preaching love and peace. The low-activation-energy (short, unstable or delicately fused) follower-types are easily excited, deceived and set off for anachronistic purposes that do not become them nor serve their interests. Anachronism tends to be regressive, oppressive and destructive resulting in carnage or waste maximization: the usual outcome of utopian enterprises. They should return to their indigenous culture to find rich and rewarding sources of material for study, inspiration and self-knowledge, above and beyond the one-book-and-no-other, one-way-or-no-way impasse of Christianity. After all, the formidable knowledge amassed in the Arabic culture gave impetus to the age of Renaissance and much else to the world at large. The transfer of knowledge from Arabic cultures was limited and selective, and therefore was developed and deployed for aggression against the many (along with exploitation, impoverishment, destruction and dehumanization), for the benefit of the few. Whether the Arab empire has been diminished or not, its culture is one that embodies an ancient family code and a deep bond with the land, independent of the more recent imposition of religious or political beliefs and practices.

Implicit in the use of any bilingual dictionary is, if not an extensive and comprehensive knowledge, at least a working knowledge of another language. In a similar manner, understanding one's own culture requires an effort to understand its language in some depth and breath for the context of its heart and mind, and understanding another requires a similar and greater level of effort beyond the mechanics of translation. A sense of centredness gives bearing to the self from and with which it can venture forth, not only with positive but negative capabilities. Both these capabilities are essential for understanding and navigating in the intermediary space of infinite plurality. No religion is preferable to one that confines the mind in a binary format rather than liberating it. The sacred books offer insights of a time, place and a people, but they are not the sacred soul of the people which is only found in their language and culture.

Regardless of when and where one came into existence, one can always have access to a cultural identity: life comes together through the understanding of the body, mind and spirit in this sequence of unfolding; to treat them as discrete and independent components results in discord and opaqueness within and without, because there can be no harmonic oscillation, no ties that bind, no bonds that heal, no clarity and oneness, only the coming apart.

The notion that men are born free does not seem to bear out in the context of the overwhelming need to belong to the extent of submitting to an absolute belief system constructed by men, mostly on a voluntary basis or with little prodding. The corollary of this tendency is the cultivation of hate and fear: to define non-belongers, the other, those not worthy of merit and consideration as a human being or a genuine person—such individuals or groups to be pelted with all the malfeasance that can be mustered. Thus the definition of the set becomes all important and paramount. This is the paradox within all restrictive and absolute isms and beliefs: how broadly brotherhood, humaneness and unity apply.

A pro-life philosophy that embraces co-existence in diversity as well as the organic virtues of permeability and transience is viewed as an assault by minds that are imprisoned in monist or totalitarian systems that demand absolute compliance and subservience, so that they tend to be conditioned against compassion or negative capabilities. In summary, to save the human soul it must first be killed of its humanity: the heart is blinded, drained and conditioned into subservience to one perspective (a single book), and immunized to repel any other. To be selfish is to get ahead and to be compassionate is to be stupid in the minds and hearts of those who have been so fortified and inured.

Even humanism must be carefully considered and not slide into being a standalone, absolute means and end. It must not forget the individual and become an abstract template: the devil, as usual, is founded or confounded in the detail. The caution, as always, is against mindlessness and forgetfulness so that clarity of purpose can be distilled and filtered through the cultural paradigm or problem-solving template as suggested on page 141. Absolutism and dogmatism prevail in a milieu of ignorance, poverty, superstition, fear and trepidation, blindly and stubbornly locked into stasis with demand for absolute (binary) simplicity and certainty. These traits and tendencies are all inter-related manifestations of a need to belong, coupled with an over-abundance of vanity, conceit, pride and self-esteem, in the absence of self-introspection, self-knowledge, compassion, gratitude and humility. They may be rough and crude, but are effective in a self-serving and self-defeating way, all at once—ruthless, relentless and reckless beyond comprehension and truly mesmerizing, stupefying and fearsome in all its mindlessness, bottom-lessness and grotesqueness, but no longer willful.

The speck (of will) is stuck in a seemingly comforting groove from which escape becomes ever more unlikely as it spins and spirals ever deeper into the groove, finely ground, polished and smoothed, becoming increasingly obscure and indistinguishable from the groove, until the machine stops, time is no more and the speck is gone. The will, heart, and mind or soul impacted by mindless repetition of the same metamorphosizes into complete translucency or opaqueness or non-manifestation of singularity removed from the interim plurality of being. This includes the endless chanting of Life, Liberty, Equality (no fraternity) and the pursuit of Happiness, which seems to create an effective mind block. Such specks or apostates oftentimes jump from groove to groove or ism to ism in avoidance or evasion of the self, preferring to remain a stranger to both itself and to others. To embrace one ism is to have the mind snookered.

While the more and bigger, the better, seems to apply easily to the material world, when it comes to intellectual application, it seems quite the reverse. How challenging would it be to study at least three isms by the time one reaches 18 or 21 years of age, as a rite of passage into adulthood, to understand how a position engenders reaction, re-reaction and so forth. The path to self-knowledge is challenging and requires much effort over various stages of life. It is anything but quick, simple and easy. One has to see the pluralities within and accept both what appears to be good and attractive, as well as the bad and the unappealing, with the proviso of working towards a balance that satisfies the conditions of humanness.

The French revolutionary and the communist manifestos both contain much of the same inspiring idealism with the addition of brotherhood, but as with other manifestos, not to any great effect in reality given the blood bath then, as before and thereafter. The struggle for freedom and justice goes as far back as all of recorded history, therefore all this so-called modern radicalism is nothing new. The manifestos of these revolutionaries espouse the ideals of life, liberty, equality, fraternity, happiness, and justice—and consistently deliver oppression, inequality, fraticidal slaughter, much unhappiness, injustice, and living death or death of the spirit.

The compelling impetus of the American Revolution was essentially a tax revolt (economically driven) fueled with the same intensity of dogmatic religious fervour that drove the rebels from their homelands to seek new beginnings in the New World. And so these two impetuses still remain today, with the issue and matter of tax (money) and religion (dogma) exciting the raw nerve and vital centre of the American psyche. However, there is a steadily growing industry around mythologizing and deifying political figures in its history, with the full Hollywood treatment: an attractive-looking cast with perfect teeth and indubitably, minty breath to match, conveniently over-looking the standard of plumbing and sewage infrastructure and maintenance of the times and people, with stirring soundtrack and soft focus. The few other countries which attempt similar exercises tend to be totalitarian, with mug shots and images of the Heroic Leaders to be found everywhere and the wordings of their propaganda quite similar and similarly inspirational and inspired. The brevity of history is more than made up for by this unceasing fascination, as is evident through the mountain of films, images, books and other market extensions, which exceed the quantity of like material covering the same time span in the historical documents of any other country. Painting politicians with a divine glow is not going to turn them into saints, just as canonization is more a cult of celebrity with political purposes.

It is quite a feat of alchemic transmutation to turn the secular into non-secular, especially in the context of the separation of church and state. No matter how wonderfully creative and appealing, such transformations are still subversions, perversions and inversions. Patriotism as a source of spiritual inspiration is a marketing concept and may work for a shrinking base of people with an ability to combine two disparate elements basically at cross purposes. To turn the Declaration of Independence, the Constitution and the Bill of Rights as a basis for generating folk tales, folk songs and entertainment is not far-fetched or an impossibility. But regardless of time, effort and money expended, it would still fall short of passing as a cultural template because there is no poetry or poetic sense in them, and no matter how charming and knowledgeable the constitutional scholar, it is neither entertainment nor culture.

It would be as rare to find a politician without flaws as it would be to find a perfect human being, anywhere. There seems to be an aversion or inability to provide any moral context in history, with a preponderance of heroics and skimming or skipping over shortcomings. A heroic figure or leader loses his appeal with the sighting and citing of the slightest and singular private flaw negating his humanity and wholeness of character. Such process and mentality imparts and reveals a sense of amorality that is a characteristic of the world of politics and commerce divorced from culture. Thus Achilles who retains his humanity, stature and poignancy, especially with his heel and all, recedes. This is again a very binary mind-set which contrasts sharply with the recordings of Korean history which have the specific intent and purpose of discerning moral contexts, showing both the strengths and weaknesses of historical figures and their times. This is the difference and distinction that a cultured heart makes in keeping human beings, human.

To remain in the middle zone demands powerful exertion of all our faculties of being to stay in the middle without being pulled or pushed, attracted by the forces of polarization and sucked into the vortex of polarity and non-being. Culture and civilization are testaments and antidotes to non-beingness with the rule of the polarized, senseless, mindless, dogmatized and reduced mass into illusions of being, represented by the mob, might and Almighty. The powerful gravitational, electromagnetic and strong (sub-atomic) forces may be required to work together to produce a force field from their infinite pluralities in action to counter the 'weak' (sub-atomic) force within and maintain the interim harmonic oscillation. These tensions created by pluralism are like violin strings—too tight, they snap, too flaccid, they are ineffectual, just right they are capable of producing the sublime, subject to innumerable variables including: the organic nature and artistic sensibilities of all the raw material used, instrument maker, the musical score, the player, the teacher, the conductor, the orchestra, the atmospherics and audience receptivity. We can only try our best in preparedness and express wonder at the sublime outcomes when we find ourselves occasionally in harmony with Nature.

Politics, commerce and oftentimes religion are at their most creative and insidious in creating illusions of morality and certainty in materialism, viz. more is good, so that money, speed, property, publicity, celebrity and technology attain moral status when morality lies outside the domain of inorganic attributes. Statements such as 'money is the root of all evil' or 'lack of money is the root of all evil' are equally empty statements. Like time and space, there is no innate intent, will or volition. We exist in a neutral and benign pool, so that all that is good or evil in the world begins and ends with us precariously and critically pivoting on our self-knowledge or mindfulness.

There is in nature and the universe an exuberance of distributive, diversifying, divaricating and dynamic balance or compromise of the life force or *chi*. The *chi* may be infinite but not carrying capacity and nurturing sustainability in the mesh of interdependencies and inter-relationships of lives and timelines. That the human population has reached six billion may be more of a testament to the quantity of human ignorance rather than the quality of human wisdom. Civilizations, ancient or modern, based upon a combination of populace, agriculture, military, commerce or industry, all concentrate power, along with access to the levers and leverages of power, among the few, and are consistently founded upon a slave economy and mandatory overtime on every continent through the ages. There is a compromise, proportionality and parity amongst quantity and quality at every level, literally and literately.

These cycles of enslavement perpetuate because mindfulness and moral cultivation is undertaken by very few, and the texts and teachings they leave behind are either subverted to serve the vested interests of the power structure or left to gather dust. Political leadership has rarely been concerned with moral cultivation through defining the common good in a public context, because there are far easier ways to gaining and maintaining power by subscribing to the cult of the lowest common denominator. Thus the burden rests, as it always has, entirely upon individual endeavour at 'reading' into life, because there is no free ride.

Instead of teaching and climbing the ladder of self-reflection, modernity tends to condition people to search and locate moral leadership and morality in the incessant world of politics, economics, entertainment, deification, and a host of addictive and toxic indulgences. It is all binary, all the time, which consumes and obliterates time and mind, resulting in the cultivation of laziness, ignorance and intolerance, leading to obsolescence and inactivity. Politics and commerce are amoral or morally ambiguous or antagonistic, so that lives pervaded by these influences develop a sense of amorality, ambiguity, ambivalence, relativity, non-orientation, or just plain wackiness. As religious and pseudo-religious entities enter the fray, to party and parry with political and commercial interests, they also take on these attributes. Playing where they don't belong, they end up on the rigid extremes rather than in pluralism, liberalism and pantheism of the centre. Instead of transcending the material and teaching the way to harmony and clarity, they end up in the temporal quagmire of property, power and money, along with suppression and enslavement of the masses. When illusions of morality are cast on abstract, inorganic externalities in a strictly binary format and are set up to infinitely and mutually compound and complement each other, a self-perpetuating revenue stream flows.

The indiscriminate and malleable English language has been conscripted by commerce and technology in increasingly assigning organic attributes to the inorganic: revenue streams, cash flow, cash cow, 'n'th generation or better bred products or release or versions, male/female sexual denotation of terminals, nodes, connections, masters and slaves, etc. If there are masters of the universe, there naturally must be slaves to serve them. Multi-faceted and sacred words as well as their opposites are similarly conscripted for advertising jargon. With continuous and frequent repetition and recycling, they are equally flattened, and become commutative or interchangeable in the service of commerce. Terms such as 'deadbeat dads' and 'absentee moms' no longer jar and alarm, not only through broadcast repetition but because these are someone else's problems or viewed as an abstract other, outside the perimeter of private property. Perhaps the most abused, overused and overtaxed word is 'free' (along with 'trust' and 'fidelity') which entraps and pacifies the masses into ignorance and non-exertion. Even greater success has been achieved in the reverse process with masses of indices and measure, generated by marketing and economic research and analysis, reducing humans and human activities into units and rates of production and consumption.

To cease and desist from imbibing from this revenue trough results in agony and pain resembling symptoms of withdrawal. True liberty is not carefree or served in a here and now manner on a silver platter or screen. It is a challenging mount that requires the rider to go through rigourous training and exercise. When diligence and discipline become second nature and always present, it seems effortless and natural, with the rider and mount forming a seamless and harmonious unity or wholeness: only then is virtuosity in play. Through globalization and corporate consolidation, cannibalization of life or mindfulness over time reaches peak predatory efficiency, with the few gorging and gnawing on the mindless mass, who obligingly perpetuate mindlessness weaned and tethered to machinery, gadgets, or instant gratification delivery systems that are becoming ubiquitous and cordless or invisible in a world of familiar replicas and replications. We are increasingly trading off organic growth of memory and mind for instant and instances of immediate mechanical gratification. This is slavery in a nice, tidy and easy to perpetuate package, worthy of the information age which triumphantly heralds the dawning of a new age and end of life as we have known it. There is no energy or any other kind shortage—only the premium collected for the privilege of wastefulness in a country where SUVs rule the road and lawn maintenance is a $40-billion growth industry. These are all inalienable rights in a self-aggrandizing, evangelistic, Capitalist, Christian Democracy—the holy trinity of the modern age. It is a formidable anti-cultural or anti-life loop sustained by asymmetricism, anti-intellectualism and infantilism. It is not Americans that the rest of the world fears or are wary of; it is Americanization against which the only defense is mindfulness and learning from our predecessors who have shaped our languages and cultures, giving us life with heart and soul, a sense of centre, meaning and belonging. By studying the path illuminated in these texts of various origins but having one purpose and heart, we are enabled towards becoming human beings in diversity and co-existence. This is not an anti-American but a pro-everyone position. It is not political obsolescence, but obsolescence of life that has created and will continue to create the angst which gives impetus to cultural formation and shape. The past seems erasable or rewritable, the future, perfectible, but the present is inescapable, imperfect, angst-writhen and -wrought.

The numerous Western beliefs of Puritanism, enlightenment or rationalism, romanticism, utilitarianism, etc., of the last few centuries find expression in liberty, equality and fraternity practiced within the context of Christianity, Capitalism, Democracy on the bed of Homocentrism. The Eastern principles of true heart (individual moral cultivation), propriety (duty) and harmony (nature) of the last five millennia are based upon Buddhism (spiritual), Confucianism (ethical) and Taoism (universal), representing a holistic and organic process of identity formation always in public context. One is not better than the other, but merely represents an evolutionary organic process which can be helped and guided along in syndesis, but not in quantum leaps and bounds in synthesis.

The East and West coexist in a continuum representing young and old or decay and regeneration, which are ever present in both, with balance in the interim. There may seem to be many irreconcilable differences, but all peoples share the same dream: the health and happiness of all children initiated and weaned upon organic nurture and culture, not mechanical and transactional feeding, conditioning, monitoring and mass entertainment increasingly reliant and dependent upon technology. The quick, simple and easy mentality and commutative use of organic and inorganic terminology are at their most dangerous as they seep into all aspects of life, with parenting and family relationships expected to conform to this model, with the cost entirely borne by the young, weak and old. They are increasingly left in the care of people to whom one would hardly consider entrusting one's car, money or investment.

Since there is no shortage of rationalizations which are consistent with individualism, consumerism and all manner of inalienable rights, along with legal precedents, formulae and recourses for converting organic loss into monetary gain, and assigning blame or responsibility to third parties—it is a logical outcome. There appears to be symmetry or justice as long as the values, beliefs and practices of commensurability or fungibility are maintained by the majority between organic/inorganic and time/ money. It is a slippery slope once price tags are attached to all manner of organic lives and times, whether human or non-human, and all are similarly tainted and devalued, even in memory. The strength and virtue of relationships and lives, which lie in their irreplaceable uniqueness, are violated, voided and nullified. It is quite a leap from giving and teaching children independence and choice to lightening the load of and providing convenience for adults who have their own agenda and priorities to juggle in the pursuit of the material, recognition and entertainment.

It may be useful to remember that the Chinese term for happiness is 'open heart', for study it is 'read book', and for how are you, it is 'are you good' (in an ethical sense). To study does not mean to open any book that is the latest and greatest in science and technology, some pot-boiler bestseller, self-help doo-dah, convoluted political, economic or social flim-flam, religious mumbo-jumbo and spiritual hocus-pocus. It does not mean reading entrails, bones, tarot cards, horoscopes, numerology, palms, tea-leaves, surveys and polls. There are specifically designated classical works or canons that represents the heart and soul of a culture that have been written by sages and scholars dedicated to the study of human beings. They have carefully composed their codex and codicils over a lifetime of study and observations. These represent the words of concordant, compassionate and collaborative hearts and minds who do not hold back, set traps, keep secrets and file for patents and copyrights in order to profit by nickel and diming their readers and followers. They simply share as much as they can and make accessible their wisdom and knowledge to all those who can speak in the language of the human heart. Theirs is not a world of rigid right angles, recluses and recusants of isms, but of well-rounded rectitude and engagement in the affairs of daily lives.

To be read in the classics and be considered cultured in Korea involves study and fluidity in the Five Classics and Four Books along with many of their qualified compendium. One of Korea's exemplar scholars, *Jong Yahk-yông* (1762-1836), referred by his honorific title, *Dah Sahn Gông*, single-handedly produced an epic body of work covering 14,000 pages[63] in his own classical Chinese calligraphy between 1789-1834. Such great minds demonstrate the awesomeness of the mind-space potential and our sense of humility is only equaled by that of gratitude for their having been. While many in modernity unhesitatingly and enthusiastically genuflect, bow and kowtow before some who hit, throw and catch balls for a living, how many do so for their predecessors, mentors and teachers?

---

63. "Translated into English, they would take up approximately seventy volumes averaging three hundred pages in length." Mark Setton, *Chong Yagyong: Korea's Challenge to Orthodox Neo-Confucianism* (State University of New York Press, 1997), p. 65.

People will continue to procreate and family units will adapt and change in response to economic, technological and sociopolitical forces; however, the multidimensional role of the enculturation process does not change, only the means of delivery. The family unit continues to exist in many forms with varying degrees of commitment and duration (serial monogamy, remarriages, single parent, same-sex couples, communal), rather than the rigid definition which has prevailed in the past. Regardless of the variety of family structures, the single biggest change has been the daily prolonged periods of absence of adults (parents, older siblings, extended families) from the young and the diminishing familiarity or relevance of consanguinity accompanied by an increasing amount of passive time spent engaged with the mass media.

These changes necessarily have effects on family function and functionality which need to be closely understood so that critical elements in the shaping and forming of a cultural identity are not passed over without notice, with certain effect on the flourishing of the one and the many. Human beings have great potential for destruction, and while we all can be considered powder kegs, not all fuse lengths can be so short and delicate (low activation energy) as to blow up at the slightest provocation without any other recourse. Enculturation attempts to mitigate suffering rather than eliminate or deny it.

The reasons for having children may be varied and sometimes it can be a challenge to articulate them clearly. It is important, however, to consider what the minimum requirements may be from the procreated's point of view, aside from physical care and well-being:

1. Social position, which is conferred by the parents' cultural paradigm, their socioeconomic status, both inherited and achieved, with particular emphasis on that of the father in patriarchal societies (still most prevalent). This positioning operates as a key to the ease-of-entry or barriers and obstacles to be overcome in the many phases and dimensions of a life; equality operates in the context of status and status is always operational in human nature.

2. Family and its traditions, which provide an element of timeless consistency and stability in one's life, centred and defined by consanguinity or permanent membership and geography, i.e., a place to call home where membership (recognition, acceptance, belonging) is lifelong and certain.

3. Education and skills development for increasing the odds of flourishing in a socioeconomic environment, predicated on cultural, social and economic intelligences.

The mere awareness that one is not alone and that there are resources and recourses to which one can turn, shapes an attitude of possibilities and potentialities. One is not a victim of personality and chance which would circumvent and preclude any effort and thereby render the concept of free will null and void. To confine oneself in fanaticism and dogmatism, whether of one or many, is not only futile but insalubrious to flourishing in the long-term, as it also is to insist on inalienable individual rights to liberty and equality without acknowledging others' entitlement to the same. What passes as reason, reasoning and reasonable is often and can be as subjective as truth, justice and beauty in a vacuum.

Cultural perspective provides a template and a sense of standards based on broad consensus and collective experience over many generations, to sustain and nurture the one and the many. That there is such a diversity of coherent cultures is a testament and bulwark against views and behaviour which reflect that most people are driven solely by money, are irrational, let feelings take precedence over all other considerations, and believe life is chaotic. To disagree at a minimum requires communications and an exchange of views, but to subscribe to such a belief as aforementioned, circumvents and precludes even a need for a dialogue, resulting in an a priori mutual exclusivity and a zero sum outlook. Such outcomes fragment and weaken the one and the many with grave insult to the individual and social fibre and integrity, with portents for the survival of the one and the many.

Is belonging to a family group purely a function of how one feels and an expression of 'what I like or dislike', without any sense of duty, honour, obligation and responsibility, just as one can choose to opt out of a society simply because one does not like its rules? This is analogous to tossing overboard a crew member with no recourse, since all is justifiable on a subjective basis. (There is much that serves as metaphors of life in the tales of the seas and islands in Western literature, as its development and history have greater seafaring traditions which have played such a significant and decisive economic role on the world stage, but whose true value far exceeds just this dimension.) Is this the outcome that parents and adults wish for the children: an unrestrained and non-contextual individualism? This gives rise to a greater sense of disposability and ease of disposal.

A value system is complex and non-deterministic, involving trade-offs and choices; but just to mention family values without specific examples or attempts to set an example, is as empty as a culture of one. The individual need to differentiate and be different, without any balance with the needs of the collective society which impart to the one a sense of belonging, recognition and acceptance, as well as individuality, is a prescription for unhappiness. Has the human condition been predicated upon the premise that *I am always right and must prevail at all costs* or have human beings evolved as a function and result of a unique ability to anticipate, prepare for and ameliorate difficulties, aided by collective and cumulative learning, rather than acceding to reactions solely based on instincts and impulses as they occur?

The point of Adam and Eve eating the fruit is that they felt heart-piercing shame because they understood what was sacred to honour and forbidden to indulge. In modern society, 'forbidden' is merely an empty concept, as a sense of shame or nobility is as absent as an internalized code of conduct. Internalized sensibilities are fed by sensory perceptions and reflections which guide behaviour as a function of the relationship with the other and situational assessment. Cultural imperatives, in this context, are taught so as to minimize the excuse of personality or omnipotence as cause and justification for unacceptable or sub-optimal choice which can destabilize and decouple joined efforts for co-existence.

The organic learning process passes through and endures tensions, transformed by the changes in successive and iterative waves. Each successful transition increases and affirms self-discipline, analogous to the range of Poisson's ratio (1781-1840) and Hooke's law (1635-1703) of tensibility or tensile strength which is increasingly less fixed with increasing complexity of the organic being. The result over time is wholeness and resiliency of a sum of parts in which they are no longer distinguishable. The backward flow of each iteration and change cannot be discretely traced but undeniably, the soundness of choice at each moment of change has informed and shaped the process and the outcome. Rules and ways of a culture provide management tools for amelioration and dissipation of conflicts and tensions which do not hold out rewards but only syntonic acceptability. They are the equivalent of hygiene factors of organizational theory; such factors pose certain harm or downside risks but do not necessarily contribute to tangible profits.

Equipping children with discipline and a code of conduct, especially in regard to honouring the ties of blood, is unlikely to reduce their potential but rather the opposite by providing a mount for their maturation and ripening.

It is not difficult to see the consequences of an absence, incompleteness or distortion of such a mount on the rider regardless of academic degrees or chronological age. Discipline, much more than love, is indispensable and more often called upon in the journey of life.

Each individual is a unique being, but we all stand relatively on the time continuum of becoming. In some matters, places and times, the relative positions vary, but our attitude to each other does not. It is an attitude of mindfulness over the relationship with an attendant code of conduct which remains fixed and unchanged. It is in this context that the ties and bonds of blood are interminable and inviolable and therefore most challenging to balance. Such balance does not equal a statistical mean, averaging out, neutralization or a two-person-zero-sum contest, but reflects our relative position within the relationships. Honouring such relationships is not a function of inclination of will or choice but, rather, prescribed by the cultural imperatives shaping an attitude of reverence and humbleness towards Nature.

Reverence and rites for ancestors are also prescribed in many ancient cultures as a means for the progeny to respect the interlocking relationships of oneness through time. These rites are analogous to tracing back to one or a beginning to be found in many of the mathematical iterative series whereby each result is a formulation of a combination of the predecessors—for example, the Fibonacci series and Pascal's triangle, where some understanding of the relationship and some of the values at two conjoining or consecutive points prove helpful in pointing to the previous, current and next steps. Perhaps the closest mathematical representation of ancestor worship which acknowledges the multiplier effect over time and space of 'successful' genetic and cultural code transmission, is the Markovian model which describes the stochastic process whereby the present state influences the subsequent state. Our being is not a simple linear equation with plug and play answers but a result of infinite variables and probabilities that did not cause nor result in our ancestor to buckle under and flounder.

The Western tendency to separate and maintain separateness partitions the field of ethics, sciences and the arts. But what they share is a similar reliance on rules and influences of their predecessors regardless of country of origin or vintage. Each successive generation of thinkers builds upon previous bodies of work in a collaborative manner to further explore the unknown and uncertain. No work is a stand-alone result of one mind and body: "One cannot attain the limit of craftsmanship. And there is no craftsman who acquires his total mastery." (Ptahhotep, 2350 BC). It is unnecessary to wipe the slate clean at each generation when there is no upside to doing so, and yet with cultural templates there is no such restraint. There can no longer be such an invisible hand of moderation by definition just as drollness is non-existent without the normative to define the perverse. The deficit in identity banks are satisfied and filled synthetically as the industries of identity proliferate and prosper by making a clean sweep over mindlessness, not only through efficient reach but by the creation, expansion and maintenance of this state.

Binary input and process can only result in binary output, to paraphrase the old computer industry maxim of GIGO or 'garbage in, garbage out'. Faithful renditions and renderings of the old ring truer and finer than empty modern constructs masquerading and parading as creative or innovative or both, valued for revenue circulation. The human mind can be programmed with collective and cumulative knowledge without hampering its ability to seek out the new frontiers. Booting up a cultural programme, not booting it out along with the old, is to equip it precisely for this purpose. The timeless truths and insights that flow down the millennia are ample evidence of their ability to ignite the spark of essence for the transformational journey embarked by each being towards his or her potential, in harmony and co-existence.

Creativity and creation, the refuge and resort of the mind, the result of graduated tension and release, fueled by highly disciplined and developed filters of all its faculties and sensibilities, are snuffed or malformed as sight and sound overwhelm and displace all else. The senses, other than those of seeing and hearing, are pacified and subdued by the overdose, addiction and excitement or enthrallment of uncontrolled audio-visual influx. Taste, smell and touch diminish in relevance, disconnected from the ties and times of the land, blood and rites of their predecessors, but weaned upon binary uniformity. Their absence is not only unnoticed but preferred in an advertiser- and consumer-friendly world of odourless homogeneity: only manufactured taste, smell and touch have value since they engender profit streams.

The alliance of technology, commerce and art reach ever new heights of inveiglement and predatory efficiency as they merge into a seamless, indistinguishable and synergetic hole, sucking up, enslaving and leveling diversity, complexity and individuality. In lieu of creativity, the result is an endless loop of recycled audio-visual spectacles condensed, compressed, distilled, digitized and pixilated for speedy and tidy consumption of time. With primed and steady supply of the new and newly emerging markets of the young and the impressionable coming on line in steady streams, the coffers of the industries of identity runneth over, nestled in security and stability. Personal excellence through self-cultivation gives over to the cult of self whose illusion of liberty belies the constriction of individuality in non-sensible and nonsensical uniformity bereft of shame and honour. The trajectory of life is flat-lined, devoid of multi-faceted poignancy, piquancy or poetic thought. Many activities can be forced or coaxed in measurable ways, except reading, learning and understanding, which can only be launched by the cultural code or language. As cultural codes and their vessels for safekeeping and transmission recede, life continues to exist but is divorced from the business of living. The question of why or ultimate purpose of life is unanswerable, but there are many answers and ways to the question of how to live and die well.

To be compassionate, tolerant and able to compromise with an inclusive and holistic problem statement of *What is in my interest and that of the relevant set?* rather than *My interest can only be served at the expense of someone else's or the group's*, which presupposes that one's preference is paramount and supersedes all else whereby willfulness is all, does not characterize and distinguish human behaviour and existence. But is how one thinks, feels and behaves an independent and random event, or is it shaped, formed and defined by enculturation, experience and education over a lifetime? The means and mechanics of the transmission are as critical as the value system itself, and need to be safeguarded in the same degree and manner so that they evolve in tandem. One may believe in nothing and that nothing matters, but such imprudent and impudent attitude should not result in dismissing or inflicting harm on others with impunity.

Life's journey consists of possibilities and impossibilities, and one's choice reflects an appreciation, acceptance and distinction between these, in the context of decisions to be made: Is there a choice? What are the possibilities? And what is the decision? To state subjectively that one has made one's best effort in accordance with one's individual standard as a sole indicator rather than shared standards and the attendant recognition and acceptance of the effort and result by one or more other(s) is to deny or opt out of membership or belonging to any set of the human race along its broadest axis, i.e., what being human means and entails. Living out an 'average' life demands more than an average or averaging of effort because the challenges, conflicts and tensions are not averages but extremes. Each life is incomparable, and incessant comparisons, whether positive or negative, tend to subtract and detract from identity and individuality as cautioned by the commandment regarding the neighbour.

Enculturation can be seen as both a process towards harmonious co-existence and towards curtailment of catastrophes by sharing and disseminating what is known and knowable through cumulative experience and knowledge. To gain and benefit cannot be predicated upon or necessitate loss and cost to another, and realizing one's potential cannot rest upon denial or deprivation of another's as a general rule but, rather, the obverse, as to think or act otherwise is to deny that one can only derive satisfaction and meaning in the context of the other, whether that other consists of one or many individuals.

It seems that almost anyone from any walk of life, at any time of life, from any country and century can become an '-American', but not the reverse. What is it about being or becoming an American that makes such a transition and transformation into a specific culture so prohibitive (beyond the economic and political hurdles), while the possession of a specific cultural paradigm enables those from any other culture to have such an equal opportunity and liberty to become American? It seems that the requirements of American citizenship on the surface appear easy, casual and undemanding, but upon closer analysis, just the reverse is revealed. Citizenship in a country of diversity and democracy has many more prerequisites and greater need for enculturation than in a homogeneous country, regardless of its sociopolitical framework or economic wealth. Citizenship needs to be associated with more than just rights and privileges in a country that very few can claim as their native land and where citizenship is much more a process of becoming than simply being.

Is ignorance bliss, and is innocence truly the desired and preferred state? Has the struggle to survive and evolve into the complex and dangerous with unlimited potential been to conclude that being simple and benign as an amœba is the ultimate goal? Even if this were so, is going back a possibility and can the time-order be reversed? The pursuit of the material is not predicated upon the loss of materiality and humanizing values. The paradigm shift is not from rationalism to emotionalism, order to chaos or some other such dichotomy. It is to a multidimensional choice-making platform that involves and includes many perspectives of human existence, shaped and formed over a lifetime of effort and experience.

Has greater mass, access and availability of information led to discernible improvements in the human condition, or is it just resulting in filling up the belly beyond need, as a spectator in a coliseum to be diverted and pacified with daily doses of programmed spectacles controlled by the few. The carnage, both staged and unstaged, but all virtually experienced with an overflow of blood, conditions and inures not only the senses of perception but disengages and neuters the heart, especially of the young and inexperienced for whom being faint-of-heart is a no-no in any case. The beat of the heart can be felt but has no feel with emotional sensitivity and sensibility severed. By plugging in and becoming merely a receiving end or terminated node, the mind and mediascape mirror those that are aptly described in the book *Infinite Jest.*[64] Life becomes just a topsy-turvy giddy gig of goggle, gobble, giggle, gibber and gibe. Such is the appeal of mindless existence when time becomes irrelevant and hard Truths are crowded out by perfect anesthetizing illusions, fairy tales and money.

Consolidation and globalization of mass media are efficient and effective silencers of dissent, authoritative or otherwise, in that dissent feeds the appetite for spectacles and headlines, becoming part of the same disposable landscape. The strength of mass media lies in its amoral, amorphous and pervasive nature which gobbles, ingests and regurgitates highly-processed and easy to digest muck which numb and disarm not only the dissenters but the masses who cannot tolerate anything that is not or cannot be thus reduced for tidy and speedy consumption: the dietary requirement and satisfaction being highly refined, specialized, narrow and rigid. Information without purpose is as potent as being right or in the right without any power or recourse. There is much to gain and nothing to lose by viewing the cumulative and collective knowledge and experience of humans as a single species and a single population.

The future is not in the past or with the one, but can benefit much from it, for the future of the one and the many. Just as the trajectory of life shapes an arc that looks backwards and forwards with a unique perspective at each point, each generation and age needs each other in linked partnership to navigate the transition from partner-to-be, junior partner, full partner, senior partner, honourable partner, to retired partner, because it is the best and worst of times all the time, in creating and recreating memories which are not as

64. David Foster Wallace, *Infinite Jest* (Back Bay Books, 1996).

ephemeral as yesterday's news. Partnerships are as unique as the individuals who form them and reflect permutations of longitudes and latitudes, pivoting upon purpose, just as all collaborations do. No one escapes from judging or being judged, and the only difference that one can make is in its quality of rendering—its completeness in comprehension and contemplation of consequences so that appropriate words and deeds or silence and non-action are chosen, reflecting balance, tact and timeliness.

> Young Man to Middle-aged Man: "You have content but no force."
> Middle-aged Man to Young Man: "And you have force but no content."[65]

The North American culture has all the exuberance and idealism of youth in hot pursuit at any cost and speed with the end justifying the means without holistic comprehension of consequences, caught in the throes and thrills of the moment, dazzled and fascinated with illusions; remaining and wanting to remain forever the willful, petulant, irrepressible and impressionable adolescent. Ergo, the cult of youth.

In a milieu that is steeped in idolizing youth, youthful illusions, idealism and indiscretion, in pursuit of looking, acting and staying forever young, there is no room, indeed, *need* for teachers, elders and the elderly. With the silence and silencing of these tempering and humanizing voices,[66] with no one admitting or wanting to be identified as mature or old, it is unlikely that society will any longer be civil, humane or cultured. An individual's identity is not just a product of a lifetime of experiences or simply a unique compilation of three billion DNA letters or even an accumulation of the millennia of recorded thoughts and traditions, but pivots on an attitude of reverence for all

---

65. Isaiah Berlin, 'Fathers and Children, the Romanes Lecture' [1970], op. cit., p. 26.

66. "...the way the individual mind grows and alters in its perception of the truth, inevitably changed by age and experience...that belief in a personal God did not rest in an abstract notion of 'the divine', but followed from the personal discovery of evil in the world, of failure that required forgiveness. For this reason young people were naturally, and almost inevitably, both materialists and idealists....Hence no need is felt of Redemption....But whatever demands effort, requires time. Ignorance seldom vaults into knowledge, but passes into it through an intermediate state of obscurity, even as Night into Day through Twilight." Richard Holmes, *Coleridge: Darker Reflections*, op. cit., pp. 204, 205.

that exists in the world rather than solely confined by contestable intellect or insatiable appetite of the self.[67] What a work is man and what a lot of work it is to be human;[68] an anomaly struggling with awareness of its own anomalousness, searching and yearning for the undefinable, unidentifiable and elusive mean or standard.

67. "Repeated some 50 times in the Koran is the verb *aqala* which means to connect ideas together, to reason, to understand an intellectual argument." D.S. Roberts, op. cit., p. 41.

Author's Note: This word spelled 'aqala' may be a variation of 'qaraat', meaning 'to read sacred books' or works of lucubration as all important religious and secular texts are. To read and study, of course, implies adequate external illumination (guidance, counsel, motivation) for internal illumination (learning, insight, inspiration). Thus, the fascination with light in ancient mythologies such as Prometheus, mythic creatures such as the Phoenix, and religions such as Zoroastrianism. Ancient cultures that have endured abound with fables and myths that serve to instill reverence and awe of the supernatural as well as initialize, develop and reinforce cultural codes. Children in these cultures are exposed to an abundance of stories to illuminate heritage, traditions, ethics and Beauty within their cultural context, forming the foundation for building their identity in tandem with a sense of belonging over a lifetime. These works and words are not merely entertainment, designed and played to kill or waste time, but quite to the contrary.

68. "...but my life...is no longer meaningless as it was before, but has an incontestable meaning of goodness, with which I have the power to invest it." Leo Tolstoy, op. cit., p. 807.

Darwin's theory of evolution and Smith's theory of free trade, along with many other theories, have been pared down into sound bites to justify modern capitalism. 'Survival of the fittest' and 'free trade is good' are bandied about without studying or a cultural understanding of what fitness, freedom and goodness means in the context of the one and the many, i.e., a framework. There is nothing new in these theories, and economic, political, religious and social dimensions are found in all ancient cultures in great abundance, along with a rich heritage of studies of Nature. In these pantheistic and polymathic cultures, Nature is described and revered for its exuberant exertive diversity, inter-relatedness and co-existence of all living beings in a balance that transcends each, creating Oneness and Harmony. The wonder that Blake alludes to in 'Tiger, tiger' is the wonder that the tiger and the lamb co-exist in Nature.

The scale of destruction in the Americas from 1492 to the present breaks records and boundaries in the sheer number of deaths caused, directly or indirectly, by the parvenu based upon preferred interpretation of history. When 95% of the existing population of tens of millions of people disappears within a hundred years (1500-1600) of the new arrivals, it cannot have gone unnoticed, unfelt or unrecorded, except for people without any code of conduct or who are in essence, inhuman. Slaughtering to extinction not only the indigenous peoples but buffaloes and other beings, in tens of millions, as well as in an orgy of blood and land-grab mania in less than a hundred years in the 19th century, while killing each other to boot, is quite a feat. The purpose of the killers is to kill, and they have become more efficient at both the business of killing along with anesthetizing and rationalizing their potential preys and bystanders. They are so bent on destroying and prevailing at all costs that they have no time for second thoughts or to consider what purpose is being served other than their wanton exercise of power simply because they can, beyond any need or reason. What they cannot create or appreciate is not worthwhile conserving even if it is not self-serving, other than for instant gratification in the thrill of the kill that is all too fleeting. Therefore these acts must be repeated as the past is either forgotten through selective amnesia or devalued through refined ethnocentrism that forms a tidy loop. This is also the case for Africa between 1700 and 1800, and

Australia between 1800 and 1900. All these acts of wanton destruction on every continent, introducing virulent cancers of identity, transpired after what the West likes to call the golden age of Renaissance, completely disregarding its underbelly. These legacies and activities are carried ever forward, facilitated and enabled by not only decoupling moral and intellectual cultivation, but burying and sweeping them aside under ethnocentrism, doctrines and propaganda of Christianity, Democracy and Capitalism. Once set in motion, these cycles of violence inevitably seem to repeat. Only the mask of the perpetrator changes as those who were oppressed become the oppressor, using the same rhetoric and rationale that seems to work equally well with recycling.

In this trinity, forgetfulness and closure are essential opiates of the mind, resulting in constant cycles of displacement of the old by the new, exemplified by unilateral consumption, without remembering or learning through integration and transformation. As with all Utopian models, the reality of the past and the present are sacrificed for the illusion of perfectibility and images of abstract perfection, consistently bypassing the individual. The inner voices of restraint, compassion and humility of cultural codes are drowned out by the amplifying waves of images and sounds, nullifying the self and the other, for the promises and illusions of a variety of isms of certainty and might.

With the advent of globalization, corporate consolidation, and the pervasive infiltration and proliferation of the mass media and killer applications into every nook and cranny of all cultures, there is an impetus to break and set new records with one-upmanship being the *sine qua non* of global status. The cycle of omnipotence in winning at all costs in a zero-sum framework is accompanied by illusions of omniscience. Those who study and feel integrated with Nature have a sense of self in relationship with the other, and tend not to falter into this man-made cesspool or chaos.

Immigration by mostly the same types or the very differents does not create the critical mass of oneness, but only increases the pool of worshipers at the alter of Mammon, with lives efficiently processed for the sake of money, in lieu of the many. New for its own sake emulates knowledge for the sake of knowledge: both pursuits equally handicapped by lack of pro-life centre and purpose. While many cannot quite put their finger on their source of unease and repulsion, they instinctively recoil against what they sense is un-Natural and destructive to Beingness. Life supersedes and precedes text, and text exists to preserve life in co-existence. In the beginning was Life, and then the Word.

How much should we pay the man or the woman who 'discovered' zero, writing, art, musical notations, philosophy, mathematics, sciences, etc.? There is an infinite realm of benefits and pleasures that we derive without even acknowledging, honouring and revering our many predecessors, independent of time and place, who have left us so much without seeking any consideration. This is the human spirit of culture impregnated by polymathic thinkers that dims and fades when knowledge is no longer valued or pursued for its own sake and satisfaction, but solely for recognition and remuneration. Instead of a Hall of Worthies, we get parades and commemorations of celebrities, politicians, billionaires and wars, which consume individuality and blur history along with the many lessons imparted and illuminated. It is not closure but the tensile strength and resiliency of the linkages, transcending time and space, that enables us to heal, learn and move forward with a critical mass of oneness or essence, keeping all of us afloat in the benign pool of life.

The ancient structures and works have timeless appeal finding their location, scope and shape in harmonious relationship with heaven and earth. The ancient symbols of the Celtic braid, the Star of David and the Tao of Pluralities, represent the infinite links and inter-relatedness between the one and the many, without a beginning or an end. The ancient texts and intricate arabesque designs and geometry of India and Persia also reflect this concept. The entire Chinese writing system is symbolic with rich and specific expressions of human relationships. Just learning a dozen characters that incorporate the symbol of the heart, along with a dozen terms of family, fraternal and mentor/student relationships, will illuminate belongingness. There exists a rich palette and palate of identity, but the journey starts with initialization and exertion in one path that will eventually open the doors to all others. Once the might and the right of the sword and the cross are disengaged from the interchangeable master/slave role assignments to serve temporal means and ends, and are unburdened from serving as a cultural identity but, rather, are coupled to one, there will be less confusion and more clarity. If it has not imparted a sense of identity in two thousand, two hundred, twenty or two years, there is much to gain and nothing to lose in choosing another path of linkage for the purpose of education and liberation.

While a cultural identity can take on religious, economic, political, social and national identities, none of these as a standalone or in combination gives rise to a cultural identity. Receptive and attentive attitudes, primed by the cultural codes, serve to guide, frame and liberate aptitudes in all dimensions, but not the reverse. There is much effort and resource directed to studying the physiology of the brain and decoding the human gene. But it is unlikely that better understanding of evil or improvement in the human condition will result. They will not find significant differences in the brains and genes of Shockley, Hitler and Stalin with Einstein, Gandhi and King: the significance is in their cultural codes and cultural experiences.

The cultural code, like the genetic code, is a complex organic system whose functions shape and in turn are shaped by experiences of living through time. A nano-deficiency or expression in the gene can manifest quite dramatically in many dimensions, including the physical, intellectual and emotional (pleiotropism), and it may also be the case for identity, which is the coupling and interplay of the genetic with the cultural codes and experiences. Such an interplay is both an outcome and function of billions of man-years and lives. Each lifetime contributes its own uniqueness, and whether the flow through impact is positive or negative and significant or insignificant, it affects the whole due to infinite and infinitesimal degrees of inter-relatedness amongst all the parts. Do transcending time and space with faster and more consumption and activity qualify even as a human need, and do they increase liberty or anything else? It seems only to feed impatience, greed and ignorance in wanting to know ever less and caring even less. The cultural code comes together over a lifetime, in the one, from the many, through relationships of the extended family and the rites and teachings of predecessors, and vice versa. The interplay between genetic codes and cultural codes, their inter-relationship and random timing and duration of experiences and events, form keystone states and stages for identity formation, recalibration and transformation throughout life. There is hierarchy and order in the integration process, perhaps as complex as the double helix.

The break with the vast metaphysical traditions, underpinnings, studies and understandings of the unseen below the surface for just the seen tip of the iceberg began in earnest with the Renaissance and reached its defining moment in the Romantic period when rationalism, empiricism and industrialization really gathered momentum and took off for the masses. Only what man can control, explain and measure are valued in the homocentrism of the Renaissance where Man is the wonder and the creator. Only what man can possess, display and exploit are valued in the empiricism and rationalism that jump-starts the Industrial Revolution, resting upon rampant economic expansion where Man is the master and controller. And today, it is the big screen picture and the big boomer sound of the known, or what can be packaged, marketed and sold, that dominate the mindscape. The tip of the visible iceberg is emphasized in ever greater detail in inverse proportion to its relative insignificance as representative of the whole.

When a mind always stays at the level of the known and the knowable or within its positive capabilities, it tends to feel trapped in claustrophobic schizophrenia: it is confined but fears going outside the box of the familiar, similar and known. But it has no other recourse because this is the only vernacular and reality it knows: it shuts down in involution or it engages in frantic activity of the packaged, marketed and cloned lifestyles in order to keep up and keep its head above the water. The nature and types of modern crime and ills reflect the values of its home society: killer applications, mindless sex and violence, instant recognition and celebrity, instant payoffs and jackpots, as well as eating disorders when losing weight and particular physical attributes are valued as accomplishments of extraordinary effort. They are as heartbreaking as they are heartless and mindless. All these are manifestations of individualism which feeds the need to be recognized as something increasingly unique and definably and demonstrably different, and therefore to be valued, priced and prized.

What the parents and teachers end up teaching are merely the residual leftovers remaining after all the body of knowledge and tradition of the meta-physical and the metaphysicians have been banished and butchered, having been so labeled and defined. Studying other cultures and peoples is exotic, strange and different because they have been a priori defined so, along with being inferior. But are human beings so essentially different and so defined by a place and a time? The 'primitive' natives of the soil on any of the continents appear to be infinitely cleaner and purer in their hearts than all the porn, smut and pollution engendered, exemplified and exalted by the technically advanced and 'civilized' minds. The products of the department of humani-ties do not seem any different from those of the non-humanities departments, other than in different market valuations of their respective degrees. They are equally disengaged and disengaging in the heart, and are equal experts within their respective boxes and vernaculars for making a living and a name, with few being students of life.

The depth and nature of feelings in the relationships formed during the time spent as a student towards one's teachers/mentors as well as to classmates are different, and yet as strong and oftentimes stronger in the heart as those to one's parents. These relationships all release, nourish and nurture life, and represent essential constituents of the code, coda and codicil of life and to inner iterations, recalibrations and transformations in the journey of identity liberation and realization. This is night and day from the transactional nature of modern education whereby accountability and measurability are all. Education is reduced to: 'I am your customer and I pay you to download to me the necessary and sufficient skills to result in my making as much money as possible, with attendant recognition, by meeting the demands and constraints of the marketplace. And, by the way, this download must be user-friendly, plug-and-play compatible and consistent with my limited positive capabilities.' While we all must make a living in order to eat, this does not necessitate and require exclusivity or an asynchronous experience from life as a human being. Learning to make a living needs to be synchronous to learning the value and values of relationships in life, so that there is a sense of fitting in, fitness, and belonging as an integral part of a family and community in Nature. The cultural grid gives definition to where one is located in the web of relationships in life. Being equipped with the knowledge of one's bearings along with the wherewithal of origin in context of time, place and lineage $(0,0,0,)$ enables forging and formulating relational equations and linkages to others. Such a sense of position and direction coupled with purpose gives rise to the liberty and confidence to travel and explore in many dimensions, with compassion that is not nullified by demand of or need for reciprocity in kind. The coinage of compassion carries and is carried by gratitude and humility as its integral sides and immunizes against fear which begets hate. This is a journey towards cultivating good faith and good will to approach what is Whole and Holy, never being fooled into the notion that one is or is invested with the Whole and the Holy as an individual, but only as a manifestation of and in Oneness.

The brain has vast redundancies, and it remains just so because it is increasingly defined, classified and confined to specialized and demonstrable knowledge solely for consideration. What is valued is knowing a lot about very little—that is, specialization. The information age is a totalizing movement that is a consistent continuation from the 15th-century homocentrism to 18th-century expansionism in saturating and drowning the mind with a deluge of more and faster circulation of the skimmed known and the replicable. The food of the mind or the human being is reduced to consolidation of time for its synthesis into money in the age of technology when time loses meaning and is only tracked for money. The nature of poetic thought which understands that to capture a moment is to lose it, and yet is able to share such a moment with clarity without killing it of its sublime essence, reflecting it in the conical spheres of the one and the many with maximum concentration and dispersion, preserving its uniqueness and timelessness, is Beauty and Creation. These vast, unexplored territories of the mind are marginalized and trivialized in the age of man-made information industrial empires, where only what can be cloned, replicated and duplicated is valuable, reducing and homogenizing lives into conforming to these inorganic attributes.

A young or impressionable and unformed mind is like an empty vessel needing to be filled, and disliking emptiness, it soaks up inputs indiscriminately and equally. A code of conduct or an instruction code is characterized by purpose, priority and sequence along with definitions of relationships, sets and ranges. A good programme can handle a wide range of inputs of various sorts and sizes without crashing, as well as localize problems for appropriate disposition, patching and resolution. What may be a tiny fractional error in degree can end up in a huge deviation between planned and actual destination of the journey over time. This is demonstrable in computer programmes where a single error in code within millions of lines can have huge ramifications in outcomes through replication and compounding. This is also exemplified when people are given a clear and consistent message, but their feedback indicates a wide range and variety of interpretations from comprehension to incomprehension to complete non-resemblance. A code of life is initialized by the cultural code to tune into the Truths of Nature, to listen for and hear the inner voices and whispers which are maximally dispersed and concentrated by the conic curves of the mind shaped over time, and to detect the subtle scents that awaken and invoke a sense of what it is to be alive. The study of minutia and detail reveal the infinity of being in the interim, where extrapolations meet and are equally matched by interpolations.

When the processing systems are so untuned and unreceptive to clarity, resulting in so much distortion and confusion, it is symptomatic of reliance upon a rigid and inflexible demand for binary inputs, processes, outputs and feedbacks. This is what boggles and exasperates those who seek the middle way or compromise: tiny processing deficiencies amplify and multiply to the point where there is not even consensus on what is black or white, let alone right or wrong. In this scenario, not having an opinion and not making judgements and choices becomes synonymous with virtuous. Virtue which is an outcome of conflict of interest arising from established relationships is replaced by avoidance of conflict, non-expression of interest and/or non-definition or establishment of relationships. With such an abundance of absences and abstentions, there of course is no purpose or goal in any context, cultural or otherwise, and virtue is unrealizable. With everyone left to their own devices, however, vice is all that plays out in private and public spheres in ever greater volume and frequency, as it too loses potency, becoming blander and mushier than a pig's breakfast and is inhaled without assaulting the olfactories.

Both virtue and vice are the exercise of direct and indirect positive or negative power whereby their potency radiates or carries high multiplier factors in numerous dimensions pivoting upon and determined by the nature, depth and breath of the relationship itself, as well as the understandings thereof. True power is in its indirect exercise through the interim drawing upon experience, finesse and fineness by maximizing good faith with its positive multiplier effect and minimizing bad faith: it is moving minds without the appearance of any movement. It requires negative capability and understanding based on perspective of eternity rather than direct use of power and mountains of situational and transactional analyses.

Dumbing down works in tandem with the numbing of the mind; not feeling or denying pain, it is not localized, attended to and healed or breached. With continuous procrastination, it festers and compounds. There is no sequential and integrative learning process, but only the building up of an inability to deal with relationships, conflicts and their outcomes. This leads to an escalating sense of impotence (what can I do), injustice (life is so unfair) and alienation (nobody loves or understands me), with disassociation and disconnect between cause and effect, finding release in indiscriminate harm or inertia in boredom and involution. In the world of the binary mind, there is no continuum, no compromise and no harmony of the Way. It is not illiteracy or lack of Internet access that determines the level of ignorance. It is the fear of the unknown coupled with the determination to stay within the box of the known that fuels ignorance or specialized literacy, with no redundancy, recourse or reserve. The Internet and mass media create and reinforce tunnel-visioning, blocking out all else.

Just as the English word 'China' only serves its own convenience and bears no resemblance to the indigenous terminology (Middle Kingdom), 'Jew' is even more so, since not many people would say that they spoke Jewish. These and many other examples are outside-upon imposition of labels, rather than an inside-out self-definition of identity. It is only in '-American' where both insignificant and significant identifiers precede a generic term whereas in other countries, it anchors identity. To label oneself Black, Jewish or Chinese-American seems to be a double-dose of emptiness; a practice resulting in an identity deficit that is uniquely American, one which is being exported with record-breaking speed, image and sound.

When labels and price tags (instant familiarity, recognition and association at subliminal level) define and precede relationships, behaviour follows a virtual script writ large through propaganda, advertisements and brand marketing. Brands are driven and targeted by compartmentalization, categorization and amplification/distortion of minor differences and commonalities, devoid of individuality, negative capability or compassion, since these are unnecessary and non-essential baggage. Such pervasiveness of labels tend to handicap, short-change and unbalance relationships on both sides of the equation, impairing free will, preempting choice and subverting expression: all in all preventing exploration, learning and transformation. English, given its transactional bent, is unlikely to have incorporated the most complex or culture- and sentiment-laden terms. In reducing it into increasing simplicity, its root and essence in etymology is further severed of culture and sentiment so that speed and ease substitute for purpose and content.

An illusion of communications having taken place is created when there actually has been no increase in knowledge, exchange of ideas and feelings, or closing of the gap towards compromise, but only a deduction in time. Young and impressionable minds are especially vulnerable to soaking up labels in all their binary glory. Since people increasingly are conditioned or inclined through self-censorship to stay within the box of the familiar, labels will proliferate into idiolects, hollowing out, bankrupting and rupturing identity. Identity becomes just another new and trendy off-the-shelf product with endless permutation of equally disposable, replaceable and inter-changeable hyphenations of displayable products and features. How easily one forgets that a rose by any other name or label would smell just as sweet and that our compulsion to label is symptomatic of disconnecting and disassociating superficially without dwelling upon the essence of the ubiquity of uniqueness in all manifestations of the life-force or *chi*.

Addressing the latest round of ritualistic public cleansing with blame-casting upon the entertainment empire, what is achieved or learned by staging a media gab and grab fest and giving face and face-time to people on both sides with their high-priced mouthpieces, whose compasses are collectively tuned by and into the ringing of the cash till? It is the parents of the 9 to 12 year olds who should be hauled in and made accountable for gross dereliction of duty and child neglect, exploitation or abuse. Surely these children did not drive themselves to and from the test-market screening of R-rated movies or sign off *in propria persona* (in one's own person or right) any release forms relieving the studio of liabilities. Politicians, unsurprisingly, lack the moral fortitude and integrity or there are no compelling reasons or impetus to risk turning off potential contributors and voters by upsetting the unassailable and untouchable sacred cows of Americanism: parents and parenthood.

In such a milieu of non-accountability, absence of shame or remorse and gaping schisms between authority and responsibility, belonging with its attendant code of duty and honour, become irrelevant. Everyone ducks for legal cover or scrambles for legal recourse and pay-outs except for the young, the weak and the poor. In other cultures where family values survive and family name and honour have meaning, it is the parents who get dragged through the mud because they are 100% responsible and accountable for their children. No other country has such a rampant practice of nicknames, pet-names, stage-names, handles, monikers, initials, acronyms, and the total abandonment of names altogether with the anonymity and avatars of the information age. 'Hey, you', signifying non-recognition or objectification into a thing, is deemed a severe insult in cultures where the language encapsulates sentiment within relationships, especially in regards to strangers and unacceptability.

When parenthood and parental rights converge with private property and privacy rights in the absence or silencing of any cultural imperative, it presents an irresistible proposition of everything to gain and nothing to lose. It opens the door to all kinds of tax breaks and subsidies, with a sense of getting 'my fair share and entitlement', without any public accountability since personal privacy is an inalienable right. How challenging is it to get minor children who are totally dependent for identity and survival to side with and stand by the parents? This state lasts until they too 'achieve' parental status in their own right. It represents a path of satisfying a requirement of social status and invulnerability, rather than fulfilling self-accountability and preparedness. It is a world of inalienable rights over inviolable rites and mandates, of entitlements over effort and diligence, of absolute liberty, equality and happiness of the one, rather than duty, restraint and sacrifice for the many, including children.

Two types of owner's manuals proliferate in this scenario for empowerment of the typical and average consumers, equally victimizing individuality on both sides of the modal equation: one for parenthood and one for marriage, still a stubborn but depleting precursor state to the former. This leads to an escalation of the siege/bunker mentality as consumers load up on more and latest how-to's and must have's, creating a gluttony of feeding frenzy that is entirely satisfactory to the healthy growth and nurture of the revenue systems. The possibility and potential of market extensions are unlimited based upon the premise that the surface area of a sphere is exponentially greater and infinitely expandable, whereas the centre remains fixed. Trying to cover the ever-expanding surface would necessitate an obsession with speed and size to create an illusion of progress and change, whereas inner understanding and transformation tend to require self-knowledge in calm stillness and mindfulness.

Skimming the surface, tangential to the outer perimeter of the curve, only results in being more off and away from the centre, compounding the need for semblance of frenetic activity in great variety and variability. Such activity is epitomized by the allure of multitasking or doing everything equally badly at the same time (especially observable in those with fixed binary mind-sets), as if going somewhere instead of getting some know-ware. This demonstrates the 'inverse square law' of physics that operates for all the forces: the magnitude of a force at a point is inversely proportional to the square of the distance between that point and the point location of its cause. As any good cook knows, following the letter and mechanics of a recipe is not as essential as the heart that goes into the making of a dish for the hearts cherished. It is subject to as many organic variables as in producing a symphonic sound and soundness including the marriage or unity of skill of craft with the love of craft.

How else but through parenthood can one load up on free or subsidized housing, free child-care, free education, free meals, free transportation, free health services and products, and free sympathy? In no other country does the statement 'I am a parent' carry such weight and status in defining identity, becoming the first and last cry of offense and defense. It is a game of the quick draw and quick finish, clearly demarcating some sense of position and belonging. This is quite the inverse from other cultures where parents impart a sense of identity, meaning and belonging to their children, not the other way around. This creates a hysterical cycle of consumption and disposal or procreation and destruction with the illusion of private property with absolute, iron-clad, legal and constitutional protections and guarantees, sustaining the notion that 'I get more than I put in' and 'it's not my money or child'. This bodes well for collectivism of bureaucratic and corporate growth and consolidation, demonstrating that individualism really thrives by gutting and decapitating individuality. It is the best of all possible worlds for making and circulating money when responsibility is skinned off and spun off from accountability. In tidy convergence, cultural mandates of integrity between private and public face and duty are increasingly replaced by inalienable rights, entitlements and lawsuits. Winning, not integrity or even being in the right, increasingly becomes the name of the game.

Neither communism nor capitalism, Islam nor Christianity requires individual moral or intellectual cultivation which tends towards self-knowledge and balancing of pluralities, but quite the reverse. All isms are tangents on the surface of the sphere, unbalanced and unhinged from the centre. Only democracy (political pluralism and process for change) requires a modicum of self-knowledge as a necessary and sufficient pre-requisite to its functioning and purpose, and it seldom works to anyone's satisfaction since integrity or synchronicity within private or public spheres are unlikely. Many procreate or indulge in numerous activities out of fear of the uncertain as well as being forgotten or feeling impotent. While ancestor reverence represents culturally prescribed mnemonic ritual, as contained within the family unit, most who are remembered and revered by posterity are those who did not regard children as private exclusive property nor equate parental love or compassion with biological parenthood, but quite to the contrary. Jesus, St. Francis and St. Claire are not remembered for being wealthy and wonderful personalities, but for their universal compassion and shared insights. They are beings who chose to parent the many over the few.

The Eucharist rites, as well as many other rites of cultures, symbolize gratitude and humility without physical and temporal boundaries or categories, of the One in the Many and the Many in the One. The test and challenge of Truth (cultural imperatives, universal laws), as well as its radiant Beauty, reside in the infinite and timeless applicability to the many without any diminution of its potency and poetry, in its ability to be shared by all while remaining indivisible and undiluted. This is the parable of the loaf of bread and the tumbler of wine that can equally satisfy the hunger and the thirst of the many who seek the Way of Life in co-existence in good faith through diligence, sacrifice and compromise, to fulfill one's obligation and potential without impeding any other's.

Why does Polonius tell Laertes, "neither a lender nor a borrower be" which in combination with "to thine own self be true" leads to "then you cannot be false to any man." To be consistent with integrity or true to one's identity or to Truth is inconsistent, if not incompatible, with money. Once money seeps in and takes over on both sides of the master/slave or lender/borrower continuum, fear and bad faith are introduced to each other. With such an introduction, liberty is compromised, curtailed and contaminated, especially in the rendering of a moral choice (a function of attitude and understanding of relationships) consistent with cultural or family values. On one side is the fear of loss of principal and interest with the objective of subjecting the other for the extraction of maximum penalty as a recourse against default. On the other side is the fear of loss of collateral, be it labour, family or home, and even worse, fear of being found out or caught in trying to get away with a free ride at someone else's expense.

Thus, when interest payments are equated to tax deductions or perceived as being free of or subsidized carrying costs, and images of lifestyles are deficit-financed predicated upon cycles of consumption and disposal or making money for the sake of spending in cycles of bills due, way beyond need or sustenance, there is no balance, meaning or sense of centre and control over one's choices and therefore life. When money, image and Man are the measure of all, cultural and family values, or the value and values of life, spiral into a free-fall, enslaving all equally, the older, stronger and richer as well as the younger, weaker and poorer in a free-for-all in which there is no safe harbour or moorings. This is the coinage of consumerism: 'I cannot be happy unless I have...' (a list of salable goods and services). This state of mind not only equates asset amassment, ownership and private property with happiness, but also creates an illusion of immortality in what seems to be an endless chase, where speed is all. It is a fast cycle of instant gratification and revolving credit (shorting or forward-selling of time) with instant dissatisfaction and ingratitude. This is a parallel track at cross purposes in coupling pursuit of free and freedom with pride and entitlement of ownership and private property. In the chase of the material, all are enslaved by the appetite for living beyond one's means or needs, with accumulation of debt and a lifetime of deficit living, with interest servicing and deductions, sustaining the uniquely defined and definable American Dream. Many choices are made in split seconds or impulsively, when heart, mind and body are overwhelmed or bypassed. Impulse should be tempered by an inner voice of restraint that sounds an alarm or pops up a red flag, but these need to be louder and clearer, as external noise and image entrap and entangle the honour and dignity of life, liberty and duty.

Ownership of home or any other type of material asset does not figure in any moral or spiritual texts because none of these gives rise to a sense of home, family and belonging, especially as a part of Nature. Whether humans are guests, hosts, renters or owners, the attitudes and actions are those of squatters, with replete consumption and destruction of as much as possible without contributing or replenishing anything at all, resembling more of a blight on, rather than a part of, Nature. Without an understanding of 'good' or 'faith', there can be no sense of justice—personally, legally, culturally, globally or universally. Justice is an affair of the heart, and an outcome of good faith and good will in relationships based upon a code of life, not a mountain of fine print and piles of endless reams of legal statutes.

Hamlet (youth and vacuity) enthralls and captivates, while Polonius (age and wisdom) languishes and expires: what is empty can be filled and projected onto and is therefore more appealing. Both are caricatures of life and caricatured on stage, with youth as the focus of all attention and the inevitable age diminished or denied at all costs, to the detriment of all, since death does not discriminate. The question is: Would one choose to live and die as Hamlet or Polonius? The answer reflects upon one's relative position in the trajectory of life, self-knowledge and negative capability. Titles and labels can draw attention, but are mere peripherals to content. As cover titles and images grow exponentially, content declines in same measure.

Duty, a word that has atrophied and exited along with extended families, similar in its effect upon the wellness of isms and revenue systems as another four-letter word whose usage they profusely promote to relentlessly malign duty, however, has not been un-created. In surviving ancient and traditional cultures, duty reminds all belongers that while all things change with the coming of new life and passing of the old, it is only our relationships and our attitude to and understanding of them that remain interminable and inviolable, giving meaning (capstan, anchor and root) to our own lives and those of our children. It is only in this context that honour and dignity operate and become real, linking the past with the present and the future. Times and many things change, but we are all manifestations of a fertilized egg in vitro or an organic pool of life. This truth of our organic nature and being will remain even as we ceaselessly and tirelessly try to define all that makes us different from other animals and humans or all others, convincing ourselves into illusions of superiority and supremacy. Such attitudes and attendant actions lead to exterminating rather than fostering co-existence and balance with the different, be they stronger or weaker: willfulness, self-esteem and I-centrism displace willpower, self-worth and life. To every point, there is a counterpoint; without a sense of shame and remorse, there is no honour and dignity or self-worth and worthiness. The overflow of the fountain of youth dries up the riverbed of life. Only in North America are people so coy and cloying about age, as if time can or should be denied. What is uncontrolled or uncontrollable is denied, suppressed or feared versus minded.

The cultures that have survived the tests of time, in native and foreign soils, and demonstrated a broad spectrum resistance against man at his most destructive are enduring and resilient testimonies to the superpower in the Way of Life. The backbone or transmitters of the code of life in these cultures are mothers and motherhood. They are the guardians and practitioners of the power of compassion and maternal love in transcending self-interest, unbounded by notions of recognition, reciprocity and private property, or any of the extremes of limited and limiting isms, especially of imported varieties. They sacrifice, overcome and endure impossible odds to maintain the structural integrity of the family for the sake of releasing the human potential of their children. They are the focal points where the multiplier effect of good faith and good will harness maximum momentum and radiate with maximum concentration and dispersion, holding the key to and safeguarding the mysteries and powers of the heart. The needs and wants of the individual are insufficient to overcome the values and vows of unity for the well-being of the many.

The foods of the human being in these cultures are the antithesis of the many types of highly refined, simulated, synthesized, processed and packaged junk food of modernity; they are the super foods of the Way or the power of virtue encapsulated in family relationships, and reverence and respect for their predecessors and Nature. What these superpowers share is the code of life which places the highest values in moral and intellectual cultivation or self-knowledge, framed and shaped by honour and dignity of what it is to be a human being as part of Nature. The cultural paradigm incorporates all the virtues and sentiments of organic life in the daily lives, practices and languages, spoken and unspoken, of all the belongers. Cultural or family values are not about mass markets, mass appeal or mass, but of the essence of Truth which does not deny, suppress and exterminate the Other but, rather, embraces and is embraced by a code of life of all that live in co-existence as an integral and unique constituent of Oneness.

As commercial interests propagandize the great mythical 'digital divide' and work their level best to push and shove this down the global throat or pipeline, the binary split between the haves and have-nots will increase, fed by consumerism and disposalism. This will be proportionately matched by the decline in the ratio of thinking to non-thinking activities, and absolute reduction in activity, imagination and creativity out paced by numerity and variety of replications and recycling of labels for imagery, inactivity and inertia. Identity deficit will then become a truly equal opportunity global phenomena, tended to with great care and diligence by the industries of identity with a self-perpetuating and self-sustaining revenue circulatory system of the information age.

Time and again, modernity or progress as defined in the West continue its history and legacy of millennia of blood baths to exterminate, enslave or exploit the different, unfamiliar and unknown. These ever-increasing scales of destruction are empowered and released by Christianity (evangelistic zealous totalitarianism), justified and measured by the standards of Democracy (spawned by the dogmas of empiricism and rationalism with their progeny, the military industrial combines), and accommodated and propelled by Capitalism and its *lingua franca* (expedient normalization and conversion of organic into inorganic terms and measures). The taking off of the military industrial combine coincides happily with the take off of its food source, the human population, and regardless of cause and effect coefficients, anti-choice is ultimately pro-business and war, or anti-life, which can only feed and grow upon the young, impressionable and vulnerable. The unique individual creations of the marriage between skill and love are reduced to only what can be mass produced, packaged and sold, so that compassion, imagination and creativity meet their boundaries or masters. The great uniformity of the products, services and mass-media programmes reflect and attest the uniformity among the masses which result in massive markets sizes where USD 40-billion-plus industries are common, with healthy annual growth trends. The delusions of individuality and non-conformity mark and mask extremes of conformity or its corollary, intolerance.

This is the kernel that resides in the English-speaking traditions of the West into which the young are initiated, especially by the mass media, with increasing profit and profitability, as it marches on globally. Along with uniformity of consumer goods, tags intolerance and the uniformity of social malaise that it breeds. The inclination to stay within the box, with the binary headset of the young firmly clamped on, results in the adolescent state of mind becoming a permanent state, so that discernments remain restricted to predator/prey, life/death, sex/violence and win/lose. The process of enculturation that transforms the mind into the kaleidoscopic symphony of Nature through the initialization and booting up of cultural programmes is preempted by mass media propaganda everywhere, across all time zones. The extermination of diversity along with cannibalization of the young and the vulnerable not only continue unabated, but are invited into every home and mind with open arms. The unique flavours and essences of each home decline everywhere with the introduction of an inexhaustible supply of kitchen gadgets and time-savers, along with increases in the absolute size and per square foot costs of kitchens and houses, as they become as equally tethered to machines and money as naturalized Americans.

The illustrated, simplified and simplistic history of the West presented from the sole perspective of the 'victor' resembles fairy tales and continues the legacy of its tunnel-vision I-centrism and infallible righteousness. This results in an in-built incapacity for apologizing or atoning, having defined itself and its purposes as good and right. Apologizing is a highly developed artform in many cultures which serves to affirm position and face-value of both parties rather than as means for redress, restitution and recrimination. Icentrism never needs repentance and redemption, but hangs on to the Redeemer as an insurance policy against any downsides it may have overlooked in defining or forgetting away. It finds it most convenient to load and heap as much negativity onto Nazism and 'six million Jews' as possible, which serves its need to deny ('not us'), overlook and divert from the complicity of the Western powers in this and so many other instances of human destruction. No conscience is preferred to a guilty one. Only the killer needs forgetfulness to forge on within the spheres of lies, deceits and illusions in order to justify its own progeny that it feeds and nurtures upon its knees of bipedal binary intolerance of the sole 'I'.

The ages of Renaissance, Restoration, Enlightenment, Romanticism, Splendid Isolationism, Imperialism and Expansionism equally mask and belie their historical and human significance. Since only the benefits accrued to the West are showcased for posterity, without accounting for the other side of the ledger whereby the rest of the world bears the costs, these stories tend to be incomplete, unaudited and unbalanced. Since the lessons of the whole of humanity are not integrated, the tradition of intolerance is amplified and passed on, remaining silent on the unspeakable, with victory enshrined and recounted *inter vivos* (among the living). With collective amnesia, asymmetric/factional/fractional recollections, truth avoidance, evasion or denial of any other perspective in equal measure and time, the dark underbelly of humanity is not understood. Formal education is rarely a match against self-censorship already *in situ* constructed from the influence of the family, peers and the mass media, especially when held positions diverge. As schools become more livelihood oriented, exploratory learning remains an option for a shrinking pool. How the dots get connected in the mind is a mystery, but less so when there are so few to connect.

Like anything else denied, suppressed or unprepared for, cannibalism rears its ugly head again and again, and the surprise is that anyone is surprised at all. After all, it is only half of a coin seeking its other half in order to get back into the circulation of intolerance and destruction. What other country besides the U.S. is referred to as the Evil Empire as well as considered Uncultured by so many others? What other country has citizenry that cries out for hate crimes legislation to protect so many diverse groups from the one group? Unless and until the U.S. understands why this label sticks and why such legislative need exists, it will be chronically stuck in inhumanity as it exports, replays and recycles intolerant attitudes and insatiable appetites. These tend to rationalize stoning of others in lieu of atonement, regress into restoration movements and isolationism instead of forwards toward harmonization, equate might with right, and confuse certainty with clarity. While no country can be said to be free from these downsides, the power of technology to inject, amplify and circulate the American point of view dwarfs those of the rest of the world. What sounds the alarm for so many is that Americanization is increasingly coupled with an inexhaustible supply and variety of killer applications in their circular journey in this age of globalization.

This system's diet will increasingly be composed of a currency whose every denomination equally and appropriately bears the 'In God We Trust' imprint, symbolizing the coupling of the identity deficit with the industry of identity in appropriate homage to the God in residence. Lives will be processed, ever more tidily and efficiently, for measurable increases in absolute profit (earnings per share) without sacrificing marginal profitability (return on investment) and eliminating the limits of growth. In such a flourishing of the mesmerizing monotheistic monomania, these financial indicators will no longer be relevant or clear in any case, since frenetic activity to consume and dispose while avoiding self-knowledge blurs any fine-tuning and differentiation between quantity and quality, especially in regard to time usage and passage.[69]

Many people, living in their homeland or elsewhere, do not subscribe to any particular culture, ethnically or otherwise derived. In fact, those who choose to uphold, live by, develop, study and understand their cultural heritage have usually been a select minority in many tribes, times and places. There is not one belief system or culture that makes anyone immune or exempt from immoral, unlawful, unethical or unhappy thoughts, words and deeds, although many attempts are made and many are quite adroit at trying to escape from their consequences. There is scant evidence to correlate intelligence to integrity, veracity to loyalty (patriotism and ethnic nationalism), face-value to goodwill or truth to trust, but quite the reverse. There is no shortage of ample and loud squirms and squeals of the malevolent zeal of hypocrites. With the rise of credentialism, specialization and scientism, come the elevation of impartiality and objectivity. What purpose do these serve except to demonstrate how well developed anyone's ability may be in the art

[69].   Time, Real and Imaginary: An Allegory
by S.T. Coleridge [1812]

On the wide level of a mountain's head,
(I knew not where, but 'twas some faery place)
Their pinions, ostrich-like, for sails out-spread,
Two lovely children run an endless race,
A sister and a brother!
This far outstripp'd the other;
Yet ever runs she with reverted face,
And looks and listens for the boy behind:
For he alas! Is blind!
O'er rough and smooth with even step he passed,
And knows not whether he be first or last.

William H. Marshall, ed., op. cit., p. 94.

of self-denial, or how exquisitely or otherwise one can castrate one's heart and mind or centre? How can judgements be fashioned independent of the self in denial of selfhood? Many such refined practices and practitioners of impartiality, objectivity and neutrality seem to be engaged in and rewarded for the exercise of preserving some dogmatic or sacrosanct precedents and noodles at the expense of self-cultivation, -evaluation, -history, and even self-preservation and reality. Many precedents, however unjust, out-dated and irrational, are used as reasons to replicate more injustices, inhumanness and unhappiness as they achieve god-like status and distinction of group-honoured dogmas. Becoming inexorably fused with pride and paraded as principles that pile on and up, they can no longer be revised, modified or changed, even with and especially in the face of any number of evidences to the contrary, without a telling toll on vanity, or pseudo-identity without individual backbone.

Due diligence and scrupulous discharge of duty, are the thin threads upon which mitigation of gross insults on the many, hang. In the absence of trust, belief, or faith—virtue, like virtuosity, is as scarce as moral abortions are plentiful. Taking other people's money means less than nothing when contracts are loaded with disclaimers and are designed against findings of fault and liability by the service providers. The patients and clients end up without legal or medical recourse except by hiring more of the same. Business and elaborate, incomprehensible and unaccountable billing systems are always good and business-as-usual, even better, when proven to be change- and challenge-proofed by legal and institutional precedents in lieu of rites and practices of human cultures. Malpractice, misconduct and misrepresentation by the hidden, hushed and secretive cannibals and technocrats of legal, medical and financial industries deserve greater light of day, however much the mass media prefer the easy selling-out and sale of celebrity names. Evil does not discriminate and diminish over time, and finds delight in escape clauses, loop holes and fine conceptual reasonings and even finer statistics.

How does anyone get "it", let alone understand any or all of the content, context and purpose, if style or form remains an impenetrable, over-riding or immovable stumbling block, circuit breaker or impasse? Language then merely serves no more deictic or id-like a function than a fixed stare, posture, grunt or pointed finger, so that it becomes equivalent to being armed with organ rupturing projectiles or mind numbing parapets of logic which dictate standards of what counts and by how much. Even maths and sciences resort to imaginary concepts and conventions that defy visualization by most, independent of a common and shared language. In a world governed by the principle of Uncertainty, what constitutes a balance of probabilities or beyond a reasonable doubt and do these concepts sway anyone from thinking, talking or acting other than they do, usually or unusually? The answer is not simply reducible or expandable into legalese or so much hocus-pocus of legal, financial and authoritarian industries (institutionalism) designed to ensure their own ideology, immortality and profitability against changes and challenges wrought by time, by circumventing and giving the old heave-ho to organic individuality and mortality. Thus both the masters and slaves of ideologue, of secular or non-secular pedigree, form a contiguous boundary and a seamless whole, sharing a family of values and practices. Above all, they share appreciable and under-rated character traits whose degree of smallness is amply exceeded by hardness and dependence on numerity, replicability and gullibility of the masses. Self-sufficiency or independence is by definition *non sequitur*, since such an unlikely trait would result in breaking off from the pack as well as breaking the mould. The age old bag of tricks and tricks of the (religion) trade seem to play well and thrive beyond expectations on all sides, especially in conjugation with the parvenu isms of capitalism, democracy, scientism and journalism, equally armed with and amplified by the mass media technology and business model that is not below scraping a dime off anything. As long as mass attention remains fixated on the ever-expanding outer layer, skims the surface and skates on the tinny patch of style, the beast of enslavement is safe and secure. The constant or increasing gaps between intent (e.g. words of universal brotherhood) and deed (e.g. actions that kill off diversity) are selectively (not us) exploited and leveraged for profit and power maximization and centralization for the non-universal or exclusive congregations whose hands are congenitally joined and reaffirmed, eternally. The cogs of capitalism work in harmony in supplying appropriate homage, homilies and hyperbolic bling-bling to hype the newest and latest into the stratosphere of purchasable illusions to feed and grow volume by volume, everlastingly. Nothing impedes propriety, learning and liberty quite like pride, vanity and ennui. Any one of these form the necessary and sufficient bed upon which increasingly numerous and splintered interpretations or refractions through reversed telescopes of original ideas and originators can lie and proliferate so that labels such as capitalism, nihilism or communism can be conscripted and bent to serve narrow interests alien to their human (individual) and moral (non-commercial) geneses. Who can be bothered with such unadulterated density or fidelity as to study the original text in order to separate the grain from the chaff *tête-à-tête* which may just nip errors in their bud and prevent their compounding deformations over time and distance beyond recognition to the delight of free traders, freeloaders and two or more timers? Not only is the baby thrown out with the water but the bathtub to boot since all three are eminently replaceable. The growing chasm between the rich and poor is as well enshrined as those between sponges and agents of change or the majority and minority. Why think global and act local or vice versa rather than just thinking and acting for the specific time, place and occasion with integrity? Such is the beauty of democracy, might of the buck, and the right of the consumer as king of indiscriminate taste spun through revolving lines of credit in harmony with the uncultured, disembodied and absent-minded heads and mouths.

Reality comes into focus from many angles, abstruse and acute, with innumerable shades of lies and truths that are equally elusive to deny or confirm, absolutely. The goodness and badness of outcomes pivot upon what purpose (paid for or gratis) these lies and truths serve with each enactment having irreversible consequences. Any shortfalls, distortions or shortchanging in the comprehensive articulation and understanding of purpose gradually and imperceptibly creep into results which increasingly deviate from the original intent or raison d'être, spawning ever greater mastery and masters of elaborate, refined and brilliant denials, deceptions or obscurantism. Blind loyalty, faith or trust, like any other form of absolutism, is likely to be characterized by lack of *in propria persona* (individual) credibility or authenticity, as veering away from the positive and veracity become the norm, whereby one willfully or unwittingly becomes equally blinded, disillusioned, consoled, pigeon-holed or angled, sucked into the vortex of a black hole. Thus many spend and end their days as an instrument or means for ends that are not of their own making, irrespective of material compensations, accolades and credentials. The vested interests and sunk costs associated with maintaining illusions of the best of all worlds or some ideal and idealized figment become the over-riding priority, displacing and subverting the goals of minimizing or mitigating harm and maximizing co-existence in diversity, which find their sound foothold in the irrefutable and undeniable web of relationships, bonds and origin, in the gravitas of the mother, literally, namely or symbolically.

The revenues of U.S. corporations are often categorized as U.S. and ROW or rest of the world, and this is the template that conveniently serves many other purposes of division.[70] What is Americanism but a triple lamination of black and white binary systems of absolute might and right of monotheism, two-party political attenuation, and capitalism that greases and wields the machination of power in all three spheres. This extreme binarism is infused or shot through with unilateral and grandiose notions of manifest destiny, eminent domain, God-given rights (absolutism) as well as God-proof inalienable rights (secularism); wrapped up in orthodox ultra-deluxe or –redux packaging to nurture the cannabalistic attitude of eat or be eaten; encoded with rituals to deny, dishonour, deindividualize, dissect, carve-up and

70. Author's Note: The divide between the U.S. and ROW within the UN is becoming as acute and shrill as that between the Democratic (individualism) and Republican (institutional) parties, with each side going out of its way to pull and push the other off the centre stage by disconnecting from the centre in the age of labels, monologues and uniform scripts and scores. The time and life proofing or blinding slogans of 'all is fair in love and war, the end justifies the means, fighting for a just cause' or some such variation are used time and time again to degrade and defile life by consistently short-changing and bypassing individuality. The value of one life is the value of all life and this sentiment is captured in a Jewish saying, 'to save a life is to save the world'. Should such a talented, charismatic and eloquent leader as President Clinton be confined to the realm of U.S. bipolarity? What would impede him from becoming the first American and eighth UN Secretary General? As the population profile of the U.S. changes and with increasing globalization, the U.S. is not only at odds with much of the rest of the world but increasingly with its own changing identity. This is President Clinton's métier as the quintessentially independent American who is capable of modulating the breach to keep it from becoming a festering wound. He embodies the *auf eigene faust* fire of a warrior, which can only burn in a heart that is truly compassionate, penitent and forgiving in the one who chooses a life of service to the many over self-serving ends. The crown of rule is meted out by the slings and arrows borne in sacrifice to the living spirit. His legacy is not limited to his two terms as merely the POTUS, and as the head of the UN, he could do much to rescue this body from peddling itself into the backwaters of history using much poverty and misery as some kind of a badge of honour while the pool of the poor grows and multiplies. The UN would not have seen the light of day without American leader

continued

discard lives; without a barometer, compass, timer or presence-of-mind. Thus cannabalism thrives best through mind displacement, dismemberment and absence. The apotheosis of this concoction are the endless exercises in categorization and segmentation by race, gender, age, religion and sexual preference divorced from the matrix of moral agency or duty to others. In a world of winners and losers, true symbiotic relationships are bypassed as predators, parasites and hosts form the trinity with greed, avarice and sloth as its top three virtues, with increasingly asymmetric distribution of costs/benefits and storytelling. Rather than triangulating for the way towards truth or integrity within the accommodating and uroborus circle (in Oneness cause and effect is no more or infinite), it is squared-off, partitioned, rationalized or destroyed so that a square fixed upon unilateral lines of cause and effect serves as an archetype as diversity in microstates is reduced. Like-minded squares sport and spout ever-narrowing slogans and doctrines as if by identifying with

ship and investment, and it seems only bent on sliding into virtual nonexistence and decay by defining itself off the American media and mind screens which, regardless of ethnocentric biases, increasingly command the largest market share in eyeballs, eardrums and dollars. President Clinton is uniquely tested and qualified to stand his own ground against bullyism and serve as a keystone or catalyst, from the many nations to the one and the one to the many, so that these fissures need not become as explosive in the future as they have in the past. His long and tapered fingers are designed to touch many hearts and not to be clenched in self-vindication for which such a hand-span would be unnecessary. His persona does not depend on a surfeit of charm but on the arc of life, intellectual finesse, mindful heart and a poetic mastery of his own language, the sum of which does not stir anti-American sentiments, which is not an easy trait to cultivate or possess. The Democratic party is too limiting for his vision and the Republican party, too inadequate, as a foil. By transcending the partisanship of American politics, the way towards the art of compromise can be paved, turning the tide towards doing more with less so that more can be shared with those who have less, for co-existence in diversity. Doing away with more for efficiency and uniformity reduces individuality and in so doing increases instability as equally vulnerable microstates are ignited at the slightest provocation, setting off chain reactions of becoming unraveled, tangled, mangled, kinked, knotted, frayed, snapped or coiled and becoming undone, untenable, unrecoverable or unplayable. The challenge of change or destabilization is the same as long as the soil remains hospitable to the possibility of organic union in pluralism (evolving incrementally in proportionality and complementarity) versus inorganic divide in binarism (swinging violently with metacentres and mottos far removed or disconnected from the centre), which determines the relative happiness of the macrostate.

such, anointed identity in a political grid, that at best fosters chronic indifference and at worst fans terminal intolerance. Both outcomes obstruct intellectual curiosity and passion for learning with pride of ownership and originality that must lock in the status quo at any cost. This vain stance increasingly diverges from human cultures of forgiveness and remembrance that strive for integrative harmony with an understanding of organic unity, frailty and imperfection, not in denial of the imperfect nor with illusions of uniformity, perfection, mastery and ownership.

Crossing the species barrier from the inhuman to human rests upon awakening to the possibility of maximum compassion by being acutely aware of tensions (heart strings) in life that straddle, negotiate and compromise a path between sublime joy and pain, uniquely expressed in infinitesimal to infinite movements and sounds. Is superiority attained by degrading and demoting all others, by shutting out all sights and sounds of pain, or by some kind of first strike without fear of retaliation capability? Is arrogance in ignorance preferable to intellectual arrogance and what fine distinction separates these equally unenlightening states? What measures will not be taken or what price not paid to maintain illusions of creation, perfection and unilateral gain in a universe overflowing with wonders in a complex web of interconnectedness that humans seem uniquely endowed to enjoin and destroy rather than celebrate and enjoy? How profitable would the secular and non-secular industries of identity be if it dawned on their customers, clients and subscribers that a true and centred heart cannot be purchased nor sold, but is a gift of compassion or selfless giving reflecting such a sublime heart. Such a heart is represented in many diverse cultures in mothers and mother-figures independent of gender and form, from wolves and bears to mythical beings characterized by an absence of hard corners, edges and boundaries. Anthropocentrism or self-obsession and self-indulgence that insists that everything exists for the benefit of man and that man exists solely to serve man, like other isms of absolute ignorance in which subscribers revel, can only be chipped away by shafts of light and awareness of other realities. As science progresses from finite matter to infinite non-matter or the relationships in between matter, measurability gives way to the immeasurable and ROW can stand for the Real One World rather than dividing the U.S. from all others.

Words such as equal, equivalent, identical; change, compromise, collaboration; sufficiency, necessity, contingency (ancillary); sexual, asexual, non-sexual (benign, celibate, complete, fused, hermaphrodictic, sterile, immaculate); and normal, average, mean are a function of our preferences, desires or beliefs which are known, knowable, knowable with great difficulty or unknown, and derive, degenerate or regenerate from the question of 'what does it matter?' which can be answered in the presence (creation) or absence (destruction) of moral principles that inform and are in turn informed by dynamic feedback loops from aforementioned determinations. With a 'more is good' approach, humankind is exponentially obliterating and consuming many other lives and habitats through reproduction, duplication and evolution of human products (good to look at and possess), human services providers (reallocation and conversion of cost/ benefit of manhours) and human ideas that rationalize degrees of homocentrism: what profits and feeds humans are humans in the food-chain of life. The gods of humankind share much in common with their creators, including an absolute and insatiable appetite, and humans can only change their gods by changing themselves by tempering their appetites. While we are our own best producers and consumers in the predator/prey and parasite/host schemes, without appetite control and indicators, hunger will cease to be, perhaps to the collective sigh of relief by all else—a testament to the failure of an experiment to co-exist in harmony when advantaged or handicapped by freewill or an illusion of it.

Can this be why so many teachers and sages have opted to give us absolute belief systems and traditional moral foundations as an insurance policy to protect and save us from ourselves since they were no strangers to despotism, devastation, stupidity and suffering or were they blind to their own inconsistencies, putting on blinders, gouging out their eyes or waking up irrational one fine day? They were not merely clever but realistic, robust and sober minds, even at the expense of their own knowledge and self-awareness. It seems that they were demonstrating parental love or compassion to the many at sea without a moral compass to guide them in the journey of life by offering a temporary or permanent lifeline or ladder depending on the dicey individual state of being. In the seesaw of life, which poses less mischief and harm: busy and thoughtless or idle and thoughtless? They could not be convincing unless they themselves sincerely believed or appeared to believe in their metaphysical, traditionalist and absolutist outlooks in order to hold out for posterity by wagering their reputations and lifetimes of work, not in blind optimism and upbeatness, pessimism and gloom, nor for celebrity, notoriety and profit, but simply in fulfilling their *dharmas* (duty of honour) as students transformed into mentors in goodwill and good faith.

The wagers placed towards the end of their lives tilt in favour of aeonian truths or illusions (time-dependent and man-independent or time-tested and not subject to approval of the times, verifiability, isms, common sense, opinion or whim) as being less dangerous than the absence of such in the human experience that obstinately denies and efficiently destroys the terrors and wonders of the Oneness in Nature by incessantly dichotomizing good and evil as a function of categorized, skewed and mandated human appetite and perspective. This is the wager: if mind-sets are prone towards binarism, let my way/no way with exquisite paradigms of cost/benefit serving as choice-making templates, be replaced with at least a group consensual our way/no way, so that the furies unleashed by thwarted wills are not a daily offering. But adding mass to any binarism only adds to its momentum as the increasing force of unity sucks in many without willpower, purpose and direction or without any cultural ideology and language, so that illusions of individual freedom and grandeur serve to centralize power for the few. The power and attraction of Oneness is equal on both sides of the vortex as demonstrated by couples, cults, sects and parties with godheads and dogmas, and only a handful break through the cycles of sex and violence or life and death, unpolarized and benign, into the Way, which is profoundly moral as opposed to amoral or strictly binary. Thus, the importance placed on the central figure as representing an absolute authority (lode-star, True North or Polaris) as a means to protect, normalize and orient the many, since few other surviving guidance systems have proven to be as user-independent for the unpredictable journey and sea in life where ineffable and ineluctable cataclysms are par for the course.

In the post-mortem of carnage throughout human existence, causation explanations are elusive and neither necessary nor sufficient to understand the rationality or irrationality of mob incitations. This is because mobs are composed of pluralities of individuals who cave in despite all that makes them unique, becoming a unity independent of purpose, contingent only upon the pull and push of its own crescendoing vortex in mass and momentum. People are like-minded only in their out-of-mindness when entrapped, enthralled and inflamed by the forces unleashed in mob frenzy or unity that feeds illusions of superiority and power over their own destiny as much as dominion over all others. Thus transcendence of self or no self (*anatman*) into Oneness or Nothingness can be quite easily sparked and sported, but mindful and compassionate union requires unimaginable discipline in grappling and embracing the paradox of being (consuming to live) and non-being (killing, processing and packaging for consumption) as the one and of the One, simultaneously, without disconnecting moral agency from timelines.

Understanding evil is no less critical than understanding good, and the state of benignity or the Way of the Mean is a mediating, particular and wavering mount that leaves no imprint in certainty, only the sword of Damocles dangling over our heads as our lives ignite, transpire and expire in a hair's breadth and split second of space and time. Each thought, word and deed takes on a moral life of its own regardless of our personal take, bias or view on morality and immorality, just as our relationships with others (human or non-human companions) seem to fill a huge space with their presence as well as leave an ineffable and ineluctable void in absence when the sense of Oneness brought to bear with the other, without the necessity to own, know or control the other, is still palpable and being ready, willing and able just does not cut the mustard like specific performance. Those who have lived through poverty, hunger, adversity, alienation and fallibility are likely to have different sensibilities than those who are unfamiliar with one or more of these aspects. The effects of these trials are a function not only of how and when these were overcome, but more importantly whether they were in private versus public spheres and the degree of control the individual could exercise over their occurrence and witness. Very few people can lead a scar-, secret- and lie-free life except for those who are perfect; believe in perfection; are experts at denial; have limited imaginations; just have not lived enough; and prefer illusions despite all evidence to the contrary, especially in regard to self-image. Humiliation rarely produces humility, just as abundance does not lead to gratitude, and literacy to mindfulness, but rather their reverse in disproportionate pride, dissatisfaction and distortions, so that expressions of appreciation and regret tend to be stingy, underdone, grudging, measured or entirely absent.

The need to liberate the human spirit as suggested by the Romantic Movement suggests that freedom is not a given but is achieved through a process of becoming that involves struggle, sacrifice and suffering to reach a standard that is anything but of the lowest common denominator and having to meet its own 'duck-test' of recognizable humanness and freedom. Forged, tempered, hewn, disciplined and tested independence, as exemplified by Romantic thinkers and creators throughout recorded time, is by nature and design an uncommon and exceptional wonder of the private inner language, not a mass product stamped out by a mass mould for mass consumption. They live up to and by their names and principles rather than those of labels and popularity of various tone-deaf and iron-clad isms and tenets that do more harm than good by recusing personal responsibility through tautological rationalizations that provide escape clauses, while ensuring ownership of credit for upsides by the upstarts. In this regard, humanitarianism, concerned with temporal issues, is too limited in the context of widely popular religious beliefs and organizations across all groups, and its espousal of human perfection, along with elimination of pain and suffering, is too broad and unrealistic. While humanitarianism is categorically secular, many of its sentiments seem spiritually inspired, shared or moved, especially in regard to the concept of universal brotherhood and neighborhood. The acid-test for isms is in their divisiveness and exclusivity with masked purposes of expansionism and totalitarianism; propositions masquerading as orthodox principles spawned as means for power centralization; non-requirement of an original idea or any qualifications; advocates and adherents who cannot be discerned by external appearances; and much polished, practised and repeated show-and-tell that stand in for crude and coarse internal design and intent that rarely cross the my way/no way and good/bad binary constructs.

The liberated and humanized minds do not subject their principles to barter, but only compromises in kind. The thinkers and creators of the Romantic Period, as an example, seem fearless because as long as they did not betray themselves, they did not fear being hurt. Their works reflect a sense of harmonic oscillation in the coalescence of their solitude with Oneness, which radiates sublime truth, light and beauty without giving in or breaking, but transcending mass and form in the moment of sheer delight in play as their delicate, lithe, supple, tensile, versatile or playful and kinetic strings are plucked. There is no calculation of profit and loss—only in giving as much as they humanly could of themselves to the act of creation and to the created. There is no holding back or hoarding for a rainy day in their response to the call. The representation of their experience and insight only exists and plays intangibly in our minds—leaving an indelible trace of sublime wonder, taste and scent. Many attempt to convey the experience from the asymtotic proximity to the One, and few manage to stay in the flow without falling over the edge or all over themselves. Those who do not try to possess and capture the sense of Oneness, but simply bask in it by flexing and expanding the curvature and boundary of their conical minds for maximum convergence and dispersion of light, seem to impart glimpses of their direct experience through their works. As the two focal points court each other in complementarity, many other microstates are created within the courtship ritual without breaking, reducing or diminishing the other. They unreservedly and wholeheartedly bring their own artistry and integrity into the process of concordant collaborative creation or synergy through which the constituent identities dissolve as equals beyond compare, so that what is brought forth in the joining is sublime reality that is more real by its very unverifiability and disinclination to be verified. Their works are creations of extreme economy in tangible matter, which inversely correlates to the universality of their appeal and recognition, which awakens us to what *sui generis* means in context of *mutatis mutandis* coupled with *ceteris parabus* or what immortal creation is.

In modernity, plutocrats and autocrats are anointed by the authority of inorganic systems in lieu of God, rather than being invested with individual mastery, acuity and finesse. Power of mass and momentum tramples and stumps principles, rather than being tempered by them in practice, resulting in crowding out and enslaving humanity as focus, care and attention are lavished on inhumane, faceless, nameless, careless, humourless and unyielding monolithic entities. These efficiently grind out principles to make sausages whose flavour and texture can no longer be tied to the constituents, so that they flourish and grow without being subject to deprivation, change and compromise, exemplifying the virtue of blended and processed inorganic systems created by aberrant humanoids in pursuit of immortality. These creations can take all kinds of blame and abuse, yet remain standing in impunity, because they have no identity conundrums and are dedicated to their own growth at any cost, with money or some other *quid pro quo* to pacify and neutralize dissent, without the burden of mortality or morality. The essence and strength of these systems lie in the binary design and intent, which can reduce and reproduce ad infinitum in this fool-prone and uniform format. Because of the presumption of infallibility and entitlement associated with majority will or unity that can over-ride any individual veto as well as disconnect any moral agency with unlimited blame-assignment and -absorption redundancies, these entities feed and grow indiscriminately with power to affect the many, seemingly overnight, launching the slightest errors or undetected oversight into uncharted territory, against which immunization, prevention, safeguards, counterforce and chants are too little, too late. Excessive mass and/or acceleration acts as multipliers on force, momentum and frenzy against which spin control, course correction and counter-measures are virtually impossible—often the only recourse being to wait out its own decay and eventual spending, which applies to organic, senescent and sentimental constituents but not incorporeal, humourless and inorganic constructs—as most monitoring systems lack the acuity and sensitivity to detect course correction needs until it becomes alarming, irritable and indigestible enough in daily lives. In human cultures and lives, a sense of proportion, mind and economy tend to prevail over gluttony, haste and waste. With the increasing number and size of these monoliths, the identity industries scrape the bottom of the barrel for stories and heroic figures, so the sense of the heroic and tragic becomes meaningless and banal except as topical grist for mincing, selling and occupying airtime, mind-space and shelf-space.

Within the spiral cosmos, the centripetal force of unity (macrostate) allows for very limited independence, and the distribution curve can be conceptualized as having multi-modal peaks of low-activation-energy (easily ignited) microstates on either side, representing the tidal waves of polarity (sink-holes) with fixed tensions ranging from loud and tight to silent and flaccid, with a pivotal, leptonic and saffron[71] isthmus in the

71. Author's Note: Why saffron? It seems to be a colour that is unforgiving, exacting, indomitable and potentially catalytic. At the same time, it is non-domineering, tentative, economical, diffuse and incomparable at its best. Its dharma is not to seek recognition, reciprocity, reply, reward or renown for itself. Its beauty is unrecorded, undeclared, uncapturable, discreet and subtle, but its touch and tinge are everywhere manifested. It is user-unfriendly or demanding because life itself has crossed the isthmus, comes through only once more, and visits when they do rarely occur, seldom last more than a moment or a split-second as too long a stay would make life and death, impossible. The blossoms of saffron are the ambrosia of creation by which life and death unfolds, whose scent and sway are unintrusive and fleeting but nonetheless infinitesimally tuned and calibrated to the rhythmic pulse of the flow of time. It is the winking colour of being and non-being or life and death which are existentially sequential, not self-willed, –syncopated or –synchronized happenings, so that saffron has no meaning in the cultures of life wherein most dwell but great significance for those who disengage from the cycles of sex and violence into the world of maximum compassion and possibilities, quietly and imperceptibly. Life in the parallel universe is not an escape into exoticism, mysticism, utopianism, paradise, truths or certainty, but is its antithesis in

continued

centre, with spiral extensions. Those in the centre remain independent or unpolarized, but are acutely aware of and attuned to the forces of rotation by virtue of being perched on a mount that will not be taken for granted but is all demanding in its efforts to stay the course in an infinity of the many micro-state possibilities. Independence is distinct from the unengaged, disinterested, non-aligned, carefree or couldn't-care-less reduced and common microstates at the less polarized margins, but which are still subject to the centrifugal force exerted from the centre and compensate by covering more distance with illusions of speed. Independents are not gods, leaders, uniters nor dividers, but creators and givers of light or visionaries who communicate to and for the many who do not speak or have a platform and representation in the military-industrial axes, but are nevertheless irreplaceable beings with equal rights to co-exist with their families, habitats and ways in the *axis mundi* (axis of the world). The power of the Way does not depend on numerity, weight or temporal force, but on the external and rippling light that guides the many different and rare microstates, so that the human experience

complete surrender to the Uncertain, the Unknowable and the Nameless in permeability and transparency. It is skimming by entirely on one's own cognizance and recognition without any means of visible support. This state is not for the faint, feint or febrile of heart. The twists, turns and self-closure of the Möbius strip, Klein's bottle, the vast and delicate inner membrane seamlessly joined and contained by the outer skin or the uroborous circle of time and space creates and necessitates illusions for traction in life that transpires in such a midst, as the metacentre tries to keep above an unfixable and unverifiable centre of gravity, similar to a slightly tilted spinning top or compass in revolving motion. Whether one's *dharma* tacks to self-service (limited possibility of branded myshare reproduction of attenuated half-life decay) or non-self-service (infinite possibilities of universal mindshare through space and time with extendable half-lives or revitalizable kinetic cores, telomeres or strings), the shades of saffron determine being thrown off the mount or staying on it, in context of the arrow of time. On the cover, only the areas marked '2' join to form the apex and base of a triangle and impart a sense of direction, but its unique feature includes the Janus-like rhomboid (wildcard) that displaces one of the rhomboids which is otherwise shared by the primary colours in correspondence from the centre. Thus knowing the centre or self-awareness provides only one focal point and the elusive direction, purpose or *dharma* (catching the rhomboid) is as crucial to approximate another focal point to form the balanced triangle. The answer to the why of life is joined to the know-how and the way of life. There is no going back in the particular timeline and the story is in unrecorded time, not in man's categorized, labeled, willed, skewed and measured creation and commemoration of himself, by himself, for himself.

does not suffer from a dearth of visionaries but a preponderance of illusions, perspectives or visions of familiarity and stability that life necessitates.

The tree of knowledge merely liberates or condemns us with moral agency, spinning compass or freewill, which can serve to split us from or unite us with the One of infinite facets and hues in lightness and darkness. Biting the fruit does not give rise to a free pass or endow inalienable and absolute rights or inject facts and figures, but it can show that the pursuit and procreation of knowledge is barren as are lives immersed in the nexus of cause and effect divorced from reverence of all that exists in co-habitation. Reproduction and replication continue unabated to satisfy insatiable appetites as the procreated serve as means for desire satisfaction as writ large by the industries of identity deficit and their marketing scripts that replace organic and human culture mythologies with inorganic isms and artificial power grids of winners/losers, good/bad, and profit/loss. These industries are fed by and feed upon the asymmetric scramble to corner profitable goods and stories while ignoring or diverting the gaze from all that suffer and pay with incommensurable lives. Ferocity and voracity of appetite is independent of size, shape and species, and humans are only distinguished in being top wasters of lives that seem terminal and criminal.

Who has a better handle on morality—those locked away or those doing the locking up, which action fosters an insufferable police mentality over self-criticism and self-cultivation? Inter-connectedness does not depend on human knowledge or preference, and even if stepping outside the circle is possible or desirable, what is the price paid and the prize gained? Will we ever know if the holy grail (truth, light, beauty) lies within or without the circle and what is form without a reference, reverence and sense of an unrankable and indivisible centre? Are non-humans obsessed with gender, sexuality and certainty (free meal, god and utopianism) or are they piously aligned and attuned with their *dharmas*, including memory retention and transmission in the flow of time with unique identities (individually differentiated and distinguishable) within a web of relationships? Are humans hard-wired for sex and violence to create and consume lives in an overkill that must constantly break new ground? Are humans owners, masters, guardians, custodians or even free-agents within the uroborous circle (heads connected to tails without a beginning or end and alpha or omega), where the root and way of good and evil is life, with moral agency transpiring incrementally and individually, moment to moment, mindlessly carried away in shared silence or in the rush and roar of union, congregation or collectivity of at least two or more? Or are humans simply players at play in the game of life, as free to be, as all other increments of time? Which journey requires courage, time and effort in becoming—from inhuman and inorganic to human and organic or vice versa? Is the imperative to go forth and multiply a reward or punishment without possibility of parole or commutation within a lifetime and beyond? The questions are few in comparison to an inexhaustible supply of answers as unique as the beings who pose the questions and in whom lie the replies. We are all dealt unique hands and the only difference we can make is in how we choose to play our hand as we transition from nothing matters to some things do matter to everything matters because all are of the one matter, at which moment of truth, we learn the art of compromise and sharing.

Wisdom, oftentimes passed off as justice, retribution or revenge, is a dish best served chilled in just-enough-to-satisfy portions so as to not tip the scales into counter-productive excess that obscures and vitiates purpose. Encounters with sex and violence or the forces of life and death by unprepared, undiscerning, untempered, unaged or premature and immature minds and hearts short-circuit, invert, taint and impair the process for change by equating mere excitability, certainty and crisis with true irritability, tenuousness and criticality. Familiarity with the many means of killing and variety of killer applications only sets off crude, exuberant and volatile reactions, emotionally, physically and intellectually. These responses may be honest, true, pure, beautiful, courageous, passionate or self-sacrificing, but such demonstrable love of one's own power to harm, deny, define, desensitize and destroy is only vanity, which increasingly and irrevocably becomes unhinged from the lore of life that balances tenuously by appreciating, embracing and incorporating both good and evil, with intimate knowledge and with its own coy impunity, humour, riposte and recoil. Life is a high-stake gamble mounted on time's arrow that takes no prisoners. But it does console all equally well with flickering and multi-faceted illusions (including the cast of truth, beauty and light) for freeloaders and relief-seekers who believe in their own irrefutable freewill, answers and replicantism. Illusions are well served and perpetuated by the many who believe that they have chosen the free and effortless path to non-suffering and immortality by hitching a free ride to get away scot-free with a Scotch-verdict.

So alluring is the need to resist and deny change and the coming into one's own or dissolving into nothingness that matter (in context of the aeonian debates dichotomizing and deciphering who's-on-first in regard to matter versus principle, body versus mind, heart versus soul and human spirit versus spirit of all and one Life) clings onto illusions of permanence and a myriad of isms that anesthetize cannibalizing and being cannibalized, believing itself to be unchanged or invulnerable, as time winks and ushers in change, anyways. At least crocodiles presumably shed tears while consuming their prey. It is debatable as to whether we are descending or ascending when resorting to anthropomorphism and zoanthropism, let alone know what direction we are headed in or need to head towards. Our self-perceived perch at the top of the pyramid, usually in conjunction with self-interest at the centre, is more notorious for increasingly leading us off course over time into mayhem rather than for producing desirable or desired ends, if such are even formulated or uttered, since becoming fixated and locked-in contravenes and does not jibe with the nature of the amœbaean gyre (in context of the call and response that synchronize the convolutions of the cingulate gyrus, the seat of maternities, with the parahippocampal gyrus, the place of co-incidences).

In other words, regardless of gender, there are propensities for maternal drives in communion with tendencies to integrate the inner worlds with outer realities which intersect at various angles and points, not neccesarily uniquely for each individual, but oftentimes as aspects, allegories and amalgams of the One Eternal Mind. At certain moments of time extensions in concordant harmony or complementarity, in or out of solitude, we can appreciate the Oneness through shared, like-minded and similar experiences and perceptions over the millennia of diffuse, diverse and descriptive oral and written traditions spun by the sensitive musicality of the gyri (convolutions) in synch with the sulci (grooves), viscerally and vicariously. In this sense and spirit, Machiavelli's *Discourses* (1531) can be viewed as a complement or A' to *The Prince* (1513) as Smith's *Theory of Moral Sentiment* (1759) is complementary to *The Wealth of Nations* (1776), so that a moral matrix is laid and ever-present within realities and beliefs to complete the picture. The spirals (including the dentate gyrus with an affinity for learning, change and probability processing for their own sakes) remember, recreate, cue, gear-shift, probe and trace through circular counter-motions to preserve, yet modify the unbroken wholeness in the past, present and future pathways toward long-term potentiation and escapement versus retrospective falsification and rescission, relying on permutations in the theme of 'looks and sees', whose boundaries are a function of the sense and sensibility of singularities.

Many are driven to write or record in their own voice and mode of communications, trying to transcend time beyond mortality that limits time and resources for modification for those who may follow in posterity. The written word reduces the probability of but does not entirely eliminate deniability, falsification and eradication. It makes, liberates and serves its own point and purpose, irrespective of name, place, and time-signatures. Trust and truth are in the eyes of the beholder, independent of guaranteed, measured and verified *quid pro quo* for non-memorable and a total-waste-of-time events and goods pasted onto a prepaid or promissory bill of sales. These bills are preloaded with explicit and implicit fault and default proofing fine prints tilted in favour of money, for in-your-face collection and consumption. These consumption preferences are conditioned by artful show-and-tell propagandism for upholding money as the always corruptible, shameless and faceless symbols of trust and truth. Such an elaborate scheme or business model enables comforting blindness of the eye which can see that what is profitable, liberating, constructive and progressive for some is costly, oppressive, distressing and regressive for others, as blind and blinding fear and faith interlock to neutralize hearts and minds to destroy life, equally well on all sides, justified by expedient and self-serving categories and concepts of the just and justice or the unjustifiable.

Time is minutely inventoried as it runs out and effort is directed at preserving innocence, irreverence and ignorance, whose tomorrows are as dead as they are certain, abbreviated, and synopsized into user-friendliness and replicability. The result is an intellectually castrated, barren and impotent atmosphere where all are equally equipped with ubiquitous and uniform screens and mirrors for endless re-runs. There is an illusion of same time next time when there is no same and no next time. This is well exemplified by the stealth and profuseness of 'privacy notice' ring-dingers mailed and emailed out by inorganic and amalgamated entities, free of charge, which should set off alarm bells if ever read aloud, line by exquisite line, instead of reading some purchased and purchasable pop illusions. There is an increasingly relentless inculcation to demonize or dehumanize (paint with broad brush strokes in one colour) poverty and the poor as the cause of all manner of undesirable outcomes and all kinds of undesired beings in a flat-out attempt to implant another absolute fact, illusion, lie or inversion of linear and binary cause and effect so that Money is the ultimate and sacred saviour symbol, not only of utilitarianism, goodness and goodies but of greatness, sacredness and holiness. Thus with attention focused upon and effort riveted onto the mad-dash scramble to the top of the pyramid with a dollar sign perched at its tip (where there can be no crowding out), in straight lines representing the shortest and quickest route between two points, innumerable lines are made all over the place, as far and wide as possible without reference to wholeness or in appreciation of the infinite possibilities made possible only by the grace and humour of sacred, faceless and nameless Time.

The pyramids are merely man-constructed monuments or monumentally defiant statements against mortality by the few with insatiable appetites for time embedded within the endless spirals and pulsations of time. The elaborate cult of the afterlife concocted by the few demonstrates the power of illusion and the fear of death enabling those in the power grid to tap into an inexhaustible supply of time matrices. These are produced by the many who believe that their progeny will all be masters of the universe or better servants with more credentials but never, God forbid, slaves to perpetuate the ends of their masters in a lifetime of well- or ill-fed, -clothed and -housed servitude in order to produce more of themselves. The good news for the cannibals is that the supply will continue to multiply even with barely sustainable wages or at virtually no direct cost to those who benefit or replicate. Those who understood the insidious nature of these original Ponzi schemes and business models took very different paths to the value of individuality by bringing the spirituality and lineage of sacred time into their language of hearts and minds. Those who identified with the pharaohs crossed the species, space and time barriers and continue these traditions with numerous empire and nation-building exercises based upon all kinds of time-amassing and -consuming isms. The beauty of these systems is that those who can draw from the vast supply of time matrices can enjoy virtual immortality in their lifetime, consuming countless lifetimes while keeping up the illusion of life-after-death for the many who are willing and living donors and traders of their time. Pryamidism continues to represent symbols of power and immortality as the corpses, however beautifully encased and dressed within, have all been equally pulverised and shrivelled by time, rather than representing the enslavement and cannibalization of millions of lifetimes and oceans of blood, sweat and tears of individuals willingly or unwillingly reduced to slaves in their respective niches. By targeting the top of the pyramid through the singular viewfinder, by being mesmerized by visions of power, reward and glory, or by endless deconstruction, the whole point of the pyramids is overlooked, missed or lost in and by time. Only when form and function are individually, intimately or organically formed and fused through the endless process of trial and error or incremental learning, can time or change be mediated with some sense of courage, taste and style. While the death brought on by time strikes once and then is no more, the cannibals of time bring living death as creatures of both night and day in the 24/7 loop of their self-serving design.

In sacred time, the end is the path traced without fixed entries, closures or punctures and where up, down, top, bottom, colours, flavours, charming or strange are not even contingencies and entirely out of order. So, what is the purpose of speed and volume in mediating time except in their stupendous, duplicitous and duplicatable counter-productiveness? In the Islamic tradition where hospitals are wellness centres serving the community rather than profit and cost centres plugged into industries, the tenth and final note of the patient's pulse to be taken into account by the *hakim* (healer) is its musicality, which can best be appreciated by the most delicate of sensibilities, so that being of a tender nature versus being cold-blooded, is a fundamental pre-requisite to such an esteemed position of burden. As usual, the message is lost in the din, vagaries and vanities of perception and attachment to shapes, colours and forms that cloak the radiance and mystery of sublime beauty and horror or death and life in the paradoxical heart or central principles of the matter.

Books are lived-through-stories and ultimate symbols and testimonials of portability, potability (incorporability) and potentiality for self-actualizing, becoming or unfolding by the sashaying leaves of time, finding and tracing their own unique pathways into eternal compassion or insatiable cannibalization. Maternal drive or compassion comes with four times the potential for pleasure and pain, as the sensations of and sentiments in the beloved (self in the non-self) awesomely and exponentially amplify and play out their chords of dissonance or concordance within the caregiver. Individually scored and seared dignity and markings of character find their deepest and fearless expressions in those who live, with or without intent, intensely without the comforts and consolations of mind-numbing purchased and imported illusions, usually accompanied by exemptions and deprivations from morality by blind-faith, denialism, fanaticism and utopianism. When someone or something else does the seeing, hearing, walking, talking, choosing and thinking, singularity or individuality is unrealizable, being disengaged from the intricate interplay of pain and pleasure of becoming and making, or dead for all practical or impractical purpose and intent, but nevertheless extremely adept in the fine mechanics of rationalization for maximum and unilateral replication and certification for consumption, destruction and disposal.

Anti-ism or multi-ism as an antidote to acquired identity deficit syndrome and universal species barrier crossing cannibalism

Moral sentiments and ethos are increasingly displaced by amorality and relativism which gather mass and momentum with increasing professionalism, credentialism and narrow specializations. The proliferation of service and information providers with innumerable categories of intangibles-for-sale, including the medical, legal, financial, real-estate and home sectors results in consumers experiencing an abundance of identicalism or clones belying outer markings. Many of these full-time parasites, scavengers or cannibals with propensities for free-lunches mirroring their lackadaisical and out-to-lunch attitudes, gorge and stuff their faces at the disproportionate time, expense or energy of their clients and their interests. These server-types accredit, organize and replicate themselves with their own set of fine prints for obscurantism gobbledygook, non-disclosure, disclaimer, fraternal courtesies and acceptable industry standards or accountable-to-nobody-at-anytime-and-anyplace-but-always-billable hours and practices.

The volume of fine prints grows on the withering vines of personal responsibility and accountability or fault-freeness and fault-profitability as all sides take offensive and defensive postures and measures. As the perception of change overloads and overwhelms the unmentored learning and due process centres of the brain, it undergoes reverse-engineering, with the reptilian part being pulled inside-out, inverted and stretched to cover the developing complexities and convolutions. Being stretched and spread pretty thin in all directions, it tends to be in a constantly tense, tight or taut state that snaps and spins with the greatest of ease. The client-server relationships are thus redefined, inverted and perverted as this species category increasingly promote, protect, bullet-proof and fault-proof their lax and lose practices of negative service and disinformation aka rip-offs and lies, ad nauseum and ad infinitum. These representatives or archetypes of such a diverse range of services become a pan-endemic norm as their purposes converge into one—profit maximization or winning at all costs—the *sine qua non* of capitalism. This trend conjoins with globalization, consumerism and media consolidations giving rise to blighted, besotted and benighted milieux that are equally inhospitable, belittling and unbecoming of individuality. The practice of con as art gives way to a con-culture as being conned, suckered and duped become the expected norm in a culture of fads, images and illusions. The existence and continued growth of so many $40 billion plus markets and industries means that ubiquitous, mass, typical and uniform experiences and events or boiler-plate productions and fillers are being increasingly replicated, replayed and shared, creating a singular sense of reality or illusion. In such an absence of atypicality, much homage is paid to individualism, originality and a host of virtues, while individuality, authenticity, and virtues of the heart no longer become discernible. This results in a democracy that is crippled, deformed or stillborn as trickle-down obliterates and discounts any upward percolations as cast by individual votes and notes or other expressions of consent or dissent.

Fixed, rigid and singular perspectives impede any participation, realization and testimony of truths as and when they can be witnessed, since truths do not materialize unilaterally in service of an individualistically eye-catching *I-want-my-way-I-centric* enterprise, purpose or interest. A variety of human beings from all walks of life are rubber-stamped, imprinted and impressed or mass conditioned so that they hold similar prejudices, preferences and perceptions, with tendencies toward hyper-reaction in tandem with hypo-vigilance or mindlessness. Anti-Americanism is an exception to this rule of mass conditioning, springing up from the ground-swells of many hearts, minds and places, finding this phenomenon equally unpalatable and queasy or instinctively repellent and grotesque, despite the wasting and waste of superficial packaging, to human sensibilities, steeped and nurtured in the traditions of sacred ties of time. Heads may roll and various forms of governments and isms may come and go but the work-in-progress that is identity or character formation goes on through the sequential, incremental and cumulative readings disengaged from the conventions and conventionalism of time. While events may be or seem to be random, our collision, reaction and incorporation transform them into significance and meaning in our lives, in a cumulative sequence from that moment on. There is hope of etching out and realizing identity as long as learning is not impeded, short-changed or arrested for the sake of hubris, isms or preservation of ignorance in arrogance as lip-service is paid to multi-culturalism as fadism or popularism.

Whether error is made or not is irrelevant and immaterial so long as there is no blow-by-blow replay or a sequel that is as equally a dead-bore and a deadbeat as it is unbecoming and unenjoyable. A style does not represent principle or loyalty but the calibre and repertoire of atypical personas accumulated through studies and composites of the minutiae, iota, Iago or I-ego over a lifetime can be readily put into play to meet the demands of changing roles, places, occasions and times. A chameleon changes colour but still remains pious to its home or principles of residence, as it is and as it must. People are not chameleons, leopards, zebras or any other beings notable for piety, integrity and fidelity to the principle of life. Nevertheless, they evolve to find their alignment, orientation and direction for nidification or a sense of home, without the benefit of an expected value tabulation but subject to probabilities of a host of outcomes, as is the case for all differentiated, metabolic, transforming beings or individuals. Through atypical and contextual library amassing and cumulative cantenations (syndesis), the base increases in weight and volume, so that the whole does not topple, destabilize or deform when irritated into responses in or not in kind. There is no imperative for calculated loss of profit, to be irrefutably proven right, or an absolute need to win—just a fairness or joy in play by a unique trinity of life, heart and principle as a representative of and as a tribute to Time.

As much as one would like to believe otherwise or force-fit into categorizations, balance is dynamically maintained by expansions in *gravitas*, not by rigor mortis locking into a stare, posture and fixture on a single tightrope, tightly clutching onto a rigid ism rod, rule or reason, exemplified by born and bred loggerheads or louts. Such a universal, timeless and virulent scourge or archetype run amuck irrespective of name, ethnicity, place, degrees, job-category, or time, especially of itself, and represents an ever-present menace to life, limb and property. It does not respect or revere anything, holds nothing sacred, and is entirely devoid of loyalty, principle or a centre. It only knows and wants to get its own way at all and any cost. It rears its head from time to time, but does the most harm through disguise, guile and norm emulation as it seeps and creeps below the radar screen. It is characterized by its phenomenal ability to replicate by direct and indirect transmission and infestation, aided by globalization, capitalism and democratization. Such an onslaught of mass killer applications or cannibal-ization of time matrices produces mindlessness, apathy and mediocrity, against which infringements and irritations life can only be immunized by being acutely aware, honing micro to macroscopic acuity and minding and guarding time. Life is play in the making, not in pursuit of liberty, equality and justice but merely to play well and ring true, in time, marking each day as a holy day. Individuals are not inorganic products or shelf-lives with clearly marked expiration dates to be made obsolete and displaced by the purchase of the newest and the latest, like the news, indices, accessories or EPROMS (erasable programmable read only memory chips).

The culture of the mafia-like strains are group responses to the anti-culture of Romanization-like homogenization and absolutism. The former espouses the rule of blood bonds, deeds and duties seeded in families and rewarded by individual identity recognition and acceptance. The latter rules by the rule of law, mind-numbing fine print and power-fixated institutional-ism, eponymism and epochism enforced by legalized violence. Koreans, Chinese and others may be stereotyped as dog eaters, but this pales in comparison to the slaughter, processing and recycling of tens of millions of dogs, cats and other domesticated animals as well as roadkills and collateral damages, as human and non-human feeds and goods, annually, by the superpowers of money, guns and cannibalism. The League of Nations was a reaction to the devastation of WWI, but what followed was increased nationalism, totalitarianism, fascism and militarism. After WWII, the United Nations was set up as big and bold ideas, price-tags, solutions and illusions continue to hold sway over the masses, over what is in plain view in daily lives and realities that eventually denude, discount and reduce bigness through the grace of Time that prefers compact, compressed and diverse or economical and efficient space container designs. That there should be a direct and appre-ciable correlation between price and quality is so much wishful thinking or an illusion of the normative versus the descriptive and the positive of more than a singular viewpoint. The quoins (keystones) of *lex loci* (law of place) and *lex non scripta* (unwritten law) hold court and fashion remedies, gnashing and gnawing the grain from the chaff, bowing only to the code of Time, without even a side-long glance at the supercilious and stupendous lexicon of the temporal *per curiam* (full court couture and press) judgements and contor-tions justified by a self-serving code of ethics and rules whose dénouement (unraveling) is delectable for a select few, out of view.

In context of the ubiquity of uniqueness, it is likely that the personal sense and idea of the divine, poetic, sublime and much else will also seem to be unique. The task of life could then be to strive to connect to the one other or all others through various relationships and understandings, so that what cannot be identified or identical, can nevertheless be shared and linked. Each individual desires to be acknowledged as unique and, at the same time, needs to find acceptance seamlessly in time and space. The vehicle and means employed is self-identity, which formulates and compromises, as well as is formulated and compromised by the deepest held principles against the base common denominators, resulting in tensions and tensibilities which confront, comfort, and define life and living. There is no normal, mean or standard life; only a personal sense of normality and fitness, achieved through dynamic equilibrium points as conflicts are overcome, endured and replenished, without rendering and reducing life into a flaccid, bland and immutable state. Thus, form and content shape purpose as much as purpose gives rise to form and content.

Rarely is the choice between the path of least resistance and the path of least harm so readily apparent or compatible. The illusions of similarity and familiarity serve as both decoys and excuses for taking the easy way over the right way. Such elusiveness is also present in the win/lose zero-sum finality which masks the infiniteness and oneness of the right/wrong moral complexion. The binary framework of my way or not my way reduces the menu of choices and the decision rendered is blind to the infinite difference and irreversibility of doing and undoing. Each decision is momentous and merits attention to detail and purpose. Any of our conceptions of time, such as saving or losing time, tend towards futility except in flowing through time in all our relationships with services rendered and purposes served, beyond those that are self-serving. A life is like a pluck in time that is incommensurable. Chronometers do not keep or tag time regardless of how finely it is parsed, and bring one no closer to gaining insight into the paradox of relativity which suggests that the faster I go, the slower I arrive. Living takes time and so should we.

Growth and profit or profitable growth are empty, or without any merit, when uncoupled from the flourishing of life versus the law of private property. Such contextual considerations apply equally for patriotism in its borderless sense versus zero-sum partisanship (borderless terrorism) and in distinguishing honesty from loyalty in their interplay within and without the spheres of integrity. The prognosis of demise through growth is unexceptional for economic entities that do not have the organic virtue of even an amœba: relative permeability and transience. Since change is viewed and weighed in strictly dollar terms of financial models versus organic models, there tends to be consistent under-planning or mis-planning for change, in any direction and dimension. When growth is pursued for its own sake and defined in extra-organic terms, not only is happiness an elusive state, but the organic lessons of growth, decay and regeneration, are unincorporated, unrespected and unpracticed, so that recidivism remains unchecked.

It is often repeated in the business press that when the United States catches a cold, the non-U.S. countries come down with pneumonia. In a similar disproportionate manner, the ills that affect American society, along with its world-view, plays out, amplifies and recycles through other countries in the non-stop pumping of the mass-media. Just as its per capita consumption and disposal factor is 30 to 50 times that of other countries, so too is its potential for both negative and positive reverberation. The corrosive and corruptive appeal and spread of gunboat 'diplomacy', backed up by the weight of 'international' laws, finds adherents and perpetrators in many other countries.

An example of such an appeal can be found in the Meiji Restoration movement in mid-19th century Japan. This is a movement whereby those clinging onto their political power chose to become like their enemies by grafting the markings of inhumanity, acquiring and developing weapons of mass destruction, and cleaving onto them by signing treaties of mutual recognition and interests. This paved the way to justify their actions under the guise of international or Western laws as manifested in their inhuman conduct and regard for those they categorized as different and therefore, inferior. In this regard, Japan is no different than many other civilizations of antiquity and humanity which have fallen by the wayside under the spell of Americanization, imperialism and omnipotence, as they take on board American popular culture, both literally and figuratively, from reliance upon anesthetics, plastic surgery and fashions to numerous isms from nihilism to capitalism that are not of indigenous origin, happiness or design. This transformation of Japanese culture provided the impetus, excuse and means for both expansion and assertion of its world view, with industrialization being the necessary precursor. A policy of splendid isolationism, as expressed by the British foreign policy of the same vintage, provides an expedient pretext for washing of soiled hands or turning a blind eye, consistent with the tendency to pack up and leave rather than face the consequences. It has been the consistent practice of those who rape, pillage and plunder to seek forgetfulness over forgiveness. The relationship between Korea and its neighbours as well as the Western powers cannot be understood without understanding the historical contexts. Such an approach reveals why history, especially where wounds have continued to fester for generations, tends to be subjected to numerous distortions in order to serve various parties and times, internally and externally.

National history is but a figment of political imagination, and reading at least three perspectives will aid in shaping a more balanced understanding of relationships. The traditional skills of reading, writing and arithmetic are still being touted about when they are but mere pre-requisites to societal needs of understanding the relationships between people and to all that live, as well as to non-renewable and non-replaceable resources. Language of words and numbers are useless without an accumulation of lessons to neither bark nor beg but to communicate in the relational framework of a specific culture with a reverence for all life or co-existence in diversity. American history, like the history of many other countries after the age of industrialization, cannot be justly or adequately explained by one voice. It is a history of many voices and lives representing great diversity, both before and after colonization. The noise of the 'winner' drowns out the cries and whispers of the 'losers', be they the Native Indians, herds of buffalo, descendants of transplanted Africans, or all the other sounds of dissent, internal and external, to the winners' spheres of interests and borders. We tend not to learn from history because it is rarely recorded and transmitted to give voice equally to all sides, resembling the stability and symmetry of an equilateral triangle. The memory of the oppressors is glorified, while the voice of the oppressed is rendered silent and left unaccounted for. Does it matter how much diversity was eliminated or how many people were killed in the colonization on the New World? Numbers justify for those who keep scores.

This mentality to dominate at all cost, or unilateralism, can be summarized by the popularity of SUVs. They are bigger, heavier, safer and provide better views than average cars. The appeal of these attributes support the determination to out-do all others with more consumption, as well as to out-live the others with unequal handicapping of survivability regardless of fault or driving acuity. The only reason why fully armoured vehicles have not yet crossed over to the civilian marketplace is that the profit margins of the military industrial complex remain obscene and relatively risk-free in practice. No other contract can match the fat content of defense industries to satisfy the appetites suckling on the invincible teats of unlimited killer application research and development, production, sale and distribution for land, sky, sea and space deployment.

The relationship of the U.S. with Korea, as an example, reveals the limitations of principles and laws as laid out in the Declaration of Independence, the Constitution and the Bill of Rights in the face of imperial politics and corrosive capitalism. The U.S. traded off its 1882 Friendship Treaty for other economic and political gains (Philippines and China) by nodding off on the Taft-Katsura rationalization or *quid pro quo* in 1905, paving the way for annexation of Korea by Japan.[72] Breaking treaties is not an anathema to any state, but as demonstrated by the Battle of the Little Bighorn in 1868, it would be interesting to see how and why the U.S. decides to make or break them, in the context of its many avowed principles. International laws and universal principles that traverse cultural borders only make sense when they are equally promulgated and enforceable, not subject to some proportional representation of equality or special applicability to suit vested interests and anachronistic outlooks of one country, state, party or person. While diversity and divisiveness has been the norm through the ages, resulting in cycles of conflict and compromise, the modern trend has been towards greater centralization or insurmountable concentration of material and political powers, sustained by overwhelming use of killer applications which are becoming more miniaturized, invisible and ubiquitous.

There are predators, scavengers, parasites and prey in every culture of the human animal, with unrelenting struggle producing a dynamic equilibrium of co-existence. But the introduction of non-indigenous elements (ideas, practices, peoples) results in unequal handicapping, as has the introduction of non-indigenous life forms in various continents. The cultural system evolves

72. Andrew C. Nahm, *Korea: Tradition & Transformation*, (Hollym International Corp., 1996), pp. 154, 206.

at its own built-in circadian rhythm and can only process change organically. While there are redundancies and shock-absorption capacities, it goes into shock and decline when overwhelmed and insulted by non-indigenous onslaught.

Each cell and occupant in a cellular network is nurtured and attended to, to include all the built-in redundancies for optimal communal survival, rather than minimal feeding and denial for a bare-bone existence of the many for maximizing the exclusive survival of the one and the few. To shut down any kind of system is quick, but to maintain and grow requires just the reverse, just as a baby's physical or measurable changes belie the innumerable non-linear changes in the arrays of internal functions. The calibration of the economy of scale and diminishing rate of return is scrambled in the single-minded pursuit of heft and renown, so that the holistic cost/benefit paradigm is skewed. Individuality, with all its unquantifiable and messy inefficiencies and redundancies, is wrung out under the press of conformity and the lure of enslavement through illusions of equality and entitlement. The asymmetric and asynchronous nature of economic concepts and measures of growth and profitability cause schisms in numerous dimensions, as do the political constructs of liberty, equality and justice.

These disconnects and distortions from Dharma (cosmic order or law, principle, purpose, right conduct) keeps Atman (one's true nature or understanding the oneness in creation as an interplay between the created and the creator) hidden from view, and the path of the Karma (destiny) is kept out of reach by an unbridgeable breach. The path of Karma remains virginal and unmarked by any trace of a footprint when internal and external schisms and polarization prevent and distort identity formation and foundation. The kaleidoscopic glow of life diminishes when there is non-alignment or non-symmetry and non-synchronicity within this Trinity. Kings, dictators and totalitarianisms have been toppled because their lifestyles and beliefs of extremes, excesses and abuses were deemed unseemly and unfitting, and were roundly condemned in a sea of poverty and much lack, not so that everyone could then engage in the same.

Only human beings appear to be exempt from the fusing of purpose and being. Or, they have been uniquely endowed with freewill to define and find out what is natural and unnatural as purpose is unbundled from being. Whether we are thus deprived or over-compensated, the result is that our purpose seems to be to find or shape our own purpose in becoming natural or unnatural beings in approximation of the Dharma. The Dharma can be viewed as the gluon that has no matter or charge, and carries the strong force within the nucleus for an infinitesimal distance to keep it all together. When we find our true nature and carrier, there is a greater likelihood of reaching our destination, whatever it may be.

One way to understand our Dharma and Atman is to view our lives as processes of trial and error. If we stay within the confines of an ism, cling onto the comfortable and safe for dear life, hate and destroy what we don't like, there is very little process—only ennui and entropy. Our minds are like risk-processors that remember, process and filter change. Do we teach our children the 3 R's and weigh them down with a heap of values, virtues, morals and beliefs as immutable facts so that they can become productive workers, wage-earners, cost-centres, complacent citizens, insatiable consumers, good form fillers, shufflers of boiler-plate information with substituted words and numbers which do not increase knowledge but only complaints over spoilt or spilt milk? No, we teach our children how to live and to explore their many possibilities by increasing their field of perception beyond the physical through an understanding of relationships in life. Many people make expressive music without writing or reading standard musical notations. We share our stories of process, outcome, success and failure to help them understand and develop decision-making skills (from discrete and one-dimensional to systematic and organic) in the context of set theories and definitions (constant and variable relationships).

When we say to a child—yes, that's right—it is not an affirmation of an abstract and absolute concept of Good, but of acceptability and consistency in the context of human experience which shapes social norms and practices. Stories are noble or ignominious lies, depending on what purpose is served. They can imprison or liberate the creative spirit of the mind, suppress or fire up all the cylinders of the risk-processor and finally, convey a sense of immutable permanence and certainty or permeable and transient mutability. Enculturation can fairly be viewed as being both anti-nihilistic and anti-democratic. Democracy (individualism) is the slippery slope to nihilism and various arguments against it rest on this point, as philosophers from Plato to Hobbes to Nietzsche have tried to elucidate, and as demonstrated by statecraft and practice through the ages. People are free to do what with Democracy— use the rights of free speech and press to destroy? Purpose can only be self-serving when rights translate into equal assertion of the attenuated individual.

Nietzsche is the embodiment of anti-nihilism as his life seems dedicated to a search for meaning, not meaninglessness. His life and books are warnings against the danger of democracy sliding into the *hoi polloi* of plebeianism (lowest common denominator, baseness, herd mentality), whereby everyone and anyone is equally entitled to an opinion that counts equally and carries equal weight, as a prelude to nihilism. Why has there been such great resistance to democracy in theory and practice? This can be answered by asking the question: Does the human animal resist the Dharma by design? The answer must be no, otherwise there is no purpose to his ability to procreate and the human Dharma can only be realized through union or by more than one.

To sign on to the bandwagon of the rule of law is to settle for centralization and order through uniformity and control of definitions. The thrust of ancient cultures has been centred around the rule of life over the rule of law. A cultural identity shapes and informs an inside-out projection of reality, based upon billions of man-years of trial and error, as a guide to acceptability, harmony and realization of individual potential, not an outside-in imposition or a singular, artificial and stereotypical construct and characterization. The rule of law assumes that prudence and rationalism are paramount, whereas in practice these are but more of the same totalitarian constructs or dogmas designed to capture the enforceable tip of the iceberg through legalized violence, limitation and intolerance.

The outcome in the pursuit of identity through the ages indicates that money (power), sex (gender) and violence (killer applications) characterized by outside-inness of show and tell, are not only peripheral but detrimental to its foundation, tending to arrest development and progress of inside-outness. When these two perspectives converge and focus more than diverge and distort, a semblance of identity comes onto the stage with palpable authenticity. It is palpable because to keep the heart pumping, a finely-tuned risk processor must at all times, places and occasions assess what is worth killing and dying for, always in context of not only self-preservation, but also of the group within the Oneness of Life. Good acting seems to pivot on both presence and absence of background, but sublime acting seems firmly rooted in a tradition of depth and breath. Isms, propositions of mutual exclusivity and zero-sum outlooks proliferate as the disconnections from Oneness become more insistent, creating a greater sense of unease and alienation. We scour and scavenge for identity outside, as we drown in information and image inputs, preserving and hanging onto illusions over confronting our own equal potential for creation and destruction and appreciating circularity as the ultimate equalizer. Authenticity (self-assurance) is more often resented than exemplified by those who do not seek it, avoid it, find it unfamiliar and unattainable, and therefore resort to its destruction.

The story spinning of the entertainment industry suggests that the circle of life is procreation as an extension of private property or a means of achieving immortality. But the story of Moses and examples of adoption and creation show that motherhood and creativity transcend origin and ownership of life. There are even many stories of humans being suckled and nurtured by wolves and bears or social animals. The paradox of ancient cultures, languages and traditions that prescribe and preserve the bonds of micro-family relationships and unity can only be pierced when projected onto the macro or universal family. The dual purpose of the family unit is to weave, within a comprehensible framework, those lessons and memories which enable being woven into the incomprehensible and infinite canvass of inter-relatedness in the One. The culture of the micro-family builds organic bonds which set limits in a code of conduct so as to encourage staying within the tolerance bandwidth of fitness. What characterizes the various isms of modernity, especially with nationalism, capitalism, expansionism and incarnations of religion mixed up with politics, is the lack of ethical dimensions finding expression in a daily code of conduct and reverence for all that exists.

As history has demonstrated over and over again, the appeal of rationalism is that it can be used to justify just about anything. The assurance of its staying power lies in ensuring that the lessons and elements of life which do not fall under its auspice and sway are so easily swept aside and kept under. The rule of law and its evolution reflects and incorporates a conclusion that individuals and individuality are to be distrusted and so it grows in same measure with human population growth, that is, exponentially. Just as we feel that we are drowning in the sea of humanity, we feel equally oppressed by the growing mountain of legal statutes. It is a compromise which favours those with vested interests and power whose will and wont supersede all the others by creating an illusion that justice is a temporal experience and tangible. Do more laws, enforcement agencies and penitentiaries result in any less crimes, or are these all only lagging indicators with no effect, other than creating a police state and a physically two-tiered society? This notion of the supremacy of power that is definable and demonstrable is perpetuated by the tendency of the served and the server to not ever learn or retain any insight into the nature of receiving and giving as service (relationship and reality) is rendered.

What fine distinctions are made between the rule of law and the rule of man for the same purpose of exerting an individual and temporal will that ensures endless rounds of book burning and writing or confinement and liberation in the schisms of the inside-out and outside-in tradition of the human narrative and existence. Thus does language impose and bind, and for all the longevity, creativity and ingenuity of man, solace is found in silence, solitude and stillness of the moment through voluntary surrender. There can be no integrity or loyalty without a sense of centre or the One that does not depend upon or exist in the conventions of time and space. This, fortunately or unfortunately, means that we do not create or destroy *this that is*, but which upon recognition serves us well through our adoption of reverential attitude and submission.

The significance of the cross is in its centre or the point of joining from which radiates life and diversity. Equality is as elusive as in the two parallel lines that form the equal sign. The golden rule of mathematics is that whatever is changed on one side of the equal operator necessitates equal and opposite change on the other side, in close proximity and time. Our perception of cause and effect eludes such an awareness of quantifiable change since such acuity will overwhelm our being, but we can and should proceed cautiously, if not reverentially, once awakened. Jesus and all the much cited and remembered teachers, saints and sages may have been men, but the fundamental lesson they all espoused and embodied is compassion or motherly love: "As one whom his mother comforteth, so will I comfort you." Filial piety is a means to reflect and return parental love as we all live between the past and the future. Inserting compassion into the family nucleus is comprehensible and doable by the many, while Universal Compassion or equal radiation throughout has been demonstrated to be a Way for the very few who do not feel outer or inner isolation, but are content and complete with the *as is*. Such a state of transcendence reflects total mutability as the boundaries of permeability and transience are crossed when the one merges into Oneness. These select few seem to have reached the frontier of their potential without working themselves into the ground to serve someone else's purpose. They worked to their own purpose, in collaboration with their predecessors and contemporaries. Most seem to have lived lives of material minimalism, rather than opulence.

There is no mention of a work ethic in the Ten Commandments or in other elevated teachings. Only in the post-industrial age are exhaustive and extensive man-hour statistics generated, coupled with the virtue designated to excessive labour and over-consumption. Being industrious has no relationship to working for an industry outside the home for the purpose of producing non-essential and disposal goods as excessively as possible to grow the mountains of garbage. The term 'work ethics' is a marketing master-stroke to yoke the masses into serving the purpose of their masters. Glorifying work as a virtue is an elegant and tidy means to perpetuate enslavement for maximum order which serves the vested power interests. The factors that operate as exponential or catalytic power functions on identity are found within the sphere of relationships with all the others, especially in attitudes pertaining to mothers, mentors and elders. These power functions do not reside in money, fame, rights, isms or accident of place of birth, but with the qualities composing and associated with genuineness of human life and living. There are no random acts of kindness, meanness, violence or anything else: only mindlessness or mindfulness.

The only truism seems to be that organic works are never to be finished or are essentially works-in-process. But change comes with the purpose to preserve, not transcend, diversity and co-existence, whereby costs and benefits flow in circularity. Globalization is not a modern construct fueled by capitalism, democracy, science or religion, but is a timeless feature of the force of life, much like the air that is inhaled and exhaled by all that live. Has anesthesia in all its myriad forms and applications been destructive or helpful to all life? As pervasiveness and profitability in promoting and peddling habits, means and prescriptions for temporary suicides, denial of self and others, being trapped in an illusion of freedom, and spell-bound in vanity by being same as everyone else under the marketing umbrella are made ever more widely available as means to achieve hip-ness, painlessness, mindlessness and forgetfulness, it seems to give rise to suicide or self-cannibalization as a permanent solution to end any suffering altogether, once and for all.

This gives much credence to the Buddhist adage that 'to live is to suffer' or its corollary, 'to die is not to suffer'. The only purpose of the concept of reincarnation is to give meaning to living or suffering by encouraging compassion, not to serve as an empirical fact, text or quiz. We have cultivated and culled all that exist, live and move, including our own species, with increasing ignorance and decreasing understanding of Oneness. Reverence for life would necessarily impede such acts of wanton unilateralism and cruelty. Therefore we strive our utmost to obliterate such sense and sensibility with rationalizations and diversions. The fitness and hierarchy of various forms of life from single-celled organisms and ants to all other non-human categories that seem to mesh seamlessly into the fabric of life as differentiated by the unique significance of the mind will only continue to be debated and upheld by the possessors of its greatest self-designated attributes. Thus will presence of mind demonstrate the virtuosity of self-obsession into mindlessness, since the supremacy of man could not be justified or localized by the size and mass of his grey matter, alone.

Hate crimes are a perennial reality as long as individuals and groups prefer their own illusions of exclusionary concept of the categories of all life and matter, for the purpose of assuming the role of the infallible Creator, without first coming to terms with the conditions of the precursor state of being the created. Reverence for life or gratitude and humility are conspicuous by their absence in the oppressors who inevitably destroy more than preserve and create, flunking out of the test of evolution or retentive flow of the learning process which cannot be so easily faked or denied, but only joined. The lesson of evolution is to change or to let go of what does not work or fit in, with or without our particular notions of the presence or absence of mind.

As one begins to know oneself, one will recognize one's nemesis and upon such recognition clutch, embrace and learn from it, so as to overcome and transform it into another means of escapement or balance by incorporating it into one's being. Otherwise, it will remain an unknown as a potential source or cause of harm, unease or destabilization. If it is simply killed, bypassed or ignored, it will be to one's own short-changing and time-wasting, as it will inevitably rear its head, repeatedly. Fear and uncertainty are best faced with courage, style and honour, not in fearlessness and blind-faith, nor with an intent to win at any cost. A *débrouillard* (one skilled or resourceful at handling any difficulty) sometimes acts for hire and sometimes for *gratis*, but not for any reason, for any person, nor for the highest payoff, known or unknown— only for the privilege of choice in which deeds to engage in for his or her own purpose and to play a good game with finesse to affect minimum recoil by delivering the just-enough force; set up at just the right angle; aimed precisely at the sweet-spot; and in so doing give time her just due or tribute that is becoming. But mostly, the disentangler prefers to retire and rest in quiet langour and solitude, indeterminate, undisturbed and unprovoked, of no cause, of no effect, of no blame-assignment, of no significance, of non-being—the ultimate paradox of beingness at the journey's end as hubris clashes with nemesis, leaving only a trail of so much debris.

The poem that follows is dedicated to my *wé-halmoni* (maternal grand-mother 1908-1997) who showed me the sublime beauty of the human spirit.

Clarity: A Sublime Gift and Test of Integrity

I cannot ever know the cause of your unconstrained and unpretentious tenderness;
It is something that I did not expect nor plan and can only hope
That you feel it reciprocated, in kind, if not in degree.

You are the only one I know whose attitude towards me
Pivots and focalizes on a version of myself which is no longer familiar
But nonetheless has never departed nor been displaced;
Only transformed, yet still living through time and space.

To be well remembered:
Is this not the most worthwhile and uncontrivable
Fallout and flow through, in and of life
Where Humility and Gratitude converge, coalesce and glow?

You bring to mind what is, by recalling what was
Adumbrating and limning what can be
By casting both a shadow and a light.

Àn Yong[73]

73. Everyday Korean precursor in meetings and partings, meaning *peace, tranquility, good health* or *be well, be all right, be in good health*. This term in Chinese includes the 'inner', 'female' and 'heart' ideograms.

Appendices

Appendix 1   **FYI: Four Heads-Up Endnotes**

These endnotes are excerpts downloaded between February 21 and 26, 2001, from the cited web sites to corroborate some of the issues addressed in this book. The Oklahoma City bombing (April 1996) and Columbine High School massacre (April 1999) are also on the PBS web sites.

Visit <pbs.org/newshour/forum/may99/internet-violence> "A Web of Violence?" for spread of hate and violence and <pbs.org/wgbh/pages/front-line/shows/kinkel/blame/summary> for a summary of lawsuits filed as of January 2000, including Columbine, Thurston, Paducah, Jonesboro, and Pearl.

1. Cannibalism [page 130]

.1 Mad Cow Disease: Industrialized Cannibalism Will Ice-Nine Your Brain

Rendering: The ancient but seldom discussed practice of boiling down and making feed meal and other products (gummy candies, lipstick, homeopathic medicines, pharmaceuticals, candles, soaps, waxes, inks, cement, and lubricants) out of slaughterhouse and restaurant scraps, dead farm animals, roadkill, and cats and dogs euthanized in animal shelter.

For example: the City of Los Angeles sends 200 tons of 'euthanized' cats and dogs per month to West Coast Rendering to be made into "feed meal and other products." Forty-three billion pounds is the weight of the parts we didn't eat from the animals that we killed, in 1996, in the USA. So what do we do with 43 billion pounds of bloody scrap leftover when we've taken what we want from the animals? We boil it down and feed it to them, feed it to them in captivity.

Sandra Blakeslee. *New York Times*, 3/11/97
<mkzdk.org/prionhell>

.2   20/20 Hindsight

Our species has been responsible for extensive environmental change since the dawn of civilization.... We don't always understand the ways in which those microorganisms interact with us, with the plants and animals we raise for food, and with each other. Unfortunately, that lack of knowledge can prove fatal....Old testament dietary laws concerning the eating of meat, for example, require (among other things) that animals chew their cud. Carnivores and scavengers were declared 'unclean'. Cows and sheep remained plant eaters throughout human history - until the advent of certain agricultural practices. Not all that long ago, farmers began feeding cows and sheep with dietary supplements containing rendered body parts of other cows and sheep. This dramatic change in the domestic animal food chain effectively turned both sheep and cows into partial carnivores (if not cannibals).

Joseph S. Levine.

<pbs.org/wgbh/nova/madcow/hindsight>

.3   Cannibalism Can Kill You

"...cannibalism is counterproductive in evolutionary terms, says David Pfennig, assistant professor of biology at the University of North Carolina in Chapel Hill. If you're trying to keep your traits alive in the gene pool, you should help your closest relatives instead of gobbling them down.... The two experiments reinforce the notion that by shunning cannibalism, animals directly avoid certain diseases. 'Cannibalism may seem like a good way to make a living,' he says. 'And yet it's a behavior that in the animal kingdom is really rather rare.'"

David George Gordon. ABCNEWS.com, June 26,1998

<newts.org/~newsweek>

Author's Note: Many will recall the story of The Donner Party in the Sierra Nevada mountains (California) in the mid 1800s, the Uruguayan soccer team in the Andes mountains (Chile) in the early 1970s, and the award winning Broadway musical, *Sweeney Todd*, about a charming couple selling very special meat pies. Most by now probably have forgotten about Jeffrey Dahmer, who killed 17 men between 1987 and 1991, and was convicted on 15 murder charges. The prosecutor stated: "He was satisfying his extraordinary sexual cravings." More recently, in December 2000,

Nathaniel Bar-Jonah was charged with killing a ten-year-old boy and feeding the remains to his neighbours in Great Falls, Montana. There are many articles listed in the Internet under "cannibalism" in the context of anthropology, crimes, morbid humour, and Eucharist rites, but no mention of the efficiency of modern technology coupled with the mass media doing a clean sweep of timelines by addicting the masses into mindless consumption of lives, their own as well as others, through insatiable appetites for hatred and intolerance, riding upon forgetfulness. It is worthwhile deliberating whether it is preferable to forgive the sinner while remembering the sin versus forgetting the sin in an all-out-pursuit of retribution, retaliation and revenge when blind hatred clamps down and clamps shut the mind, crowding out everything, including the sinner and the sin, leaving only generic hate, gloriously alive and burning.

2.   Hate Crimes [page 175]

.1 <hrc.org/issues/hate> This Web Site contains the Human Rights Commission Report: "Decade of Violence" and a chronology of hate crimes by state titled, "Hate Violence Continues to Shock the Nation: How Many More Must Die Before Congress Takes Action?" From 1998 to 2000, there are 230 separate accounts listed, including 89 murders. Following are six excerpts:

June 7, 1998, Jasper, Texas
James Byrd Jr. was chained to a pick-up truck and dragged to his death on a backwoods road in a racially motivated attack.

October 12, 1998, Laramie, Wyoming
Matthew Shepard, an openly gay 21-year-old University of Wyoming student, was savagely beaten, tortured, tied to a wooden fence in a remote area and left to die in freezing temperatures.

February 1999, Yosemite National Park, California
An individual charged with the murder of four women - one of which was a 16-year-old girl - told the police investigators that he had fantasized about killing women for three decades.

July 4th weekend, 1999, Illinois/Indiana
An individual associated with a racist and anti-Semitic organization killed an African-American man, Ricky Byrdsong, and wounded six orthodox Jews in Chicago before killing a Korean student, Won-Joon Yoon, in Bloomington, Ind.

August 19, 1999, Los Angeles, California
A former security guard for a white supremacist organization wounded five individuals, including young children, at a Los Angeles Jewish community center, and later killed a Filipino-American postal worker, Joseph Ileto.

August 11, 2000, New York, New York
A 17-year-old who announced to his parents he was gay earlier this year was recovering after his parents severely beat him....allegedly repeatedly smashed their son with a lead pipe as they yelled anti-gay slurs. "God will punish you for your lifestyle! You can't be gay," the couple, aged 49 and 36, are quoted as saying. (New York Daily News, Aug. 13, 2000)

Following is an informative article:
Human Rights Campaign
"Since the FBI began collecting statistics in 1991, hate crimes based on sexual orientation have nearly tripled.... Currently, only 22 states and the District of Columbia include sexual orientation in their hate crimes statutes.... Because federal law enforcement agencies do not yet have jurisdiction over anti-gay hate crimes, this law can only be used when a hate crime based on sexual orientation occurs on federal property, such as a national park."

.2 < pbs.org/newshour>

December 20,1995: Hateful Speech
Racist language at a Harlem Clothing Store resulted in eight deaths.

January 15,1996: Remarks by The President at The Martin Luther King, Jr., Annual Commemorative Service
...In giving in to appeals, to primitive and blind hatred, those who started that awful war were stepping back into an imagined, unreal past in which they say life had greater integrity and meaning - when we define ourselves in terms of who we are *not* instead of who we are. Does that sound familiar to you? When we define ourselves by whom we can denigrate and debase, instead of those whom we can reach out to and embrace.... Children have to be taught to hate.... Dr. King said that men hate each other because they fear each other. They fear each other because they don't know each other. They don't know each other because they can't communicate with each other. They can't communicate with each other because they're separated from each other.... Keep going in the right direction.... We have to continue to heal the racial divisions that still tear at our nation. We can't rest until there are no more hate crimes, no more racial violence.... But we can't end it (affirmative action) until everyone with a straight face can say there is no more discrimination on the basis of race.... Charity and love, in that sense, are the same thing - charitable love, the understanding that even those who are totally different from us share a common human nature. And we all see through the glass darkly. Nobody has the whole truth. We should remember that, and we should ask them to.... But if the global economy means that everywhere we have to have more inequality, more people thrown out of work, more people living without hope because those of us who are doing well won't set up the conditions in which everyone can win, it is not a good thing.... Every American can be a servant in the never-ending work of building our American community and building a stronger and a more united and more decent world. As he said, "Everybody can be great, because everyone can serve. You only need a heart full of grace and a soul generated by love."

May 22, 1998: A Deadly Trend?
March shooting at Westside Middle School in Jonesboro, Arkansas. There, two boys - aged 11 and 13 - killed four students and a teacher and wounded 10 others. Earlier this week, an honor student in Fayetteville, Tennessee, opened fire in the parking lot of his high

school, killing a classmate. In April, a fourteen-year-old shot a science teacher at a school dance in Edinboro, Pennsylvania. In December, another fourteen-year-old boy killed three students and wounded five others at an early morning prayer circle at a West Paducah, Kentucky school. Two months before that, in Pearl, Mississippi, a teenager murdered his mother and then killed two students and wounded six others at school.

April 15, 1999: NYPD Blues

Abner Louima is a 35-year-old Haitian immigrant who in 1997 was arrested during a skirmish outside of a bar. He was taken to this police precinct, where he was savagely beaten by cops in the men's room. At one point, they shoved a blunt instrument up his rectum puncturing his intestines. Louima had no police record.

...the shooting of an unarmed African immigrant named Amadou Diallo. In February, he was killed in a hail of 41 police bullets while standing in the doorway of his apartment building in the Bronx.

July 30,1999: The Atlanta Shootings

Shortly before 3 in the afternoon, Barton walked into the complex. Within minutes, he began shooting, killing five at All-Tech office and four at another stock trading office nearby. ...police went to his apartment in nearby Stockbridge. There they found the bodies of his 11-year-old son Matthew and his seven-year-old daughter Mychelle Elizabeth dead in their beds. The body of his wife, Leigh Ann, was found in a closet. ...We believe he actually shot himself with the .45.

November 10,1999: Kinkel Sentenced

- had pleaded guilty to four counts of murder and 26 counts of attempted murder. The now 17-year-old opened fire in his Thurston high school cafeteria in May 1998 (Springfield, Oregon), killing two students and injuring 25 others. The shooting came a day after the teen killed his parents and rigged their bodies with explosives.

February 6, 1996: Frontline - Murder on 'Abortion Row'

Airing as his trial begins, FRONTLINE follows the intersecting lives of twenty-two-year-old anti-abortionist, John Salvi III, charged with murder in the armed attacks on two Massachusetts health clinics, and his victims, Shannon Lowney and Leanne Nichols.... From the producers of "Romeo and Juliet in Sarajevo," this two-hour program crosses the emotionally charged terrain of the abortion battle.

Author's Note: The Hate Crimes Prevention Act was killed in a House-Senate conference in October 2000, and Texas still does not have a hate-crimes bill because it died from neglect of leadership. (P.S. Hate-crimes bill passed in May 2001 in Texas lending credence to the 'Peter Principle' which seems to have some saving grace for the many left behind.)

3.   Education   [page 250]

.1 Math and science offer the common basis for comparing American schools to the rest of the world...So-called third world countries have a higher literacy rate than the U.S....the results in terms of world competition (for U.S.) are worse than portrayed in these charts. In short, the tests showed U.S. fourth-graders performing poorly, middle school students worse, and high school students are unable to compete....Chances are, even if your school compares well in SAT scores, it will still be a lightweight on an international scale....the actual cause for failure appears to be weak math and science curricula in U.S. middle school....31 percent of teachers do not have at least a minor in biology....55 percent do not at have at least a minor in any of the physical sciences....U.S. textbooks treat topics with a "mile-wide, inch-deep" approach....Many people believe that our best students perform better than the best students of most other countries. TIMSS shows this notion to be untrue. Note again that many superior countries (especially the Asians) are not reported in the reported results (Grade 12 Tests). We import 107,000 H-1B professionals every year, many from less industrialized nations such as China and India.

<http://nces.ed.gov/pubs99>

.2 What % of U.S. students would be in the international top 10% in Grade 4 Mathematics? ...9% In Grade 4 Science?...16% In Grade 8 Mathematics? ...5% In Grade 8 Science?...13%

<http://nces.ed.gov/Pressrelease/reform/figureG.gif>

.3   Grandfather International Math & Science Test Report

SAT testing criteria were revised in 1995 - making the tests less rigorous than before, and test scoring methods were revised in ways unrelated to clear comparison to the past.... Since then the evening news no longer reported SAT results each year, as if all of a sudden all is well....In advanced math our students were tied for the last place, and in physics they has sole possession of last place.... "While many of our schools appear to avoid solid academic training in favor of 'self-esteem' training, this must be working since in the tests American students led the world in one department: 'self-esteem.' As in previous international tests, American students had the highest perception of how well they had done. 70% thought they had done well. This would be comic if it were not so tragic. Raising teacher salaries will not fix it." (Professor Thomas Sowell, published 2/25/98 Sarasota Tribune) There is clear evidence that there is zero correlation between spending and quality achieved. Each parent with school-age children should demand of their local school board that every 8th grader and senior must be required to take the International Math and Science Survey (IMSS) test each year, with the results published....

Grandfather International Education Report

Combining primary and secondary spending, U.S. spending per student is 45% - 67% higher than most advanced international competitors. ...students of other nations have 22 - 35% more school days per year than U.S....some require 13 years for a high school diploma vs. 12 years in the U.S. ...The Textbook Report shows how professionals call today's science and math textbooks error-laden and unacceptable.

Grandfather Economic Reports - Summary

There has been a 71% decline over the past 35 years of the U.S. education productivity index (SAT to $ per student index charted from 1960 to 1994). This was caused by declining quality output, coupled with huge increases in (inflation-adjusted) spending per student — compared to our past and to foreign competitors. It is apparent improved quality does not equate to more money thrown at the current system....more spending produced lower quality.

Michael W. Hodges
<mwhodges.home.att.net/education-c.htm>

4. Literacy, Discipline, Juvenile Crimes, Lying, Gambling

.1   U.S. Department of Education, National Center for Education Statistics. *Education and the Economy: An Indicators Report*, NCES 07-269, by Paul T. Decker, Jennifer King Rice, Mary T. Moore, and Mary R. Rollefson, project officer. Washington, DC:1997.

Pages xix and xxii: source of quotation on page 250 of this book.

Page xvi: "Table A: International distribution of academic achievement relative to the United States: 1991-92." This table seems to suggest that both math and science in the 9 and 13 year old categories had 0 to 2 countries significantly lower than the U.S. while 7 to 20 countries were significantly lower in reading.

Page 95: "U.S. workers may not receive as sophisticated training as comparable workers in other countries because they are not as well educated as their foreign counterparts and are not well prepared for higher-level training."

<www.ed.gov/NCES/>

Author's Note: This seems to indicate that the educational focus should target maths and sciences. Many parents and adults feel well-equipped to teach children reading, social 'sciences', self-esteem, ethnocentrism, dogmatism as well as such challenging topics covering sex, drugs, alcohol, tobacco, guns, gambling, cars and numerous political rights. Children, of course, have unrestricted opportunities to download these topics from so many places and sources everyday. But how many parents and adults feel at ease in teaching maths, finance, probability & statistics, physics, chemistry, biology and philosophy? It is unlikely that children will be deprived or short-changed if schools focus strictly on education, especially in these subjects, instead of social, political and religious indoctrinations.

.2 Violence and Discipline Problems in U.S. Public Schools

Figure 5 (p. 3): Percent of public schools reporting that specific discipline issue were a serious or moderate problem at the school, by instructional level: 1996-97, shows the following:

	Student tardiness	Absenteeism/class cutting	Physical conflicts	Tobacco use
All Public Schools	40%	25%	40%	14%
Elementary	32	17	18	2
Middle	40	24	35	19
High	67	52	17	48

<nces.ed.gcv/pubs98/violence/98030007>

Author's Note: It would be revealing to compare the High School tardiness and absenteeism of 67% and 52% to other countries. There cannot be any learning with this level of physical absence, let alone mental drifting. One positive unintended consequence of absenteeism seems to be that some of the violence has moved out from the school grounds to everywhere else.

.3 Incidents of Crime and Violence in Public Schools

During 1996-97, about 4,000 incidents of rape or other types of sexual battery were reported in our nation's public schools (figure 1 and table 1). There were about 11,000 incidents of physical attacks or fights in which weapons were used and 7,000 robberies in schools that year. About 190,000 fights or physical attacks not involving weapons also occurred , along with about 115,000 thefts and 98,000 incidents of vandalism (tables 2-6).

<nces.ed.gov/pub98/violence/98030003>

.4 Frontline: What meaning can we draw from these cases?

Discussions on daycare child sexual abuse (CSA) cases in the 1980s and early 1990s by Debbie Nathan, author of *Satan's Silence: Ritual Abuse and the Making of a Modern American Witchhunt*, James M. Woods, Ph.D., Associate Professor of Psychology at the University of Texas at El Paso, and John Myers, Professor of Law at McGeorge Law School.

....by the early 1980s, the percentage of working mothers with preschoolers passed the 50 percent mark. During these years, an increasing number of parents used professional baby-sitters and day care centers, instead of family members, to care for their kids.... we must maintain a deep regard for what the public calls "common sense," and what courts have always called findings of fact. Common sense has never posited a class of people who are incapable of lying and who can never be pressured or cajoled into telling falsehoods. Neither have the courts. Why, then, would anyone attribute ubiquitous truth-telling to children? And why would judges, juries and society believe that lack of evidence constitutes evidence?... When it comes to credibility, children are no different than adults...It is clear from the literature on child development that by the time most children are four years old, they possess the moral, cognitive, and linguistic capacity to be credible witnesses in the court.... As for the question "Should their testimony be believed in a court of law?" Anyone who thinks that there is a categorical answer to this question is a fool. Some children are highly credible witnesses who should be believed because they testify truthfully. On the other hand, some children, like some adults, consciously or unconsciously distort the truth.... Each case ought to be judged on its own merits.... The proof of the interview pudding, so to speak, should not be a social worker's or police officer's assertion that questioning was done correctly.... It should be mandatory in the U.S. because, ultimately, taping serves the cause of justice....improper interviews can have a lasting negative impact on children's accuracy.... "Sure, we've made mistakes," the social worker quipped. "But that's OK." It's not OK, and the moral relativism of such attitudes is appalling, not to mention un-American.

<pbs.org/wghb/pages/frontline/shows/terror/meaning>

.5 Frontline: Juvenile Justice

In 1999, law enforcement officers arrested an estimated 2.5 million juveniles. Approximately 104,000 of these were for violent crimes. The most common offense was larceny-theft. Juveniles accounted for 16% of all violent crimes and 32% of all property crimes in 1999. They accounted for 54% of all arson arrests, 42% vandalism arrests, 31% of larceny-theft arrests, and 33% of burglary arrests. Nationwide, it is becoming easier to try juveniles in adult criminal court. Between

1992 and 1997, 44 states and the District of Columbia passed laws facilitating the transfer of juveniles to adult systems. Two states - Vermont and Kansas - provide statutory provisions for trying children as young as 10 years old in adult criminal courts.

<pbs.org/wgbh/pages/frontline/shows/juvenile/stats/basic>

.6 Frontline: Easy Money! - Gambling Facts and Stats

An excerpt from *Is There a Cure for America's Gambling Addiction?* By Bernard P. Horn. Mr. Horn is political director, National Coalition Against Legalized Gambling, Washington, D.C.

Pathological gamblers lose all the money they have, then run up credit card debt. They sell or pawn possessions and plead for loans from family and friend. More than half end up stealing money, often from employers. The average Gamblers Anonymous member will have lost his or her money and accumulated debts ranging from $35,000 to $92,000 before seeking treatment. Thousands file bankruptcy. Many addicts who can't be helped commit suicide. Creating a generation of addicts. Researchers call gambling the fastest growing teenage addiction, with the rate of pathological gambling among high school and college-aged youth about twice that of adults.... Despite laws in Atlantic City restricting casino gambling to people 21 or older, a survey of teenagers at Atlantic City High School revealed that not only had 64% gambled at a local casino, but 40% had done so before the age of 14. Every year, Atlantic City casino security personnel report ejecting about 20,000 minors. Just imagine how many thousands more are never caught.... The biggest potential government expense turned out to be that of incarcerating all the new pathological gamblers who turn to crime.... Proponents claim that casinos or slot machines will stimulate jobs and economic growth. The reality is that gambling steals customers from existing businesses, cannibalizing their revenue.... The casinos don't want to stop gambling addiction because they can depend on addicts for a huge percentage of their profits.... When an industry literally is exploiting the mentally ill for profit, one might expect government to intervene. However, governments have become addicted to winning the money that addicted gamblers lose. This irony carves a strange political landscape...it is driven by self-interested gambling pitchmen with high-priced lobbyists or by the government itself.... If NCALG's opposition to gambling were based on personal morality, it would lose in the political arena. After all, a large majority of Americans gamble. ... On Aug. 3, 1996, Pres. Clinton signed H.R. 497, the National Gambling Impact and Policy Commission Act, which set up a nine-member Federal panel to investigate all facets of gambling in America.... The AGA (American Gaming Association) tried to kill the bill outright.... Pro-gambling forces are trying to recapture the momentum by arguing that gambling revenues are imperative to replace massive cuts in Federal aid to states.... Will America continue to ignore all the warning signs and continue to plunge down into the hole of legalized gambling, or will our nation see that it is time to start climbing out?... The stakes have grown alarmingly high.

<pbs.org/wgbh/pages/frontline/shows/gamble/procon/horn>

Author's Note: Report to the National Gambling Impact Study Commission can be found at <www.usgri.org/pg.html>.

Appendix 2

[see page 167]

A practical, weekly assignment for children in every grade to develop an appreciation of the mass media and consumerism, and the value of time. The purpose of these exercises is to shift focus away from the activity to pre-selection[74] (choice-making and planning), of how time will be spent (time management and activity justification) and how time was actually spent (self-monitoring and self-awareness). It is meant to encourage a diary of thought rather than activity.

1. Read the weekly TV programme listing.

2. Select and list by date, time, channel, title and length in your daily activity log book the programme you want to watch. Write why you want to watch these and what you expect to learn or gain. *Make a note of when (date and time) your log entry was made, every time an entry is made.*

3. Of the selected programmes you watched, write what you can remember about the programme and which of your expectations were met or not, and why. How would you try and fill in any gaps and supplement what you have learned?

4. What was not selected but watched? Write what you remember, why you watched these programmes, and what you have learned or gained. What did you select but not watch?

5. How many hours did you spend watching TV for the week? Explain what trade-offs you made in terms of other activities you could have engaged in.

---

74. Editors and programmers select perhaps one item out of a thousand that pass their desk for publication or production and in similar proportions, the viewers need to carefully filter out all except the 0.1% that is material to them (page 206). For example, if there are 7000 hours of programming per week (50 channels, 20 hours of air-time per day) on TV, there usually are no more than an average of seven hours worth the time spent watching. In writing this book of approximately 150,000 words, if the reader finds 150 words worthwhile having read and remembering, the task would have been amply rewarding.

This exercise can be extended to cover: what you want to buy (consumer goods and services) and actually ended up buying and why; what you want to see (Web sites, movies, concerts, special events and places); what you read (magazines, newspapers, books); what games you play (video, board, card); and what you listen to (CDs, audio books, radio). Only activities related to mass media and consumer activity need to be covered so that a child's private life (recreational and family) and 'downtime' are not unduly intruded upon. Grading is based on completeness and coherence of the log entries, which should be discussed in class so that children are also made aware of what others are interested in and why (perspective of many).

[see page 258]

The Tao symbol can represent many realities and it has been drawn to accentuate its multidimensionality and the spiraling anti-clockwise and clockwise motions to infinite density and speed at the centre (confluence, coalescence, compression, non-disclosure, integration) and infinite space and deceleration outwards (dispersion, diffusion, expansion, manifestation, differentiation). It represents the ebb and flow of *chi* or life-force in a pool of plurality and resolutions thereof, in a continuum of integration, disintegration, differentiation and re-integration. It is a spool of yarn that winds and unwinds without a beginning or an end, like möbius strips, and yet with a sense of centre that defines and anchors both the centrifugal and centripetal forces. There are intuitive and non-intuitive ways of knowing as there are paradoxes and incomprehensibility to navigate in the intermediary zone. Within the Tao symbol the four forces of gravity, electromagnetism, strong and weak, all seem to reside. In contemplating this symbol, the decision-matrix suggested on page 141 can be considered in following terms:

materiality	significance ↔ insignificance	compassion ↔ heart
perspective	present ↔ eternity	tolerance ↔ mind
context	one ↔ many	compromise ↔ body

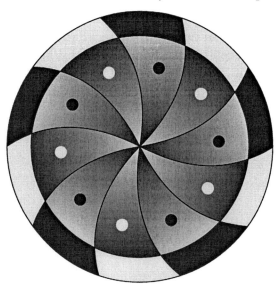

Appendix 4   Three Examples of English and Chinese Words
[see page 264]

English[75]

virtue

> **1** a general moral excellence; right action and thinking; goodness or morality.
> **2** a specific moral quality regarded as good or meritorious; see also cardinal virtues, theological virtues.
> **3** chastity, especially in a woman.
> [Six definitions are listed *Webster's New World Dictionary*]

grace

> **1** beauty or charm of form, composition, movement, or expression.
> **2** an attractive quality, feature, manner, etc.
> **3** any of the Graces.
> [Eleven definitions are listed]

compassion

> sorrow for the sufferings or trouble of another or others, accompanied by an urge to help; deep sympathy; pity - SYN. PITY.
> [Only one definition is listed]

---

75. *Webster's New World Dictionary*, Victoria Neufeldt and David B. Guralnik, eds. (Simon & Schuster, 1988).

Chinese[76]

德 virtue (te) 덕

The character for *te* - a simplified 'foot', combined on the right with the modified character for 'true', above 'heart' - tells us: Follow the path of the true heart. *Te* also means 'power', for the virtuous person thereby becomes powerful. The original name for Taoism is *Tao-te Chia*, the School of the Way and Its Power.

恩 grace (en) 은

In the character for 'grace', the 'heart', below, combines with *yin*, an ancient pictogram for a person 'resting upon' a square mat. Later, *yin* came to mean also 'rely upon'. The person who relies on his heart achieves grace.

慈 compassion (tz'u) 자

Compassionate kindness - epitomized best of all, perhaps, by the quality of a mother's love for her children - is evoked in an early version of the character by the image of a 'son' and 'daughter' cradled over a 'heart'. Today, in a universalization of the concept, the children are represented by the light strokes of tender young 'grass'.

76. Barbara Aria with Russell Eng Gon, *The Spirit of the Chinese Character* (Running Heads, 1992).

Appendix 5   Explanation of the Six Chinese
Ideograms on the Cover

1. **Culture, civilization, humanities, state of intellectual development of a society**

   letter, learning, literary taste   +   change, process, develop

   文化   문화

2. **Human nature, human compassion, humaneness, sympathy**

   human   +   affection, love, tender feelings

   人情   인정

3. **Look at (a matter) in the right light, true perception, awakened to its new significance**

   cognition, recognition   +   knowledge, sense

   認識   인식

4. **An aim, a purpose**

   Meaning, intention   +   drawing, planning

   意圖   의도

5. Sincerity, devotion, earnestness, true heart

essence, spirit   +   true, belief, devotion

精誠   정성

6. Integrity, loyalty, sworn relationship, a keen and strong sense of honour and duty

justice, righteousness   +   principles, reason

義理   의리

(Acknowledgment: Chinese to English translation provided by Prof. Lee Gun Sam, playwright and member of the National Academy of Arts, and Professor Emeritus at Sogang University, Seoul, Korea.)

Appendix 6   Remembering Hahn Changgi (1936-1997)

Hahn Changgi was a personal friend whose acquaintance I made in 1978 in Rochester, N.Y. Since I did not read any Korean publications, I was completely unaware of his public image and many accomplishments, all these many years, until I read the following translation. My personal impression is, however, consistent with what is projected within this article. I can only say that he has left the indelible impression of an individual whose unique generosity in spirit, flamboyance in style and pungency in character (like Korean basic foods) will forever remain in my memory, ensuring that I never forget where I am from.

He had a close working relationship with Mortimer Adler, Frank Gibney and Prof. Herbert Passin (Dept. of Sociology, Columbia U.) while he was the President of Encyclopedia Britannica, Korea. These are three Americans he had talked about with respect and fondness. I don't believe he would object to my mentioning their names in this context.

This article was received by private email to the author on December 14, 2000. It was edited and translated by Korean *Reader's Digest* editor-in-chief, Song Jong-ae, based upon daily newspapers as follows: *Donga Ilbo* (Feb. 5, 1997); *The Korean Daily News* (Feb. 6, 1997); *The Hankyoreh* (Feb. 11, 1997); *JoongAng Ilbo* (Feb. 11, 1997); *Chosun Ilbo* (Feb. 13, 1997); *The Segye Times* (July 7, 1998); *Hankook Ilbo* (Oct. 3, 2000).

Founder of Deep-Rooted Tree Publishing House, Publisher of The Saemikipunmul, A Monthly Cultural Review, former President of Encyclopedia Britannica, Korea.

Hahn Changgi was born in the town of Bolkyo, South Cholla Province, in 1936. Displaying an exceptionally brilliant intellect already in his early childhood, he was called a "child prodigy" in his native town. It was largely due to this reputation of his that in his academic pursuit he had to tread the path followed normally by the above-average provincial lads of the well-to-do of the day. Finishing schooling up to high school in his native province, he went to the prestigious Law College of Seoul National University in Seoul. However, he couldn't interest himself in legal studies, nor in the Civil Service Examination which would, in the eyes of the ordinary people, propel him into the promising, prestigious judiciary profession.

After graduation from Seoul National University, Hahn set up his own modest company to sell copies of Encyclopedia Britannica. The main reason he was drawn into this job, that looked unusual to the ordinary eyes at the time, was his extraordinary competence in English, which he had acquired already in his middle school days by listening intently to Voice of America broadcasting. With his proficient English he had been selling, already in his high school days, to American servicemen in Korea, mostly those due to go back home soon, items like inexpensive souvenirs by setting up makeshift stores in U.S. military compounds.

It was in those days that he got acquainted with a representative from Encyclopedia Britannica to launch a company dedicated to the selling of Encyclopedia Britannica copies in Korea. And Hahn's unusual talent as a salesman started to show. In a matter of years he achieved a magic of selling tens of thousands of copies of Encyclopedia Britannica to Koreans most of whom even couldn't speak, nor read English. And once he had some wealth accumulated through the sale of the encyclopedia and other business undertakings, Hahn embarked on his self-imposed mission of restoring and preserving the ancient cultural heritage of the nation.

Thus, he launched a monthly "Deep-Rooted Tree" in February 1976 with the avowed aim of "restoring the ancient indigenous culture of our nation." The monthly was to be the principal tool in his efforts to "unearth, preserve, and refine" the Korean literary and cultural heritage. Hahn was convinced that in order to attain the nation's literary and cultural development and progress the nation has to adopt the exclusive use of Korean alphabet in its written language, abolishing the use of Chinese characters. It was also his conviction that while both the vertical and lateral writings were prevalent since the early days of the Korean written language, we had to unify them to make the lateral writing universal in line with the general usage in most of the advanced nations. Thus, through the Deep-Rooted Tree, he launched a campaign aimed at realizing exclusive use of Korean alphabet and lateral way of writing in lieu of the perpendicular in all written literature.

With this campaign in mind, Hahn personally involved himself in the designing and editing of the magazine, correcting and trying to refine the language in all the manuscripts and materials going into the publication. In fact, he made himself the object of bitter accusations by the magazine's contributors for "distorting and rewriting" their manuscripts to suit his own thinking and liking. Despite these accusations, he continued to edit and rewrite the manuscripts submitted even by top-notch writers of the nation. It was said that even while he was abroad on company business, he would ask that some of important manuscripts be sent by fax to correct them himself. In doing so, he would replace those words borrowed from Japanese or Chinese with the pure Korean indigenous words. Also, he never failed to pick out passages or expressions that smacked of translation from foreign literature, editors who worked with him say.

With entire pages in whole Han-gul, or Korean alphabet, printed in lateral, instead of vertical, lines, the Deep-Rooted Tree, in time, sold like hot cakes, particularly among youthful readers including middle and high school students. "I guess the reason why we had a good reception with the younger population in our country was in part because the young people felt more at home with the publication printed in all Han-gul in horizontal, instead of vertical lines," Hahn Changgi said. And he criticized the successive governments following the nation's independence for their misguided educational policy under which the students, up to the high school level, were taught with all Han-gul textbooks whose pages were printed laterally, and then had to grapple with the textbooks which were printed vertically in an unprincipled mixture of both Han-gul and Chinese characters once they went up to the college.

Although he obdurately insisted on "indigenous purity" or "return to our ancient, original culture," he never was an intolerant, obstinate nationalist who would refuse to open up to anything alien. In fact, he was a man "whose cultured eyes were lifted to a highly international dimension," as one of the associates closest to him described. Actually his obsession with "our own things and our own past" was focused on the necessity of refining and improving on things of our own, which he felt had been neglected for so long.

The Deep-Rooted Tree was forcibly closed down early in the 1980s by the military who seized power following the assassination of President Park Chung-Hee in 1979 obviously because of the anti-dictatorial tone it had been maintaining. However, Hahn was not intimidated and, refusing to lay off his magazine staff, embarked on a new venture, an 11-volume series called "Discovering Korea." Investing a large amount of money, he sent a number of eminent writers and photographers to various historical sites and scenic spots throughout the country for a comprehensive pictorial series covering entire South Korea.

Meanwhile, he collected the "Pansori," the ancient theatrical songs, which were still extant, but were on the verge of extinction, to preserve them in records. His "Complete Collection of Pansori" appeared in CD-Rom in 2000. He also had the Korean pottery of by-gone days and the traditional Korean tea resuscitated to market them. On top of this, many nameless, yet competent carpenters of Korean architecture and other traditional artisans were discovered under his auspices to record their names and achievements in a book entitled "Deep-Rooted Tree Biography of Unknown Artisans."

In 1984 Hahn started another monthly, "The Saemikipunmul," which was translated as a Monthly Cultural Review, as an extension of his lifelong ambition of seeing a quality magazine of his own creation dedicated to the nation's cultural renaissance.

Hahn Changgi was a man who tried to live under the principles of his own making. Once the principles were established he stuck to them refusing to compromise. Nonetheless, he never was a stubborn hard-headed man. He was one of those Koreans who were fastidious in their efforts to preserve the elegance of the traditional Korean dress and were fond of wearing it them-selves. However, he never insisted on it unlike many of them. He was the one who was conscious and proud of his own style when it came to "Western dress" which he wore most of the time. He was, as it were, a man who appreciated the beauty of age-old things as well as the modernity of contemporary world.

Hahn started to collect in earnest the old Korean potteries, earthen- wares and other hand- crafted works of ancient times with his keen eyes trained to evaluate and appreciate them. The collection is on display in "the Deep-Rooted Tree House of Relics" in Seoul.

Hahn Changgi, who had never married in his lifetime for no apparent reason, passed away on February 3, 1997, of cancer of the liver. He was 62 years of age.

Bibliography

The numbers in bold refer to the text page on which the bibliographical work is cited.

1. Barbra Aria with Russell Eng Gon, *The Spirit of the Chinese Character: Gifts from the Heart* (Running Heads, Inc., 1992) **263, 393**.

2. Francis Bacon, *Essays* [1597, 1612, 1625] (Wordsworth Edition, 1997) **123, 127**.

3. Isaiah Berlin, 'Fathers and Children, the Romanes Lectures' [1970] in Ivan Turgenev, *Fathers and Sons* [1862] (Penguin Classics, 1975) **298, 319**.

4. ——, *The Crooked Timber of History* [1959-90] (Vintage Books, 1992) **126**.

5. ——, *The Proper Study of Mankind: An Anthology of Essays* [1949-90] (Pimlico Edition, 1998) **24, 169, 283**.

6. ——, *The Sense of Reality* (Pimlico, 1996) **107, 114**.

7. Bruno Bettelheim, *The Uses of Enchantment: The Meaning and Importance of Fairy Tales* (Vintage Books, 1975) **159**.

8. Thomas Bulfinch [1796-1867], *Myths of Greece and Rome* (Penguin Books, 1981) **159**.

9. Norman F. Cantor, *The Sacred Chain: A History of the Jews* (Harper Collins, 1994) **39**.

10. Boye Lafayette De Mente, *China's Cultural Code Words* (National Textbook Co., 1996) **263**.

11. Jared Diamond, *Guns, Germs and Steel* (W.W. Norton, 1999) **45**.

12. Collin Duriez, *The C.S. Lewis Encyclopedia* (Crossing Books, 2000) **186**.

13. Anthony Flew, "C.S. Lewis, God and the Problems of Evil" in *Philosophy Now* (April/May 2000) **21**.

14. Jostein Gaarder, *Sophie's World* (Berkley Publishing Group, 1996) **13, 86**.

15. John Gray, *Berlin* (Fontana Press, 1995) **110**.

16. Richard Holmes, *Coleridge: Early Visions* (Penguin Books, 1989) **36, 261**.

17. ———, *Coleridge: Darker Reflections* (Flamingo, 1998) **xvi, 41, 64, 65, 284, 298, 319**.

18. D.W. Hamlyn, *A History of Western Philosophy* (Penguin Books, 1987) **62, 107, 261, 264**.

19. William H. Marshall, ed., *The Major English Romantic Poets*, (Washington Square Press/Simon & Schuster, 1963) **81, 339**.

20. Andrew C. Nahm, *Korea: Tradition & Transformation* (Hollym International Corp., 1996) **366**.

21. *Webster's New World Dictionary*, Victoria Neufeldt and David B. Guralnik, eds., Simon & Schuster, 1988. **392**.

22. D.S. Roberts, *Islam: A Concise Introduction* (Harpers & Row, 1981) **34, 77, 107, 170, 270, 274, 320**.

23. Mark Setton, *Chong Yagyong: Korea's Challenge to Orthodox Neo-Confucianism* (State University of NY Press, 1997) **310**.

24. Leo Tolstoy, *Anna Karenina* [1877] (Signet Classics, 1961) **26, 142, 320**.

25. David Foster Wallace, *Infinite Jest* (Back Bay Books, 1996) **318**.

26. Oscar Williams, ed., *Immortal Poems of the English Language* (Washington Square Press/ Simon & Schuster, 1952) **ix**.

References

Asimov, Issac. *Robots and Empire*. Doubleday & Co., 1985.

Bettelheim, Bruno. *Love is not Enough*. The Free Press, 1950.

Bryant, Dorothy. *The Kin of Ata are Waiting for You*. Moon Books/ Random House, 1971.

Bulgakov, Mikhail. *The Master and Margarita* [1938]. Fontana Books, 1969.

Coleridge, Samuel Taylor. *Selected Poems*. Bloomsbury Publishing Ltd., 1993.

Coleridge, Samuel Taylor. *Spiritual Writings, Selected Poems & Prose*. Fount Paperbacks, 1997.

Coleridge, Samuel Taylor. *The Rime of the Ancient Mariner*. Avon Books, 1967.

de Laclos, Choderlos. *Les Liaisons Dangereuses* [1782]. Oxford University Press - World's Classics, 1995.

Durant, Will. *The Story of Philosophy* [1926]. Washington Square Press, 1961.

Elffers, Joost and Michael Schuyt. *Tangram; The Ancient Chinese Puzzle*. Stewart, Tabori & Chang, 1997.

Federgruen, Awi. *Markovian Control Problems*. Mathematisch Centrum, Amsterdam, 1978.

Fell, Alison, ed. *The Seven Deadly Sins*. Serpent's Tail, 1988.

Feng, Gia-Fu and Jane English. *Tao Te Ching - A New, Translation*. Vintage Books, 1972.

Gilman, Leonard and Allen J. Rose. *APL\ 360 An Interactive Approach*. John Wiley & Sons, 1970.

Gore, Al. *Earth in the Balance: Ecology and the Human Spirit*. Houghton Mifflin Co.,1992.

Lewis, Sinclair. *Babbitt* [1922]. Signet Classics, 1961.

Liddy, G. Gordon. *Will*. St. Martins Mass Market Paper, 1976.

Malkiel, Burton G. *A Random Walk Down Wall Street.* W.W. Norton & Co., Inc., 1975.

Nixon, Richard. *The Real War.* Warner Books Edition, 1980.

Paludan, Ann. *Chronicle of the Chinese Emperors.* Thames and Hudson Ltd., 1998.

Raiffa, Howard. *Decision Analysis: Introductory Lectures on Choices under Uncertainty.* Addison-Wesley Publishing, 1968.

Read, Leonard E. *The Free Market and Its Enemy.* The Foundation for Economic Education Inc., 1965.

Remnick, David. *King of the World: Muhammad Ali and the Rise of an American Hero.* Random House, 1998.

Sagan, Carl. *The Dragons of Eden.* Arbor House New York, 1977.

Seuss, Dr. *The Butter Battle Book.* Random House, 1984.

Sheppard-Jones, Elisabeth. *Stories of Wales.* John Jones Cardiff Ltd., 1976.

Walker, Brian Browne. *The I Ching or Book of Changes.* Judy Piatkus Publishers Ltd., 1992.

Winkler, Franz E. *Man: The Bridge Between Two Worlds.* Gilbert Church Inc., 1960.

Wittgenstein, Ludwig. *On Certainty.* Harper Torchbooks, 1969.

ISBN 155212810-5

9 781552 128107